Tell it like it was

A conceptual
framework for
financial accounting

The Anthony-Graham Series in Accounting

Tell it like it was

A conceptual framework for financial accounting

Robert N. Anthony

Ross Graham Walker Professor Emeritus
Graduate School of Business Administration
Harvard University

1983

RICHARD D. IRWIN, INC.
Homewood, Illinois 60430

© RICHARD D. IRWIN, INC., 1983

ISBN 0-256-03090-1
Library of Congress Catalog Card No. 83–81733

Printed in the United States of America

1 2 3 4 5 6 7 8 9 0   ML   0 9 8 7 6 5 4 3

Preface

This book has two main themes. The first is that accounting should recognize equity interest as a cost and treat equity interest just like other items of cost. The second is that business and nonbusiness accounting are essentially similar. Although I have developed the first theme in another book and in several articles, I find that it has little appeal as a separate proposition. It can be sold, I conclude, only if people are convinced that a conceptual framework incorporating this theme provides more useful information than the present accounting framework. The book describes such a framework and, I hope, demonstrates that it is superior to that now used.

Background

Tracing my involvement with this proposal over the past 30 years may help to explain why I believe it to be so important. Two incidents in the 1950s started me off.

One was an assignment to write a chapter in a finance text explaining the technique for analyzing proposed capital acquisitions. At that time the use of present value techniques was relatively new. As I worked out the explanation and examples, it was disturbing to realize that the present value technique was fundamentally inconsistent with the way financial accounting reported the cost of using capital assets. The analytical technique included interest cost and, implicitly, annuity depreciation, whereas financial accounting omitted interest cost and usually involved straight line depreciation. At the time I merely pointed out the inconsistency, believing that nothing could be done about it.

The other incident was an assignment for the Air Force to appraise the policy for reimbursing defense contractors. Leasing was then a relatively new device. At that time, the rules stated that contractors could not be reimbursed for interest costs of any type. Nevertheless, lessors obviously included in lease charges a component to recover their interest costs incurred in tying up capital in the leased asset. We did not resolve this inconsistency, and the Department of Defense continued to allow the full lease payment on leased assets but only the depreciation on owned assets. The effect was to motivate contractors to lease assets rather than own them, a practice which in many cases resulted in substantially higher costs.

For a time I was hung up on the idea that equity interest was not a cost. Financial accounting recognized only debt interest and then only as a period cost; contract reimbursement rules did not recognize interest at all. In 1965, as Assistant Secretary of Defense, Comptroller, I again became involved in contract reimbursement policies. At that time there was an indirect recognition of interest cost: the weighted guidelines that determined the profit on a contract did provide for a higher profit rate for contractors that used a considerable amount of owned assets. The allowance was rough, and many contracting officers did not apply it as was intended, but it was a beginning.

In the early 1970s, I ran across an historical reference explaining that accounting was not always this way. Back in the 1920s there had been a movement to recognize interest as a cost; there was much discussion of it, but the concept vanished with the death of its leading proponent. I asked myself: why not revive this idea?

I proceeded to develop the idea, first in a 1973 *Harvard Business Review* article and then in a 1975 monograph, *Accounting for the Cost of Interest*.

In the monograph I briefly referred to the advantage of allowing a tax deduction for equity interest as a device for overcoming the inequities caused by the double taxation of dividends. Some people became interested in this possibility, particularly my friend, the late Dan Throop Smith, a leading tax authority (although he did not unqualifiedly embrace it). This led to several articles and appearances before groups and congressional staffs. However, the Congress was not about to adopt a change in the tax laws that was inconsistent with generally accepted accounting principles.

My 1975 proposal recommended that the credit portion of the journal entry for equity interest be made to shareholder equity. Discussing the idea in class one day, a student (unfortunately I cannot recall the name) asked, "Why don't you separate equity into two parts, the equity contributed by the shareholders and the equity generated by the entity's own efforts?" My first reaction was that this was merely a complicated way of reclassifying retained earnings, but I eventually realized that this separation was by no means complicated and that it resulted in a much more sensible view of the right-hand side of the balance sheet. This led to a modification of my 1975 proposal.

Management accounting

Until 1970, most of my writing and professional work was in management accounting. In texts I emphasized the differences between management accounting and financial accounting. It did not occur to me that these differences might not be justified. If companies went to the trouble of developing internal systems whose principles differed from those of financial accounting, I surmised that they probably had good reasons for doing so. The most important of these differences was, and is, that many management accounting systems explicitly recognized interest as a cost in calculating the profit of profit centers. I had thought that the difficulty of arriving at the cost of equity funds was the reason why interest was not recognized in financial accounting. Work done by my associates at the Harvard Business School and elsewhere demonstrated that this supposed difficulty was by no means serious.

Thus, although financial accounting does differ in several ways from management accounting, I see no inherent reason why this particular difference is warranted.

In 1971–72, I participated in the development of Price Commission policies and procedures for controlling selling prices. Because most companies did not incorporate equity interest as a cost in their accounting systems, we could not make an allowance for this cost and this led to inequities in the price control regulations.

Progress

In the 1970s three important steps were taken in the direction of recognizing interest as a cost (see Chapter 4). The first was Cost Accounting Standard (CAS) 414, which made interest on both debt and equity funds an allowable cost for defense contracts. The principle was later adopted by the General Services Administration for use in contracts by other government agencies.

Second, in Statement 34 the Financial Accounting Standards Board required that interest be included as a cost in self-constructed capital assets and certain projects.

Third, the Office of Management and Budget made interest an allowable cost, under certain circumstances, in federal contracts with several types of organizations. This further eroded the traditional notion that interest was not a cost.

Promulgation of CAS 414 and Statement 34 was a beginning. The next step would be the recognition of interest as an element of inventory cost. The Cost Accounting Standard Board had this topic on its agenda when its life expired. The Financial Accounting Standards Board (FASB) included the possibility in the exposure draft of Statement 34 but excluded it from the final draft. The topic is not on the active FASB agenda.

Financial Accounting Standards Board

The Concepts Task Force was the first task force appointed by the Financial Accounting Standards Board. I have participated in all but one of its meetings over the past ten years. Although the job is difficult, my impression is that the concepts project has not made as much progress as reasonably could have been expected. I think there are three reasons for the lack of accomplishment. One is that the board and staff devoted a great deal of time to the price-level problem; this probably was unavoidable. The other two led indirectly to this book.

First, from the beginning the staff embraced the "asset/liability" approach to income measurement, even though the majority of respondents to its initial Discussion Memorandum and the majority of task force members favored the "revenue/expense" approach. For reasons explained in Chapter 3, I do not think the asset/liability approach is an efficient way of thinking about how important conceptual issues should be resolved.

Second, it became apparent that the views of many participants in task force meetings conflicted because they were based on different premises about the nature and behavior of accounting entities. These differences were almost always implicit, rather than explicit. Because they were implicit, the discussions usually did not come to grips with the question of which premises were correct. In the absence of agreed upon premises, there was no way of deciding on the concepts themselves. Arguments slid by one another, rather than addressing conceptual issues directly.

These considerations, together with lack of further progress in the recognition of interest, convinced me that the best way of advancing the cause further was to develop an alternative conceptual framework. The recognition of the problem caused by different unstated premises led me to base this framework on an explicit set of premises. By getting these out in the open, I hope interested parties can see whether differences of opinion stem from different premises or from different conclusions about the concepts that follow from these premises.

Similarity of business and nonbusiness accounting

The second theme of the book is that accounting concepts for both business and nonbusiness accounting can be stated using a single framework. A separate FASB activity helped greatly in developing this theme. In 1977 the FASB hired me to develop an exploratory study of accounting issues related to nonbusiness organizations. At the outset, I thought there would be many significant issues, but by the conclusion of the study I became convinced that few problems were unique to nonbusiness organizations. Thus, the conceptual framework described here applies to both business and nonbusiness organizations. Such a unified framework has rarely been attempted previously. I think the reason is that authors did not have a background in both business and nonbusiness accounting; they were knowledgeable about one type and surmised that the other type was fundamentally different.

Acknowledgments

At the risk of inadvertently omitting someone, I list people who have been especially helpful: Norton Bedford, University of Illinois; Charles J. Christenson, Harvard Business School; Lewis Davidson, University of North Carolina; Philip L. Defliese, Columbia University, former managing partner, Coopers & Lybrand; Walter F. Frese, Harvard Business School; Oscar S. Gellein, former member of FASB; Yuji Ijiri, Carnegie Mellon University; Henry R. Jaenicke, Drexel University; Rev. Richard T. Lawrence, Catholic Diocese of Baltimore; James S. Reece, University of Michigan; David Sherman, Massachusetts Institute of Technology; Edward Stamp, The University of Lancaster; George H. Sorter, New York University; Ross M. Skinner, Clarkson, Gordon & Co.; Robert T. Sprouse, Vice Chairman, FASB; Reed Storey, FASB staff; and William Weekes, Deakin University.

Many of the above participated in the conceptual framework conference at the Harvard Business School on October 1 and 2, 1982. Other participants, all of whom made helpful comments, were: A. Rashad Abdel-khalik, University of Florida; William W. Holder, University of Southern California; Charles T. Horngren, Stanford University; Kermit D. Larson, University of Texas at Austin; Rene Manes, University of Illinois at Urbana-Champaign; Maurice Moonitz, University of California, Berkeley; Lawrence Revsine, Northwestern University; David Solomons, University of Pennsylvania; Clyde P. Stickney, Dartmouth College; Gary L. Sundem, University of Washington; Thomas H. Williams, University of Wisconsin; and Roman L. Weil, University of Chicago.

In addition to Chuck Christenson and Walt Frese, the following colleagues at Harvard Business School provided helpful comments: Alfred Chandler, Robin Cooper, Kenneth Merchant, Denise Nitterhouse, Howard Raiffa, and Michael Sandretto.

Work done in developing Cost Accounting Standard 414 was directly relevant to this book. Cost Accounting Standards Board personnel involved included Elmer B. Staats, Chairman; Arthur Schoenhaut, Executive Director; and David Li.

I have discussed the propositions in this book in doctoral seminars at the Harvard Business School, in two annual meetings of the American Accounting Association, at a doctoral consortium sponsored by the American Accounting Association, and at seminars at other universities. At most of these meetings, the interchange gave me valuable new ideas.

Judith Uhl and Kathryn May of the Harvard Business School Division of Research, made many arrangements for help that facilitated the project. Dina Dublon did most of the historical research and tracked down much other needed information. V. G. Govindarajan conducted the research on the relative importance of earnings versus cash flow and also the research on the use of full costs for pricing. Nancy Anthony checked literature references and did editorial work. Michael E. Mikolajczyk did research of FASB records.

Marcia Lightbody and Nancy Jackson, edited the manuscript. And Pat Lougee processed draft after draft, over a three-year period.

I appreciate the support and encouragement of the two Harvard Business School Deans under whom this research was conducted, Lawrence E. Fouraker and John H. McArthur.

As the above indicates, I had a tremendous amount of valuable help. This does not, however, relieve me of responsibility for the final product.

Versions of Chapter 4 have appeared in *Journal of Accountancy* and *Harvard Business Review*.

Robert N. Anthony

Summary

Chapter 1:   The what and why of this framework

This book describes a conceptual framework to guide the preparation of general purpose financial statements of organizations. General purpose financial statements are prepared for external users in accordance with standards prescribed by a standards-setting body. The concepts guide the development of standards, but they are not themselves standards.

The framework applies to all organizations, both business and nonbusiness. The framework is limited to the financial statements; it does not deal with primary supplementary information that accompanies these statements.

All conceptual frameworks are based on the author's premises about the real world. In this framework, premises are stated and the relationship between concepts and premises is made explicit. *Premises* are descriptive statements based on the best available evidence. They are subject to change as new evidence develops. In this framework, *concepts* are normative statements; they say what financial statement information should be. Concepts are deduced from the premises and they must be consistent with the premises and with one another.

Current practice in business organizations is consistent with most of the concepts in this framework, although some of the concepts are described in terms different from those ordinarily used. The principal conceptual differences from current practice are the recognition of equity interest, the recognition of both debt and equity interest as an element of cost, and the classification of the right-hand side of the balance sheet into three sources of funds: liabilities, shareholder equity, and entity equity.

This framework suggests that several changes should be made in the practices of nonbusiness organizations.

Chapter 2:   Premises
Premises about the entity and its environment
1.   Financial accounting reports on an economic entity, which is an organization that has one or more goals and that acquires and uses economic resources in seeking to attain these goals.

1A.   The organization on which financial accounting reports is not necessarily a legal entity.

1B.   Financial accounting focuses on a single organization, not on a collection of organizations such as an industry, and not on the whole economy.

1C.   Financial accounting concepts do not necessarily apply to financial statements of individual persons.

2.   Accounting measures and reports on one or more of the properties of an entity that can be stated as monetary amounts.

3.   Entities have capital, which they have acquired with funds supplied either directly from outside parties or from their own income-producing activities. Most funds supplied directly by outside parties have a cost to the entity.

3A.   With rare exceptions, an entity cannot increase its capital by activities that do not involve outside parties.

4.   Financial accounting reports on the economic activities and the economic status of an economic entity.

4A.   Financial accounting does not provide information about the social activities of an organization.

5.   A primary economic goal of a nonprofit entity is to provide a satisfactory amount of services with available resources or to provide a specified amount of services with reasonably few resources. A primary economic goal of a profit-oriented entity is to earn a satisfactory return on the funds that investors have supplied to it.

5A.   Some entities are more successful than others in attaining their goals.

6.   Managers normally arrive at the selling price of a product on the basis of its full cost. Full cost includes a fair return on capital employed.

7.   The value of monetary amounts due from or owed to other parties is the present value of the payments that are expected to be received or paid.

8.   Although the fair value of an entity's monetary resources usually can be measured at any time, the fair value of most nonmonetary resources can be measured objectively only at the time they are acquired or sold.

8A.   The fair value of an entity that has nonmonetary resources cannot be reliably measured.

8B.   The performance of an entity during a period cannot be measured as the difference between its value at the beginning of the period and its value at the end of the period.

9.   In the absence of evidence to the contrary, an economic entity is likely to continue operating indefinitely.

10.   Managers are motivated to report favorable information about the performance and status of their organizations.

11.   The purchasing power of money varies through time.

Premises about users and their needs

12.   Users of financial statements have a reasonable understanding of accounting principles and of the nature of the entity being reported on and are willing to devote a reasonable amount of time to studying the information.

13.   Users need accounting information about the economic activities and status of an entity, but the type of information they need is not precisely known.

14.   Users need information about the past performance and financial condition of an entity, because information about the past helps users predict the future of the entity and appraise the performance of its managers.

14A.   Users do not expect financial statements, per se, to forecast the future.

15.   Users are primarily interested in the performance of an entity and secondarily in its status.

15A.   Between competing accounting practices, the one that provides users with more useful information about performance is preferable to the one that provides more useful information about status.

16.   Users believe that income provides a better measure of an entity's performance than does cash flow.

17.   Users need information that helps them make judgements about an entity's ability to meet its obligations.

17A.   Some users need information on the order of priority of each major class of obligations and the amount of the obligations of that class.

18. Users need information that is measured fairly.

19. Users need timely information.

20. Users need reliable information.

21. Users need comparable information.

22. Users do not want accounting standards to be changed unless there is a strong reason to do so.

Chapter 3:   Basic concepts

3.01. Financial statements should report on an accounting entity, which is an economic entity whose resources are controlled by a single person or governing body or by several governing bodies responsible to the same constituency.

3.02. Financial statements should summarize the economic performance and status of the entity as a consequence of those events that have occurred during an accounting period whose monetary amounts can be reliably measured. Financial statements should report the substance of economic events, even if their substance differs from their legal form.

3.03. The primary focus of financial accounting should be on the measurement of income, which is the increase in an entity's equity during an accounting period arising from the entity's operating activities during the period. Pending the analysis of results of experiments now being conducted, income should be measured in actual monetary units and should not attempt to reflect current costs.

3.04. Income should be measured directly by measuring revenues and expenses rather than indirectly by measuring changes in assets and liabilities.

3.05. The calendar period covered by a set of financial statements should be one year.

3.06. Financial statements should be based on information that is available by the end of an accounting period or shortly thereafter.

3.07. Unless there is contrary evidence, financial accounting should assume that the entity will continue to operate indefinitely.

3.08. Amounts on the primary financial statements should articulate.

3.09. To the extent feasible, financial statements should meet the information needs of the most important classes of users, as perceived by those who establish accounting standards.

3.10. An entity should use consistent accounting practices from one period to the next unless a preferable practice becomes accepted.

3.11. Similar events should be treated similarly by all entities.

3.12. Any accounting standard may be disregarded if the effect of doing so is not material.

3.13. Recognition of increases in an entity's equity requires more reliable evidence than recognition of decreases.

3.14. In deciding on accounting standards and on the application of standards to specific events, an appropriate balance should be sought between the need for relevance and the need for reliability.

3.15. The benefits from information should exceed the costs of furnishing it.

Chapter 4:   Entity equity and equity interest

4.01. Shareholder equity reports the amount of funds furnished by shareholders. It consists of their direct contributions plus accrued interest on these funds.

4.02. Interest is the cost of using funds. Equity interest is the cost of using shareholder equity funds.

4.03. Entity equity is the difference between total assets and the sum of liabilities plus shareholder equity. Its principal source is the entity's operating activities.

4.04. Interest should be recognized as an element of cost. The cost of using funds in the acquisition or production of goods and services should be an element of their cost. Interest cost that is not capitalized should be an expense of the period.

4.05. The amount of equity interest in a period should be credited to shareholder equity.

4.06. The rate used in calculating the interest cost that is capitalized should be either the entity's pretax debt rate or a rate designated by the Financial Accounting Standards Board.

Chapter 5:   Cost and cost assignment

5.01. Cost is a monetary measure of the amount of resources used for a cost object. A cost object is an object whose cost is measured.

5.02. An expenditure is the increase in a liability or shareholder equity or the decrease in an asset that results when the entity acquires goods or services.

5.03. Expenses are costs that are applicable to the current accounting period.

5.04. The cost of a resource acquired for use by an entity should be the total of the expenditures that make the resource ready for its intended use.

5.05. The amount of an expenditure should be the price in an exchange with an unrelated party. If such a price is not determinable, the amount should be the fair value of the resource acquired. If the fair value of the resource acquired is not determinable, the amount should be the fair value of the resource given up by the entity.

5.06. Donated goods or services should be recorded at their fair value.

5.07. Expenditures that require future outlays should be measured as the present value of the expected value of these outlays.

5.08. The cost of a product produced by an entity should be its full production cost, that is, its direct costs plus a fair share of indirect costs.

5.09. Temporal Fairness: if a resource is used for several accounting periods, the amount of its cost assigned to any one period should be in proportion to the estimated benefits provided in that period.

5.10. Object Fairness: indirect costs of an accounting period should be allocated to cost objects in proportion to the amount of these costs that each cost object caused. If a causal relationship cannot be identified, another equitable basis of allocation should be used.

5.11. A by-product is a secondary product from a process whose primary purpose is to produce one or more main products. If the by-product is intended to be sold, its cost should be set equal to its net realizable value. The cost of other by-products should be the direct costs of producing them.

5.12. The cost of using a depreciable asset in an accounting period should include both depreciation and the cost of interest on the funds committed to the asset.

5.13. If the benefits of using a depreciable asset are presumed to be equal in each year of its life, the depreciation component of the cost should be calculated by the annuity method.

Chapter 6: Net income measurement

6.01. Net income is the increase in entity equity arising from the financial effects of those operating activities of an accounting period that can be reliably measured. Net income is measured as the difference between revenues of the period and expenses of the period.

6.02. When a given event affects both revenues and expenses, the effect on each should be recorded in the same accounting period.

6.03. The revenues of an accounting period are those additions to entity equity resulting from operating activities of the period that can be reliably measured.

6.04. Revenues from products should be recognized in the earliest period in which (a) the entity has performed substantially what is required in order to earn income and (b) the amount of income can be reliably estimated.

6.05. Gains from the discovery of a mineral resource should be recognized in the earliest period in which a reasonable value for the resource can be reliably estimated.

6.06. Other nonmonetary gains should be recognized in the period in which they are realized.

6.07. Other resource inflows intended for operating purposes should be recognized as revenues in the period in which income is realized.

6.08. The amount of revenue should be the present value of the amount that is highly likely to be realized.

6.09. If there is a reasonable possibility that an asset will not be associated with revenue in a future period in an amount at least equal to its recorded cost, the difference between its recorded cost and the probable future revenue should be reported as an expense.

6.10. If there is a reasonable possibility that a loss (other than a loss on a monetary asset) has occurred during the current period, or if a loss occurring in a prior period is discovered during the current period, the amount of loss that is reasonably possible should be recognized as an expense of the current period.

6.11. Monetary gains and losses should be recognized as revenue or expense in the period in which they occur unless they are unlikely to be realized, in which case they should not be recognized until realized.

Chapter 7: Assets and sources of funds

7.01. A balance sheet reports the amount of funds supplied to the entity from various sources, and the forms in which its capital existed as of the balance sheet date.

7.02. Assets are the forms in which an entity's capital exists. Assets consist of monetary items, unexpired costs, and investments. The amounts reported are the amount of capital tied up in each form.

7.03. Liabilities report the amounts of funds supplied by those external parties who do not receive equity rights in return.

7.04. Contracts, the two sides of which are proportionately unperformed, should not be recognized.

7.05. Contributions intended for nonoperating purposes should be credited to entity equity.

7.06. A direct entry to entity equity should be made only if it corrects an error in the amount of entity equity at the beginning of the period or if the effect of including the amount in net income would be to distort seriously the measurement of net income.

7.07. Events involving increases in assets whose recognition is not guided by other concepts should be reported in the period in which the entity acquires the right to use the resources. Events involving increases in liabilities whose recognition is not guided by other concepts should be reported in the period in which the entity becomes obligated to pay another party.

7.08. Monetary items are money and claims to specified amounts of money. They should be reported at the present value of the amounts highly likely to be received.

7.09. Investments are interests in other entities. Investments that do not involve a promise to pay money should be reported at the amount originally invested plus amounts due from the other entity.

7.10. Liabilities whose amount is not governed by other concepts should be reported at the present value of the entity's obligation to those who supplied the funds.

7.11. In measuring the amount to be reported for a liability, the future amount of the obligation should ordinarily be discounted at the interest rate implicit in the amount of funds received. If this rate is not apparent from the transaction itself, the discount rate should be the interest rate on obligations of similar risk prevailing at the time the obligation was entered into.

7.12. The amount reported for shareholder equity should be the fair value of the capital originally supplied by equity investors, calculated at the time the funds were committed, plus equity interest, less dividends or other distributions to shareholders.

Chapter 8: Financial statements

8.01. An operating statement should summarize the revenues and the expenses of an accounting period and the difference between them.

8.02. The net effect on entity equity of each principal type of extraordinary gains and losses should be reported separately and below other items on an operating statement.

8.03. If the principal activities of an entity are to carry out identifiable programs, the operating statement should summarize the expenses and, if applicable, the revenues for each major program.

8.04. A balance sheet should identify current assets and current liabilities separately from noncurrent assets and noncurrent liabilities.

8.05. Nonoperating assets are assets acquired with nonoperating contributions. Nonoperating assets should be reported separately from operating assets, and the related sources of funds should be reported separately from the entity equity generated by operating activities.

8.06. An entity should report a funds flow statement that summarizes investing and financing activities associated with its operations during an accounting period if these activities have been significant.

8.07. If the causes of significant changes in shareholder equity or entity equity are not readily discernible from other statements, these should be reported on one or more statements of changes in equity.

Contents

accounting. Direct versus indirect approach to income measurement. Other basic concepts.

Appendix A: Some implications of the basic concepts.

Appendix B: An analysis of inflation accounting.

4 Entity equity and equity interest 91

Unrealism of current practice. Proposed balance sheet structure. The measurement problem. Advantages for the conceptual framework. Advantages for financial reporting. Other advantages. Arguments against the concepts. Transition steps.

Appendix: Accounting procedures.

5 Cost and cost assignment 120

Definitions. Acquisition cost concepts. Cost assignment. Allocation concepts. Application of the allocation concepts. Interest and depreciation. Interest on entity equity.

Appendix: Some implications of cost concepts.

6 Net income measurement 148

Approach to the analysis. Relevant considerations. Red herrings. Definition of net income. Matching concept. Definition revenue. Revenue recognition: Timing. Recognition of revenue: Amount. Expenses: Losses. Monetary gains and losses.

Appendix: Some implications of income measurement concepts.

7 Assets and sources of funds 175

Balance sheet. Recognition concepts. Unperformed contracts. Nonoperating contributions. Other changes in entity equity. Other balance sheet events. Measurement concepts. Shareholder equity. Endowment earnings.

Appendix: Some implications of assets and funds sources concepts.

8 Financial statements   194

Operating statement. Balance sheet. Funds flow statement. Statement of changes in equity. Conclusion.

1

The what and why of this framework

This book describes a conceptual framework for general purpose financial statements; the framework applies to both profit-oriented and nonprofit organizations. The objective of financial statements is to provide financial information about an economic entity.

PURPOSES OF A CONCEPTUAL FRAMEWORK

Most people agree that standards governing the nature and content of financial statements are necessary and that the standards should be developed within a conceptual framework. As Oscar S. Gellein has remarked, "A framework of concepts comprises ideas that coordinate to form the fabric of a system—the fabric that determines the bounds of the system and makes it hang together." [1]

In the United States the Financial Accounting Standards Board (FASB) is responsible for developing standards. Each of the seven board members has a mental conceptual framework that, whether articulated or not, guides his analysis of a proposed standard. Those who comment on proposed standards usually do so in terms of their personal conceptual frameworks. Thus, concepts provide guidance in the development of standards (also

---

[1]Notes begin on Page 207.

referred to as generally accepted accounting principles, or GAAP), although concepts are at a higher level of generality than standards.[2]

At present, there is no authoritative conceptual framework that is sufficiently comprehensive to provide a guide to the development of standards. (The present situation is summarized in a later section of this chapter.) In the absence of such a framework, accounting issues are resolved on an ad hoc basis. Those who comment on proposed accounting standards do so in terms of their personal conceptual frameworks, and the members of the Financial Accounting Standards Board vote in accordance with their personal conceptual frameworks. These frameworks differ one from another.

Many of the disagreements among accountants about a proposed standard stem from these differences, even though they may not be apparent to those stating the arguments. A comprehensive, authoritative framework would limit these disagreements to matters not resolved by reference to the framework and thus would reduce considerably the time involved in discussing a proposed standard. Established concepts provide an agreed-upon takeoff point for such a discussion.[3] In their absence, a conceptual issue may be raised at any time, and the discussion cannot proceed until controversy about that issue has been resolved. For example, current discussions about pension cost and pension liability often flounder because of disagreement as to the concepts of "cost" and "liability."[4]

Moreover, adoption of an authoritative, comprehensive conceptual framework reduces the need for detailed standards. In 1981, for example, the FASB considered five proposed standards that related to the recognition of revenue in various circumstances. If there were a concept on the nature of revenue itself, some of these separate standards would be unnecessary, and the others would be narrowed to issues not clearly resolved by the concept.

A reduction in detailed standards would lead to an accounting structure with less of a "cookbook" flavor than the current set of standards. When entities report events in a way that is consistent with broad concepts, they can take into account nuances in their particular circumstances. In this complicated world, standards setters have great difficulty in identifying and formulating detailed standards for all the possible circumstances.

Moreover, a conceptual framework would help students to understand accounting; it would help them see how individual topics fit into an overall picture.

SCOPE OF THIS FRAMEWORK

This framework for financial statements is limited to matters within the purview of the Financial Accounting Standards Board, but not to all such matters. The framework's boundaries are described in the following paragraphs.

Information for external users

Financial statements provide information about an entity that is intended to meet the needs of external parties. In ordinary circumstances these external parties cannot require the entity to provide information consistent with their individual preferences. Moreover, external parties rarely have either the time or the inclination to develop a set of specifications for the information they need. On the other hand, they are unwilling to have the entity decide the nature and content of the information it reports because of the possibility that such information will be biased and inadequate. External parties therefore must rely on an authoritative body, such as the FASB, to prescribe standards for reporting financial information. Unless an authoritative body performs this function, the financial statements for an entity will be at worst incomprehensible or misleading and at best not comparable with those of other entities.[5]

Limiting this framework to information furnished to external parties does not imply that information prepared for management is inherently different from that in an entity's published financial statements. Management, of course, uses accounting information, and unless there is good reason to do otherwise, it tends to use information prepared in accordance with FASB standards. However, because management can specify the type of information and manner in which it is to be reported, an authoritative standards-setting body is not needed for internal accounting information.[6]

General purpose statements

This conceptual framework applies to general purpose financial statements. Financial statements prepared for parties who can prescribe the statements' contents—such as the Internal Revenue Service, regulatory commissions, legislative bodies, and grantors—are excluded. Such reports are special purpose reports. Nevertheless, to the extent that general purpose reporting concepts are sensible, these agencies are likely to be guided by them in establishing their requirements unless their objective is different from that which governs financial reporting. The income tax, for example, is often used for social objectives, and some income tax regulations designed to accomplish these objectives—such as those relating to depreciation—are inconsistent with general purpose financial accounting standards.

Special purpose statements are not a substitute for general purpose statements. A state legislature may prescribe the content of financial statements prepared by municipalities, and these municipalities must by law conform to the state's rules. If, however, these rules are not consistent with GAAP, the resulting statements are special purpose statements. If a municipality is required by bond rating agencies to supply financial statements prepared in accordance with GAAP, it must prepare separate statements for the bond rating agencies. These are general purpose statements.

Financial statements

A financial report consists of a set of financial statements plus notes and other supplementary information. Although the jurisdiction of the FASB encompasses all the information in financial reports, this book is limited to the financial statements (often referred to as primary financial statements in order to distinguish them from the supplementary information).

My omission of supplementary information does not mean that this information is unimportant. On the contrary, a principal thrust of the FASB in recent years has been to expand requirements for supplementary information. Rather, the sole purpose of this limitation is to narrow the focus of the analysis. This narrower focus makes it unnecessary to discuss a number of issues, such as the amount of detail that should be disclosed in notes, supplementary information required of some entities but not others, nonfinancial information, and so forth.

Limiting the analysis to financial statements also requires that I present a more rigorous analysis. It is one thing to state that information about the effect of inflation on the entity is useful and therefore should be disclosed somewhere. It is much more difficult to decide whether such information, on balance, meets the criteria that govern the primary financial statements.[7] In particular, since the several financial statements must articulate, difficult choices must be made on some issues, as will be seen.

Focus on an entity

Financial statements focus on a single entity, rather than on broader economic groupings such as an industry or an entire economy. National income accounts are prepared from reports on individual entities, but concepts governing the preparation of these accounts are outside the scope of this analysis.

Financial, not social

Accounting information is financial information. Accounting reports are therefore limited to phenomena that can be described in monetary terms. If fines are imposed on an entity for polluting a river, these are relevant to financial accounting. If the entity pollutes the river without suffering a financial penalty, its poor social performance is not reflected in its financial statements. (This point is developed further in Chapter 2.)

Limiting this analysis to financial information does not imply that nonfinancial information is unimportant. Indeed, relatively little information about the overall performance of a nonbusiness organization is conveyed in its financial statements; most such information is nonfinancial.

Both business and nonbusiness

This framework is intended to apply to the general purpose financial statements of all organizations except the federal government. Most accounting texts and conceptual frameworks limit their coverage to profit-oriented companies. Hendriksen, the most widely used text on accounting theory, does not list "nonprofit" or "nonbusiness" in the index, nor did I find mention of these organizations in the text itself.[8]

Since the framework applies to both, there is no need to define business and nonbusiness organizations, except to note that the approximate line between them is that one is profit-oriented and the other is not. Governments, hospitals, educational organizations, and other nonbusiness organizations comprise about a third of the entire economic activity in this country. Nonbusiness organizations issue more debt securities than do profit-oriented organizations.[9]

Although most nonbusiness organizations prepare financial statements, there is a tendency to presume that these financial statements should be governed by concepts that are only loosely related, if related at all, to those applicable to business organizations. Unusual accounting practices exist in nonbusiness organizations, especially in state and municipal governments, and there has been little effort to fit these practices into a conceptual framework. I shall deal with both business and nonbusiness entities and describe an overall framework that applies in general to both of them, although there are some differences in detail.[10] Actually, the differences in detail between accounting for manufacturing companies and accounting for financial institutions are considerably greater than differences in the accounting appropriate for business organizations in general and those appropriate for nonbusiness organizations in general.

The fact that accounting texts typically focus on profit-oriented organizations probably reflects the background of the authors rather than their conviction that accounting in nonbusiness organizations is essentially different from that in businesses.[11] This focus also results from the fact that until fairly recently investors, who are the principal users of accounting information, were primarily interested in business organizations.

The federal government is excluded because some aspects of the framework do not apply to financial reporting for federal agencies. Unlike any other entity, the federal government has the power to print money; it cannot go bankrupt. For this reason, those interested in the financial status of the federal government do not look to its financial statements for information on the government's liquidity or solvency. Furthermore, the Comptroller General has statutory authority to set accounting standards for federal agencies, and the FASB therefore has no jurisdiction in this area.[12] In most respects, however, concepts for financial reporting in the federal government are similar to those in other entities.

Regulated entities included

Some argue that regulated industries require a unique conceptual framework. Although regulated industries do have some unique characteristics, the accounting problems associated with them can be dealt with in the context of a framework that applies to all organizations. This framework, therefore, is intended to be applicable to regulated industries.[13]

Focus on American environment

Although I have some knowledge of accounting practice in Europe (including the Soviet Union), Latin America, Canada, Asia, and Australia, I do not know enough about the economic environment to assert that the conceptual framework described here should apply to countries other than the United States. So far as I am aware, however, except in countries with hyperinflation, such as Argentina, Brazil, and Israel, there are no unique characteristics in other countries that lead to substantially different accounting concepts. In Western Europe investors tend to be interested more in dividends than in net income, but this is a matter of degree that does not affect the nature of reported income.

STRUCTURE OF THE ANALYSIS

Some say that accounting is a science; others, that it is an art. For our present purpose, the difference is unimportant. If accounting is a science, it is an applied science, and if it is an art, it is a practical art.[14] Although not always described in these terms, standards in most disciplines are developed in the following way: First, *premises* about the "state of nature" are developed by the process of *induction*. Second, *concepts* are *deduced* from these premises. Third, *standards* are developed that guide the application of these concepts to practice.[15] The approach in this book comprises the first two of these steps.[16]

Premises, the inductive statements, are supposed to describe the way things are. Concepts, the deductive statements, are ideas about what accounting standards should be. Premises are descriptive; concepts are prescriptive, normative.[17] The metallurgist induces premises about the properties of various types of material; the physicist induces premises about the load-bearing limits of various geometric shapes. From these and other premises, the engineer deduces concepts for building bridges that will not collapse, and these concepts are the basis for standards of bridge construction.

Premises

Premises are statements about an area of interest that are believed to be valid. They are also called postulates, assumptions, theorems, or axioms. (Most of the "objectives" in FASB Concepts Statements No. 1 and No. 4 are actually premises.) They are beliefs, not eternal truths. Some premises are developed on the basis of scientific observation or experiment, and they are valid in the sense that they are not contradicted by the current weight of scientific evidence.

Few scientific premises are valid forever. Although a premise may persist for a long time, new evidence eventually comes to light that requires that the premise be either revised or discarded. Although for many years the atom was believed to be the smallest unit of matter, this premise was superseded by the premise that the electron and proton were the basic units. This premise was, in turn, superseded by others, the most recent of which is that the basic units of matter are three particles. At any given time, physicists accepted the premise that is consistent with the available evidence at that time.[18]

Chapter 2 describes premises that I believe to be relevant to the development of financial accounting concepts and gives the evidence for these premises. Although this evidence may be inadequate, contradictory, and inconclusive, I believe it is the best available.

Concepts

Concepts do not follow unequivocally and clearly from the premises. Some premises conflict with other premises, and in developing concepts one must decide which premise should be given the greater weight. In environmental matters, the need to preserve endangered species conflicts with the need for use of resources; the need for oil from shale conflicts with the need to preserve the landscape and to maintain the water table. The areas of conflict grow as society and its interests become more complex.

In accounting, the principal conflict is between the need for information that is relevant and the requirement that information be reasonably reliable. Although the best evidence of the value of a business is the judgment of competent top management as to its future earnings, there is no reasonably reliable way that external users can obtain this information.

Accounting concepts are described in Chapters 3 through 8. They comprise two types of statements. One type is a definition. Although definitions are given as declarative sentences, the way in which a term is defined is a normative conclusion about it. The second type of statement expresses the concept itself as a normative statement in the form, "Assuming that the premises are valid, then financial accounting *should* report. . . ."

OTHER CONCEPTUAL FRAMEWORKS

Few attempts to develop a conceptual framework for accounting have used the approach I use in this book; namely, explicitly to state a set of premises and then to deduce concepts that are consistent with these premises. Although conceptual frameworks are necessarily based on premises about the nature of accounting entities and about the needs of users of accounting information, in most of them the underlying premises are not made explicit. When the premises are implicit, it is difficult to know whether a critic's dissatisfaction with the concepts is based on disagreement with the premises themselves or on the belief that the concepts are not consistent with the premises.

The principal conceptual frameworks developed in recent years can be grouped under two headings: unofficial and official.

Unofficial frameworks

Unofficial frameworks are those not developed by, or at the request of, an authoritative body. (This book describes an unofficial framework.) Most accounting textbooks are written around some such conceptual framework, although the framework may not be explicit.[19] References to unofficial frameworks are given in the Appendix to this chapter.

Official conceptual frameworks

In the United States the first set of accounting standards by a professional body was *Uniform Accounting*, a document developed in 1917 by the American Institute of Accountants (predecessor of the American Institute of CPAs) and published by the Federal Reserve Board. This document focused on the balance sheet. It was revised from time to time, and its focus gradually shifted to the measurement of income.

In 1934 the Securities and Exchange Commission was given statutory authority to develop accounting standards. It decided, however, to rely primarily on the private sector for this work. Thus, the "official" standard-setting body remained the American Institute of CPAs, which in 1936 formed a Committee on Accounting Procedures for this purpose.

Committee on Accounting Procedures. Between 1939 and 1959 the Committee on Accounting Procedures issued 51 Accounting Research Bulletins, each on a specific topic. Beginning about 1950 the committee attempted to develop a conceptual framework that would guide its work in developing bulletins. It did not succeed. In lieu of such a framework, in 1953 it issued Accounting Research Bulletin 43; this was titled a *Restatement and Revision* of the 42 bulletins issued up to that time, and as the title indicates, it was not a set of concepts.

Accounting Principles Board. The Accounting Principles Board (APB) superseded the Committee on Accounting Procedures as of September 1, 1959. Shortly before that, the AICPA commissioned Professor Maurice Moonitz to prepare analyses on accounting principles and postulates. Professor Moonitz enlisted the help of Professor Robert Sprouse on the principles project. Two monographs resulted.[20] Although these postulates and concepts were discussed by the APB, they were not accepted. A subsequent effort to develop a conceptual statement was launched, but it did not produce results.

In a move that was intended to provide source material for the development of concepts, the APB commissioned Paul Grady, partner of Price Waterhouse & Co., to develop an inventory of currently accepted accounting principles; this was published in 1965.[21] It was never blessed as an authoritative statement, even of existing principles.

The APB published its Statement No. 4 in 1970. This was a codification of existing concepts, rather than a statement of what concepts should be. Although often quoted, and in fact frequently referred to by the FASB as if it were authoritative, Statement No. 4 was never accepted as an authoritative set of normative concepts or even as an accurate description of concepts underlying current practice.[22]

Trueblood Committee. The report of the Trueblood Committee in 1973, *Objectives of Financial Statements,* [23] was an important document. It was primarily a statement of premises, rather than of concepts, but it did contain a few concepts. Although it influenced the early work of the FASB, the report was not itself an authoritative document.[24]

Financial Accounting Standards Board. The four FASB concepts statements published through 1982 are primarily statements of premises. Concepts Statement No. 3 does define the principal terms used in financial statements, and Concepts Statements No. 1 and No. 4 have a few concepts.

Transnational bodies also are developing conceptual frameworks.[25]

WHY ANOTHER FRAMEWORK?

The Financial Accounting Standards Board is the authoritative standards-setting body in the United States. It is so recognized by the Securities and Exchange Commission. Rule 203 of the American Institute of CPAs prohibits auditors in most circumstances from giving a clean opinion on financial statements not prepared in accordance with FASB standards. The FASB is developing a conceptual framework. The question naturally arises: Why should an individual like myself presume to develop a different framework?

My reason is that the FASB conceptual framework does not seem likely to provide the guidance that is needed to develop a sound body of standards. Although the FASB has been developing a framework since 1973, the results 10 years later have not had a noticeable effect on the promulgation of standards.

For example, in 1981, shortly after the publication of Concepts Statement No. 3, the FASB issued a Discussion Memorandum on accounting for pensions.[26] This memorandum had a whole chapter on the liability aspect of pensions and another on the expense aspect. Since *liability* and *expense* were defined and discussed at great length in Concepts Statement No. 3, one would expect that the subsequent Discussion Memorandum would simply state that most issues on these topics were no longer debatable and that the discussion would be confined to those matters not properly addressed in a concepts statement. This Discussion Memorandum imposed no such restrictions. Although there were references to Concepts Statement No. 3, this statement was not used to limit the discussion in any way. Furthermore, the term *expense* was used in this Discussion Memorandum in a sense that was inconsistent with the definition in Concepts Statement No. 3.[27]

This example illustrates a basic defect of FASB concepts statements: they are not incorrect, but they are so vague that practically any proposed standard can be said to be consistent with them. Although their stated purpose is to provide guidance in the development of standards, they do not provide much guidance.

There is today no agreement among theorists as to the basic ideas that should govern financial accounting for general purpose statements. One can get a feel for the current state of thinking by reading the report of a symposium arranged in 1978 by Robert R. Sterling.[28] The 17 papers presented at this symposium were written by leading scholars who were active in discussing accounting theory. Each was asked by Sterling to describe what accounting should report for a company whose only assets were cash and taxicabs and whose only activity was providing taxi service. No author simply said, "I agree with Professor X," and let it go at that.

There were 17 different answers to Sterling's question. Five participants said that the question could not be answered; any answer would be "unscientific," they claimed, if it did not describe an accounting system that met the information needs of users, yet these needs were not known. The five suggested various ways, all different, of discovering what information users needed. Three participants proposed frameworks based on cash flows.

Five outlined systems that included price-level adjustments, replacement costs, net realizable values, deprival values, or other departures from historical cost. In one paper, the emphasis was on forecasts, rather than recorded data. One favored the current framework, without describing what it was. One favored the current framework modified to incorporate annuity depreciation. And one advocated three different frameworks, to be used concurrently.

In short, despite the efforts of the FASB over the past 8 to 10 years, there is no consensus about financial accounting concepts. Perhaps my framework will merely add to the confusion, but my hope is that it will lead to discussion and a coalescing of views. Such an alternative framework may provide the Board with an opportunity to take a fresh look at the concepts problem. My hope is that the Board will consider this framework in such a light. The Board will not, of course, adopt it entirely. Any attempt such as this is at best a first approximation, one that surely will be modified substantially after discussion.

EVALUATION OF THIS FRAMEWORK

This book is organized to facilitate discussion. First, readers are asked to agree or disagree with the premises in Chapter 2. If they disagree, readers are asked to decide if the weight of the evidence supports a different premise or if additional premises are necessary for the development of accounting concepts. Implications of these proposed changes can then be traced to the concepts stated in later chapters and presumably would lead to revisions of certain concepts.

If the premises are accepted as valid and sufficient, then readers who disagree with a concept are asked to decide if: (a) it is inconsistent with the premises or with other concepts, (b) it does not strike the proper balance between conflicting premises, or (c) it is not needed as the basis for arriving at standards.

Readers can also criticize the set of concepts on the grounds that it omits a necessary concept.

ARGUMENTS AGAINST A CONCEPTUAL FRAMEWORK

Although most people grant the usefulness of a conceptual framework for financial accounting, a few think that efforts to construct such a framework are not worthwhile. Some argue that development of a framework is not feasible; others that it is not necessary or desirable. Arguments of these critics are cited frequently enough that discussion of them is warranted.

Concepts not feasible

Some who doubt the feasibility of developing an acceptable conceptual framework point out that none of the attempts by various persons and organizations has succeeded. No official framework exists, and unofficial frameworks have had little impact on the development of accounting. This defeatist argument, however, really says only that history shows that the development of a conceptual framework is difficult, not that it is impossible.

Although previous efforts have not been successful, it must be recognized that an authoritative body has existed only in the past 25 years. Without official acceptance by an authoritative body, it is unrealistic to expect the acceptance of any conceptual framework. The failure of the Accounting Principles Board to develop a conceptual framework is a bad omen, but despite this failure the FASB has, since its inception, stressed the need for a conceptual framework.

Another reason advanced for the infeasibility of developing a conceptual framework is the assertion that the purpose of financial accounting is to measure "true income" and the claim that this goal cannot be achieved because no one knows what true income is.[29] Those who take this position expect too much of accounting. Although it is almost inconceivable that conclusive evidence will be developed proving that one way of measuring income is more valid than all others, it is reasonable to conclude—in fact, obviously essential to any accounting framework—that some ways are more useful than others. Premises are not eternal truths. Acceptable premises are, however, as close to the truth as the current state of knowledge permits.

A sophisticated version of this argument takes off from the "impossibility theorem" of Kenneth Arrow and attempts to show that conditions similar to those that allegedly prohibit the development of a rational theory of choice in economics apply as well to accounting. Although some economists take Arrow's theorem seriously, actually it is nothing more than an elaborate statement of the obvious: in the real world, criteria conflict with one another and people differ in their perceptions and beliefs; therefore, it is impossible to devise perfect decision rules.[30]

Perfection is indeed impossible because accounting concepts are based on premises that cannot be verified and also because some premises conflict with others, and a balance must be struck. The members of the FASB have to make the best judgments they can. (For similar reasons the Constitution of the United States sets forth a mechanism whereby the Congress and the judiciary may modify and interpret its provisions.)

A number of theorists, called "positivists," urge that development of a conceptual framework for accounting be delayed until research has established "why accounting is what it is, why accountants do what they do, and what effects these phenomena have on people and resource utilization."[31] Since it seems unlikely that these questions can ever be answered by research, acceptance of this view would postpone development of a conceptual framework indefinitely. As with the preceding arguments, the basic trouble with this one is that its proponents are unwilling to settle for anything less than perfection, whereas accounting needs a conceptual framework, even if imperfect, as a guide in resolving important outstanding issues.

A less extreme version of this proposition is that only the objectives and criteria of accounting can be set forth as concepts and that standards consistent with the objectives and criteria should emerge from a process similar to that of the common law. The standards-setting body would resolve specific issues on the basis of these objectives and criteria.[32] I believe that a conceptual framework can do more than state objectives and criteria and that a coherent body of standards cannot be developed unless it does so. As I explain in Chapter 2, because some criteria conflict with others, a set of criteria is inadequate as a basis for resolving issues. A conceptual framework should suggest how these conflicts should be resolved.

Concepts not necessary or desirable

A political process. A second argument against the development of a conceptual framework is that accounting progresses by dealing with specific issues. The resolution of these issues is essentially a political process, it is said, and advocates with the strongest clout have issues resolved in their favor. In these circumstances, a conceptual framework is irrelevant, and its development is therefore a waste of time. A recent example is the 1970s controversy over accounting for oil and gas exploration costs. The issue was settled as much by pressure exerted by industry on the federal legislative and executive branches as by reasoning from a conceptual framework.

Although the development of accounting standards is in part a political process, this is the case with any discipline whose premises are not verifiable. Even in the natural sciences, certain premises, such as the theory of evolution, are accepted only after what is essentially a political debate. And the words of written documents such as the United States Constitution are changed through amendment and interpretation to reflect current social and political conditions.

Rely on accountants. The Accounting Principles Board was the first body to establish accounting standards that the profession was required to follow. (Adherence to the Accounting Research Bulletins was voluntary.) During its life, there were those who argued that the APB never should have undertaken the task of developing standards.

A few people continue to advance these arguments. Abraham Briloff has described this view as the theory of "let many flowers bloom."[33] By this, he means that public accounting firms should prepare the financial reports of the firms they audit in whatever way they think is best. Since there are about 20 major accounting firms, each of whom would necessarily develop a set of standards in order to promote consistent treatment by its own partners, the result would be 20 sets of standards rather than one.

Disaggregated data.   An even more extreme proposal is that entities should report essentially raw data, and users could then arrange these data in whatever way they found most useful.[34] For example, instead of reporting a number for depreciation expense, the entity would report the cost of assets acquired and perhaps a frequency distribution of the possible life of each type of asset; the user might use these data as a basis for constructing a depreciation number, or if so inclined, the user could exclude depreciation. It seems unlikely that users have the time, the inclination, or the ability to construct their own financial statements from disaggregated data. They expect accountants to do this. Assuming only 10 items are reported on an operating statement, with three alternative numbers for each item, approximately 1,000 "bottom lines" would be possible. The result would be chaotic.

Let users adjust   Several research studies are said to show that users "see through" the effects of certain accounting alternatives, such as LIFO versus FIFO inventory valuation, accelerated versus straight-line depreciation, and pooling versus purchase. Users are said mentally to allow for the effect of these alternatives in comparing companies that use different methods or in comparing the current earnings of a company with earnings reported in prior years under a different method. These studies are used by some as arguments against the need for accounting standards.[35]

These arguments are weak. Some of the studies are inconclusive. All of them focus on dramatic changes in accounting practices, each of which had a substantial effect on reported income. They do not deal with the possible effect of the numerous small-scale alternatives which would be likely in the absence of standards. Users could not adjust for such changes and most certainly do not want to make adjustments in order to develop comparable financial statements for all the entities they analyze. They expect accountants to provide comparable statements.

Possible rigidity.   Another argument is that the development of a conceptual framework is undesirable because it would lead to too much rigidity in accounting. This rigidity not only would inhibit those who want to report faithfully the results of certain transactions that do not fit nicely into the accepted framework, but it also would freeze accounting into a mold that would prevent further progress.

Although a conceptual framework can lead to rigidity, this danger is less grave than the alternative of attempting to develop standards without a framework. Although a written framework can indeed be an obstacle to progress (because there is a strong burden of proof on anyone who wants to change it), on balance the resulting stability is probably desirable.

Critics of efforts to develop a conceptual framework are too pessimistic. There is already a considerable degree of agreement on concepts. If these noncontroversial aspects are properly articulated, and if the controversial aspects are thoroughly discussed, a consensus should emerge.

OVERVIEW OF THE FRAMEWORK

This book is an attempt to present those concepts that are generally agreed upon and to state the case for the recommended resolution of the few controversial matters. It aims to develop a conceptual framework that will guide future decisions on accounting standards and on the application of standards to specific entities.

For the noncontroversial topics, I merely state the concepts as clearly as I can and show how they fit into the overall framework. My main effort will be focused on a few controversial topics. For these, I shall describe the various points of view and provide what I think is the proper resolution, consistent with the premises and other concepts.

This framework differs from the accounting concepts that are now generally accepted for nonbusiness organizations in several respects. One of my themes is that accounting in nonbusiness organizations should be similar to that in business organizations, and not for the reason of "forcing nonbusiness into the business mold," as some assert.[36]

My framework differs from accounting as currently practiced in business entities in only one substantial way. Its basic theme is that financial accounting should focus on the entity as such, rather than on the interest of equity investors in the entity, as is the present focus. In my framework, equity investors are regarded as one source of funds. They provide these funds at a cost, and I maintain that accounting should include this cost (here called equity interest) and also the cost of using funds obtained from debt (debt interest), just as other elements of cost are accounted for.

This focus leads one to report on the right-hand side of the balance sheet the amount of funds furnished by equity investors, both their direct contribution and the amount of equity interest that has not yet been distributed to them as dividends. It leads to a new category on the right-hand side, the amount of funds that the entity has generated through its own activities, called entity equity. Since the cost of using funds would be treated as other elements of cost are now treated, an appropriate amount of interest cost would be capitalized on the left-hand side of the balance sheet.

As suggested in Paragraph 43 of FASB Concepts Statement No. 1, the primary focus of financial accounting should be on the entity's success in maintaining its equity through its operating activities, as measured by its net income. That is also the focus of this framework. However, as it appears on the present operating statement, net income includes both the cost of using shareholder equity funds and the addition to equity that has resulted from the entity's own activities. With the explicit recognition of equity interest as a cost, net income would be only the addition to equity arising from the entity's activities during an accounting period.

"Current value" models are not accepted as the basis for primary financial statements, at least until more evidence about their usefulness has been obtained. Revenues would be measured essentially as is done in current practice (although the framework spells out concepts for revenue measurement that are not explicitly stated in current authoritative pronouncements). Inventory would be measured at its full cost, also a current practice. Expenses would include the cost of equity interest, which is not recognized currently, so net income would be reduced by the amount of this new charge. Concepts for the allocation of costs are made more explicit than is currently the case, at least so far as the FASB standards are concerned. The recognition of equity interest as a cost leads to annuity depreciation as the preferred method for assets that are expected to provide approximately equal benefits for each year of their service life.[37]

Of these themes, the following appear to be the most controversial:

Equity interest.

Focus on income measurement, rather than on the balance sheet.

Inventory measured at full cost.

Continuation of historical cost basis.

Same concepts for business and nonbusiness.

Although the preceding summary of changes from current practice is short, it involves the most drastic change in accounting since the introduction of depreciation and therefore will not be accepted without wide discussion. The arguments and evidence presented in the remaining chapters will, I hope, provide a basis for such a discussion.

Appendix

UNOFFICIAL CONCEPTUAL FRAMEWORKS

Although aspects of a conceptual framework can be found in the 1494 treatise by Pacioli (and earlier in Chinese and Indian works that are not well known in the Western world), frameworks that are relevant to the modern environment date from the 1920s and 1930s. For a summary of these, see Eldon S. Hendriksen, *Accounting Theory*, 4th ed. (1982), Chapters 1 and 2; Kenneth S. Most, *Accounting Theory*, 2d ed. (Columbus, Ohio: Grid Publishing, 1982), Chapter 1–7; A. C. Littleton and V. K. Zimmerman, *Accounting Theory: Continuity and Change* (Englewood Cliffs, N.J.: Prentice-Hall, 1962); and American Accounting Association Committee Report, *Statement of Accounting Theory and Theory Acceptance* (1977).

The earliest American text that was built on a conceptual framework (as contrasted with a description of practices) probably was Charles E. Sprague, *The Philosophy of Accounts*, 5th ed. (1923).

Among the most influential of the early efforts was the monograph by William A. Paton and A. C. Littleton, *An Introduction to Corporate Accounting Standards* (1940), based on a 1936 article in *The Accounting Review*. Some sentences from it continue to be widely quoted. For example, the following statement applies equally well to the present effort: "Accounting standards should be systematic and coherent, impartial and impersonal, and in harmony with observable, objective conditions" (p. 1). The monograph has a list of articles on specific topics appearing in the 1930s, but none of these describes a complete conceptual framework.

The American Accounting Association is not a standards-setting body, so the Paton and Littleton monograph never received an official seal of approval. Nevertheless, probably 90 percent of its ideas are reflected in current practice. Its principal weaknesses as a modern document are that it takes a different view of the shareholder equity section of the balance sheet than that accepted today, and it does not deal with some problems, such as capital leases and deferred income taxes, that did not exist at that time. For an appreciation of Paton and Littleton, see the review article by Yuji Ijiri and the comment by William A. Paton, *The Accounting Review*, October 1980. A similar concepts statement was Thomas H. Sanders, Henry R. Hatfield, and Underhill Moore, *A Statement of Accounting Principles* (1938).

Another important early work was John B. Canning, *The Economics of Accountancy* (1929). Canning's objective was to explain accounting concepts to economists. This book did not have much impact at the time, although its merit has been increasingly recognized in recent years.

Frameworks by Chambers, Ijiri, and Mattesich explicitly set forth premises; they were called "axioms" by Ijiri and "assumptions" by Mattesich. Neither of these authors carried the analysis to the point of developing a complete set of concepts, however. An axiomatic approach is helpful in testing the internal consistency of certain concepts, but it cannot provide a complete conceptual framework because there is no way in such an approach of resolving conflicts among premises. Raymond J. Chambers, "Accounting Principles and Practices—Negotiated or Dictated?" in *Proceedings of the Second Annual Accounting Research Convocation* (1977) had a short list, at a high level of generality. References to the others are: Richard Mattessich, *Accounting and Analytical Methods: Measurement and Projection of Income and Wealth in the Micro- and Macro-Economy* (1964); Yuji Ijiri, *The Foundations of Accounting Measurement: A Mathematical, Economic and Behavioral Inquiry* (1967); and Ijiri, *Theory of Accounting Measurement*, AAA Studies in Accounting Research No. 10 (1975).

Ijiri's axiomatic framework published in 1967, revised and extended in 1975, is "written from the viewpoint that accounting is a system designed to facilitate the smooth functioning of *accountability* relationships among interested parties . . . in contrast to the widespread idea that accounting is a system for providing information useful for economic decisions" (p. ix). Ijiri develops an axiomatic model of existing accounting practice, deals with some extensions of historical cost accounting (for example, commitments and human resource accounting), and explores some methodological improvements needed in future accounting research. The book does not attempt to resolve controversial issues. A recent Ijiri framework is *Historical Cost Accounting and its Rationality*, Research Monograph No. 1, the Canadian Certified General Accountants' Research Foundation (1981).

James W. Pattillo deduced concepts from a single premise, "fairness to all parties," in *The Foundations of Financial Accounting* (1965).

Several authors have based frameworks on some version of "current values." Among these are: Edgar O. Edwards, Philip W. Bell, and L. Todd Johnson, *Accounting for Economic Events* (1979); this is an updated version of the widely quoted book by Edgar O. Edwards and Philip W. Bell, *The Theory and Measurement of Business Income* (1961); Robert R. Sterling, *Theory of the Measurement of Enterprise Income* (1970); Raymond J.

Chambers, *Accounting, Evaluation and Economic Behavior* (1966); George J. Staubus, *Making Accounting Decisions* (1977).

Conceptual frameworks not cited in the sources given at the beginning of this appendix include: Herman W. Bevis, *Corporate Financial Reporting in a Competitive Economy* (1965); George J. Staubus, *Making Accounting Decisions* (previously cited); Ross M. Skinner, *Accounting Principles: A Canadian Viewpoint* (1972); and William H. Beaver, *Financial Reporting: An Accounting Revolution* (1981). The Beaver book deals primarily with disclosure; the title notwithstanding, it does not suggest that there has been or soon will be a "revolution" in accounting concepts.

Louis Goldberg, *An Inquiry into The Nature of Accounting*, AAA Monograph No. 7 (1965), has an approach similar to mine; that is, it states premises and then develops a conceptual framework by reasoning from these premises. However, the premises are at a high level of generality, as for example: "In accounting we deal with activity—principally, but not solely, human activity—and therefore we must examine our concept of activity." The concepts deduced from these premises are also necessarily at a high level of generality.

Committees of the American Accounting Association have written several reports on financial accounting concepts, the most recent of which is the Committee to Prepare a Statement of Basic Accounting Theory, *A Statement of Basic Accounting Theory* (1966). ASOBAT, as it is called, is highly regarded by academics, but it has had little impact on practice.

Frameworks built around the idea of measuring current values differ fundamentally from those built around the idea of measuring the flow of costs. Within each of these two broad groups, however, differences are mostly in matters of detail. None of these frameworks includes the idea of shareholder equity as a source of funds that is separate from entity equity and that has a cost, equity interest, that is treated just like other elements of cost. None of these frameworks attempts to encompass both profit-oriented and nonprofit entities.

2

Premises

This chapter starts with a discussion of the nature of premises. It then states and supports a set of premises that underlie the concepts that should govern the preparation of general purpose financial statements.

GENERAL COMMENTS ABOUT PREMISES

As explained in Chapter 1, the premises on which a set of accounting concepts is based are derived by the process of induction (as contrasted with deduction). Although they are based on what appears to be the best available evidence as to the state of nature, their validity is not necessarily flawless; this is because the available evidence is incomplete and inconclusive. Premises may change as new evidence accumulates.

Premises as a source of controversy

Many of the important accounting controversies relate to the validity of premises, rather than to the accounting concepts deduced from an agreed set of premises. Proponents and opponents of a certain concept argue from different premises, yet quite often these differences are not made explicit. For example, those who support the concept that financial accounting should measure the present value of the future stream of the entity's earnings must implicitly accept the premise that this amount can be reliably measured; those who oppose this concept do so, at least in part, because they do not accept this premise.

Other controversies arise from disagreements about the relative importance of conflicting premises. Such disagreements show up most often in arguments that involve the relative importance of the reliability of information and the relevance of information. Examples will be given in Chapter 3.

Premises as generalizations

Most premises are generalizations; that is, they are believed to be valid in the majority of instances but not necessarily in all instances. The existence of exceptions to a premise is not a sufficient reason for rejecting it. In medicine, for instance, the generalization that cigarette smokers are likely to die from lung cancer is valid, even though not all smokers get lung cancer, even though not all lung cancer sufferers die from this disease, and even though lung cancer is also caused by factors other than cigarette smoking.

Premises not immutable

There are few external truths. In a recent Phi Beta Kappa oration, Lewis Thomas, M.D., expressed this idea well:

> The great body of science, built like a vast hill over the past three hundred years, is a mobile, unsteady structure, made up of solid-enough single bits of information, but with all the bits always moving about, fitting together in different ways, adding new bits. . . . Human knowledge doesn't stay put.[1]

Many premises eventually become outmoded, either because the world changes or because our knowledge about the world changes.

The need to revise premises because the world itself has changed is the more obvious of the two types of causes. The development of steam and electric power, of the telegraph and telephone, of precision machinery, and of institutional arrangements for acquiring large amounts of capital, led to the formation of large industrial organizations. Premises about the nature and behavior of organizations that were based on preindustrial conditions had to be revised to reflect the new reality.[2] The development of automatic data processing has led to the revision of premises about the uses of information.

Less obvious are the premises that are changed because of new knowledge, that is, discoveries that revise our ideas about the state of nature. The discovery of black holes, for example, is revolutionizing astronomy and astrophysics. (Indeed, in a 1980 draft of this book, I stated that the existence of black holes was speculative. By 1982, their existence had become widely accepted.) The discovery of DNA revolutionized biology; the discovery of plate tectonics revolutionized geology.

Acceptance of new premises

Changes in premises tend to be more quickly accepted in the natural sciences than in the behavioral sciences. In the natural sciences, most new ideas are either accepted or rejected on the basis of observations or experiments, shortly after their formulation. (There are exceptions. Experimental evidence did not validate the special theory of relativity until many years after Einstein stated it. Some people still do not accept the idea of biological evolution.)

In the behavioral sciences, particularly those disciplines that relate to organizations, important new ideas can seldom be satisfactorily validated by statistically sound observations, much less by experiments. Few organizations will permit controlled experiments about their activities. If undertaken at all, experiments are usually on trivial topics, and the results are difficult to interpret because so many variables influence them.[3]

Because of the lack of experimental evidence, new ideas in the behavioral sciences are not accepted quickly. Kuhn makes the case that a conceptual revolution is required.[4] This point is especially significant for the development of accounting concepts because there are basic disagreements about the nature of economic entities, particularly business organizations. Until fairly recently, economists assumed that most businesses were essentially like the pin factory that Adam Smith described in *The Wealth of Nations* (1776). Their employees had no emotions. Their managements strove only to maximize profits. They sold their products, without sales effort, at prices determined by the rules of pure and perfect competition.

Although business organizations probably never were like this, many of the premises in current economics texts implicitly accept this description. Students who have been exposed to these texts believe them. Some of these students become accounting theorists and base their theories on these obsolete premises. In developing a conceptual framework and, more importantly, in gaining acceptance of this framework by academics, burying the premises of classical economics is perhaps the most difficult problem that must be overcome.

Theory and practice

Some people make a distinction between theory and practice. The premises stated here are intended to describe what the world really is like, and the conceptual framework is based on these perceptions of reality. If the perceptions are correct, and if the theoretical framework is, in fact, based upon them, then there should be no difference between accounting theory and good accounting practices.

Accounting concepts and practices that are based on unrealistic ideas about the real world are not sound. There is, of course, no implication that current accounting practice is entirely sound; if this were so, there would be no need to develop a conceptual framework. What I mean to imply by this statement is that accounting practice should be based on sound concepts and that these concepts should be derived from realistic views of the world.

Evidence for accounting premises

Two types of premises are necessary for the development of an accounting conceptual framework: (1) beliefs about the nature and behavior of economic entities and (2) beliefs about the needs of users of accounting information.

Accounting is an applied science. Premises in an applied science should be based on evidence from relevant underlying disciplines. Premises about the nature and behavior of economic entities should be developed from evidence gathered and analyzed by economists, particularly microeconomists, and by sociologists and social psychologists. Presumably they are the experts on this subject in the same sense that physicists are the experts who develop premises about physical phenomena. Premises about the needs of users of accounting information should also be derived from economics and from that branch of psychology that studies how individuals process information. Finally, some research directly focuses on accounting topics, and this should be relevant in the development of premises.

Because entities are systems, ideas from general systems theory are also relevant. General systems theory does not have a set of concepts in its own right. Rather, its purpose is to investigate the similarity (technically, the isomorphy) of models and systems in various fields so that concepts from one field can be usefully transferred to another field.

Evidence from economics. Unfortunately, economists disagree among themselves about the nature of economic entities. As a general indication of the state of this discipline, consider the fact that the Nobel prize was awarded in 1976 to Milton Friedman, an economist who had one view of the nature of economic entities, and in 1978 to Herbert Simon, an economist who had a diametrically opposing view. Professor Friedman describes a model built on the assumption of pure and perfect competition and the goal of profit maximization.[5] Professor Simon describes a different model, one that is based on the goal of satisfactory profits, and argues that Friedman's model is unrealistic.[6]

In no other discipline would Nobel prizes be awarded for such different views of the state of nature unless new evidence had convinced the scientific community that a new model was superior to that hitherto accepted. Although the Simon model is newer than the Friedman model (which is rooted in Adam Smith's 1776 book), economists disagree as to whether or not it is superior.

Kenneth Boulding, an economist, has argued that economics and accounting are so dissimilar that economics concepts cannot be used to formulate accounting concepts.[7] Since economics is supposed to describe the nature and behavior of an economic entity and since accounting is supposed to report information about an economic entity, I do not accept Boulding's conclusion. The trouble is that many economists do not describe reality, and it is their unrealistic descriptions that are useless in developing accounting concepts.[8]

Information economics.   Some years ago a discipline called information theory was developed. This discipline relates to the transmission of information by telephone or electronic devices, and it provides extremely useful insights for telecommunication scientists and engineers. Recently, attempts have been made to develop an analogous discipline about the transmission and use of information in general. It is called information economics. These attempts have not amounted to much, however. Although information economists have developed an impressive jargon (information overload, information inductance, the cognitive conflict paradigm), the underlying ideas are trivial or obvious. For example: "Information should be worth more than the cost of providing it."[9] Information economics is not, in my view, useful in developing a conceptual framework of accounting.

Evidence from social psychology.   Social psychology focuses on the behavior of people in groups. Organization behavior is the branch that deals specifically with organizations. The development of valid evidence in this discipline is extraordinarily difficult, and little of it is relevant to accounting issues. Some insights, although not supported by "scientific" evidence, are useful in thinking about the nature of organizations, however.[10]

Human information processing.   One branch of psychology studies how humans process information. These studies should provide evidence about the information that users of accounting information need. Unfortunately, the studies made to date have provided only generalizations that are so broad that they do not help resolve accounting issues.[11]

Accounting research

In the last two decades much research in financial accounting has focused on the relationship of accounting information to stock market prices.

This is a logical focus because investors use accounting information in decisions to buy or sell securities. Unfortunately, none of this research helps to develop a conceptual framework for accounting. Commenting on a paper by Robert Kaplan that summarized some 60 research efforts, Robert K. Mautz said: "Not one of these conclusions, nor all of them together, are likely to impress many practitioners as any great contribution to his knowledge."[12]

Other research has attempted to identify the information needs of investors and creditors. A recent review of this research by Paul A. Griffin concludes that "it is doubtful that the empirical research has produced tangible results of direct applicability to those who must evaluate or select accounting alternatives."[13]

Premises not supported by evidence

As the above summary makes clear, the evidence needed to substantiate a set of premises about accounting entities and the needs of users of accounting information is inadequate. The gaps must therefore be filled on the basis of an author's personal beliefs. This is the way all conceptual frameworks are constructed, although in most of them the premises are only implicit.[14]

Scarcity of evidence is not an insurmountable handicap in developing a framework, however. A well-developed set of accounting practices does exist, and users of accounting reports find most of these practices satisfactory. A major task in developing a conceptual framework is to articulate the concepts implicit in these acceptable practices. Although there can be disagreements, most will be disagreements as to phrasing rather than substance.

Ideas from general systems theory

An economic entity is a system, and general systems theory provides insights into the nature and behavior of systems that have relevance to accounting.[15] As used in general systems theory, a "system" is any set of elements that are related to one another. A system is either closed or open. A closed system, like a storage battery, is self-contained. An open system interacts with its environment.

All living systems are open systems. Living systems can be arranged in a hierarchy, in terms of their complexity. The hierarchy is: viruses, cells, organs, organisms (e.g., human beings), groups (e.g., families), organizations, societies, and supranational organizations. An organization is relatively high in this hierarchy and is therefore relatively complex and difficult to understand.

All living systems are teleological, that is, they have goals. In lower order systems, the goals are innate. Higher order systems, such as organizations, determine their own goals. All living systems receive resources from the environment and use these resources in seeking to attain their goals.

The desirable state of a system is a steady state. This does not mean a static state; a human being grows from infancy to adulthood, but desirable growth proceeds in an orderly manner. Control mechanisms are designed to keep the system in the desired state, that is, a state in which the system is in equilibrium with its environment and the elements of the system are in equilibrium with one another. This process is called homeostasis.

Related to the system itself is information about the system. This information is of two types, flow information and state information. Flow information describes the inputs to the system, the work done with these inputs, and the outputs of the system during a period of time. State information describes the status of the system as of a moment in time. Models of atmospheric systems, geological systems, chemical reactions, and many physiological systems focus on flow information rather than on state information.

Flows through a system can be measured either directly or indirectly. The performance for a certain period of an oil-fired electrical generator can be measured directly by comparing its inputs (amount of fuel used) with its outputs (kilowatt hours). The flow of grain from a grain elevator, assuming no additions during the period, can be measured either indirectly as the difference between the height of grain at the beginning and at the end of the period, or directly as the quantity of grain flowing out.

Criteria for premises

Premises must be consistent with the available evidence, and they must be consistent with one another. The set of premises should be necessary and sufficient for the development of a conceptual framework.

Necessary. If a proposed premise is not needed in order to resolve a conceptual issue, there is no need to state it. For example, FASB Concepts Statement No. 1 says (paragraph 10): "The United States has a highly developed exchange economy." Although this is a valid statement, it is not helpful in resolving conceptual issues. Although books, even encyclopedias, have been written about the nature and functioning of organizations, most of the material in them is not necessary to explain what the concepts governing the reporting of financial information about organizations should be.

Obvious, noncontroversial premises need not be stated. Premises about which there may be some disagreement probably need to be made explicit even though the majority agrees with them. In preparing a weather map, it seems obvious that forecasters do not care whether or not the air is fragrant (although this is of interest to poets), so fragrance can be disregarded. In contrast, not many years ago it seemed obvious that the weather was adequately described by conditions at the earth's surface, but this has turned out not to be so. Air temperature, wind direction, and wind velocity, as measured at various altitudes, are now recognized as an important part of reporting weather conditions.

Sufficient. A set of premises is sufficient if it provides an adequate basis for resolving conceptual issues; if it does not, this is an indication that something is missing. In some cases the missing premise can be found by exploring the source of beliefs of the advocates on each side of the conceptual issue. In other cases, there is no defensible basis for a premise, and the issue is necessarily resolved by fiat or compromise.

Readers may disagree with one or more of the premises stated here. If they do, they probably will not accept the concepts based on the premise(s) with which they disagree. I trust, however, that rejection of one, or even several, premises will not cause a reader to reject the whole conceptual framework. The controversial premises are relevant to only a few of the concepts, and most of these concepts can be modified without seriously damaging the structure of the framework as a whole.

PREMISES ABOUT THE ENTITY AND ITS ENVIRONMENT

The topic selected as the first item in a set of premises tends to influence the whole set. I have decided to start with the entity for which accounting information is reported because such a starting point makes it possible to relate accounting to general systems theory. This relationship provides insights, both as to the nature of organizations, and as to the appropriate accounting information about organizations.

Economic entities

Some of the inferences about accounting that can be drawn from general systems theory are obvious; others, not so obvious. The theory does provide a starting point for stating a set of premises about the entities for which financial statements are prepared.

> **Premise 1.** *Financial accounting reports on an economic entity, which is an organization that has one or more goals and that acquires and uses economic resources in seeking to attain these goals.*

The entity is an organization, an association of individuals. (Some accounting entities, such as mutual funds, are not literally organizations, and accounting concepts apply to proprietorships with no employees, but these are minor exceptions.) The entity is not a person and should not be personified.[16]

The premise states that the focus is on the entity as such, and not on one party to the entity, such as its owners.[17] This point will be discussed at length in Chapter 4. Failure to make a distinction between the entity and its owners is a major defect of current accounting practice.

A premise of general systems theory is that all living systems have goals. This belief is substantiated for organizations by all writers on organization behavior. Literally, the goals are the goals of top management or of governing bodies, rather than the goals of the organization as such. It is customary, however, to refer to them as organization goals.

No distinction is made in this premise between business enterprises and nonbusiness or nonprofit organizations. Accounting concepts apply to economic organizations of all types.

> **Corollary 1A.**   *The organization on which financial accounting reports is not necessarily a legal entity.*

Proprietorships are not legal entities; in law, the liabilities of the economic entity are not differentiated from the liabilities of the proprietor. At the other extreme, a consolidated corporation is regarded as being a single economic entity, even though it is a collection of legally distinct subsidiaries.

> **Corollary 1B.**   *Financial accounting focuses on a single organization, not on a collection of organizations such as an industry, and not on the whole economy.*

The significance of this point is that financial accounting concepts are properly limited to matters relating to an individual entity; they are not concerned with macroeconomic matters. Whether national income accounting should follow the concepts applicable to a single entity is not a relevant question in the development of a conceptual framework for financial accounting.

> **Corollary 1C.**   *Financial accounting concepts do not necessarily apply to financial statements of individual persons.*

Individuals are not organizations, and the type of economic activity in which they engage is substantially different from that of organizations. The goal of an individual is to satisfy his or her personal needs. Although most individuals engage in economic activity in order to satisfy these needs, the economic activity is only a means to an end, not, for most people, an end in itself.

This corollary suggests that it is dangerous to draw analogies between the activities of individuals and the activities of organizations. For example, the following statement from J. R. Hicks is often quoted: "A person's income is what he can consume during the week and still expect to be as well off at the end of the week as he was at the beginning."[18] Although this may be a valid statement for an individual, its emphasis on consumption means that it is not relevant in thinking about the income of an organization.

Financial reports required of individuals by credit grantors and financial disclosures required of public officials by legislative bodies focus on the balance sheet. In financial reportinf for organizations, however, the focus is on the operating statement. An individual's wealth is the sum of the value of each of his or her assets, which usually can be measured reliably. The wealth of a business organization, however, is the present value of its future income, which no one knows how to measure. Individuals live for a span of years, and then they die; organizations have no inherent limit to their life span.[19]

Measurable property

> **Premise 2.** *Accounting measures and reports on one or more of the properties of an entity that can be stated as monetary amounts.*

Accounting is a process of measurement.[20] As is the case with any measurement process, accounting seeks to "assign numerals to aspects of objects or events according to rule."[21] The minimum essential of a valid measurement process is that, within reasonable limits, it permits the objects to be arrayed in order according to the specified aspect or property that the objects have in common. The paragraphs that follow explain this criterion and can be skipped if the criterion seems self-evident.

Once numbers have been assigned to objects (e.g., "assets") according to the property being measured, objects can be arrayed according to these numbers since the basic rules of arithmetic state whether one number is greater than, equal to, or less than another number. Thus, for the objects called persons and the property called height, there is a measurement process (e.g., a yardstick) which assigns a number for the height of each person and permits people to be arrayed according to their height. A person 72 inches high is taller than a person 71 inches high. Other measurement processes permit us to say that one object is heavier, sharper, warmer, louder, bigger, brighter, denser, etc., than another. Unless some valid measurement process can be devised that will permit objects to be arrayed according to the specified property, the property is not measurable.

The application of this criterion to accounting is simple but crucial. Consider the property "net income." If when measured according to a certain accounting process, Company A has reported net income of $1.5 million and Company B has reported net income of $1 million, the process is valid only if Company A's net income is in some sense, and within reasonable tolerances, higher than Company B's.

Two other criteria are desirable but not essential in a measurement process: objectivity and precision.

Objectivity.   Most, but not all, measurements are objectively determined. Skill in figure skating is measured according to the subjective opinion of judges, but figure skaters in a meet are arrayed (first, second, etc.) according to the number of points awarded by the judges, and this is a valid measuring system. We must strain to find such examples, however. Usually, if an objective process is not known, the property is not measured. Thus, we rarely attempt to measure a woman's beauty. Instead, we measure what are believed to be related properties that can be measured objectively. In such cases, we must take care not to assume that the property being measured is the same as the property in which we are actually interested. A woman with the measurements 36–24–36 might be said to have a perfect figure, but it by no means follows that all women with such measurements are beautiful.

Similarly, we do not attempt to measure college aptitude as such for purposes of college admission. Instead, in the Scholastic Aptitude Tests (SAT) we measure two subproperties called quantitative aptitude and verbal aptitude. In using the results of these two tests, we know full well that they do not correspond exactly to the property, "aptitude," or "likelihood of success in college," although we have reason to believe that they are related to these properties.

I shall mention another aspect of the SAT here since it bears on an argument that I will make later. It is conceivable that some day we shall test a third subproperty, such as social skill, and rank college applicants according to their score on this test, and on the average of the three tests, quantitative, verbal, and social. This would be valid measurement process. It would not be valid, however, to construct a single ranking in which applicants whose scores were determined from the two old tests were intermingled with applicants whose scores were based on all three tests. To do so would be to mix two sets of properties in the same measuring system and therefore to violate the principle that the measurement is always related to properties that the objects have in common.

An entity's "well-offness" is conceptually a measurable property. Even if this idea could be clearly defined, however, it is doubtful if anyone would recommend that accounting construct a monetary measure of this property because of the practical difficulties in doing so.

Precision.   The other attribute that is not essential is precision. No measurement (as distinguished from a count) is absolutely precise; nevertheless, a measurement process can be valid even if it gives rather broad approximations. All measurements from samples are approximations, but objects can be ordered according to a sample measurement so long as there is a likelihood that the ordering of the objects based on the sample is the true order. In some sampling plans, this likelihood is stated in terms of p, or confidence intervals, but this is not the case in all samples (for example, many reported public opinion polls), and this refinement is not essential to a valid measurement.

In a sample measurement, we admit that the sample results will not necessarily order the objects correctly, but the measurement process is nevertheless valid unless something in the process itself is responsible for the error in ordering. In this case, the results are said to be biased. For example, a properly designed and executed television viewing survey can give a valid, unbiased measurement of the size of the audiences of Networks A, B, and C, even though the measurement is quite rough.

Capital

The next premise uses the word *capital*. In the literature of economics and accounting, this word is used with any of four different meanings. Considered in the context of a balance sheet, capital can refer to: (1) all items on the left-hand side, (2) some items on the left-hand side, (3) all items on the right-hand side, or (4) some items on the right-hand side. I shall use the word with the first meaning.

Capital as resources.   In carefully written economics texts, capital is defined as an entity's wealth, that is, the resources that it controls.[22] Assets are those resources that are recognized in accounting. Assets do not include, for example, the value of a management team, which is a valuable resource. This is the meaning of *capital* used in this book, except when it is necessary to refer to other meanings in common usage. (The meaning of *assets* will be discussed in Chapters 4 and 7.)

Capital as certain assets.   Capital is often used to designate one type of assets. Plant and equipment are often referred to as *capital assets*. When costs are added to plant and equipment, the costs are said to be *capitalized*. Capital used in this way ordinarily does not lead to confusion, unless it causes the reader to infer that other assets are not capital.

Working capital or *circulating capital* is the excess of current assets over current liabilities. To some people, these terms refer to the resources themselves, as contrasted with fixed capital or permanent capital. To others, the terms refer not to the resources but rather to the means of financing them.

Economists refer to labor, land, and capital, which may be a valid classification scheme for an entire economy. When applied to an individual entity, however, this classification implies that its land is not capital; this is incorrect.

Capital as equities.   Capital is sometimes used to refer to all the items on the right-hand side of the balance sheet. Actually, these are sources of the funds used to acquire capital, not capital itself, and it is confusing to use the same word for the thing itself and for its source. More precisely, the right-hand side reports the sources from which the entity received one form of capital, called funds. The entity used these funds to acquire other forms of capital, and these are the amounts reported on the left-hand side.

Terms such as *debt capital, equity capital,* and *contributed capital* do not refer to capital as such, but rather to certain sources of capital. *Cost of capital* is a weighted average of the cost of using debt funds and equity funds; it does not refer to the cost of equity funds alone. *Return on capital* can mean the return on total assets (or total equities), on funds supplied by equity investors, or on funds supplied by both debt and equity investors.

Capital as one type of equity.   Use of the term *capital* for one category of items on the right-hand side is especially confusing. Capital is often used in the sense of shareholder equity. An entity is *undercapitalized* if it does not have enough shareholder equity. Investors who furnish equity funds are *capitalists,* and *capitalism* is an economic system in which equity funds are supplied by private investors. (In socialist countries the government is the principal source of both debt and equity funds.) It is said that an entity has not maintained its physical capital unless its retained earnings, a component of shareholder equity, is large enough to replace its physical plant.[23]

The latter concept is seriously incorrect. Entities obtain funds from a mix of debt and equity, not from shareholder equity alone. In order to replace plant, even in periods of inflation, entities need not rely solely on equity financing; they can also use debt financing for part of the funds required. Most discussions of distributable income or sustainable income overlook this point and thus lead to incorrect concepts for the measurement of income.

Funds used to acquire other forms of capital come not only from lenders and equity investors but also from vendors who sell on credit, from those who provide services in advance of payment for them (salaries and fringe benefits), from the government as a consequence of income tax incentives, from contributions, and from the entity's own income earning activities.

Part of the confusion about capital stems from a related confusion about wealth. For an individual, *wealth* refers to the person's equity, that is the difference between assets and liabilities. With reference to a corporation, however, *wealth* can have either of two meanings. It can refer to shareholder equity, which corresponds to the meaning applicable to an individual's wealth. Or, it can refer to total resources, without subtracting the liabilities. In the latter sense, but only in this sense, wealth means the same as capital, as I shall use the term. Often, one has to speculate which meaning the author intends, because the context does not make this clear.

Capital and income.   The distinction between capital and income can be confusing. Capitalizing a cost does add to capital, but earning income also adds to capital. A more accurate way of stating the intended distinction would be to refer to "capital and expense." For income tax purposes the recipient must know whether a distribution made by an entity is a distribution of income, or a return of capital; but this distinction is relatively unimportant to the entity that makes the distribution. In either case the distribution reduces the entity's capital.

> *Premise 3.*   *Entities have capital, which they have acquired with funds supplied either directly from outside parties or from their own income-producing activities. Most funds supplied directly by outside parties have a cost to the entity.*

Creditors and equity investors furnish funds directly. In most circumstances the earning of income involves an inflow from an outside party. Thus, in almost all cases, increases in capital come from outside parties, either directly or indirectly. The following corollary emphasizes this idea.

> *Corollary 3A.*   *With rare exceptions, an entity cannot increase its capital by activities that do not involve outside parties.*

The corollary says that an entity cannot pull itself up by its own bootstraps. Production involves changing various elements of capital from one form (material and equipment) to another form (finished goods and services). Production by itself does not increase an entity's total capital. Exceptions to this generalization will be discussed in Chapter 6.

Economic activities and status

The next premise relates the general ideas of flows and stocks from general systems theory to the subject matter of accounting.

> *Premise 4.*   *Financial accounting reports on the economic activities and the economic status of an economic entity.*

The economic activities of an entity involve obtaining funds, using these funds to acquire resources, and using these resources to provide goods and services to external parties. The word *economic* means that these resources are scarce; accounting is not concerned with free resources, such as air in the atmosphere.

Social accounting. Although Premise 4 is believed to be noncontroversial, it has a corollary that not everyone accepts:

> *Corollary 4A.* *Financial accounting does not report information about the social activities of an organization.*

A branch of accounting, called social accounting, does attempt to measure the benefits to society that an organization provides (for example, through training programs and research/development) and the costs to society that an organization levies (for example, air pollution). These considerations are not properly a part of financial accounting.

The goals of many nonbusiness organizations are primarily social rather than economic. This is obviously the case with legitimate religious and charitable organizations, and it is probably the case with many governmental, educational, and health care organizations. These organizations do use resources in attaining their goals, and to this extent their activities are economic, but these activities are secondary to the social activities. It follows that financial statements of many organizations do not contain the most important information about the activities of these organizations, namely their success in attaining social goals.[24]

Entity goals

The next premise is highly controversial. I will therefore discuss it at some length.

> *Premise 5.* *A primary economic goal of a nonprofit entity is to provide a satisfactory amount of services with available resources or to provide a specified amount of services with reasonably few resources. A primary economic goal of a profit-oriented entity is to earn a satisfactory return on the funds that investors have supplied to it.*

The entity's goals are those of the organization and are not the same as the goals of employees of the organization. The latter have personal goals that are not always entirely consistent with the organization's goals. The premise is restricted to economic goals; organizations, especially nonprofit organizations, may have noneconomic goals that are more important than their economic goals.

Nonprofit organizations.   This premise is, I believe, noncontroversial with respect to nonprofit organizations. Some readers may feel that the terms *satisfactory amount of services* and *reasonably few resources* are too weak. They would prefer something like *as much service as possible* and *as few resources as possible*. These alternatives are, I think, not quite realistic. In any event, this possible disagreement has no effect on the conceptual framework.

Profit-oriented organizations.   A contrary view of the premise regarding the goals of a profit-oriented organization is that its primary goal is to maximize its profits. The Trueblood report asserts that:

> The primary and continuing goal of every commercial enterprise is to increase its monetary wealth so that over time it can return the maximum amount of cash to its owners. (*Objectives of Financial Statements*, p. 21)

This view stems from classical economics, more precisely from the branch of economics called microeconomics.[25] With respect to the behavior of costs, the classical economists are on sound ground. Their analyses have led to important advances in operations research, management science, and similar subjects.

However, when economists extend their analyses to revenue, the other component of profit, their conclusions are not valid. Their models are based on the assumption that a business can estimate its demand curve, that is, the quantity of product that will be sold at various prices. In their writings, classical economists usually do not attempt to support their assumptions; they simply assert that the selling price is, or should be, set at the point at which marginal revenue equals marginal cost, and they let it go at that.[26] They grant that accounting systems are not consistent with this pricing policy but imply that this indicates that accountants have below average intelligence.[27]

Herbert A. Simon, in his speech accepting the Nobel prize in Economic Science, made a strong argument against the profit maximization premise. In summary, he said:

> What then is the present status of the classical theory of the firm? There can no longer be any doubt that the microassumptions of the theory, the assumptions of perfect rationality, are contrary to fact. It is not a question of approximations; they do not even remotely describe the processes that human beings use for making decisions in complex situations.[28]

Simon gives two bases for this conclusion. First, managers cannot know enough to make rational decisions of the type necessary to maximize profits. In particular, the shape of the demand curve rarely can be estimated, even within wide limits.[29] Second, available empirical evidence about the behavior of people in organizations is not consistent with the profit maximization premise.

To these, I would add a third point, namely, that some profit-maximizing decisions would be unethical, and most managers will not make unethical decisions. For example, the price of the first models of kidney dialysis machines, although high, was nowhere near as high as it could have been in view of the fact that without these machines desperately ill patients would have died.

Bounded rationality.   Simon suggests that the alternative to profit maximization is the idea of "bounded rationality." Included within this is the premise that participants in an organization do not have a single-minded devotion to the goal of pleasing the owners. Rather, employees, including managers, have their personal goals. They recognize that a business must earn an adequate return on funds invested in it to survive, but subject to this constraint they act to achieve their own goals. As one obvious example, employees bargain to make their own compensation as high as they can, even though the result is to reduce the profits that otherwise would be earned for the owners.

Satisficing.   Included also is the idea of "satisficing." The variables relevant to most important business problems are so numerous, so interrelated, and so difficult to identify and to estimate, that managers despair of reaching an optimal solution, even with the most sophisticated decision rules and computational tools.

Instead, the manager searches for an alternative that provides a satisfactory solution. Such a solution is expected to provide a fair return on funds invested in the entity, a return that is at least as high as the cost of using those funds. Although some other, unidentified solution might provide an even higher return, the manager has neither the time nor the resources to defer the decision until all the possible alternatives have been identified. Nor does the manager have the knowledge required to estimate the consequences of each alternative, even if all could be identified.

This does not mean that the manager is uninterested in a solution that provides more than a satisfactory return. If such an alternative is identified and if it is ethically acceptable, it is preferred. What satisficing does mean is that there is no guarantee, or even expectation, that the course of action decided upon is optimal. The most that can be said is that it is satisfactory.

As for the empirical evidence, Simon in his Nobel lecture refers to a vast body of empirical evidence about the behavior of firms and of individuals within firms. He concludes that none of this evidence supports the premise that profit maximization is the governing objective of business.

One reference Simon does not cite is Alfred Chandler's *The Visible Hand*, a Pulitzer prize-winning analysis of the behavior of American corporations from 1850 to 1950.[30] The "visible hand" is the hand of management. Chandler demonstrates that management action is a much better explanation of the behavior of the modern corporation than the "invisible hand" of the marketplace that classical economists assume to be the governing factor.

> *Corollary 5A.* *Some entities are more successful than others in attaining their goals.*

This obvious statement follows from the fact that economic resources are scarce. Entities must compete with one another for the funds needed to attain their goals. Some are more successful than others in this competition. The corollary applies both to profit-oriented and nonprofit entities; all entities compete for scarce resources.

The corollary suggests that interested parties want to know which among several competing entities performed better than others in some sense.

Pricing behavior

Although there is not much hard evidence about the behavior of prices in individual firms, what evidence there is does not support the idea of profit maximization.[31]

The relationship between supply, demand, and price that is assumed by classical economists is of some use in explaining the behavior of the economy as a whole and of general forces at work in particular industries. At this macroeconomic level, there is a tendency for prices to fall in periods of overcapacity and to rise when capacity limits are approached (although there are many situations in which this relationship does not hold).[32] Our focus, however, is on the individual firm, and at this level the relationships postulated in macroeconomic analysis do not usually exist.

The controversy about certain financial accounting issues arises because persons on each side support alternative views of the business goals stated above: the profit maximization view or the satisfactory-return view. Those who, despite the weight of contrary evidence, continue to hold to the profit-maximization view will disagree with a few of the accounting concepts stated in the following chapters, particularly those related to the allocation of costs. The basis for the disagreement is sharpened by the following premise, which is closely related to Premise 5.

> *Premise 6.* *Managers normally arrive at the selling price of a product on the basis of its full cost. Full cost includes a fair return on capital employed.*

This premise follows from Premise 5 because if the selling prices of the products of a profit-oriented entity, on average, equal the full costs of these products, including a fair return on capital employed, and if the entity sells its planned quantity of these products, the entity will attain its economic goal of earning a satisfactory return.

This is a controversial statement. It is also highly emotional because many people have been brought up with opposite beliefs. Challenging these beliefs is like challenging the virtues of "the American way." One version of the classical view is that the marketplace sets prices. If pressed, the classical economist will admit that this statement is not correct because prices are set by people, not by some impersonal force. The correct statement of the classical approach is that the manager finds the marginal cost (or variable cost, which is usually taken as approximately equivalent to marginal cost) and then sets selling prices so as to get as much additional revenue above this cost as is possible. In the typical situation, however, the marginal cost is so much lower than the attainable selling price that this approach provides no practical guidance.[33]

The alternative view is that selling prices are normally arrived at by adding together estimates of direct costs, a fair share of indirect costs, and a profit margin. The price arrived at in this way is a target price, which is then adjusted upward or downward according to the firm's current pricing strategy. This full-cost approach provides a useful guide to managers in arriving at selling prices, whereas the marginal cost approach does not. In one direction, the full-cost approach provides some assurance that a satisfactory profit will be earned. In the other direction, it lessens the likelihood that profits will be so high that competitors are attracted to the product, which will drive down profit margins.

Although it might be argued that the same result can be obtained by adding a constant margin percentage to estimated direct costs, this is so only if all products use proportionately the same amount of the resources that are represented by the indirect costs. This is the case in single-product firms and in certain service companies, such as TV repair, but this simple approach will not provide valid results in more complex situations. If, for example, a company produces some products using expensive machinery and other products with inexpensive assembly operations, and if the same margin were added to each product, the expensive machinery products would not bear a fair share of indirect costs and the assembly products would bear so much more than their fair share that the price would tend to be too high to be competitive.

As noted above, empirical evidence supports the premise that prices tend to be based on full costs. The situations in which this is not the case are relatively uncommon. In purely competitive markets, such as auctions, stock exchanges, and commodity exchanges, prices are set by individuals' reactions to market forces. No costs are relevant to the pricing decision (except in the unusual situation in which market prices are close to the firm's marginal cost).[34]

Departures from the average may be based on marginal costs. An example is off-peak pricing in public utilities. Indeed, despite the writings of economists about marginal-cost pricing, the economic literature contains few examples of circumstances in which this is the usual practice.[35] Distress prices are sometimes related to marginal costs, but these situations are inherently abnormal. Furthermore, although auction prices are not based on cost, an auction transaction is unusual in that all variables except price have been resolved in advance so that the price element is the single element to be negotiated; in most business sales transactions, a number of variables are involved.

On the other hand, we know that regulated prices are based on full cost and that such transactions constitute a large fraction of exchange transactions in the economy. There is voluminous evidence that most manufacturing prices are based on full costs. Companies that publish catalogues or that otherwise announce prices at the beginning of a selling season must have some basis for arriving at these prices; they cannot wait until the price set by the marketplace becomes known. Companies that are price followers, rather than price leaders, must make calculations on whether they can produce and sell their products at a satisfactory profit margin. These calculations work backwards from the market price. If the market price does not cover full costs and an adequate profit margin, the price follower is likely either to redesign the product or eventually to discontinue it.

Valuation

The following Premises, 7 and 8, relate to valuation. Premise 8 is controversial. Those who advocate some version of current cost as the basis for asset measurement probably disagree with it.

> **Premise 7.** *The value of monetary amounts due from or owed to other parties is the present value of the payments that are expected to be received or paid.*[36]

> **Premise 8.** *Although the fair value of an entity's monetary resources usually can be measured at any time, the fair value of most nonmonetary resources can be measured objectively only at the time they are acquired or sold.*

Fair value is "the highest price at which property would change hands between a willing buyer and a willing seller when the latter is not under any compulsion to sell, both parties having reasonable knowledge of the relevant facts."[37]

There are numerous exceptions to Premise 8. The fair value of accounts receivable, a monetary resource, can be measured only if the amount of uncollectible accounts can be reliably estimated. The fair value of a commodity traded on an organized exchange, a nonmonetary resource, can be reliably measured. (Because the entity may not plan to sell such commodities as of the measurement date, the price on a commodity exchange as of a given date may be irrelevant, however.)

The premise says that prices in arm's-length transactions (or in established auction markets) are reliable measures of value, but that estimates of values in other circumstances are likely to be unreliable. The disagreement is on the word *reliable*. Some people point out that assessed values and insurance values, although estimates, are reliable enough to be used as a basis for property taxation and payment of insurance claims. However, a measurement error that is a small fraction of an asset amount may be a much greater fraction of income, and, as I will argue later, the primary focus of accounting should be on the measurement of income. Not many people would argue that insurance values are sufficiently reliable to be the basis for resource measurement in financial accounting, or that there are enough competent appraisers to estimate such values annually for all accounting entities.

The impossibility of reliably measuring the fair value of nonmonetary assets is a sufficient reason for rejecting this approach to accounting. The question of whether this would be a good approach if it were feasible therefore need not be addressed.

Authors of the considerable body of literature advocating current-value accounting implicitly reject Premise 8. Most of them do not explicitly discuss it.[38]

> ***Corollary 8A.*** *The fair value of an entity that has nonmonetary resources cannot be reliably measured.*

The corollary follows directly from the premise. If the value of some of an entity's resources cannot be reliably measured, the total, which contains those resources, likewise cannot be reliably measured. The corollary also follows from the fact that the value of an entire entity is different from the sum of the values of individual resources. The value of a profit-oriented entity derives partly from the skill of its management, its position in the market, the products that it is developing, and other nonquantitative considerations. Nonquantitative factors are also important in determining the value of a nonprofit entity; for example, the value of a college is partly determined by the competence of its faculty and its reputation.

Conceptually, the value of a business entity is the present value of the stream of future earnings that it will generate. However, there is no way that anyone can estimate the numbers in this earnings stream. It might be argued that the market value of the company's stock is an estimate of the entity's value, but such a value is based, in part, on accounting information about the company, and to use it as a basis for accounting measurements would be circular. In any event, only a thousand or so companies have stock that is traded broadly enough so that the company's market value can be regarded as a reliable measure of its true value. An accounting framework cannot be based on information that is available for only a thousand entities.

Except in certain financial institutions whose resources are almost entirely monetary, such as mutual funds, the sum of the values of individual assets is not the value of the entity. Even in broadly traded companies, there is not the correspondence between market value and book value that one would find if this were the case.

> **Corollary 8B.** *The performance of an entity during a period cannot be measured as the difference between its value at the beginning of the period and its value at the end of the period.*

General systems theory explains that flows through a system can be measured in either of two ways: (1) directly or (2) indirectly, as the difference between its beginning and ending states. Premise 8 states that indirect measurement is not feasible in an economic entity. Since neither of the two points required to obtain such a difference can be measured, it follows that the difference itself cannot be calculated. Calculation of a meaningful difference would be possible if, but only if, the percentage of book value (in some sense) to real value at the end of the period were the same as the percentage at the beginning of the period. However, there is no reason to believe that these relationships are constant.

Going concern

Premise 9 is noncontroversial. It is needed as a basis for ruling out accounting concepts that assume the opposite premise.

> **Premise 9.** *In the absence of evidence to the contrary, an economic entity is likely to continue operating indefinitely.*

This premise rules out various types of liquidation values as a basis for a conceptual framework because unless the entity is going to be liquidated, such values are irrelevant.

The word *indefinitely* need not be made explicit. In general, it means that the entity will continue to operate at least as long as the remaining useful life of its principal productive resources.

Management bias

Premise 10 is the rationale for accounting concepts with which the word *conservatism* is usually associated. To some people, conservatism means that the entity's performance should be deliberately understated: "Anticipate no profit, but provide for all losses." Without a justification, such a concept cannot be defended. There is a justification for conservatism, however. The idea is warranted as a way of offsetting the bias stated in the following premise:

> *Premise 10. Managers are motivated to report favorable information about the performance and status of their organizations.*

Behavioral research clearly demonstrates that most people give optimistic reports of their own performance. For example, more than a half (some say two thirds) of college alumni will report that their grades were in the upper half of their college class. Although not all managers exhibit this behavior, in general they are motivated to report optimistically because accounting information about the entity is one basis for judging their own performance. Also, they tend to report optimistically about short run performance, even though they know such reports will probably require a subsequent downward adjustment. Reactions to current reports will become apparent quickly, whereas much can happen that affects future reports.[39]

In its Concepts Statement No. 2 the FASB states: "Conservatism in financial reporting should no longer connote deliberate, consistent understatement of net assets and profits" (paragraph 93). This is so. The Board did not, however, point out that unless some restraints were placed on the way in which management judgments can be incorporated in the reports, the reported assets and income are likely to be overstated. This follows from Premise 10.

Purchasing power of money

Premise 11 is obvious, but it needs to be expressed in order to contrast it with an alternative often found in the literature. The alternative premise is incorrect.

> *Premise 11. The purchasing power of money varies through time.*

The alternative wording would be, "Accounting assumes that the dollar is a stable measure of value," or words to that effect. Since everyone knows that the purchasing power of the dollar is affected by inflation, accountants would be stupid if they made the alternative assumption, and accountants are not stupid. The fact is that accounting amounts are reported in dollars for some reason other than the assumption that the dollar is stable. One reason is that alternative units of measurement are not believed to be sufficiently reliable to be incorporated into an accounting system.

PREMISES ABOUT USERS AND THEIR NEEDS

This section states and explains certain premises about the users of accounting information and the nature of the information that users need or want. Most of these premises describe user needs rather than user wants because users of any type of information tend to want the information they are currently getting. Thus, if the premises were based primarily on wants, they would tend to describe existing practice. An analysis of needs is more difficult than an analysis of wants because evidence on the latter can be obtained by observing the information that users currently use, whereas the former requires speculation about the nature of information that would be useful it it were available.

Certain requirements for supplementary information are based on the belief that users may need this information, but the belief is not strong enough to warrant including the information in the primary financial statements. This is the rationale, for example, for the FASB's requirement in Statement 33 for constant dollar and current cost information from a sample of companies.

Identity of users

As noted in Chapter 1, the focus here is on external users, that is, users "who lack the authority to prescribe the financial information they want from an enterprise and therefore must use the information that management communicates to them." [40]

The FASB identifies investors and creditors as the users of financial accounting information about business enterprises. In my research report on nonbusiness organizations, I identified resource providers as users of financial accounting information about nonbusiness organizations. [41] Although both these statements probably are valid, I now see no reason to attempt to identify classes of users. Although differences in the needs or wants of various classes of users do exist, these differences do not lead to separate conceptual frameworks. Unless differences in information needs affect the conceptual framework, there is no point in attempting to identify user groups nor to classify information needs according to user groups.

Relation to qualitative characteristics

Among the premises relating to user needs are the "Qualitative Characteristics of Accounting Information" given in FASB Concepts Statement No. 2. Paragraph 1 of that Statement says that its purpose is ". . . to examine the characteristics of accounting information that make that information useful." Although a case can be made for setting out these qualitative characteristics in a separate document, they logically are premises in the sense of this framework. Accounting information has certain qualitative characteristics because, and only because, it is presumed that users need information with these characteristics.

Informed users

Premise 12 is taken from FASB Concepts Statement No. 1, and its rationale is explained in paragraphs 24–27 of that statement.

> **Premise 12.** *Users of financial statements have a reasonable understanding of accounting principles and of the nature of the entity being reported on and are willing to devote a reasonable amount of time to studying the information.*

If financial accounting had to be limited to what is comprehensible to uninformed users, the information would be overly simplified. Simplified reports can be prepared from sophisticated financial statements, but the needs of sophisticated users cannot be met if accounting is limited to presenting information that is comprehensible to uninformed users.

This conceptual framework does not discuss principles for the construction of such simplified statements.

Information needs not precisely known

There is much discussion in the literature about the types of information that users need. The fact is, however, that no one knows what information various classes of users need, and that within a given class of users, individual preferences differ. Premise 13 states this idea.

> **Premise 13.** *Users need accounting information about the economic activities and status of an entity, but the type of information they need is not precisely known.*

Most statements of a similar premise indicate that users need information as an aid to decision making. Although this is a valid statement, it is almost a tautology. Technically, any quantity is a datum, but only a datum that adds to knowledge is information. Anything that adds to knowledge may be useful in decision making.

The important point is that we do not know how users employ financial accounting information. Although it is probably safe to assume that decisions made by most users relate to their interest or potential interest in an entity, this statement does not convey the idea of how information is ana-

lyzed as a basis for user decisions. Even if the class of users is more narrowly defined as investors, we do not know, nor are we likely to find out,
what the best method of analysis is.

This lack of precise knowledge of user needs is not a serious impediment
to the development of a conceptual framework for accounting, however.
Accounting is history, and few historians claim to know precisely what the
needs of their readers are.

As a general statement, it seems safe to say that fixed-income investors
are primarily interested in assessing the risk of an investment in the entity,
and that equity investors are interested in assessing both risk and return.
We do not know, however, much about how either type of investor goes
about the process of making these assessments.

Although more specific statements of users needs are given in the following premises, they must be interpreted as generalizations, and they should
not be used to restrict accounting information unnecessarily. Such restrictions may result in the omission of useful information.[42]

Information about the past

Although an obvious idea, the fact that accounting reports on the past
needs to be stated.

> **Premise 14.** *Users need information about the past performance
> and financial condition of an entity because information about the
> past helps users predict the future of the entity and appraise the
> performance of its managers.*

This premise has the same thrust as, but is more precise than, the usual
statement to the effect that accounting information helps the user make
decisions.[43]

Implicit in this premise is the idea that economic entities exist in a society that has a certain amount of order. In an environment of disorder,
such as a country in which established institutions are in the process of
being wiped out by revolution, historical information is of little use as an
aid in predicting the future.

Stewardship. This premise is also related to the vague concept of "stewardship." Literally, as suggested by the Biblical parable of the steward, the
idea of stewardship relates to the performance of a person, or to a group of
people known collectively as the management. Accounting does give some
clues about the performance of management, but management activity is
only one of many factors that affects the performance of the entity. A report
on performance reflects both how well the management has performed and
how well the entity has performed. Entity performance may not be closely

related to the performance of the management, however, because the entity may be affected by any number of outside influences as well as by the actions of its managers.[44]

Thus, accounting information has two overlapping bases for predictions. It helps to predict the performance of the entity, and it helps to predict the performance of the management. The former is of interest to those who must make decisions about the entity. The latter is of interest to those who are thinking of hiring members of management and those who question the past performance of management.

Both uses of accounting information rest on the belief that information about the past helps predict the future. An entity that has performed well in the past is likely to perform well in the future. A person who has been an able manager in the past is likely to be an able manager in the future. (Both statements, of course, are subject to strong qualifications. A baseball player who hit .300 last year may not bat well this year for any of a number of reasons; nevertheless, knowledge of the batting average tells us something about the likelihood that the player will do well.)

> *Corollary 14A.* Users do not expect financial statements, per se, to forecast the future.

Although some accounting information, such as the entity's depreciation expense in a year and its estimated amount of bad-debt losses, requires estimates of future conditions, these forecasts are made only as a necessary step in the task of preparing historical reports. The entity's financial statements are not intended to be forecasts of what future performance will be. Forecasts of future performance may be extremely useful information, but forecasts as such are reported elsewhere than in the primary financial statements.[45]

The accountant is like the person who prepares a weather map, not like the meteorologist who analyzes it and makes a forecast. The analytical function is that of the investment analyst, the loan officer, or other users of accounting information. The job of the accountant is solely to "tell it like it was." Although accounting information is used by decision makers as a basis for their inferences about the future, it is the decision maker, not the accountant, who makes these inferences.

Primary focus on performance

> *Premise 15.* Users are primarily interested in the performance of an entity and secondarily in its status.

This is a short way of stating the relative importance of income as reported on the operating statement as contrasted with status information as reported on the balance sheet. The balance sheet was the dominant financial statement until the 1920s, but there is now general recognition of the greater importance of the operating statement.[46]

The predominance of performance measurement over status measurement is even stronger in nonbusiness organizations than in business organizations. Although analysts are interested in monetary assets and liabilities on nonbusiness balance sheets, they seem to pay relatively little attention to the balance sheet as a whole. For example, the value of a museum collection is ordinarily not reported, but users make satisfactory economic analyses of museums without this information. More generally, many nonbusiness organizations do not report the book value of depreciable assets, but there seems to be no great demand for such reporting.

This premise is consistent with the central idea of FASB Concepts Statement No. 1: "The primary focus of financial reporting is information about an enterprise's performance provided by measures of earnings and its components" (paragraph 43).

> **Corollary 15A.** *Between competing accounting practices, the one that provides users with more useful information about performance is preferable to the one that provides more useful information about status.*

In most situations, there is no conflict between providing useful information about performance and about status. In a few, however, a conflict does exist. The claim that LIFO provides a more useful measurement of income, even though it results in unrealistic inventory amounts on the balance sheet, is perhaps the best example. Corollary 15A says that if LIFO does provide a more useful income measurement performance, it should be required, even though it results in a less meaningful balance sheet. Of course, a method that provides equally useful balance sheets and income statements would be even better, if such a method could be devised.[47]

Income versus cash flow

Discussion of the next premise tends to get bogged down in semantics, and many people take issue with what they understand to be the idea behind it.

> **Premise 16.** *Users believe that income provides a better measure of an entity's performance than does cash flow.*

On the surface, there appears to be a controversy on this point, but the controversy is relevant to the development of a conceptual framework only if cash flow advocates propose this measure in lieu of income measured on an accrual basis. Most people admit that both measures are necessary; if this is granted, there is no issue. Cash flow information always can be derived from accrual information, whereas accrual information cannot be derived from a cash-based accounting system. For example, an accrual accounting system collects information on both the acquisition of inventory and its consumption, and a cash flow statement can be derived from it by disregarding the consumption information. By contrast, a cash-based accounting system records only the acquisition of inventory, so the consumption information needed to measure income cannot be derived from it. Similarly, a cash flow system would not record depreciation, so the depreciation component of income would not be available.

Cash flow advocates point out that the correct analysis of a proposed investment requires that the present value of its cash flows be calculated. They fail to appreciate the fundamental difference between this problem in investment analysis and the problem of accounting. Investment analysis (i.e., capital budgeting) estimates the total return over the life of the project. Accounting must measure what the income was during *each year* of the project's life. Most accounting problems stem from this requirement.

The current controversy has a strange history. In 1971 the Accounting Principles Board, in Opinion No. 19, stated that cash flow information should not be the primary way of reporting the results of operations:

> The amount of working capital or cash provided from operations is not a substitute for or an improvement upon properly determined net income as a measure of results of operations and the consequent effect on financial position.[48]

The SEC took a similar position in 1973.[49] Nevertheless, FASB Concepts Statement No. 1 states (paragraph 25) that users are "interested in its [an enterprise's] ability to generate favorable cash flows because their decisions relate to amounts, timing, and uncertainties of expected cash flows." This assertion stems from the AICPA's 1973 Trueblood report, which placed a heavy emphasis on cash flows and recommended a de-emphasis of income.[50]

Notwithstanding the many references to cash flows in FASB Concepts Statement No. 1, a careful reading of the statement shows that the primary emphasis is on income. The quotation in the preceding paragraph suggests that investors are interested in cash flows to themselves (through dividends, interest, repayment of principal, or sale of securities), and that they are therefore interested in cash flows of the entity. As a matter of logic, this conclusion does not follow from the premise. Cash flows of the entity may or may not be related to, or provide the most useful information about, cash flows to the investor.

Whatever the logic, it has become fashionable to talk about cash flows. A recent chairman of the Securities and Exchange Commission said: "In my view, cash flow from operations is a better measure of performance than earnings per share."[51]

There are two disturbing things about the current emphasis on cash flows. First, the term means vastly different things to different people. To some, it means income plus depreciation; to others, it means income plus depreciation less capital expenditures; to still others, it means the difference between cash receipts and cash disbursements. Only the latter construction is literally "cash flow."[52]

The second disturbing thing about the emphasis on cash flows is that there is little evidence in support of the assertion that cash flow is more important than earnings, and much evidence that it is less important. Vijayaraghavan Govindarajan studied all the security analysts' comments published in *The Wall Street Transcript* for January through June 1976 and July through December 1977. Using content analysis techniques, he classified the 976 comments into categories that ranged from no mention of cash flows, through equal emphasis on cash flows and earnings, to no mention of earnings. In only 3 percent of the comments was the emphasis on cash flows, in 10 percent the emphasis was equal, and in 87 percent the emphasis was on earnings.[53]

The Louis Harris study prepared for the Financial Accounting Foundation has been used by some to support the assertion that users are primarily interested in cash flows rather than earnings.[54] A careful reading of this study shows that it does not support this assertion.[55]

A number of other studies of investor preferences conclude that although many investors believe that cash flow information is useful, few of them feel that cash flow information should be a substitute for information on earnings, as contrasted with providing information in addition to that provided by earnings.[56]

Ability to meet obligations

The emphasis on income measurement in the preceding premises may imply that the balance sheet is unimportant. In order to correct this impression, Premise 17 is a noncontroversial statement about the need for balance sheet information.

> *Premise 17.* *Users need information that helps them make judgments about an entity's ability to meet its obligations.*

This premise is often stated in terms of liquidity and solvency. Liquidity indicates an entity's ability to meet obligations that become due in the near future, usually within one year. Solvency indicates an entity's ability to meet all its obligations when they become due. Accounting information does not provide a direct and complete measure of either liquidity or solvency because there is no feasible way of measuring routinely amounts that could be realized from the liquidation or sale of certain types of assets, such as inventory. Accounting provides relatively little information about solvency for those entities whose solvency is doubtful, because solvency depends heavily on events that have not yet happened. Despite these limitations, studies have shown that certain accounting ratios are statistically significant predictors of bankruptcy.[57]

> *Corollary 17A. Some users need information on the order of priority of each major class of obligations and the amount of the obligations of that class.*

This corollary is the rationale for classifying obligations in terms of the priority of their claims.

Fairness

> *Premise 18. Users need information that is measured fairly.*

The idea of fairness or equity underlies many measurement practices, especially the allocation of costs to time periods and to cost objects within a time period. This notion will be discussed at length in Chapter 5. It is, of course, basically noncontroversial since few would argue that accounting measurements should be unfair. Some argue that the idea of fairness is implicit in several of the other premises, and that this one is therefore redundant. Although this may be the case, no harm is done by stating it separately.

Timely, reliable, and comparable information

Premises 19, 20, and 21 are noncontroversial as stated, but there is considerable controversy about how they should be interpreted and particularly about the weight that should be given to them when they conflict with other premises.

> *Premise 19. Users need timely information.*

Although accounting information is historical, it is not the type of history that can be written long after the event. Users need information relatively soon after an accounting period has ended. Since the full consequences of some events in an accounting period cannot be known with certainty until a considerable time has elapsed, the accountant necessarily must estimate these consequences on the basis of the information available at, or shortly after, the end of the period.

The desire of users for timely information suggests that accounting focuses on short-run results, rather than on long-run performance. Such a focus does indeed exist, but there is nothing that accountants can, or should, do about it. Users do not want to wait for the judgment of history, and accountants should give them what they want, despite the inherent limitations of short-run reports.

Premise 20. *Users need reliable information.*

As we shall see, Premise 20 conflicts with several other premises, and this conflict is at the heart of most of the problems involved in constructing a conceptual framework.

FASB Concepts Statement No. 2 states: "The reliability of a measure rests on the faithfulness with which it represents what it purports to represent, coupled with an assurance for the user, which comes through verification, that it has that representational quality. Of course, degrees of reliability must be recognized" (paragraph 59). The problem arises in deciding how much reliability is adequate.

Completely unreliable information is obviously not useful. Completely reliable information is often not obtainable. For example, the most useful information about a business would be the present value of its future earnings; however, as stated in Premise 8, there is no reliable way of obtaining this information. The most reliable information about a depreciable asset is its acquisition cost, and the most reliable accounting rule would be either to write off that cost immediately or to hold the asset at cost until it was disposed of, without depreciating it. Any depreciation rule involves judgments as to the asset's life, its residual value, and the pattern used to write off the cost over the useful life. Because of these judgments, an accounting system that incorporates depreciation is less reliable than one that does not. Nevertheless, as I will show in later chapters, including depreciation provides a better way of measuring performance than the alternative of not making such judgments.

A few accountants deplore the use of judgment in an accounting system. They regard any numbers resulting from such judgments as arbitrary. Their position is, I believe, untenable, and I will discuss it in appropriate places in later chapters, particularly Chapter 5.

I know of no way of stating how much reliability users need. Although there is a strong trend toward including more soft information in supplementary notes to the financial statements, there seems to be no enthusiasm for reducing the hardness of information included in the primary financial statements. (Recall that this framework is limited to the primary statements.)

Clearly, users do not need exact information, for no measurement system provides exact information. Indeed, critics of the inexactness of accounting numbers often do not appreciate the inadequacies that exist in most measurement systems, including even those in the natural sciences.[58]

Premise 21. *Users need comparable information.*

Most uses of accounting information are comparative. Amounts of one period are compared with those of a previous period; amounts for one entity are compared with those for other entities. These comparisons may involve either absolute amounts or they may be ratios. In either case, the validity of the comparisons is lessened (and often the comparisons become completely invalid) if different rules are used from one period to the next, or if different rules are used by various entities.

As used here, comparability incorporates the idea of consistency, which often is stated as a separate premise. Consistency means that a given entity records transactions in the current period in the same way that it recorded similar transactions in the previous period. When consistency is given as a separate premise, the comparability premise is that all entities record similar transactions in a similar way.

The need for comparability is a principal justification for an authoritative set of accounting standards. It is particularly important in intercompany comparisons. For an individual company, comparability could be attained simply by leaving the rules, whatever they are, unchanged from year to year. To permit useful intercompany comparisons, however, entities should use the same standards.

Despite the need for comparability, it is unlikely that accounting standards can be developed for industries as industries, although they can be developed for those types of transactions that are peculiar to a given industry. For example, standards are appropriate for reporting franchise fee revenues, which is one type of transaction in the franchise industry, and for the capitalization of oil and gas reserves, which is one type of transaction in the petroleum industry. These industries should, however, account for such items as pension costs in the same way that all entities do. There is nothing unique about pension costs in a given industry.

A serious, often insurmountable, problem in developing standards for specified industries is the difficulty of defining industries in such a way that a given entity knows the industry to which it belongs. This problem does not arise if an accounting standard applies to a type of transaction, wherever it occurs.

Comparability does not mean uniformity. Uniformity could be achieved only by the development of detailed accounting rules, such as those promulgated by the Interstate Commerce Commission. Economic entities are so diverse that it is beyond human ability to develop rules that prescribe the treatment of all types of transactions. Even if this were feasible, changes in circumstances would soon make any set of rules obsolete (as has happened to the Interstate Commerce Commission's rules). Thus, comparability is never precise; the most that users have a right to expect is that financial statements of different entities have approximately similar meanings.

The comparability premise implies a point that perhaps should be stated separately as a corollary. Although in some circumstances users could increase the comparability among statements by making adjustments to the reported numbers, users do not want to take the time for making these changes. This fact is another reason for having accounting standards that lead to comparable information. Users prefer that an entity's accountant prepare the information. according to a common set of standards in the first instance. Economists point out that if users were required to adjust the statements, the cost of accounting information to society as a whole would increase.

Reluctance to change

Changes in accounting standards inevitably lead to information that is not comparable with information reported previously. When a rule is changed, users who have become accustomed to a certain basis of reporting have to learn the implications of the new rule.[59] Only if the new information is significantly more useful, should they be asked to undertake the task of understanding its implications. This leads to the following premise:

> **Premise 22.**   *Users do not want accounting standards to be changed unless there is a strong reason to do so.*

The 1980 Harris survey asked about the speed of the FASB's action, and only 19 percent of the respondents said that it was moving too slowly. Other studies confirm the impression that there is a reluctance to change unless a persuasive reason exists to do so.[60]

It follows that there is a burden of proof on anyone who proposes a change in current practice. Some changes are proposed in this framework, and I recognize the importance of sustaining this burden.

Premise 22 implies that users are reasonably well satisfied with most current accounting practices. If this were not the case, they would clamor for improvements. There is dissatisfaction with some aspects of accounting; for example, the whole system of accounting for state and local governments is widely criticized, and in this area there are strong pressures for change. In contrast, widespread dissatisfaction with accounting for business enterprises is confined to a few topics, rather than to the overall approach.

Some attempts to construct a conceptual framework start with a clean slate; that is, they disregard all existing practices. Such an approach is unrealistic. An accounting system exists, and there is no strong movement for abandoning it entirely. The task is to improve what now exists, not to start from scratch.

The premise does not imply that acquiescence is a sufficient justification for existing standards. For example, APB Statement No. 4, which describes existing standards, is criticized by many.[61] Justification for standards should be based on the fact that they are consistent with a conceptual framework and that the framework is, in turn, consistent with valid premises.

Neither does Premise 22 imply that changes are not needed. The purpose of this book is to propose certain changes in concepts that will lead to changes in current practice.[62]

CONFLICT AMONG PREMISES

A principal problem in constructing a conceptual framework is that some premises conflict with others. Basically, the problem is that users need timely, reliable information about an entity's performance, but the difficulty of measuring nonmonetary resources and the optimistic bias of management stands in the way of providing the desired information. As it is often stated, the need for reliability conflicts with the need for relevance.[63]

Failure to appreciate this conflict lies behind many of the unrealistic proposals that are currently made. For example, Robert Sterling has written prize-winning papers advocating that accounting should be based on the market value of assets, although he knows, or should know, that there is no feasible way of determining the market value of most nonmonetary assets.[64]

Another conflict is between, on the one hand, the perception that changes in current practice might result in better financial statements and, on the other hand, the premise that users are reluctant to accept changes. I propose no change in current practice here unless I believe that the change will result in substantially better financial statements, enough better to warrant the trauma of adjusting to it. The message implicit in each proposed change is: "Try it; you'll like it."

PREMISES NOT INCLUDED

In developing the concepts given in the following chapters, many more premises than those given in this chapter were considered. Items are in the final list only if they are relevant in developing a concept or in resolving a conceptual issue.

Moonitz has a list of 14 postulates; some of them correspond to the premises given here, and others are not stated here because I do not believe they are necessary.[65] The only postulate inconsistent with those stated here is his stable unit postulate: "Accounting reports should be based on a stable measurement unit." Moonitz indicates that he does not regard the dollar as a stable unit if its purchasing power changes significantly. This conclusion differs from my Premise 11.

Mattessich has a set of 18 basic assumptions.[66] They are at a higher level of abstraction than the premises stated here and include several topics not mentioned in my list.

Paton has a list of eight postulates. All are consistent with mine.[67]

Premises omitted

Following is a discussion of possible premises that I have not included, together with my reasons for not referring explicitly to them.

Materiality. It is taken for granted that accounting need not report on immaterial matters. Although there are severe problems in prescribing standards for materiality, a premise about materiality does not help resolve conceptual issues. In other words, no concept is stated in a certain way because that way results in material information, whereas an alternative way would not.

Significance. Closely related to the idea of materiality is the idea of significance. Accounting should report significant financial events. However, I know of no way of generalizing as to what events are significant. Significant events—those that make a difference—are best understood in the context of specific concepts.

Point estimates. Thirty years ago, I suggested that financial statements might well be stated in probabilistic terms, such as an expected value with a standard deviation.[68] Although others have mentioned this possibility from time to time, interest in it on the part of users has been practically nonexistent. The reason probably is that users do not believe that reliable estimates of the dispersion can be made. Since Premise 22 implies that a change in current practice will be accepted only if there is a strong reason to do so, this possibility is omitted. Its time has not yet come, and it may never come.

Summary information. In an entity of even moderate size, millions of individual events occur in an accounting period. Users cannot make sense from reports that merely list the effect of these individual events. They expect the accountant to summarize them, so that they can assimilate the significant information in a relatively short period of study. The need for summary information has a great influence on accounting practices, but the need itself does not involve a conceptual issue.

Economic impact. Although accounting information unquestionably affects the way people behave, the idea by no means follows that accounting concepts should be designed for social or political purposes. Public opinion polling has been criticized on the grounds that the results of the polls affect how people vote, but few people, if any, would suggest that polling practices should be deliberately structured to produce results favorable to one political party. Similarly, accounting should tell it like it was, without regard to what the impact of the accounting numbers may be. Thus, I rule out the possibility of slanting accounting information to deliberately induce a certain impact.[69]

FASB premises

The list of premises given in this chapter is considerably shorter than those stated or implied in FASB Concepts Statement No. 1, *Objectives for Business Enterprises,* in its Concepts Statement No. 2, *Qualitative Characteristics,* and in its Concepts Statement No. 4, *Objectives for Nonbusiness Organizations.* Except for the points specifically discussed in Chapter 2, I do not disagree with the FASB list. The topics omitted from my list are, I believe, unnecessary as a foundation for accounting concepts. Since some readers may wish to consider whether I have omitted an important premise, I summarize these omissions in Note 70.

3

Basic concepts

This chapter lays the foundation for the conceptual framework. It describes basic concepts relating to: (1) the nature of the accounting entity, (2) the content of financial statements of the entity, and (3) the primary focus on the measurement of income. Concepts given in later chapters are essentially an expansion of these ideas. The chapter also states and describes briefly a number of basic but noncontroversial concepts and terms.[1]

The conceptual framework is developed within the boundaries described in Chapter 1. The framework relates to general purpose financial statements prepared for external users. It is limited to the primary financial statements. It relates to both business and nonbusiness entities. It does not relate to the financial statements of individual persons.

GENERAL COMMENTS ABOUT CONCEPTS

As explained in Chapter 1, the concepts in this framework are stated in normative terms: "Accounting *should* do such and such." Some concepts are derived from other concepts. The definitions, although stated as declarative sentences as is customary, have normative implications.

Most of these concepts are generalizations; they are not necessarily valid in all circumstances or in all types of entities. Some entities seek profits;

others do not. Some entities, such as life insurance companies, do not know the outcome of a sales transaction for many years; others, such as those that provide services for cash, may know the outcome immediately. In financial institutions, assets are primarily monetary; in capital intensive manufacturing companies, assets are primarily nonmonetary. Some entities speculate; others do their best to avoid speculation. The list of differences could be extended indefinitely. Despite these differences, I believe that the concepts stated are applicable to accounting for most events in most entities.

Criteria for concepts

The following criteria governed the development of the concepts: [2]

1. The concepts should be consistent with the premises.

2. The concepts should be consistent with one another.

3. The concepts should be comprehensive; that is, they should encompass the entire domain of the information reported on the primary financial statements of an organization.

4. The concepts should be fairly general. If they are overly specific or detailed, they are not likely to have wide applicability.

5. Each concept statement should be brief. The nature of a concept is such that it can be stated in a sentence or at most a brief paragraph. The accompanying explanation and rationale can be lengthy, but this material should be entirely separate from the statement of the concept, so that the reader will not miss the central point.

6. The concepts should guide those who develop accounting standards. Although concepts do not automatically lead to the standards, they do suggest boundaries within which standards should be developed. The framework of a house governs the general shape and usefulness of the house, but it does not prescribe how the house is to be furnished and decorated. It does, however, limit the decorating possibilities. Similarly, a conceptual framework limits the rational alternatives for resolving an accounting standards issue.

Tests of the concepts

It is difficult to test whether a set of concepts meets these criteria. Much depends on a person's own perception. One objective test is to examine how the concepts affect the financial statements of a steady-state entity, that is, an entity that is neither growing nor shrinking in size in any meaningful sense. If application of a concept does not portray such an entity to be in a steady-state situation, there is probably something wrong with the concept.

An excellent way of testing whether a concept, or a standard based on a concept, is biased is to listen to the views of parties whose inherent interests are in conflict. For example, some regulatory commissions want concepts that lead to relatively low reported income, and hence to lower allowed rates; whereas the entities they regulate want the opposite. The appropriate concept for a given issue can be arrived at by judging the validity of arguments made by these parties.

Caution on shorthand characterizations. In discussing this or any other set of concepts, there is a natural tendency to characterize the set with a brief phrase. This set can be roughly described as an historical cost model. As a general description, this is a satisfactory label. However, if this general term is then used as a precise description, serious misconceptions can result. For example, in several places I shall state concepts that do not involve historical costs. These concepts should not be criticized as being inconsistent with the historical cost model. They should be evaluated on their own terms. I know of no short phrase that precisely describes this framework.

Conflicting premises

The concepts given here are not the only concepts that can be deduced from the premises. This is because some of the premises conflict with other premises, and in these circumstances the concept reflects a judgment as to the relative importance of the conflicting premises. The most important source of conflict is that between the need for relevant information (Premises 12–17), and the need for reliable information (Premise 20).

In resolving these conflicts, I give considerable weight to the status quo; that is, a departure from current practice is not recommended unless there is a strong reason to do so. Some may characterize this policy as undue reverence for the past. Its actual rationale follows from Premise 22: "Users do not want accounting standards to be changed unless there is a strong reason to do so." Consistent with this premise, certain concepts that reflect acceptable current practice are merely stated, without justification.

Implications of concepts

Appendix A to this chapter states certain implications that follow from the concepts. They suggest logical consequences of a concept and help to explain its import.

THE ACCOUNTING ENTITY

Premise 1 defined an *economic* entity as "an organization that has one or more goals and that acquires and uses economic resources in seeking to attain these goals." In order to set boundaries around the entity for which a set of financial statements is to be prepared, the word *organization* needs to be described more specifically.

If an organization has owners, the accounting entity is, in most circumstances satisfactorily defined in terms of ownership interests. For example, consolidated financial statements are prepared for a parent corporation and its subsidiaries based on the percentage of equity interest that is owned by the parent (with certain exceptions). In some organizations, however, control may be exercised even without a parent/subsidiary relationship.[3]

Most nonbusiness organizations do not have owners. Since this framework is intended to apply to organizations of all types, the entity therefore cannot be defined in terms of ownership interest. Owners presumably control an entity. Entities without owners are controlled by some sort of governing body. Thus, by shifting the central idea from "ownership" to "control," the concept can be broadened to encompass entities of all types. An individual or group controls an entity if it has the ability to direct how the economic resources of the entity will be used. The following concept states this idea:[4]

> ***Concept 3.01.*** *Financial statements should report on an accounting entity, which is an economic entity whose resources are controlled by a single person or governing body or by several governing bodies responsible to the same constituency.*

This concept is consistent with the current concept of the accounting entity in profit-oriented organizations. It suggests the answers to some, but not all, entity issues in nonbusiness organizations. It suggests that universities, hospitals, charitable organizations, arts organizations, museums, and other organizations whose resources are controlled by boards of trustees or regents are accounting entities. It suggests that local religious, fraternal, and public service organizations are accounting entities if they are relatively independent of a national headquarters, but that these local organizations are part of the larger entity if the headquarters controls their resources.

Determining the appropriate accounting entity for governmental units is an especially difficult problem. In many municipalities, for example, one group of elected officials is responsible for the public schools, and the mayor or city council is responsible for all other government functions. Although there are two distinct governing bodies, the financial activities and status of the whole municipality cannot be understood if these two groups are treated separately. It is for this reason that the definition includes the phrase: "several governing bodies responsible to the same constituency."

The concept defines the *largest* organization that qualifies as an accounting entity. Financial statements are often prepared for components of an entity. Thus, although financial statements for a consolidated corporation are prepared for individual corporations in the "family," the set of financial statements of primary interest is that of the consolidated entity. Similarly, in a municipality, financial statements may be prepared for the public schools separately from those prepared for other activities. In an organization with a national headquarters that controls local branches, financial statements may be prepared for each branch as well as for the entity as a whole.

The concept by no means solves all the problems that arise in defining the accounting entity; it leaves many problems to be solved by appropriate standards. APB Opinion No. 18 provides such standards for corporations, and AICPA Statement of Position 81–2 provides a standard for hospitals. Standards have yet to be developed for organizations with national headquarters and local units, for separate foundations affiliated with universities and similar nonprofit organizations, and for governmental organizations.

Fund accounting.   The definition suggests that the idea of the fund as the accounting entity in nonbusiness organizations is inappropriate. The entity includes all the funds that are controlled by its governing body or by governing bodies responsible to the same constituency. (Although financial reports may be prepared for funds or other subentities within the accounting entity, the primary focus is on the organization as a whole.) Funds that are controlled by another body are not a part of the entity, however. Thus, a company's pension fund is not part of the company entity if it is controlled by separate trustees.

Focus on the entity

The concept refers to the entity as such. This is intentional and suggests that accounting should focus on the entity itself, as contrasted with present practice in profit-oriented entities, in which accounting, at least implicitly, focuses on the interests of owners.

Proprietary view versus entity view.   In the 1930s the focus of financial accounting shifted from the proprietary view to the entity view. The proprietary view is that the fundamental purpose of accounting is to report the interests of an entity's proprietors. Although this view dominated accounting thought until fairly recently, most writers now support the entity view.[5]

The entity view is the only view that makes sense in accounting for nonbusiness organizations because these organizations have no proprietors. It also corresponds to the modern view of the corporation, namely that the corporation exists apart from its owners, and that the shareholders are one source of capital.

Although the superiority of the entity view is generally recognized in the literature, current accounting practices continue to be consistent with the proprietary view. The basic accounting equation is: Assets − Liabilities = Owners' equity; that is, owners' equity is the difference between assets and liabilities. Accounting focuses on measuring changes in this difference during the accounting period. Under the entity view, the equation should be Assets = Equities; that is, owners' equity should not be given more prominence than other forms of equity.

Alternative entity views. Actually, there are two versions of the entity view. The predominant view suggests that all financial events occurring in the entity should be reported, and in particular that net income is income of the entity. The alternative view is that events related to the earning of income should be reported separately from the distribution of that income to the parties who have a claim on it.[6] This view leads to an income statement in which income before interest expense is the bottom line; interest expense is treated the same as dividends. Some who hold this view regard income taxes as an expense, and others regard income taxes as a distribution of income to the government; this is a minor variation within this school of thought.

The alternative version of the entity view is not consistent with the premise that users want information on the economic activities and status of the entity (Premise 13). Interest is one of the entity's costs, and interest should be reported along with other items of cost.

This alternative view is supported by only a few writers. It is not consistent with the premises, and Concept 3.01 rejects it.

NATURE OF FINANCIAL STATEMENTS

Premise 15 states that users primarily need information about performance during a given period, and Premise 17 states that they also need information about the entity's ability to meet its obligations, which suggests information about the status of the entity. Together, these premises indicate that users need both flow information and status, or stock, information. Premise 14 says that accounting reports history; Premise 2 says that this history is necessarily expressed in monetary amounts; and Premise 20 stresses the need for reliable information. The following concept is consistent with these ideas:

> **Concept 3.02.** *Financial statements should summarize the economic performance and status of the entity as a consequence of those events that have occurred during an accounting period whose monetary amounts can be reliably measured. Financial statements should report the substance of economic events, even if their substance differs from their legal form.*

The concept refers to events whose effects can be reliably measured. This statement will be made more specific in the discussion of later concepts.

THE PRIMARY FOCUS OF FINANCIAL ACCOUNTING

Ideally, standards should provide equally valid information about both activity and status. In the following chapters, I will describe several situations in which this ideal cannot be attained, however. In these circumstances, one must focus on either one or the other. When alternative concepts or practices are being considered, this primary focus helps one decide which is more important and which is less important. Concept 3.03 states a primary focus:

> **Concept 3.03.** *The primary focus of financial accounting should be on the measurement of income, which is the increase in an entity's equity during an accounting period arising from the entity's operating activities during the period. Pending the analysis of results of experiments now being conducted, income should be measured in actual monetary units and should not attempt to reflect current costs.*

Concept 3.03 states that financial accounting should focus on the measurement of income. As applied to profit-oriented entities, there is widespread acceptance of this idea, but considerable disagreement as to what it actually means. As applied to nonprofit entities, there is disagreement as to its applicability.

Focus on income measurement

Until fairly recently, the principal focus of accounting was on the balance sheet; the income statement was either not published at all or was published in abbreviated form and not regarded as an important document.[7] It is now generally agreed that the measurement of income is of primary importance. This is emphasized in paragraph 43 of FASB Concepts Statement No. 1: "The primary focus of financial reporting is information about an enterprise's performance provided by measures of earnings and its components."[8]

There is such general agreement on this point that there is little need to elaborate on it. The rationale is given in the discussion of Premise 15; namely, that although financial accounting reports both on the economic activities and on the economic status of an entity, users are primarily interested in the entity's performance and only secondarily in its status. Stated more simply, the operating statement takes precedence over the balance sheet.

Although there is agreement with this general idea, there is considerable disagreement at the conceptual level as to the nature of the information concerning an entity's activities that should be reported. Collections of readings on accounting theory published in the recent past contain a substantial section on income measurement. At least one collection is entirely on this subject.[9] The person who reads these collections is likely to become confused and frustrated.

Some articles on income measurement are written by economists; others by accountants. Economists tend to base their argument on either Fisher's definition, "A stock of wealth existing at a given instant of time is called *capital;* a flow of benefits from wealth through a period of time is called *income*" or Hicks's definition, "a person's income is what he can consume during the week and still expect to be as well off at the end of the week as he was at the beginning." [10]

Unfortunately, there seems to be no agreement on how to make these ideas operational. Hicks himself, in the section immediately following the definition quoted above, gives three alternative approaches to the measurement of income and says he is not certain which one is preferable. For every accounting theorist who sets up an operational definition, there is another who shoots it down by setting up a hypothetical situation and demonstrating that the proposed concept leads to an absurd result in that situation.

Some theorists go so far as to conclude that it is impossible to arrive at an operational definition of income. The most that can be done, they say, is to define revenue and expense and define income as the difference between revenue and expense, without explaining the meaning of this difference. These writers tend to disregard the fact that entities do go to considerable trouble to prepare an income statement, and users of accounting information pay much attention to the bottom line on this statement. Neither reporting entities nor users would devote this amount of effort to a useless exercise. In essence, preparers and users both accept the idea that although an income number is not perfect, it does provide valuable information.

The Scholastic Aptitude Test score (SAT) is a good analogy. No one can state the exact meaning of a SAT score of 600, but most people believe, and act on the belief, that by and large, with allowance for other factors, a student with a score of 600 is more likely to do well in college than a student with a score of 500 and less likely to do well than a student with a score of 700. Similarly, if two profit-oriented companies have the same amount of capital, and if one reports income of $2 million and the other reports income of $1 million, it is a plausible conclusion, with due allowance for other factors, that the former has performed better in some significant sense. Income is therefore a measurable property, as this term was defined in Premise 2.

Maintenance of equity   How can this general idea be made operational? I think the "maintenance of capital" idea provides the best approach. However, the word *capital* in that phrase means shareholder equity, as used in this framework, rather than resources. I therefore refer to the idea as "maintenance of an entity's equity." The concept goes back at least to the work of Alfred Marshall.[11]

Each year a profit-oriented entity has inflows and outflows of resources related to its operating activities. If, during a year, the stream of inflows is sufficiently larger than the stream of outflows, so as to provide a satisfactory return on its equity investment, the entity has maintained its equity investment during that year. Alternatively, if the cost of using equity funds is counted as one of the outflows, the entity has maintained its equity if its inflows during the year at least equal its outflows.

Viewed in this way, "maintenance of an entity's equity" provides a concrete meaning to the number labelled net income in a profit-oriented entity. Taking the alternative in which the cost of using funds is counted as an outflow, an entity that reports zero income was in a steady state. If the factors causing inflows and outflows remain unchanged, the entity can continue to operate indefinitely. Assuming that in the long run the average entity operates so as to earn a satisfactory return on its investment, zero income represents average performance. An income greater than zero represents above-average performance, and the higher the income the better the performance. Conversely, an entity that has less than zero income has not maintained its equity, and if it continues to operate in this fashion, it will go bankrupt.

Cash flows.   Financial activities can be measured in various ways, but, with one exception, all the descriptions are different ways of wording what is essentially the same concept. The exception is the proposal to focus on cash flows. I discussed this proposal at length in Chapter 2, and the analysis there led to Premise 16: "Income provides a better measure of an entity's performance than does cash flow." The basic point is that financial performance is measured by comparing the resource inflows from operations during an accounting period with the amount of resources used up during the period, and neither resource inflows nor resources used up is correctly measured by cash receipts or cash disbursements.

Nonprofit organizations.   Since most sets of accounting concepts focus on profit-oriented entities, they describe performance measurement in terms of earnings or net income as in the sentence from paragraph 43 of FASB Concepts Statement No. 1 quoted earlier. Such a focus is appropriate for profit-oriented entities because a primary economic goal of these organizations is to earn income. The relevance of such a focus to nonprofit organizations may not be apparent, however, because by definition these organizations do not have the goal of earning profits.

Although there is general agreement that a primary goal of a nonprofit
organization is to provide services, there is also general agreement that
financial accounting cannot report how well an entity performed in attaining this goal. Financial accounting can measure the resources used by the
organization, but it cannot measure how much service the organization
provided. In a profit-oriented entity, revenue is a good measure of the
amount of goods and services provided. In many nonprofit entities, however, a significant amount of revenues may arise through taxation, contributions, grants, and other sources that are not directly related to services
provided.[12]

Nevertheless, the idea of maintaining an entity's equity does apply to
nonprofit organizations. All economic entities have equity. As described
above, a profit-oriented entity that has operated so as to earn zero income
during an accounting period has maintained its equity; income above zero
(or loss below zero) is a measure of how well it has performed.

A nonprofit entity that has operated so as to earn zero income also has
maintained its equity. Although the amount of income above zero (or loss
below zero) is not a measure of its performance, this positive or negative
amount does convey important information about the entity's financial activities. If positive, it indicates the amount of cushion that the entity has
generated, perhaps in anticipation of possible adverse conditions in the
future. (A large positive amount may also indicate that the entity is not
providing as many services as it could with available resources.) If negative, the amount indicates that the entity has not maintained its equity; that
is, it has not lived within its means. If such a situation continues indefinitely, the entity will go bankrupt.[13]

Thus, although the meaning of the bottom line on the income statement
is different in a profit-oriented entity than in a nonprofit entity, the bottom
line does have an important meaning in both types of entities, and the
method of arriving at it is the same in both types.

In the preceding paragraphs I have discussed the equity maintenance
idea in general terms. In some entities it is important that accounting distinguish the effect of operating activities from the effect of other events
that, although not associated with operating activities of the accounting
period, nevertheless change an entity's equity. In nonprofit organizations,
for example, receipts for endowment purposes, contributions of plant, and
donations of museum pieces add to the entity's equity, but the effect of
these events should be separated from the effect of events that produce
operating revenue. This topic is discussed in Chapter 7.

Inflation accounting

In Statement No. 33, the Financial Accounting Standards Board required
large companies to present supplementary financial statements that showed

the effects of general inflation and also adjusted certain items to a current cost basis. These reports began in 1979, and the board stated that it intended to review Statement 33 "no later than five years after its publication."

Some people believe that this experiment will lead to a shift away from the historical cost basis in the primary financial statements. Pending the results of the experiment instituted by Statement 33, it would be premature to develop a framework on the assumption that these results will provide substantial evidence in support of such a drastic change. Therefore, I exclude this possibility from the framework.

Lest this exclusion be regarded as a cop-out, Appendix B to this chapter gives my reasons for believing that a shift away from the historical cost basis is undersirable.

DIRECT VERSUS INDIRECT APPROACH TO INCOME MEASUREMENT.

The literature describes two approaches to measuring income: the asset/liability approach and the revenue/expense approach. Under the former, income is measured indirectly as the increase in net assets during an accounting period (net assets being the difference between assets and liabilities). Under the latter approach, income is measured directly as the difference between revenues and expenses during the period.

In its initial Discussion Memorandum on Concepts (December 2, 1976), the FASB asked, as Issue One, which approach should be adopted. Of some 300 respondents, the great majority favored the revenue/expense approach.[14] Nevertheless, in subsequent writings about concepts, the FASB has adopted the asset/liability approach (although it has not said so explicitly, nor has it given any reason for its choice). It is possible that the FASB concluded that there was no difference between the two approaches. Although algebraically this is the case, in practice the two approaches lead to quite different concepts.

Asset/liability approach

With the asset/liability approach one must first define assets and liabilities, state when changes in them are to be recognized, and state how the amount of each change is to be measured. Income is then the change in net assets, which is the difference between assets and liabilities. FASB Concepts Statement No. 3 takes this approach. It defines assets as "probable future economic benefits" (paragraph 19), and liabilities as "probable future sacrifices of economic benefits arising from present obligations" (paragraph 28).

The references to "benefits" implies that the balance sheet amounts measure *future* benefits. This is inconsistent with Premise 4, which suggests that accounting should focus on what has happened, not what might happen in the future.

Attempts to use these definitions to arrive at an income concept have led to peculiar results. For example, this approach leads FASB staff members to the conclusion that income should be recognized in the period in which a firm sales order is booked, whereas most people would not recognize income until the entity has delivered the goods.[15]

The asset/liability approach also requires that a sharp line be drawn between liabilities and shareholder equity. A transaction that increases or decreases liabilities, with no effect on assets, automatically decreases or increases income. In practice, drawing such a line is extremely difficult.[16]

Revenue/expense approach

The revenue/expense approach avoids these problems. It is possible to make operational definitions of revenues and expenses and to use these definitions to measure income directly. The focus is on when revenue should be recognized, when expense should be recognized, the amount of revenue to be recognized, and the amount of expense to be recognized. The effect on assets and liabilities then becomes an automatic consequence of the measurement of income.

Take depreciation as an example. The asset/liability view suggests that depreciation should be measured by observing the amount of change in a depreciable asset during a period. But there is no way of making such an observation for most depreciable assets. The revenue/expense view looks at depreciation as an expense associated with the periods during which the asset provides service. This is the conventional view and the correct view.

Nonprofit organizations

In nonprofit organizations there is no question about the primacy of the income statement and hence of the desirability of the revenue/expense approach. Managers and interested external parties rarely examine the balance sheet as a whole (although they do, of course, examine selected items, particularly monetary items). Many nonprofit organizations do not even report a balance sheet.

Resistance to the revenue/expense approach

Why, despite the overall sentiment for its acceptance, do the FASB and many other people reject the revenue/expense approach—the direct approach—to the measurement of income? I think a basic reason, perhaps the only reason, is that the revenue/expense approach plays down the importance of the balance sheet, yet there is a deeply held belief that the balance sheet should be a report of values in some meaningful sense. Paton, Littleton, Grady, and other authors who take the revenue/expense approach make it clear that this approach does result in a balance sheet that does not state values.[17]

Robert Sprouse, vice chairman of FASB, in a speech entitled "the Balance Sheet—Embodiment of the Most Fundamental Element of Accounting Theory," states that the balance sheet should be truly a "statement of financial position."[18] He castigates those who hold that it is merely a "sheet of balances." Unfortunately, the balance sheet could be a statement of financial position only if the value of assets could be measured in a meaningful way, and Premise 8 states that for nonmonetary assets this is not possible.[19]

Unfortunately also, there are events that if recorded so as to give meaningful balance sheet amounts, would distort income. For example, Kern County Land Company for many years owned a million acres of land that it carried on its balance sheet at an average cost of $3 per acre. The land was eventually sold for 100 times this amount. Critics of accounting point to this balance sheet understatement as evidence of the abominable state of the art; accounting did not recognize this increase in value during the years in which it was occurring. These critics do not appreciate that the principal alternative would have been to revalue the land periodically, and to reflect the gain on operating statements. These revaluations would have been highly subjective, and the resulting income amount correspondingly unreliable. (Another alternative would have been to record the gain as a direct credit to equity, but this would have been inconsistent with the clean-surplus idea, discussed further in Chapter 7.)

Similarly, former Chairman Harold Williams of the SEC says it is ridiculous to publish balance sheets for petroleum companies that do not report the current value of their crude oil and gas reserves. The proposed SEC solution, reserve recognition accounting, leads to even more ridiculous gyrations in the amount of reported income when the balance sheet amounts are adjusted to reflect changes in the estimated present value of a barrel of oil as market prices change and in the estimated number of barrels of reserves as geologists revise their calculations. The weaknesses of reserve recognition accounting became so apparent that in 1981 the SEC abandoned efforts to develop it.

The definition of a "measurable property" in Premise 2 says that one essential characteristic is that individual elements can be added together to produce a meaningful total. Since Premise 8 states that the fair value of nonmonetary assets cannot be measured, nonmonetary assets cannot be defined collectively as "values," and this approach therefore does not lead to a measurable property that applies to assets as a class.

Concept

Thus, I conclude that the weight of the argument based on the premises supports the following concept:

> **Concept 3.04.** *Income should be measured directly by measuring revenues and expenses rather than indirectly by measuring changes in assets and liabilities.*

Implications for the balance sheet

A basic difficulty with an approach that starts with a definition of assets is that any definition suggests that assets must be valued in some sense, but there is, in fact, no way of determining a value of many types of non-monetary assets (Premise 8). If, however, one starts with the right-hand side of the balance sheet, there is a straightforward way of arriving at a definition of the elements on the balance sheet, which describes the actual nature of these elements.

Rather than defining liabilities as obligations to outside parties and shareholder equity as the residual claim of owners, the entire right-hand side of the balance sheet can be described as reporting the sources from which the entity has obtained its funds as of the balance sheet date. Some of these funds—the type labeled liabilities—were furnished by creditors; some were furnished by shareholders; and some of them were acquired by the entity's own effort. I shall expand on this general idea in Chapter 4.

With this concept, the nonmonetary assets on a balance sheet represent expenditures that are applicable to future periods. Some say that assets are "bundles of benefits," but this implies that the amount reported for the asset is the amount of its benefit, which is not the case. The amount reported for the asset actually is the unexpired amount of the expenditure. These items are held as assets until they are charged off as expenses in future periods. The concept says nothing about the economic significance of these amounts. They are not the values of the items named; they are simply unamortized expenditures.

Proponents of the asset/liability view intensely dislike this implication. They do not want the balance sheet to be merely a repository of expenditures that are going to be expenses in future periods. They want the balance sheet to show meaningful values. This goal would be fine if the balance sheet could have such a meaning, but this is not possible. This fact might as well be faced.

It seems unlikely that an entity's wealth can be measured with sufficient reliability to be reported in the primary financial statements. Accounting can measure income, the values of monetary assets, and the amounts of funds obtained from various sources; that is the most that should be expected of it. Measurement of income is similar to measuring the amount of oil and gas flowing out of an oil well. These amounts can be measured directly, even though we do not know either how much was in the ground at the beginning the period nor how much was there at the end. The asset/liability view implies that we do know how to measure the beginning and ending amounts.

I believe that Concept 3.04 reflects what accountants actually do in preparing the financial statements of profit-oriented companies (with one important exception, which is the subject of Chapter 4). Concept 3.04 also reflects practice in certain nonprofit organizations although many of them, particularly governmental units, prepare financial statements for which no primary focus is discernible.

OTHER BASIC CONCEPTS

This section lists other basic concepts that govern financial statements. Some of them flow obviously from the premises in Chapter 2; others are so widely accepted that there is no need to support them. Unless there is controversy about a concept, it is simply listed and explained briefly.

Accounting period

There is almost universal acceptance of the year as the time period to be covered by the primary financial statements. The Trueblood report did raise the possibility of reporting in terms of "earning cycles," an earning cycle being the interval between cash disbursements intended to generate earnings and the resulting cash receipts.[20] It did not, however, end up by recommending that financial statements be prepared on this basis, and there does not seem to be a practical way of implementing such a concept.

Annual financial statements provide an acceptable balance between the need for timely information (Premise 19) and the need for reliable information (Premise 20). The shorter the time interval, the higher the degree of estimation that is necessary. The longer the interval, the longer the user has to wait. Also, the annual period eliminates the effect of seasonal influences which can have a substantial impact on shorter periods.

> **Concept 3.05.** *The calendar period covered by a set of financial statements should be one year.*

This concept allows for the preparation of interim statements, but it implies that when the term *accounting period* is used, the time interval referred to is one year. The concept also allows for the presentation of comparative financial statements. Minor variations, such as 52 weeks, are consistent with the concept.

Timely information

The financial consequences of some events that occur during an account-ing period cannot be known with certainty for a long time. If a defective product is sold, the cost of repairing or replacing it or the cost of settling a product liability suit may not be known for years. Nevertheless, as stated in Premise 19, users want information quickly, and they prefer that esti-mates of the future consequences of past events be made, rather than wait-ing until the consequences are known with certainty.

> *Concept 3.06.* *Financial statements should be based on informa-tion that is available by the end of an accounting period or shortly thereafter.*

Going concern

Although not always understood by nonaccountants, the idea that an en-tity will continue to function indefinitely is a desirable concept in a finan-cial accounting system. If financial accounting were developed around the alternative concept—namely, that the entity is about to go out of exis-tence—then it would be necessary to measure the fair value of assets as of the end of the accounting period. Premise 8 states that such measurements ordinarily are not feasible. The following concept merely restates Premise 9:

> *Concept 3.07.* *Unless there is contrary evidence, financial ac-counting should assume that the entity will continue to operate indefinitely.*

It follows that if there is evidence that an entity will probably cease op-erations, accounting should disclose this likelihood. In these circumstances many of the concepts applicable to a going concern may not be relevant. The modifications required are outside the scope of this framework.

Articulation

Articulation means that there is a basic relationship between the operat-ing statement and the balance sheet, governed by the fundamental equa-tion, Assets = Sources of funds. Changes in an entity's equity between two balance sheets should be reconcilable with the amount of income reported for the intervening period.

In its original discussion memorandum on the conceptual framework, the FASB raised the question of whether articulation was a necessary and desirable concept.[21] Respondents showed no inclination to abandon the ar-ticulation concept, and the possibility has not been raised in subsequent FASB documents.

Concept 3.08. Amounts on the primary financial statements should articulate.

Nonaccountants do not appreciate the importance of the articulation concept. Not only is it required conceptually because the flow statements explain changes on the status statement, but also it is an excellent mechanical way of assuring that part of a transaction does not "fall through a crack," a frequent failing of single-entry accounting systems.

Information needs not known precisely

Premise 13 states that the nature of the information needed by users is not known precisely, and some authors have used this fact as an argument against an attempt to develop a conceptual framework.[22] Such a position is too extreme. Based on years of experience, standards-setting bodies have developed their personal judgments about the types of information that users need. The validity of these judgments cannot be verified, and they probably are not entirely accurate. Furthermore, needs vary among users, and the needs of a particular user vary with the situation being analyzed.

Nevertheless, these judgments are sufficiently reliable to serve as a basis for setting standards. The concept that follows states a middle ground between the assertion that accounting information should meet user needs perfectly and the assertion that unless needs can be clearly specified, standard setting is impossible.

Concept 3.09. To the extent feasible, financial statements should meet the information needs of the most important classes of users, as perceived by those who establish accounting standards.

No set of accounting standards can claim to be perfect; there is no way of knowing the needs of all users, much less knowing how to meet these needs. It follows that critics whose perception of user needs differs from that of the standards-setting body may have legitimate grounds for criticism. If these critics can convince the standards-setting body of the merits of their perception, they may succeed in modifying a standard. The process is analogous to that used to revise legislated statutes, and, as is the case with statutes, the revision must be consistent with the underlying concepts.

Consistency

Premise 21 states that users need comparable information. If financial information for an entity in one period is to be compared with that in a previous period, the standards governing the preparation of the information must be the same in both periods. On the other hand, the requirement for consistency cannot be so rigid that desirable changes in standards, or in the application of standards to particular situations, are ruled out.[23]

> *Concept 3.10. An entity should use consistent accounting practices from one period to the next unless a preferable practice becomes accepted.*

A preferable practice is one that is more nearly in accord with the standards and the conceptual framework from which the standards were derived than is an alternative practice. This is a vague statement, but I do not know how to state the idea more concretely. Partly because the statement is vague, entities change their accounting practices for reasons that cannot be defended strongly on conceptual grounds. For example, entities shift to LIFO strictly for its income tax advantages, even though they believe the LIFO is conceptually less desirable than FIFO. A change required by a new standard is inherently a preferable change.

Comparability

The preceding concept refers to accounting for a given entity in different time periods. Users also need to compare financial statement information of various entities. The validity of such comparisons is lessened if each of these entities did not prepare its financial statements according to the same standards.

> *Concept 3.11. Similar events should be treated similarly by all entities.*

This concept focuses on the nature of the event, not on the nature of the entity. Thus, the standards-setting body appropriately develops a standard for the treatment of exploration costs associated with the discovery of oil and gas, and this standard applies to any entity that conducts such activities. The standards-setting body need not develop standards for a petroleum company as such, because many of the events in such a company are similar to those in other companies. Nevertheless, an industry association may develop preferred accounting practices for its members.

The aggregation problem. The concept begs the question of what constitutes a similar event, which is more clearly described as the aggregation problem. The most important example is recording the events relating to exploration for oil and gas. Some companies treat each hole as a separate event, others treat all the holes in one field as one event, others treat all the holes in one country as an event, and still others treat all the holes owned by the entity as one event. The FASB issued Statement 19 on this question, but it encountered so much opposition that Statement 19 was suspended by Statement 25. The issue is still unresolved.

Similar aggregation problems exist in the case of certain asset categories. Should the portfolio of marketable securities be treated as a single asset, with gains and losses to be recognized for the portfolio as a whole, or should gains and losses on individual securities be accounted for separately? Should inventory items be treated separately, aggregated into classes of similar items, or treated as a single portfolio? Should depreciation be calculated on individual items, on groups of similar items, or on the composite of all items?

A concept regarding aggregation is needed. I confess, however, that I do not have a sound enough view on what the concept should be to justify an attempt to state it.

Materiality

The FASB includes in each of its standards the statement: "The Provisions of the Statement need not be applied to immaterial items." This is almost a tautology because users obviously do not care if a departure from a standard makes no material difference in the information. Nevertheless, a concept about materiality is desirable in order to avoid giving the impression that standards must be adhered to in all circumstances.

> ***Concept 3.12.*** *Any accounting standard may be disregarded if the effect of doing so is not material.*

Information is material if it is likely to influence decisions made by users. Although there have been many attempts to make the materiality concept more specific, so far no one has succeeded in doing so.[24]

Conservatism

Traditionally, the idea of conservatism has been stated in such terms as "anticipate no profits but provide for all losses." Such a statement is too strong; it leads to a deliberate understatement of income. The other extreme, a concept that states that the most probable results should be reported, is also unacceptable. It disregards the fact that managers tend to be motivated to report favorable results (Premise 10). The concept stated below takes a middle ground. It is consistent with the thrust of the seven paragraphs about conservatism in FASB Concepts Statement No. 2.

> ***Concept 3.13.*** *Recognition of increases in an entity's equity requires more reliable evidence than recognition of decreases.*

A concept along the lines of the above is criticized by some people who assert that it misleads current investors and favors future investors who benefit if actual performance eventually turns out to be better than that originally reported. Such an assertion disregards Premise 10, about management optimism. If equally reliable evidence were required for revenues as for expenses, reported performance would tend to be better than actual performance.

Balance between relevance and reliability

Information is not useful if it is not relevant to the needs of users. As Premise 20 states, users also need reliable information. In resolving many important accounting issues, the basic problem is to arrive at the proper balance between these two criteria. For example, FASB Statement 2 requires that research/development costs be expensed, notwithstanding the fact that in some circumstances a portion of such costs are properly capitalized; a capitalized amount would be relevant information. The Board evidently concluded that there was no sufficiently reliable way of distinguishing between the circumstances in which research/development costs should be capitalized and those in which these costs should be expensed.

The problem of balancing relevance and reliability is by no means unique to accounting. Physicians routinely report certain relevant information about a patient that can be reliably measured: temperature, pulse rate, blood pressure, blood composition, and so on. They do not report routinely other important information such as degree of happiness, optimism, diligence, and the like because there is no way of measuring these attributes reliably. (For special purposes, physicians do develop subjective measures of emotions.)

> *Concept 3.14.* In deciding on accounting standards and on the application of standards to specific events, an appropriate balance should be sought between the need for relevance and the need for reliability.

Both relevance and reliability are relative terms, not absolutes. A concepts statement cannot describe precisely the degree of either that is acceptable. The acquisition cost of a piece of equipment is both relevant and reliable. The amount of annual depreciation expense for that equipment is much less reliable, but is sufficiently relevant to be included in the measurement of income.

Because of management's optimistic bias (Premise 10), the reliability criterion is stronger for revenues than for expenses. For example, provisions for warranties and various contingencies are recorded even though the estimates of the amounts are relatively unreliable, whereas unrealized gains are rarely recorded. The defendant in a law suit reports a possible loss as soon as the suit is filed, but the plaintiff does not report the possible gain until the suit has been settled.

Costs and benefits

Although the benefits that users derive from an item of information obviously should exceed the costs of furnishing it, this idea should be stated explicitly because the point has a bearing on certain concepts to be discussed in later chapters.

> **Concept 3.15.** *The benefits from information should exceed the costs of furnishing it.*

The costs of furnishing information include not only the cost of collecting and reporting the information, but also the cost of auditing and the opportunity loss from disclosure, which can result in loss of competitive advantage, or losses from a weakened negotiating or legal position. Since no one knows how to calculate the benefits of accounting information, the concept is at most a general statement of a desired state of affairs.[25]

Accountability. Ijiri expands on this idea in a concept that he labels *accountability*. He points out that although users have certain rights to financial information, the entity also has certain rights with respect to the privacy of information.[26] In deciding on whether to require the disclosure of certain information, the standards-setting body must weigh the benefits to the user, whom Ijiri calls the *accountee*, against the costs to the entity, the *accountor*.

Appendix A

SOME IMPLICATIONS OF THE BASIC CONCEPTS

A conceptual framework provides guidance in the development of standards. Standards spell out circumstances and conditions for reporting specific events in accordance with the concepts. Listed below are certain implications that follow from the concepts discussed in this chapter. These implications are not appropriately stated as concepts because the concepts lead to them without separate analyses. They are not standards because they suggest only the general nature of standards. My purposes in stating them are both to clarify the meaning of the concepts and to suggest how the concepts serve as guidelines in resolving accounting issues.

Monetary amounts. Financial statements report only monetary amounts. Financial statements require that all amounts be expressed in a common denominator. The obvious common denominator is money. Accounting systems based on other measures, such as units of energy (quads), have been developed, but these are for special purposes.[27]

Exclusion of social responsibility. Concept 3.02 implies that reports on corporate social responsibility are not part of the primary financial statements because information about social responsibility cannot be expressed in monetary terms. Such reports are supplementary information.[28]

Historical. Financial statements reflect the financial effects of events that already have happened as of the end of the accounting period. As pointed out in the discussion of Premise 14, although financial statement information is used as a basis for predicting future performance, the information itself relates to events that have already happened. Accounting is historical.

New information.   Information that comes to light after the end of the year is properly included in the financial statements provided that it relates to events that happened before the end of the year. Discovery of an inventory shortage that existed at the end of the year is properly included; a theft of inventory that occurred after the end of the year should not be included, although it should be disclosed as supplementary information if material.

Budgets.   Although budgets or forecasts, as such, are not part of the primary financial statements, they may, of course, be reported as supplementary information.

Substance over form.   Financial statements should report the substance of economic events, even if their substance differs from their legal form. The concept refers to summaries of economic performance and status. These summaries may differ from the legal interpretation of what has happened. In a conditional sale agreement, for example, title does not pass until the final installment payment, but in substance many sales are made when delivery occurs.

Stewardship.   Financial statements do not necessarily report on management's stewardship. As I mentioned in the discussion of Premise 14, there are references in the literature to financial statements as a report on stewardship, by which is presumably meant the performance of management. Since financial statements focus on the entity, and since entity performance may be affected by forces that are outside of management's control, the financial statements may or may not report how well management performed. If the focus were on management performance, the financial statements presumably would have to be adjusted to allow for the effect of these noncontrollable forces.

Conflicts in emphasis.   If there is a conflict between reporting an event in a way that satisfies the primary need for information on an entity's performance, and reporting it in a way that satisfies some other information need, the method that satisfies the performance need should take precedence. Concept 3.03 suggests that the recognition of purchased goodwill as an asset is desirable if this leads to the recognition of the proper amount of income, even though the resulting asset is, to some people, not really an asset at all.

Balance sheet amounts.   Amounts of individual assets reported on the balance sheet do not purport to measure the value of these assets, nor does the total of net assets purport to measure the value of the entity. The amounts reported on the balance sheet for many items are not values in the usual sense, but rather are the consequences of entries made to satisfy the primary need for information about performance. (Incidentally, in introducing accounting to beginning students, the usual approach is, and probably will continue to be, to start with the balance sheet. This is the best way of introducing the fundamental theme that debits always equal credits. This pedagogical purpose does not imply that the balance sheet is more important than the income statement.)

AN ANALYSIS OF INFLATION ACCOUNTING

Concept 3.03 specifically excluded inflation adjusted numbers from the framework. There are two reasons for this exclusion. First, as stated in the text, experiments with inflation accounting are currently being made, and it seems inappropriate to recommend a change from the historical cost basis until the results of these experiments have been analyzed. Second, and as a practical matter more important, this topic is currently controversial and if any conclusion on it were stated in the main framework, discussion would probably focus on that conclusion to the neglect of other topics. Such a focus would be unfortunate because it would detract attention from other aspects of accounting that need to be improved.

My analysis of inflation accounting is therefore given separately in this Appendix.[29] My conclusion is that, subject to the unlikely development of contrary evidence from the current experiments, historical costs should continue to be the central focus of accounting, with the possibility of a few exceptions for certain types of monetary and inventory transactions.

Boundaries of the analysis

Two topics are explicitly excluded from this framework, and these exclusions apply also to the discussion of inflation accounting.

First, the analysis relates solely to the primary financial statements. It seems likely that information about the effects of inflation will continue to be included in the supplementary material, at least for large companies, but the nature of such information is outside the boundaries of this framework. A few people propose that there be two sets of primary financial statements, but this seems to me to be a self-contradiction and a way of avoiding the central issue, namely, which set should govern the way in which the entity's basic accounts are kept.

Second, the framework does not discuss issues relating to the measurement of taxable income. Income tax regulations now make allowances for the effects of inflation and probably will continue to do so in the future. These include the investment tax credit, accelerated cost recovery of depreciable assets, and the use of LIFO. Some allegations about the defects of historical cost accounting overlook this fact. Some people assert, for example, that income tax rules result in "eating our seed corn," that is, the income tax is taxing away the funds that are needed for new capital investments.[30] This assertion overlooks the fact that if some form of current cost accounting were permitted for tax purposes, the favorable treatment of depreciable assets and inventory undoubtedly would be eliminated.

A few decades ago proposals for inflation accounting involved the adjustment of all items on the financial statements. Currently, the proposals are limited to three types of items: (1) inventory and the related cost of sales; (2) property, plant and equipment, and related depreciation, and (3) monetary items.[31] There is general agreement that adjustments of other items involve complexities that are not worth the effort. This analysis will be limited to these three categories of items.

For simplicity, I shall assume that prices tend to rise, that is, a condition of inflation exists. Statements relevant to the opposite situation are omitted, but they are, of course, the converse of those given here.

Proposals for inflation accounting

Although there are many differences in details, proposals for recognizing the effects of inflation can be grouped into three categories, with two permutations in one of the categories, making a total of four alternatives. They are not mutually exclusive.

Constant dollar.   One proposal is to state the financial accounting amounts in units of constant purchasing power, rather than in units of actual dollars. (Actual dollars are often referred to as *nominal dollars*, which is a subtle way of prejudging the issue.)

Current cost.   This proposal is that inventories, plant, and related income statement items be measured in terms of their current costs, rather than at their historical acquisition cost. There are many variants of this basic idea, going under such names as current reproduction cost, current replacement cost, net realizable value, net present value of expected future cash flows, and recoverable amount. They are not discussed separately because the same general considerations apply to all of them.

There are two important alternatives in a current cost system: (1) the amount of the write-up of historical cost to current cost is credited to income; or (2) the amount of the write-up is credited to shareholder equity, and current income is affected only by the increased depreciation and cost of sales.

Monetary adjustments. This proposal is that changes in the purchasing power of net monetary assets or net monetary liabilities be recognized in the measurement of income.

Constant dollars

In any system, transactions are originally entered in the accounts at the number of dollars involved when the transaction occurred. Since the value of the dollar changes with time, the accounts reflect amounts whose purchasing power differs. The purchasing power of $1,000 used to buy a machine in 1960 was much greater than the purchasing power of $1,000 used to buy a machine in 1980. Constant dollar accounting recasts these dollar amounts into units that have the same purchasing power, that is, each unit presumably commands the same amount of goods and services as other units. These units may represent either the purchasing power of the current period or the purchasing power of some specified base period. The restated asset amounts have no necessary relationship to the value of the assets; they simply convert the dollars paid for the asset into other units, just as gallons can be converted to liters.

For our purpose, the important point is that constant dollar accounting is a restatement. Transactions are originally recorded at actual dollar amounts, and financial statements are prepared that summarize the effect of these transactions, also in actual dollar amounts. The constant-dollar statements are developed from these original statements.

Since the actual dollar statements must be prepared in any event, the only issue relevant to the present analysis is whether the *primary* financial statements are to be the constant dollar statements or the actual dollar statements. In either event, the underlying accounts contain actual dollar amounts.

In countries with high inflation rates, such as Brazil and Israel, financial statements are in effect expressed in units of constant purchasing power because transactions are reported at amounts that are adjusted by indices that reflect changes in purchasing power; however, this practice is not quite the same as restating amounts from actual currency units to units of constant purchasing power.[32]

There is little evidence that investors in the United States want the primary statements to be stated in constant dollars. In the late 1960s companies were urged to experiment with such statements, but only a handful did so. There have been a number of surveys on this question, and in none of them did a majority of respondents state that constant dollar statements would be more useful than actual dollar statements.[33]

As Premise 22 states, however, users of accounting information are reluctant to accept changes. It is conceivable that the experimental preparation of constant dollar information by 1,000 large companies may lead eventually to the acceptance of this method of presentation. Although I think this result unlikely, there is no need, for our present purpose, to hazard a guess on this matter.

Current cost

A second set of proposals would account for inventory and plant, and the related operating statement items, at something other than their historical costs. Supplementary statements prepared on this basis are encouraged by the Fourth Directive of the European Economic Community and by International Accounting Standard No. 15. Statement of Standard Accounting Practice No. 16 in the United Kingdom requires companies to report current cost information, either alone or accompanied by historical cost information. Many companies in Europe, Australia, and New Zealand periodically revalue their plant, which has the effect of incorporating current costs. In France, periodic revaluation is required by statute. The Phillips Company, one of the largest in the Netherlands, has for many years used an accounting system that incorporates replacement costs (a version of current costs). A few other Dutch companies use this approach. The Broken Hill Proprietary Company, Ltd., the largest Australian company, restates annually the amount of property, plant, and equipment at estimated current costs.

Some of the current cost proposals are both conceptually unsound and impractical. An attempt to report the current value (often called exit value) of assets is both unsound and unworkable: unsound because current values would be relevant only if the assets were about to be sold, which is contrary to Premise 19, the going concern premise; and unworkable because the current market value of most used productive assets cannot be reliably measured (Premise 8). Measuring the present value of the future earnings on productive assets is even less practical and is conceptually unsound because the value of an entity is not, in most cases, the sum of the value of individual assets.

Excluding the above alternatives, there remains the possibility of converting the actual dollar cost of plant and inventory to some version of current cost. Although this might be either the cost of reproducing the same asset or the cost of acquiring an asset with the same productive capacity, we can disregard these nuances and discuss the general proposition that assets should be reported at their current cost.

In Statement 33, the FASB required large companies to experiment with supplemental disclosure of current costs of inventory and plant. Previously, the SEC, in Accounting Series Release 190, required similar experiments.[34] Many individuals, including probably the majority of economics and accounting professors, favor the use of current costs. Harold M. Williams, former chairman of the SEC, said, "Inflation renders superficially illuminating financial figures virtually meaningless, since historic-based earnings bear little necessary correlation to economic reality."[35]

Conceptual and practical problems with this approach are discussed below.

Physical capital maintenance

The basic rationale for the current cost approach is that it purportedly shows whether an entity has maintained its capacity to operate at the same level as in prior periods, that is, whether the entity has maintained its physical capital. When they refer to capital maintenance, current cost advocates mean that an entity has maintained its capital if its income is adequate to recover the current cost of assets. Income is an addition to shareholder equity. They therefore are using "capital" in the sense of shareholder equity. As I pointed out earlier, shareholder equity is not capital; it is one source of the funds used to acquire capital. In effect, the proponents are saying that the shareholders are responsible for furnishing all the funds required to maintain the entity's operating capacity.

This argument is weak. In an inflationary economy, additional funds are indeed required to maintain a given level of capacity, but these funds come from a mixture of debt and equity, not from equity alone. The accounting required in the current cost concept is based on the unsound premise that only equity provides these funds.[36]

Even more importantly, the funds required to replace existing assets can come ultimately from revenues earned from the use of those assets after they have been acquired; they need not be provided for from current revenues. If selling prices are such that historical costs are recovered, an entity can maintain its capacity by increasing prices when new assets are acquired.[37] The discussion of Premise 6 gave evidence in support of the proposition that this is normal pricing practice. The evidence cited there further indicates that companies typically set selling prices so as to recover historical costs plus a normal profit. An accounting system based on some other premise, such as the premise that companies price to recover current costs, would not reflect reality.

Generational equity. This point can be sharpened by considering questions of generational equity that arise in nonprofit organizations. In these organizations, revenues should approximate expenses. If expenses were measured on a current cost basis, hospital patients would be required to pay for the more expensive equipment that the next generation would use, students would be required to pay tuition adequate to cover the cost of future buildings and equipment, and taxpayers would be required to pay for the cost of infrastructure to be used by the next generation. Under an historical cost basis, hospital patients, students, and taxpayers pay for the cost of the assets that they use. They surely would regard as inequitable the proposition that they should pay for the higher cost of the next generation of equipment.

Distributable income. A related argument for current costs—actually, another way of stating the preceding argument—is that when current costs are subtracted from revenues, the remainder is the amount that can be distributed as dividends and still maintain an entity's operating capacity. As with the above argument, this assumes that funds for capital maintenance come only from equity, which is incorrect. Furthermore, those who make the distributable income argument assume, without evidence, that investors want this information. In practice, the amount of dividends actually distributed depends on the directors' assessment of future cash needs, the effect of dividends on stock prices, and other considerations that are unrelated to the amount that theoretically could be distributed.

Measurement problems. Estimates of the current cost of assets are obviously more subjective than records of their actual cost. The issue is whether these estimates are sufficiently reliable to be incorporated in the primary financial statements. There is little evidence that reliable estimates can be made. In 1898 the U.S. Supreme Court ruled that regulated utilities were entitled to a fair return on the "fair value" of their properties. Fair value is roughly similar to current cost. Courts and regulatory commissions struggled with the problem of determining fair value for the next 45 years, without success. In 1944, in the Hope Natural Gas case, the Court, in effect, abandoned this approach, and most rate regulation is now based on historical cost.[38] (A "fuel adjustment charge" is a charge for the actual cost of fuel used, not for its replacement cost.)

In the 1920s, a period of inflation, many American companies wrote up the value of their assets to an approximation of current cost, only to write them down again in the 1930s.

A basic problem with measuring current costs is that the conceptually correct amount is the amount that needs to be booked in the current year to provide for asset replacements that will occur in an unknown future year, with unknown physical characteristics, and at unknown prices. Attempts to approximate this amount by using price indices are flawed, because there is at most a tenuous connection between current price indices and the cost of the future replacement. The use of insurance values, assessed values, or appraisal values assumes that these amounts are sufficiently reliable, which is a dubious assumption.[39]

Holding gains

When asset amounts are increased, the articulation concept requires that the offsetting credit, which is called a holding gain, goes somewhere. There are two possibilities: (1) record the holding gain as a component of income in the current period or (2) credit it directly to shareholder equity.

E. O. Edwards and P. W. Bell recommended that the holding gain be credited to the current period's income. The effect of such a practice, however, is to destroy the message of capital erosion, which is the main justification for accounting for current costs. The additional expense resulting from depreciation and cost of sales based on current cost is at least partially, and in some cases entirely, offset by the holding gain. (To be fair, Edwards and Bell were not attempting to convey this message; their objective was to separate holding gains from operating income.)

Furthermore, errors in the estimate of holding gains have a magnified effect on income. For current cost depreciation, only a fraction of the estimating error affects the operating statement in a single year; for the holding gain, the whole error does. A holding gain that included an estimating error of 10 percent in the current cost of plant could easily double or wipe out reported income. As a practical matter, therefore, crediting the holding gain to income is unlikely to command much support, and indeed is prohibited in most, if not all, systems based on current costs.

An estimating error does not have as severe an impact if the credit is to shareholder equity, because presumably it is largely disregarded in an appraisal of the entity's performance. But such a practice raises a question. What is the nature of this beast? It is not funds contributed by shareholders. It is, at most, an indication that their equity has increased because of the increase in the current cost of assets. Since the basic thesis is that this amount can never be distributed to them, the logic of recording such an increase escapes me.

Inventories

Some authorities maintain that cost of goods sold should be measured at the current cost of the items sold, or on the LIFO basis, which approximates current cost. They argue that an entity has not maintained its shareholder equity unless its sales revenue is adequate to provide for the replacement of the goods sold. (In analyzing this view, the fact that many companies do use the LIFO method is irrelevant. LIFO usually reduces taxable income, but it can be used for income tax purposes only if LIFO is used in its financial statements, which is the reason many companies use it.)

The simple, straightforward way of regarding a sales transaction says that if a company buys something for $1.00 and sells it for $1.50, it has made a profit of 50 cents.[40] The LIFO (or current cost) advocate says that this is misleading; if the item has to be replaced at a cost of $1.10, only 40 cents is profit. This reasoning, I believe, implicitly assumes that accounting should measure the maintenance of physical capital, for in order to maintain its physical inventory, the company does indeed have to spend $1.10. The argument is valid if, but only if, the central focus of accounting were on physical capital maintainance. For reasons already given, this approach has doubtful merit as applied to the entity as a whole, and it would be equally wrong to account for one item on such a basis.

Some argue that a company cannot maintain its shareholder equity if it treats the whole 50 cents as profit. The 50 cents cannot be distributed as dividends because 10 cents of it must be retained to provide new inventory; it is an *inventory profit* and is so labelled in the Gross National Product statistics. The counterargument is that the focus of financial accounting is not on measuring the amount that can be paid as dividends; dividend policy is a matter for the board of directors, not for the accountant. The fact is that the company has increased its financial capital by 50 cents.

More important than these arguments, however, is the question of fact. Do companies normally set their selling prices on the basis of current costs or on historical costs? The evidence referred to in the discussion of Premise 5 strongly suggests that the historical cost basis predominates. Since accounting should reflect economic reality, this is the strongest argument for the use of the historical cost basis.

For these reasons I conclude that cost of goods sold should be measured at the actual dollar cost of the items sold.

Some argue that the lower-of-cost-or-market rule is a departure from the historical cost concept. This is not so. The rationale for this rule is Concept 3.13, which suggests that a probable decrease in equity should be recognized as soon as it becomes known. When the realizable value of inventory becomes lower than its cost, such a decrease is probable.

Monetary items

Premise 8 states that the current value of monetary items can be reliably measured, thus negating the argument about feasibility, which was an important reason for rejecting the current cost approach. Moreover, it can be argued that a company has, in fact, increased its equity if its monetary assets have increased in value; financial capital is close to being money.

The financial statements of some entities, such as mutual funds, make no sense unless monetary amounts are stated at current values. In consolidating foreign subsidiaries, many believe that monetary amounts should be converted at current values. These are reasons for considering monetary items separately from nonmonetary items.

I therefore believe that the possibility of using current values for monetary items should not be foreclosed. However, the problem essentially involves questions of income recognition. When should gains or losses on monetary items be recognized? The problem can be discussed best in the context of Chapter 6, in which I address the whole question of income measurement, and it is therefore deferred to that chapter.

A few people argue that an increase in interest rates results in a decline in the market value of a company's debt, that this in effect increases shareholder equity, and that this increase therefore should be recognized in the accounts.[41] This is a fallacious argument. Although the market value of the debt may have changed, the company is obligated to pay the principal and interest on the debt as stated in actual dollars, and it is the present value of this obligation that is reported on the balance sheet. Only if the company refinances the debt, does its obligations change.

User interest

Whatever the conceptual merits of a constant dollar or current cost approach, and notwithstanding the support for such an approach by academics, by the FASB, and by some prominent accountants, there is little evidence that company managements think that either of these approaches is superior to the historical cost model. There is also little evidence that investment analysts regard the amounts reported under such an approach as important information.[42]

Despite the strong encouragement of the Accounting Principles Board in 1969, few companies published constant dollar information, and there did not seem to be pressure from users for such information. Although large companies have been required to publish certain current cost information since 1976, first by the SEC and later by the FASB, there is little evidence that users attach much importance to this information. Earnings and price/earnings ratios continue to be published on an historical cost basis, and reports of financial analysts emphasize estimates of earnings on an historical cost basis (although they occasionally mention current costs). In reporting the required supplementary information, the majority of companies caution the reader about placing heavy reliance on it.

Although the FASB has published a book and its members have spoken frequently on what constant dollar accounting and current cost accounting mean, few of these statements explain how this information is more useful than historical costs, either in comparing one company with another or in comparing a company's current performance with its past performance. Such comparisons are an important part of financial analysis.

In nonprofit entities, the only group that has shown the slightest interest in current costs is the hospitals. The Hospital Financial Management Association has proposed that supplementary statements show the replacement cost of plant and equipment. It has not, however, described practical ways of estimating these costs. Its obvious motivation is to make the case that hospitals should be reimbursed for replacement costs, rather than for actual costs incurred.[43]

4

Entity equity and equity interest

The concepts described in this chapter differ considerably from those underlying current accounting standards and practice; they therefore are discussed in some depth. My thesis is that the right-hand side of the balance sheet of profit-oriented companies should be modified by dividing shareholder equity into two components, called shareholder equity and entity equity. Separate identification of these components suggests that the cost of using shareholder equity funds—called equity interest—should be explicitly recognized as a cost. Interest cost, of both debt and equity funds, should be accounted for in the same way as other elements of cost.

UNREALISM OF CURRENT PRACTICE

In Chapter 2 I described premises regarding the nature of economic entities and the needs of users for information about those entities. These premises lead to Concept 3.01, which states that financial statements should report on the activities and status of an entity as such. The statements should not be primarily concerned with the interests of the shareholders, who are one of several parties who supply funds to the entity. This is the "entity view," and in the accounting literature it superseded the "proprietary view" many years ago.[1]

Nevertheless, in actual practice, and in the conceptual framework of the FASB, the proprietary view is still dominant. The proprietary view leads to the interpretation that assets are resources and that liabilities and shareholder equity are the two types of claims against these resources. Under this view, the shareholder equity item on the balance sheet purports to reflect the residual interests of the owners, that is, their claims after the liabilities have been subtracted from the assets.[2]

Not all equities are claims

Some, but not all, of the items on the right-hand side of the balance sheet represent claims. Although most liabilities are indeed claims against the assets and reflect the financial interests of creditors, and although the amount for preferred stock is sort of a claim of the preferred shareholders, the amount reported as common shareholder equity is not a claim and does not reflect the financial interests of the common shareholders in any meaningful sense.[3]

The common shareholders cannot claim the amount stated as their equity, or any sizable fraction of it, without destroying the entity. The amount reported is *not* the shareholders' equity in the entity; the shareholders' rights extend to the entity as a whole, even though they are junior to the rights of creditors. And since the left-hand side of the balnce sheet does not show the fair value of the assets, the balancing amount on the right-hand side does not represent the monetary amount of the shareholders' claim, equity, or rights. If the entity ceases to be a going concern, the amount, if any, that the shareholders receive in liquidation will not be the amount reported as shareholder equity, except in the unusual case in which a corporation is sold at its book value.

Furthermore, the shareholders whose interests are allegedly reported on the balance sheet, are not usually the same persons as those who furnished funds in exchange for stock. In a publicly traded company, many of the original shareholders have long since sold their stock. The amounts invested by current shareholders are the amounts they paid former shareholders for the stock, and these amounts are unlikely to correspond to the amount of shareholder equity reported on the balance sheet. Current shareholders are interested in the current market price of the stock, which is only coincidentally related to the amount reported as shareholder equity.

PROPOSED BALANCE SHEET STRUCTURE

The foundation laid in Chapter 3 leads to a fundamentally different view of the balance sheet. If the accounting entity is viewed as an organization distinct from its owners, the entity, not the owners, owns the assets, and the entity, not the owners, owes the amounts due to outside parties. The balance sheet of an entity therefore should report the financial interests of the entity, not the financial interests of its owners.

From the viewpoint of the entity, the right-hand side of the balance sheet reports sources of the entity's funds, and amounts on the left-hand side report the forms in which these funds are invested as of the balance sheet date. The balance sheet does not purport to reflect the interests or rights of the various parties in the entity. Instead, it is a summary statement of the results of the investment and financing activities of the entity as a whole.[4] The balance sheet equation is not Assets = Liabilities + Shareholder equity; rather, it is Assets = Sources of funds.

Assets and liabilities

This view of the balance sheet is more realistic than the view implicit in current practice, and corresponds to the nature of assets and liabilities as currently reported. The liabilities report the amount of funds furnished by lenders, by vendors (in the form of accounts payable), by employees (in the form of accrued salaries and unfunded pension benefits), and by the government (in the form of deferred income taxes).

Shareholder equity

The shareholder equity section of the present balance sheet, however, does not report the amount of funds supplied by shareholders. Although the paid-in capital item shows the amount shareholders supplied initially, the retained earnings number does not represent a shareholder contribution. Earnings were earned by the entity itself, not by its shareholders. Shareholders in a publicly owned corporation have little to say about what fraction of these earnings is retained. (The idea that shareholders consented to this retention is true, but naive.)

Equity interest

The amount of funds supplied by shareholders is greater than the amount reported as paid-in capital. In addition to their direct contribution, shareholders also have furnished funds to the extent that the cost associated with the use of these funds has not been repaid to them in the form of dividends. I refer to the cost of using shareholder equity funds as equity interest.

Unpaid equity interest is a source of funds, just like unpaid debt interest. To the extent that shareholders receive preferred stock, and the dividends on this stock correspond to the cost of these funds, unpaid preferred dividends is a component of equity interest. Unpaid interest on common stock does not appear on the balance sheet as presently constituted. It should.

The amount reported as common shareholder equity should be measured in essentially the same way that the amount of the liability to bondholders is currently reported, that is, the amount originally contributed plus the amount of unpaid costs. The principal difference is that the cost of funds supplied by bondholders is, in many cases, the debt interest, which can be easily measured, whereas the amount of equity interest on funds supplied by common shareholders poses new measurement problems.

Shareholder equity is a measured amount of funds. Unlike equity as defined in FASB Concepts Statement No. 3, it is not a residual. It is not the difference between assets and liabilities. It is measured directly as the sum of paid-in capital and unpaid equity interest.[5]

The following concepts, stated as definitions, contain these ideas:

> ***Concept 4.01.*** *Shareholder equity reports the amount of funds furnished by shareholders. It consists of their direct contributions plus accrued interest on these funds.*

> ***Concept 4.02.*** *Interest is the cost of using funds. Equity interest is the cost of using shareholder equity funds.*

Entity equity

Actually, an entity has three, not two, types of sources of funds. Some funds are supplied by creditors, some by shareholders, and some are generated by the entity's own efforts. The first two types are liabilities and shareholder equity. I shall refer to the third type as entity equity.[6] As will be explained, entity equity does not correspond to retained earnings in current practice.

The amount of funds generated by an entity's own operations during a period is measured by net income. Net income should be calculated as the difference between revenues (including gains) and expenses (including losses and equity interest). Each year's net income should be added to entity equity, just as net income is added to retained earnings in current practice. Because equity interest is recognized as a cost, however, the amount added to entity equity would be much smaller than the amount added to retained earnings as currently reported. Entity equity as of a given date is the sum of all net incomes to date. (It is also affected by certain other events as I shall discuss in Chapter 7.)

As the following concept indicates, entity equity is the residual:

> ***Concept 4.03.*** *Entity equity is the difference between total assets and the sum of liabilities plus shareholder equity. Its principal source is the entity's operating activities.*

Interest

Interest should be recognized as an element of cost, just as the costs of material, labor, and other services are recognized. Interest on debt funds is now recognized as a cost, but under most circumstances equity interest is not. Both debt interest and equity interest represent the cost of using funds, and I shall use the unmodified word *interest* to apply to both of them.[7] Since interest is the cost of using funds for specified time periods, interest cost should be charged to cost objects in proportion to the funds used by these cost objects during a time period. Specifically,

- Interest is an element of the cost of newly acquired plant and equipment and is now treated as such in FASB Statement No. 34. The cost should include the interest cost of funds tied up during the construction period for self-constructed plant and the interest cost of advance payments or progress payments on purchased plant.
- The interest cost of funds tied up in the capital assets used in the production process is an element of product cost and should be assigned to products in the same way that depreciation on plant and equipment is assigned.
- When assets are held in inventory for significant lengths of time, an interest cost is incurred, and it should be added to the cost of the inventory items. Inventory is here used broadly to include projects, mineral reserves, growing timber, nursery stocks, and similar assets, as well as inventory of material, work in process, and finished goods. (Statement No. 34 now recognizes interest as a cost of projects.)
- That part of the interest cost of a period that is not capitalized for one of the above reasons is an expense of the period, just as other noncapitalized overhead costs are expenses.

These ideas are summarized in the following concept:

> *Concept 4.04.* Interest should be recognized as an element of cost. The cost of using funds in the acquisition or production of goods and services should be an element of their cost. Interest cost that is not capitalized should be an expense of the period.

Accounting for interest cost. Once the fact that interest is a cost has been accepted, its recognition in the accounts is straightforward. The process is described in the appendix to this chapter, and may be summarized as follows:

1. An average interest rate for all funds is determined, using one of the methods described in the next section.
2. The interest cost assigned to a cost object is found by multiplying this average interest rate by the funds used for the cost object. (If funds can

be identified with a specific cost object, the cost of these funds, rather than the average cost, is the interest cost assigned to the cost object.)

3. That portion of the interest cost for an accounting period that is not assigned to cost objects in accordance with the above principles is a general expense of the period.

4. The annual equity interest cost is credited to shareholder equity.[8]

Although the last step follows automatically from the nature of equity interest, its novelty warrants an explicit statement:

> **Concept 4.05.** *The amount of equity interest in a period should be credited to shareholder equity.*

Curiously, I can find nothing in current authoritative statements that prohibits the above treatment of interest costs. It is a fact, however, that few, if any, accountants would agree that these procedures are currently acceptable. The accountants' reluctance is based on longstanding tradition, not on any specific prohibition.

THE MEASUREMENT PROBLEM

The use of shareholder equity funds certainly does involve a cost. Shareholders would not furnish funds to a company unless they expected to earn a return on these funds. The cost of using funds furnished by preferred stockholders is basically the preferred dividend. For funds furnished by common shareholders, however, there is no readily observable amount. The amount of dividends paid understates the cost of using shareholder equity funds in most companies.[9]

The absence of an easy measurement method does not deter accountants from reporting such items as the current cost incurred for employee pension plans. In measuring this cost, assumptions must be made about the service life and mortality of plan participants, about interest rates, about inflation rates (and, hence, future benefits), and about other factors. Differences in expert judgments on these assumptions can result in pension cost estimates that differ for a given company by 50 percent or more.[10]

Although, conceptually, the shareholder equity interest rate should correspond to the cost of shareholder equity funds, it is generally agreed that a direct estimate of this cost can be made only in special circumstances, principally in rate-regulated companies. For actively traded companies the capital asset pricing model has been used in attempts to estimate the cost of using equity funds. Many believe the model is worthless. At most it is applicable only to companies whose shares are actively traded, and even for these companies, serious problems arise in measuring the cost of equity under real world conditions.[11] In any event, a conceptual framework cannot require information that is available only for a few large companies.

There are at least two practical approaches to this problem, however, and the FASB should consider each of them. It could prescribe either (1) that entities should use their pretax debt interest cost or (2) that entities should use a rate based on some published indication of the cost of obtaining funds.

Pretax debt rate

The first approach is implicit in Statement No. 34, which specifies that the interest cost included in the acquisition cost of capital assets be calculated by applying the entity's pretax debt interest cost to all the funds used in acquiring such assets.[12] In a given company, the equity interest rate is higher than the debt interest rate because an equity investment is riskier to the investor than is debt. Debt interest is tax deductible, however, while equity interest is not. As will be shown, the pretax debt rate is an approximation of the aftertax equity cost.

Specified, published rate

The other approach is used in Cost Accounting Standard 414. All entities are required to use a specified published rate, which varies with interest rate movements. Such a rate is not as closely related to the actual interest cost in a given entity as the one in the Statement No. 34 approach, but a specified rate eliminates judgment in its determination and applies even to companies that have no debt. The rate prescribed by the Cost Accounting Standards Board is set by the U.S. Treasury. It has been a little lower than the pretax debt cost in the average company.[13]

Concept

Neither alternative is perfect. Either, however, gives at least as close an approximation to the true amount as the estimate of pension cost. A good approximation is preferable to the assumption that the cost of using shareholder equity funds is zero, which is the implication of present practice.

Thus, the following concept encompasses either of the alternatives discussed above:

> *Concept 4.06.* *The rate used in calculating the interest cost that is capitalized should be either the entity's pretax debt rate or a rate designated by the Financial Accounting Standards Board.*

Adequacy of the approximation

Although the theoretically correct rate is a weighted average of the aftertax rates for debt and equity funds, the pretax debt rate turns out to be a satisfactory approximation of this ideal. The pretax debt rate overstates the cost of the debt component, but it understates the cost of the equity component by an approximately equal amount.

These relationships can be illustrated by an example. Assume that a company obtained 40 percent of its permanent funds from debt, with a pretax cost of 12 percent, and 60 percent from equity. Assume a tax rate of 50 percent. The cost of equity funds is higher than the pretax cost of debt, but by an unknown amount. Assume that the equity interest rate if it could be calculated, would turn out to be 15 percent. The theoretically correct interest cost is then 11.4 percent, calculated as follows:

	Pretax cost	Aftertax cost	Weight	Weighted amount
Debt	12%	6%	.4	2.4%
Equity	15	15	.6	9.0
		True interest cost		11.4%

In this example, the pretax debt rate is within six-tenths of a percentage point of the true interest cost of 11.4 percent. Exhibit 4–1 shows how closely the pretax debt rate approximates the theoretically correct rate under a variety of assumptions about the mix of debt and equity funds and the spread between debt and equity interest costs.

In the great majority of companies, the proportion of debt is within the range of 20 to 50 percent of total permanent funds, and the risk premium for shareholder equity over debt is between 2 and 4 percentage points. For such companies, the use of a pretax debt rate produces a *maximum* error of 2 percentage points. This is less than the *probable* error inherent in the calculation of pension costs.

Having started down the road of using a pretax debt rate in arriving at equity interest cost in Statement 34, the FASB seems likely to continue with this approach. Indeed, in paragraph 83 of Statement No. 71, the Board stated: "In most cases the effect on net income [of capitalizing interest as required by Statement No. 34] would be similar to capitalizing an allowance that included a cost of equity funds." There is no need to decide on one of these alternatives now, however. The important point for the present purpose is that a satisfactory way of arriving at an interest rate does exist.

ADVANTAGES FOR THE CONCEPTUAL FRAMEWORK

The recognition of interest as an element of cost and of entity equity as a distinct source of funds is the one significant departure from current practice proposed in this book. With such recognition, the pieces fit together into a coherent whole; without it, I see no way of developing a framework

Exhibit 4–1

**Difference between true interest cost and pretax debt
cost of 12 percent under various assumptions**

Assumed percent of debt	Assumed equity cost			
	14%	16%	18%	20%
10	−1.2*	−3.0	−4.8	−6.6
20	− .4	−2.0	−3.6	−5.2
30	.4	−1.0	−2.4	−3.8
40	1.2	0	−1.2	−2.4
50	2.0	1.0	0	−1.0
60	2.8	2.0	1.2	.4
70	3.6	3.0	2.4	1.8
80	4.4	4.0	3.6	2.2
90	5.2	5.0	4.8	4.6

*Example: Assume 10 percent debt (90 percent equity) and 14 percent actual
cost of equity:

	Aftertax cost	Weight	Weighted percentage
Debt	6%	.1	.6%
Equity	14	.9	12.6
Actual cost			13.2%
Pretax debt cost			12.0
Understatement of actual cost			1.2 points

Note: The capital structure of most companies is within the shaded area.

that provides information explaining what has actually happened in an accounting entity.

The FASB framework has only three categories of balance sheet items: assets, liabilities, and equity. I have described the problems that such a framework creates in Chapter 3.[14] The FASB framework does not specifically address the matter of equity interest.[15]

Similarity of liabilities and shareholder equity

Implicit in this restructuring of balance sheet categories is the proposition that funds furnished by shareholders are similar to funds furnished by creditors, and that they should be treated in a similar way. Although there are some differences between the two external sources of funds, the distinction is not basic. The many contexts in which liabilities and share-holder equity are considered together include the following:

- Economists regard debt and equity as two sources of funds. In the leading texts no sharp distinction is made between these two sources.[16]
- Investment bankers devise new financial instruments that increasingly blur the distinction between debt and equity.[17]
- Managers regard fixed-income investors and equity investors as alternative sources of funds, with the relative proportions of each being determined by the appropriate balance between risk and cost.[18]
- In analyzing proposed investments in plant, managers usually consider the cost of the total pool of funds required without distinguishing between debt and equity.[19]
- In analyzing the profitability of investment centers, managers usually take account of the total capital employed, without regard to the mix of debt and equity funds used to acquire this capital.[20]
- In a closely held corporation, the decision as to whether funds supplied by shareholders are to be recorded as debt or as equity depends heavily on income tax and estate planning considerations, rather than on a fundamental distinction between the two types.[21]
- If a company goes private, it often substitutes debt for equity without substantially changing the economic characteristics of the entity.
- Regulatory agencies permit rates that provide a return on both debt and equity.[22]
- As already noted, Statement No. 34 capitalizes both debt interest and equity interest in certain circumstances.[23]
- Cost Accounting Standard 414 permits a return on capital as an element of cost, without regard for the source of funds used to acquire the capital.[24]
- Since debt interest is a tax-deductible expense but payments made to equity investors are not, the Internal Revenue Service (IRS) must draw a line between instruments that qualify as debt and those that do not. After struggling with this problem for more than 10 years, the IRS issued a complicated proposed regulation (Sec. 385) in 1980.[25] In 1981 it suspended the effective date of this regulation and went back to the drawing board. In 1982 it tried again with a draft that is 109 pages long.

No need for a sharp line.   In the proposed framework, standards setters need not be concerned with drawing a sharp line between liabilities and shareholder equity, because both are treated in the same way and because the line does not affect the measurement of net income, as is the case in the present framework. For example, convertible bonds do not have the required characteristics of a liability, but they are treated as liabilities, whereas redeemable preferred stocks have the characteristics of liabilities but ordinarily are not treated as such. In the proposed framework, both would be treated in the same way, whether classified as liabilities or share-holder equity.

Separation of internal and external fund sources

Both liabilities and shareholder equity are *external* sources of funds. They represent funds supplied by external parties, either directly as loans or paid-in capital or indirectly as various types of accruals. Entity equity reports the *internal* source of funds, that is, funds that the entity has accumulated as a result of its own activities.

Income is then defined as the increase in entity equity that results from operating activities during an accounting period. The amount of entity eq-uity as of the balance sheet date represents the cumulative amount of in-come, net of any distributions of it, since the inception of the entity. (As will be explained in Chapter 7, entity equity is also affected by a few events unrelated to income.)

A line drawn between shareholder equity and entity equity therefore sep-arates external from internal sources of funds. This line reflects a much more basic distinction than the line drawn between liabilities and share-holder equity on the balance sheet as it is now structured.

Nature of the balance sheet

The change proposed here implies that the right-hand side of the balance sheet should show sources of an entity's funds, and the left-hand side the forms in which this capital exists as of the balance sheet date. It follows from this view that the asset side does not purport to show what the entity is worth in total, nor that the amounts for individual assets represent the value of these assets. Although this is indeed the nature of the asset side of the present balance sheet, many readers do not appreciate this fact. They regard assets as values in some sense, whereas most nonmonetary assets are not values in any sense. Readers should be helped by this proposal to appreciate the real nature of accounting assets.

Many balance sheet amounts are an automatic consequence of the mea-surement of income. Nonmonetary assets are resources that will become expenses in future periods; certain liabilities are estimate of future obliga-tions resulting from identifying expenses and revenues that relate to the current period (such as the liability for warranty expenses and for deferred revenues). I will develop this point further in Chapter 7.

Entity equity maintenance

The concept that the income statement should explain changes in entity equity leads to a logical focus on the idea that is usually called *financial capital maintenance*, and that is here called *entity equity maintenance*. As explained in the discussion of Concept 3.03, this idea should be the primary focus of financial accounting. If, as in current practice, net income is the increase in owners' equity, there is no good way of applying a capital maintenance concept to the financial statements. The conventional way of measuring net income implies that an entity has maintained its capital if it earns any positive amount of net income. This is not so. With zero income, an entity has recovered the cost of using debt, but it has not provided anything for the cost of using equity. Such an entity is not viable. As FASB Statement No. 33 states, "Capital is maintained when revenues are at least equal to all costs and expenses." (paragraph 100). The use of shareholder equity funds does involve a cost, and this cost should be included in the measurement of capital maintenance.

Harmonizing business and nonbusiness accounting

Nonbusiness organizations do not have equity investors. Describing accounting principles for these organizations in the context of a conceptual framework that focuses on shareholder equity is therefore awkward. Using a framework that does not distinguish between funds supplied by equity investors and funds that the organization has generated through its own activities is particularly awkward.

When such a distinction is made, nonbusiness accounting concepts become consistent with business accounting concepts. In both, the basic focus is the measurement of the entity's success or failure in maintaining entity equity during a period.[26] This statement does not imply that the proposal "forces nonbusiness accounting into the business accounting mode," as some have alleged. The statement merely stresses the similarity between both types of accounting.

ADVANTAGES FOR FINANCIAL REPORTING

Premise 21 states that users want comparable information. The equity interest concept increases the comparability of the financial statements of different entities in several ways, some of which are described below.

Effect of leverage

Recognition of equity interest increases the comparability of results reported by companies with different debt/equity ratios. If two companies have identical real economic performance and identical assets employed, but one obtains most of its funds from equity and the other is highly leveraged, then in conventional accounting the unleveraged company will report a higher dollar income than the leveraged company because its income is not reduced by an interest charge. The reported net incomes of these companies therefore is not a valid basis for comparing their performance. Recognition of equity interest leads to net income amounts that are not distorted by differences in the sources of funds.

Capitalized costs

The proposal makes appropriate allowance for costs that should be capitalized. This is especially significant for capital-intensive companies, that is, companies with long time intervals between the commitment of funds to an investment and the recovery of these funds. For example, the longer an item remains in inventory, the greater is its real cost to the company, because of the cost of the funds that are tied up in it. The movement to recognize this cost has already started, as illustrated in Statement No. 34.

Some people advocate the recognition of "holding gains." For reasons given in the appendix to Chapter 3, I do not believe that such recognition is feasible for nonmonetary assets. By capitalizing interest costs, this proposal recognizes "holding costs." Holding costs can be reliably measured and their recognition is consistent with the idea that accounting measures costs incurred.[27]

Realistic income

The proposal leads to a more meaningful net income number for companies that own timberland and nurseries; reserves of oil, gas and other minerals; and real estate held for sale. Under present practice, when revenue from the sale of these assets is recognized, net income is overstated because no recognition is given to the cost that was incurred by tying up funds in these assets in prior periods. Failure to recognize this cost is one of the reasons why the profits of some of these companies are regarded as obscenely high.[28]

Under current concepts, there is no way of recognizing accretion of such assets as timber and nursery stock. Unless interest is recognized as a cost, the only way to recognize accretion would be to credit income, but accretion does not generate income per se, any more than the production process does. The proposal does not recognize accretion as such, but it does lead to a similar result by recognizing a cost.

The proposal leads to better public understanding of the nature of corporate profits for companies generally. The general public does not understand that a large portion of reported profits is a return for the use of shareholder equity funds. Many people believe that a municipal power plant can provide electricity at lower rates than an investor-owned utility, because the municipal plant does not have to earn a profit. This is of course fallacious; both the muncipal and the investor-owned plant must earn a satisfactory return on whatever funds are committed to it. With explicit recognition of equity interest, these misconconceptions will be reduced.[29]

Studies of differential impact

In current practice, the amount of equity interest cost is an unidentified part of net income. If equity interest is included as an element of cost, income obviously will be lower than currently reported. However, one cannot generalize either as to how much lower it will be or as to the effect on asset amounts. Income will be affected by (1) the amount of interest cost that is capitalized in newly constructed assets, (2) inventory size and turnover, (3) the entity's capital intensity (that is, plant in relation to sales volume), (4) the cost of debt, and (5) the debt/equity ratio.

Several studies have investigated the impact of these influences, and they demonstrate that the effect on income is substantial. They also show that there is no way of tracing the approximate impact in a given entity without taking into account the joint effect of the above factors in that entity. Here are three examples:

1. David W. Young adjusted the published data for three timber companies over a long period of time (at least 17 years) so as to allow for the full impact of the interest cost that would be added annually to the book value of the timberland asset.[30] A summary of the results is given in Exhibit 4–2. It shows that although the effects on both the timerland asset and on income were substantial, the effects differed significantly among the three companies, even though they were in the same industry.

Exhibit 4–2

Summary comparison of three timber companies ($ millions)

Item	Weyerhaeuser 1951–1974	Georgia Pacific 1955–1974	Boise Cascade 1958–1974
Timberland:			
Timberland as a percentage of total assets (prior to revisions), 1974	16%	15%	8%
Reported ending value of timberland	$ 453	$ 337	$ 121
Revised ending value of timberland	$ 831	$ 493	$ 182
Percentage increase	83%	46%	50%
Net income:			
Reported total income for period	$2,128	$1,101	$ 262
Revised total income for period	$ 862	$ 541	$(199)
Percentage reduction	60%	51%	176%

---

2. J. A. Hayes studied the impact on the financial statements of 22 integrated oil companies for 1970, 1971, and 1972.[31] Results for 1970 are summarized in Exhibit 4–3. Although the effect was to decrease reported net income in all cases, the relative amount of decrease varied greatly among companies.

3. Cornelius J. Casey simulated the impact on the financial statements of 189 companies in 16 industries over the period 1974 to 1976.[32] As in the other studies, significant and unsystematic differences resulted both for firms within an industry and across industries. (He assumed that equity interest was credited to retained earnings.) Results for 1974 are summarized in Exhibit 4–4.

Difficulty of approximating these results. An analyst could adjust financial statements for the recognition of equity interest only by making a study

Exhibit 4–3

Net income of integrated oil companies, 1970 ($ millions)

	Net income as reported	Net income as proposed	Percent change
Amerada Hess Corp.	$114.0	$127.1*	+ 11
APCO Oil Corp.	9.6	5.8	− 40
Ashland Oil Co.	51.1	24.7	− 52
ARCO	205.6	32.0	− 52
Belco Petroleum Corp.	13.0	7.2	− 45
Cities Service Co.	118.6	18.4	− 84
Continental Oil Co.	160.5	51.5	− 68
Crown Central Petroleum Corp.	3.6	1.3	− 64
Crystal Oil Co.	−0.2	− 0.7	−292
Getty Oil Co.	101.9	2.0	− 98
Kerr-McGee Corp.	35.9	10.7	− 70
Marathon Oil Co.	84.6	29.0	− 66
Murphy Oil Co.	9.3	− 0.3	−103
Phillips Petroleum Co.	117.1	− 16.2	−114
Quaker State Oil Refining	10.8	6.8	− 7
Reserve Oil and Gas	3.6	− 0.7	−119
Shell Oil Co.	237.2	38.5	− 84
Skelly Oil Co.	36.2	− 2.7	−107
Standard Oil Co. (Indiana)	314.0	56.8	− 82
Standard Oil Co. (Ohio)	64.4	− 8.6	−113
Sun Oil Co.	139.1	51.9	− 63
Union Oil Co. of California	114.5	19.5	− 83

Note: For 1970, Amerada Hess Corp. presents an unusual case of negative common equity. The effect of equity capital cost calculations based on negative common equity is to increase net income over what it would otherwise be, when the interest cost of negative common equity is greater than the sum of preferred dividends and one half of the fixed charges. Consequently adjustments to the income statement deflate costs rather than increase them, leading to an increase in net income.

Exhibit 4–4

**Percentage change in retained earnings resulting from
use of proposed method (1974)**

Industry	Number of firms	−10% to 0	0 to 5%	5% to 10%	10% to 15%	15% to 20%	20% to 25%	Over 25%
Motor vehicles	6	—	1	—	1	—	1	3
Aircraft parts	4	1	1	—	2	—	—	—
Aircraft	3	—	2	1	—	—	—	—
Aircraft equipment	10	2	1	3	1	1	1	1
Flat glass	4	—	1	—	1	—	1	1
Glass containers	14	—	—	3	8	—	1	2
Blast furnace and steel	35	3	21	7	1	1	—	2
Paper and allied products	18	—	7	5	3	—	—	3
Petroleum refining	35	—	5	18	7	1	2	2
Cigars	3	—	2	—	—	1	—	—
Lead and zinc ores	4	1	2	1	—	—	—	—
Construction	5	—	3	1	—	—	—	1
Cigarettes	7	—	2	1	2	1	—	1
Gas transmission	12	—	—	2	5	1	1	3
Meat products	17	1	6	7	—	—	—	3
Nonbuilding construction	12	—	—	3	5	—	2	2
Totals	189	8	54	52	36	6	9	24

such as those described above. Few analysts have the time to do this. More-over, if it is recognized that equity interest is a cost, analysts expect ac-countants to account for this cost; they do not want to be required to make the adjustment outside of the accounts.

Correspondence with investment decisions

A concept that is consistent with the premises should be preferred over one that is not. I have demonstrated that the separation of shareholder eq-uity from entity equity is consistent with Premises 1 and 2, regarding the nature of an entity and its sources of funds, and that equity interest, which is needed to implement this idea, can be reliably measured (Premise 17). I have also shown that current practice is inconsistent with these premises. These facts should be sufficient reason for adopting the proposal.

The case would be even stronger if I could refer to statistically significant research that showed that financial statements prepared in accordance with this concept are more useful than those currently prepared—useful in the sense that they incorporate information that investors use in making in-vestment decisions. Unfortunately, there are few studies that demonstrate that any accounting practice is superior to an alternative. Indeed, G. J. Ben-ston went so far as to try to show statistically that even the publication of sales revenue is not more useful than omission of this item, a conclusion that few users are likely to accept.[33] The problem is that our research tools are not sensitive enough to identify the results of an accounting alternative separately from the other influences on stock market prices.

Despite the difficulties, two recent studies do indicate that the proposed approach provides useful information:[34]

1. J. W. Bartley compared the conventional and the adusted income numbers of 200 companies on the basis of their ability to produce accounting risk measures closely associated with measures of market risk.[35] The results of this study suggest that recognition of equity interest as a cost may reveal information about market risk that is not revealed by conventional measures of income.

2. J. W. Bartley and L. F. Davidson examined the absolute and distributional impacts of alternative methods of accounting for interest on net income, income per share and the rate of return on sales.[36] Calculations were made for 210 companies for 1963, 1973, and 1963 through 1976. The results of this study suggest that the recognition of equity interest as a cost provides useful information. The elimination of the effect of variations in capital structure reduces the misleading messages given by the conventional ratios of income to sales and of income to net assets that do not allow for these variations.

In this study, several interest rates were used. The comparisons were relatively unaffected by varying assumptions about the equity interest rate. This is a further indication that the approximation inherent in the equity interest rate does not negate the usefulness of the approach. It therefore tends to rebut the argument that the proposal is not workable because the exact interest rate cannot be calculated.

These two studies indicate that the recognition of equity interest does provide better information. It is better since the results reflect the market's perception of the actual risk characteristics of the companies more closely than income as measured conventionally.

OTHER ADVANTAGES

The concepts given here have other advantages. Although strictly speaking, these are outside the boundaries of this analysis, I shall mention them briefly.

Harmonizing economics and accounting

Accounting is supposed to measure, as closely as feasible, the economic status and performance of an entity. It cannot do this perfectly, principally because measurement of the true economic status and performance requires highly subjective estimates of the present value of future earnings, and accounting must be reasonably objective.[37] Nevertheless, accounting should not depart from economic reality unless there is a good reason for doing so. Recognition of equity interest in accounting brings accounting closer to economics. In economics, interest is the cost of using funds, regardless of whether these funds came from bondholders or from shareholders.[38] At present, the cost of using equity funds does not enter into accounting calculations.

Harmonizing management accounting and financial accounting

In measuring the profitability of profit centers, well-managed companies include a capital charge that is related to the total amount of assets employed, not merely to the fraction of those assets that were financed with debt.[39] The recognition of equity interest in financial accounting would remove this inconsistency between internal and external accounting.

The recognition of this capital charge in the income statement, together with the use of annuity depreciation, would remove a serious dysfunctional aspect of current financial accounting. Under current practice, a company that makes a large capital investment may report a decrease in net income in the first year, even though the investment is profitable. This possibility is sometimes a deterrent to making economically sound investments. The proposal cures this problem. (This point will be explained and illustrated in Chapter 5.)

Harmonizing American and other accounting systems

The emphasis on shareholder equity is not consistent with the way many other countries, capitalist as well as socialist, view a business entity. Most European Economic Community countries and Japan do not view the corporation as being operated primarily by or for equity investors; they regard employees, government, and society generally as important parties at interest.[40] Moreover, in socialist countries, the government rather than private investors provides funds for many enterprises; some of these funds are supplied on terms that resemble debt, and others resemble equity.

The focus suggested here is consistent with that of most industrial countries. Funds supplied by investors or the government would be reported as such. Funds generated by the entity's own efforts would be shown separately. This concept is already incorporated in the accounting system used in the Soviet Union and in other Soviet bloc countries and in accounting in government-financed entities in other countries.

Equity interest as a tax deduction

In calculating taxable income, a corporation can deduct interest on debt, but it cannot deduct the cost of using equity funds. The aftertax cost of debt funds is therefore about half their pretax cost, whereas the aftertax cost of shareholder equity funds is the same as their pretax cost. This makes the cost of new equity financing about double the cost of debt financing.

One consequence of this situation has already been mentioned. Corporations devise financing devices that qualify as debt but that have many characteristics of equity, and the Internal Revenue Service has been unsuccessful in its attempt to draw a practical line between instruments whose interest is tax deductible and equity instruments. If both debt and equity financing were treated in the same way, there would be no need to worry about the distinction between them.

A much more important consequence is the effect of the current income tax regulations on the formation of equity capital. Because equity funds cost twice as much as debt funds, corporations rarely seek equity funds from external sources.[41] Most additions to equity come from the entity's profitable operations, and the excess over dividend payments is currently reflected in retained earnings.

Since corporations want to maintain a prudent debt/equity ratio, their total funds for expansion are ordinarily limited by the amount of their retained earnings. Because replacing plant and maintaining working capital require considerable funds in an inflationary economy, relatively little is available for true corporate expansion. Thus, the tax structure inhibits raising the huge amount of new funds needed to keep the economy vigorous.

Moreover, only profitable, established companies have significant amounts of retained earnings. New companies need equity funds badly, but they have the most difficulty obtaining them. Established companies tend to invest the available amount of new funds in less risky ventures. Both of these tendencies handicap the flow of new products and processes that is vital to progress in the economy.

A tax-deductible allowance for equity interest would lessen the discrepancy between the cost of debt funds and equity funds and thus mitigate this problem. Those who are pushing for this change have not made much progress, however.

One reason for their lack of success is that members of the relevant congressional committees, their staffs, and their advisors are committed to one of two other ways of solving this problem, both of which have been around for a long time: the dividend exemption approach or the constructive partnership approach. Neither of these is as good a solution as a deduction for equity interest.[42]

Dividend exemption. If dividends were exempted from the recipients' taxable income, shareholders would exert pressure for high payouts, thus reducing a company's retained earnings, by far the largest source of new equity funds. New, growing companies, which need equity funds the most, are not in a position to pay sizable dividends. Furthermore, according to this approach, dividends would be treated the opposite of debt interest: not deducted in the corporate tax calculation but not income to the recipient. This lack of symmetry opens tax loopholes.

Constructive partnership. In the constructive partnership approach, the corporation itself would not pay an income tax. Instead, its income would be attributed to its shareholders, and they would pay the tax as individuals. Although advocated by some theoretical economists, the practical problems of implementing such a scheme are stupendous. The corporation's taxable income must be calculated in the usual way. Then, each owner of stock for all or some part of the year must be informed of the amount of taxable income for which he or she is responsible. This Herculean task must be done in time to include the amount on the individual's return due April 15. It boggles the mind!

Deduction for equity interest. A deduction for equity interest does not have the weaknesses of either of these alternatives. It would be a straightforward calculation at the corporate level, it would be symmetrical with the treatment of debt interest, and it would not result in pressure for unwise dividend payouts. Why hasn't it attracted more supporters?

By far the most important reason, I believe, is that equity interest is not recognized as a cost in financial accounting. The tax people say: "How can you expect us to take this proposal seriously when the FASB does not recognize equity interest in financial reporting?" They have a point.[43]

Moreover, the change would result in a substantial decrease in receipts from the corporate income tax, and alternative revenue sources would have to be considered. In order to lessen the shock, the equity interest deduction should be phased in gradually, starting at a rate of perhaps 2 percent of shareholder equity.

I cannot report any substantial acceptance of the idea of a corporate tax deduction for equity interest, and I do not expect progress until the FASB recognizes the concept of equity interest more broadly than it now does.

ARGUMENTS AGAINST THE CONCEPTS

The inexact interest rate

The difficulty of deciding on the rate to be used in calculating equity interest is an argument some use against the proposal. I have discussed this criticism above. Some purists are reluctant to accept any proposal that does not report a firm's actual cost of using equity funds. Because no one knows how to calculate such a cost accurately (except possibly in rate-regulated companies), these people reject the proposal. Although logically one would expect them to reject other approximations, such as those made for warranties and pensions, they do not. As the two studies reported above show, an exact interest rate is unnecessary; a reasonable approximation will suffice.[44]

Misleading or missing information

Some people assert that the proposal may hide debt interest cost, which is important information in judging an entity's liquidity and solvency. This argument is not valid; the total amount of debt interest cost should be disclosed, as is done currently.

Others assert that the proposal blurs the distinction between return *on* capital and return *of* capital. Although the basis for this assertion is not clear, the fact is that this distinction is unimportant in financial accounting in any event. For income tax purposes, distributions that are income must be distinguished from those that are a return on capital, but this distinction is governed by income tax regulations, not by generally accepted accounting principles. For other purposes, the relevant amount of capital is the amount the particular investor paid for the stock, but unless he or she was an original investor, this amount does not appear on the corporation's records.

Some people believe that the capitalization of equity interest "would be tantamount to an enterprise recording a profit on dealings with itself."[45] Those who make this argument view the organization and its shareholders as a single entity; they do not recognize that the entity is separate from its shareholders. The practice of recording equity interest as a component of revenue, which is followed by some regulated companies, does result in a profit on dealings with itself, but this practice is incorrect. Equity interest is not *revenue* to the entity; on the contrary, it is a *cost* to the entity.

A related argument is that the capitalization of interest inflates inventory and plant amounts. Behind this argument is the lingering idea that equity interest is a component of profit, rather than an element of cost. Furthermore, the lower-of-cost-or-market rule establishes a ceiling on inventory amounts that prohibits inventory from being carried at more than its realizable value.

A more subtle argument is that the amount of net income reported under the proposed approach may be regarded by the public as excess profits, by labor unions as an amount to which they are entitled, and by the Congress as a basis for an excess profits tax since provision of the amount due equity investors has been included in the calculation of net income. Such misconceptions may indeed exist. They require educational efforts to counter them, just as education is currently required to explain that there is no necessary connection between reported profits and dividend policy. It is inconceivable to me that Congress would pass an excess profits tax; such a tax has been tried before and found to be counterproductive.

Interest a special type of cost

Some people argue that interest is inherently different from labor, material, and overhead costs; it is a financing cost rather than a product cost. The origin and present status of this notion is discussed under two headings, business accounting and Federal statutes.

Business accounting.   As noted in Chapter 3, one early version of the entity concept was that income should be measured as an amount before interest, dividends, and income taxes, on the grounds that these items represented distributions of income rather than costs. This idea never did influence the format of the operating statement or the definition of net income; interest and income taxes were, and are, reported as expenses and deducted from revenue in arriving at net income. Nevertheless, the idea that there is something special about interest persists in some people's thinking.[46]

To me, a cost is a cost. Cost represents the use of resources. If a resource, such as interest, is used for a cost object, such as the construction of a plant, the resource is part of the cost of that cost object. This point is developed in depth in Chapter 5.

Furthermore, interest is imbedded in the cost of many resources, such as leased assets of all types, and winds up as a part of the cost of the cost objects for which these resources are used. The lease charge includes a financing component. I see no reason for including interest as a component of the cost of leased assets but not of purchased assets.

Federal statutes and regulations.   Until a decade or so ago, the Federal government maintained that interest was not a cost, except in setting public utility rates. Consequently, government contractors could not recover interest costs, as such, in cost-reimbursement contracts. This motivated contractors to acquire production assets by lease rather than purchase because the lease charge, which included interest, was an allowable contract cost. It also motivated contractors against investing in labor-saving equipment because labor was an allowable cost, but interest on the new investment was not.

This attitude is changing. Cost Accounting Standard 414 specifically allows interest on plant used in government contracts. Recent regulations of the Office of Management and Budget and of the Department of Health and Human Services allow interest, under certain circumstances, in contracts with educational institutions, state and local governments, and providers of health care. One reason for advocating the recognition of interest as a cost in financial accounting is that this would give further impetus to this desirable movement.[47]

Imputed costs

There is also the argument that equity interest is an imputed cost and that accounting does not recognize imputed costs. This criticism is not valid. Accounting does record imputed costs in transactions involving capitalized leases, notes payable with unrealistic interest rates, donated assets, future pension benefits, warranties, write-down of inventories to market, and many other items in which documented evidence of an exchange price does not exist.

Resistance to change

The proposal is rejected by many people simply because it involves a major change in accounting, the most significant change since the acceptance of depreciation. The evidence that supports Premise 22 shows that managements will resist a change unless they perceive it to be in their self interest. The basic argument for the change proposed here is that it provides a more realistic portrayal of the economic performance and status of an entity. The proposal's merits should be judged on those grounds. Proponents of any change have an obligation to demonstrate that the change is sufficiently beneficial to warrant the trauma involved in adjusting to the new financial statements; I think I have done this. The change should not be rejected just because of a reverence for the status quo.

TRANSITION STEPS

The magnitude of the change proposed here is so great that an expectation that it will be adopted all at once is unrealistic. Therefore the goal, which is the full recognition of equity interest as a cost, should be attained by a series of steps.

The first of these steps has already been taken; Statement No. 34 requires that interest cost be capitalized as an element of the cost of new plant and of major projects, such as film productions and real estate developments. The interest that is capitalized includes a mix of both debt interest and equity interest. The interest rate is the pretax rate of debt.

The next logical step is to recognize the interest cost of holding assets in inventory for a long time. Indeed, such recognition was proposed in the Exposure Draft that preceded Statement No. 34, but this idea was eliminated from the final draft. As used here, "inventory" includes all assets that are held for eventual sale; not only tobacco, wine, and liquor, which are usually given as examples of long-lived inventory, but also petroleum and other mineral reserves, growing timber, and nursery stocks.

Recognition of the interest cost of holding these assets not only is consistent with economic reality, but, as mentioned above, has the additional advantage of reducing a distortion of income that currently exists and that leads to public criticism of obscene profits reported by, for example, petroleum companies. The reported profits of these companies are vastly overstated because the amounts do not allow for the real cost the company incurs in holding reserves, in many cases for decades.

Offset to capitalized interest

Recognition of additional interest cost will require the solution of an accounting problem that already causes some difficulty in the implementation of Statement No. 34; namely, where to record the credit that offsets the interest costs debited to asset accounts. Statement No. 34 requires that this credit be made to debt interest cost. Even though the interest is a mix of debt and equity, treating the interest as if it were all debt makes no difference in the measurement of net income, provided that the amount of debt interest is large enough to absorb the credit. The problem arises when the amount of interest that should be capitalized exceeds the amount of debt interest cost.

This problem arises occasionally in the implementation of Statement No. 34, and the solution in that Statement is to prohibit the capitalization of interest in excess of the amount of debt interest. This solution is not logically consistent with the rationale for capitalizing interest, but it is preferable to the alternative of crediting a cost account with an amount in excess of its debit balance. Although this practice has been followed by certain public utilities (its continuance has been blessed by FASB Statement No. 71), its effect is to record capitalized interest as income, which clearly is not the case. An entity cannot earn income by dealing with itself.

There is another alternative that avoids this illogical result. It is to credit the equity interest portion of the capitalized cost directly to retained earnings. There will then be no illogical credit to income, and the practice will be a step toward the ultimate goal of full recognition of equity interest as a cost.

In the final step, the retained earnings account as such disappears, and the amount of equity interest becomes a component of the funds supplied by shareholders. This amount is recognized by a credit to shareholder equity.

Appendix

ACCOUNTING PROCEDURES

This appendix describes the mechanics of accounting for the cost of interest, and contrasts financial statements prepared on the basis of this accounting with those prepared in accordance with current practice. It is based on Chapter 7 of my book, *Accounting for the Cost of Interest* (1975), modified to incorporate improvements that have been suggested since the publication of that book.

Interest pool account

The mechanics can be visualized by thinking of an interest pool account that is similar to the conventional overhead pool. Elements of interest cost are debited to the interest pool account, and the total amount accumulated in it during an accounting period is allocated to various asset and expense accounts. Assume that entries to the interest pool account for 19x1 are as follows (omitting $000 or $000,000 as you prefer):

Interest Pool

Debits		Credits	
Debt interest	25	To cost of sales	32
Equity interest	35	To inventory	8
Total	60	To plant	4
		To general expense	16
		Total	60

Debits to the interest pool

Debt interest ($25). This is the actual amount of debt interest cost incurred during the year. In some versions of the proposal, this amount is calculated at its aftertax cost. Although a good conceptual argument can be made for this alternative, it is more complicated, and the tendency, as indicated in Statement No. 34 and elsewhere, is to use the pretax cost. In the example, $25 is the pretax cost.

Equity interest ($35). This is the cost of using shareholder equity funds. The amount is calculated by applying a rate to the amount of shareholder equity. The credit of $35 is to shareholder equity.

The rate is here assumed to be 10 percent, the same as the rate for long-term debt. Alternatively, as explained in the text, this rate might be designated by the FASB.

The amount is here taken as the amount of shareholder equity at the beginning of the year. It would be increased if new shareholder equity funds were obtained during the year. Conceivably, it could be adjusted by the difference between additions (equity interest) and subtractions (dividends) during the year; however, this refinement is in the nature of compound interest and is probably not warranted.

It could be argued that this rate should be applied to entity equity funds as well as to shareholder equity funds. Discussion of this debatable point is deferred to Chapter 5.

Interest allocation rate

Interest is charged to cost objects at a rate similar to an overhead rate. The rate is established at the beginning of the year, by dividing the estimated interest cost ($60) by the estimated average amount of capital employed during the year. The assumed average capital employed during 19x1 is as follows:

Inventory	$105
Other current assets	168
Plant under construction	44
Other assets (at book value)	350
Total capital employed	$667

These amounts are averages for the year. They are estimated in a manner that is similar to that used in estimating the basis of overhead allocations.

The allocation rate is therefore:

$$\frac{\text{Annual interest cost}}{\text{Capital employed}} = \frac{\$\ 60}{\$667} = 9 \text{ percent}$$

This 9 percent rate is less than the assumed debt and equity interest rate because some funds (such as those from vendors, that is, accounts payable) are obtained at zero explicit interest cost.

Because noncurrent assets have a lower turnover and hence a higher risk exposure than current assets, a good conceptual case can be made for establishing two allocation rates, one for current assets and a higher rate for noncurrent assets. This possible refinement is omitted here.

Charges to cost objects

The principal items to which an interest cost is charged are (a) inventory, (b) plant under construction, and (c) expense.

Inventory ($40). Interest is a component of production cost. It becomes a part of the cost of products in the same way that depreciation is charged. As I will explain in Chapter 5, the best mechanism in many circumstances is to apply a rate to depreciable assets that is the sum of the depreciation and interest components. An interest charge is also added to the cost of products that remain in inventory for a relatively long time. (For items that turn over rapidly, the charge is not necessary because the amount is immaterial) Inventory is used here in a broad sense and includes mineral reserves, growing timber and nursery stock, and projects in process, such as motion picture films and real estate developments.

Plant under construction ($4). Interest is a component of the cost of constructing plant. It is charged to construction in progress in the manner described in Statement No. 34. No interest is added to plant account after the plant goes on stream. The cost of using the funds committed to the plant is an element of the plant cost and eventually of the products produced in the plant as is the case with other items of construction cost.

Expense ($16). After the above charges have been made, the balance in the interest pool account is an expense of the period. The amount of interest associated with the capital used in marketing, administrative, and other nonmanufacturing activities could be charged as a cost of these activities, but the effect on net income is the same whether the charge is made directly to these items or whether the amount is shown separately as interest expense.

Financial statements

Exhibit 4–5 shows financial statements as prepared according to current practice, and as they will look when interest is recognized as a cost. The

Exhibit 4–5

Current and proposed financial statements

	As now reported		As proposed	
Operating Statement, 19x1				
Sales revenue		$1,000		$1,000
Cost of sales	$700		$732	
Selling, general, administrative	220		211	
Income tax expense	40	960	40	983
Net income		$ 40		$ 17
Balance Sheet, December 31, 19x1				
		Assets		Assets
Inventory		$135		$143
Plant and equipment (net)		300		304
Other assets		300		300
Total assets		$735		$747
		Equities		Sources of funds
Current liabilities		$115		$115
Long-term debt		250		250
Shareholder equity....................................		370		365
Entity equity		0 *		17
Total		$735		$747

* Incorporated in shareholder equity as now reported.

adjustment assumes that this is the first year under the new system. The effect on future years and on differences between the two sets of statements are explained below.

Operating statement

Cost of sales.   On the operating statement, cost of sales increases by the amount of the interest component in cost of the goods sold. The total interest cost charged to production was $40, of which $8 remains in inventory, so the additional cost of sales is $32. In future years, the cost of sales will be higher than under current practice, by the amount of the interest component.

Selling, general and administrative expense.   This decreases by $9. It is the net of two items: (1) The amount decreases by $25 because debt interest, as such, is no longer charged, and (2) it increases by $16, representing the interest cost not charged to asset accounts.

Income tax expense.   This is unchanged. It is assumed that, at least initially, equity interest will not be allowed as a tax deductible item. (In order to emphasize this point, no adjustment for deferred taxes has been made.)

Net income.   This decreases by $23, primarily because equity interest is now recognized as a cost. The decrease does not correspond to the amount of equity interest because some equity interest ends up in asset accounts. In future years, net income will be lower than under current practice.

Balance sheet

Total assets.   On the balance sheet this increases by $12, the amount of interest included in asset costs.

Inventory.   This increases by $8, the amount of interest cost charged to products that remain in inventory. In future balance sheets, inventory amounts will be higher than under current practice because of the inclusion of this item.

Plant.   This increases by $4, the amount of interest capitalized in plant under construction.

Shareholder Equity.   On the present balance sheet, shareholder equity is not separated from entity equity. In the proposed balance sheet, it is assumed for simplicity, that entity equity at the beginning of the first year was zero; therefore, shareholder equity was $350. Changes in shareholder equity during the year are as follows:

	Present	Proposed	Difference
Beginning balance	$350	$350	$ 0
Net income	+40	*	−40
Equity interest	*	+35	+35
Dividends	−20	−20	0
Ending balance	$370	$365	$− 5

* Not included in shareholder equity.

Since it is assumed that entity equity starts at zero, the balance at the end of the year is equal to the net income, $17. The balance in entity equity will increase in each year in which there is a positive amount of net income.

5

Cost and cost assignment

This chapter describes concepts for measuring the amount of cost at the time an asset is acquired and concepts governing the subsequent assignment of this cost to accounting periods and to cost objects within an accounting period. Some implications of these concepts are given in the appendix.

DEFINITIONS

Cost

Although *cost* is one of the most slippery terms used in accounting, attempts to define it carefully are rarely found in the authoritative literature.[1] The following concept defines *cost* and *cost object* as the terms are used in practice:

> **Concept 5.01.** *Cost is a monetary measure of the amount of resources used for a cost object. A cost object is an object whose cost is measured.*

Three important ideas are included in these definitions. First, and most basic, is the notion that cost measures the use of resources. The resources used in producing tangible goods or intangible services are physical quantities of material, hours of labor service, and quantities of other services. Cost measures how many of these resources were used for the cost object.

The second idea is that cost measurements are expressed in monetary terms. Money provides a common denominator that permits the amounts of individual resources, each measured according to its own scale (pounds of material, hours of labor, kilowatt hours of electricity) to be aggregated so that the total amount of resources used can be determined. Of course, many resources are acquired in exchange for money or promises to pay money, and for these the money amount is the cost.

The third idea is that cost measurement is always related to a purpose, that is, to a cost object. A cost is always the cost *of* something. An amount labeled "cost," without an indication of what the cost object is, conveys no information. A cost object can be a thing, such as a product or an asset; it can be the provision of a service; it can be a segment, such as a profit center, a department, or other organizational unit; it can be the conduct of a program or it can be the operation of an entire entity. The terms *cost objective* and *cost unit* have the same meaning as *cost object*.

Cost objects in financial accounting.   The same cost element may simultaneously be part of the cost of several cost objects: a final product, an intermediate product, a department, or an activity performed within a department. In financial accounting, three types of cost objects are relevant: (1) those for products, (2) those for productive assets, and (3) expenses, which are cost objects for an accounting period.

Sacrifice.   Unlike some definitions, the one given here makes no mention of "sacrifice," or "effort." *Acquisition cost,* the cost of acquiring an asset, involves a sacrifice, but other types of cost may or may not involve a sacrifice. For example, depreciation is an element of cost for some cost objects, but depreciation may not involve a sacrifice with respect to these objects. When a machine is purchased, the entity made a sacrifice, but when the machine is used subsequently to manufacture a product or for some other cost object, depreciation on the machine does not necessarily involve an additional sacrifice at that time or for that cost object. Although this distinction may appear to be a small point, cost definitions containing the word *sacrifice* have been used to argue that depreciation is not an element of cost. Similarly, depreciation does not measure *effort* in the usual meaning of this term.

Expenditure and expense

When a cost is incurred, there is a related expenditure. When a cost expires, the cost becomes an expense. The terms *expenditure* and *expense* are sometimes, but erroneously, viewed as meaning the same thing, and so are the terms *cost* and *expense*. They are distinguished in the following concepts:

> **Concept 5.02.** *An expenditure is the increase in a liability or shareholder equity or the decrease in an asset that results when the entity acquires goods or services.*

When an entity acquires a resource from another entity, it makes an expenditure (unless the resource was a gift); thus, acquisition cost and expenditure are two aspects of the same event. At the moment of acquisition, the resource for which an expenditure is made is an asset. It may remain an asset for many years, or, as in the case of a service, its life may be very short.

If the expenditure creates a liability, the discharge of that liability is usually by means of a disbursement (or outlay) of cash. Thus, "disbursement" is not synonymous with "expenditure." If a resource is acquired for cash, disbursement and expenditure occur at the same time. If not acquired for cash, the disbursement occurs either subsequent to the expenditure (as in the payment to a vendor) or prior to the expenditure (as in a travel advance).[2]

> **Concept 5.03.** *Expenses are costs that are applicable to the current accounting period.*

This concept could be stated equally well as: Expenses are costs that do not benefit future periods. Since resources that benefit future periods are assets, and since costs cannot benefit periods that have already passed, this statement says that costs incurred in a period are either expenses of the period or they are assets as of the end of the period. Thus, all expenses are costs, but not all costs are expenses.[3]

An expenditure results in an asset if it benefits a future accounting period and in an expense if it does not. The acquisition of material for inventory is an expenditure in the period of acquisition. There is an expense in the period in which the material is used. If the material is used to produce goods, its use for this cost object transforms the asset to another form, but it remains part of the cost of the goods until they are sold. Until the period in which the goods are sold, the material is part of the cost of the asset; in the period of sale it becomes an expense.

Further discussion of the circumstances in which costs are applicable to the current period is deferred to Chapter 6.

ACQUISITION COST CONCEPTS

There are two sets of cost concepts: (1) those relating to the measurement of cost at the time a resource is acquired, which is its acquisition cost, and (2) those relating to the subsequent assignment of costs to cost objects. This section gives the first set of concepts. Since they are consistent with the premises and other concepts, are accepted in current practice, and are believed to be noncontroversial, little elaboration or justification is given.

> **Concept 5.04.** *The cost of a resource acquired for use by an entity should be the total of the expenditures that make the resource ready for its intended use.*

Although many problems arise in deciding what elements of cost are incurred in making a resource ready for its intended use, these problems are properly dealt with at the level of standards, rather than as concepts. Except for FASB Statement No. 14, which provides clear guidance for measuring the cost of segments of an entity, and Statement No. 34 on the capitalization of interest cost, current standards provide little guidance, a situation that should be corrected.

This is a financial accounting concept. It does not necessarily apply to special-purpose cost measurements. For example, for measuring the cost that is reimbursable under a cost-type contract, the term *reasonable cost* or *necessary cost* is often, and properly, used. In financial accounting, cost is usually measured by the amount expended, and no judgment is made as to whether the amount was reasonable. An exception to this generalization occurs for certain experimental assets. When an entity builds the first unit of a new machine intended for its own use, costs in the nature of research/development costs may be incurred, in addition to the production costs of the machine itself. These costs should be excluded from the amount recorded as an asset.

> **Concept 5.05.** *The amount of an expenditure should be the price in an exchange with an unrelated party. If such a price is not determinable, the amount should be the fair value of the resource acquired. If the fair value of the resource acquired is not determinable, the amount should be the fair value of the resource given up by the entity.*

Concept 5.05 implies a hierarchy of alternatives. This is necessary to guide the measurement of acquisition cost, when there is no arm's-length transaction. It is consistent with present standards.[4]

Note that this concept is not based on *opportunity cost*, which is the sacrifice involved in using a resource for the cost object in question as compared with its next best use. To the extent feasible, financial accounting measures incurred cost, not opportunity cost.

> *Concept 5.06.* *Donated goods or services should be recorded at their fair value.*

Concept 5.06 is an exception to the general rule that assets are recorded at their cost to the entity. Donations of assets are rare in profit-oriented entities but are common in nonbusiness organizations. The question of which donated goods or services should be recognized is complicated and is properly the subject of a standard. For example, services donated by an unpaid board of trustees of a hospital or university should not be recognized in the accounts, but medical or teaching services donated by members of a religious order who have taken vows of poverty should be recognized.

> *Concept 5.07.* *Expenditures that require future outlays should be measured as the present value of the expected value of these outlays.*

Concept 5.07 follows from Premise 6: "The value of monetary amounts due from or owed to other parties is the present value of the payments that are expected to be received or paid."

COST ASSIGNMENT

Terminology

In discussing concepts relating to the assignment of costs to cost objects, I shall use terms with the following meanings:

An item of cost that is specifically traced to a cost object is a *direct cost* of that cost object.

An item of cost that is traced to several cost objects collectively, but not to any one of of them specifically, is an *indirect cost* of those cost objects. *Common cost* and *joint cost* are other terms for indirect cost.

The terms *direct* and *indirect* always relate to a specified cost object; there is no such thing as direct costs or indirect costs in general. The cost incurred in operating the factory superintendent's office is a direct cost of the factory, but it is an indirect cost of products made in the factory. In practice there are many problems in distinguishing between direct and indirect costs, but these are not appropriately discussed at the level of concepts.

Costs are *assigned* to cost objects. Direct costs are *assigned directly;* indirect costs are *allocated.* Thus, *allocated cost* is another term for *indirect cost.*[5]

There are two types of allocation problems, *temporal allocation* and *object allocation.* Temporal allocation is the allocation of an item of cost among time periods. Depreciation is a device for temporal allocation. Object allocation is the allocation of the costs of an accounting period to cost objects. An overhead rate is a device for object allocation.

Product cost concept

The following concept is generally accepted in practice but not in the literature. It therefore will be discussed in some depth.

> **Concept 5.08.**   *The cost of a product produced by an entity should be its full production cost, that is, its direct costs plus a fair share of indirect costs.*

Products include both goods and services, and they include goods and services that the entity produces for its own use, as well as those produced as outputs. Any output of an entity is a product. For example, a product of a college is education.

This concept is consistent with the concept of an organization as set forth in general systems theory.[6] An organization obtains resources and works with these resources to produce outputs. Cost measures the amount of resources used in producing the outputs.

The concept is also consistent with the idea in economics that the production process adds value. It says that as resources are added to a cost object, such as a product, the value of *that product* increases. The concept does *not* suggest that the value of the whole entity increases through the production process. The increase in value of the product cost object is exactly offset by the decreases in other assets or increases in liabilities. This is an accounting way of saying that the production process changes the form of capital, rather than adding to the total stock of capital.[7]

Historical background

For about 100 years prior to the 1940s there was general acceptance, in the literature and in good practice, of the idea of allocating indirect costs to products. Beginning in the 1940s, however, many scholarly articles and some accounting textbooks took the position that allocations were undesirable. Although reasons for any such change are speculative, my guess is that they originated in textbooks in managerial economics, the first of which were published about that time. They certainly did not originate with a change in practice; in practice, organizations did, and do, allocate costs.

The managerial economics (later called microeconomics) textbooks dealt with costs that were relevant for choosing among alternative courses of action; allocations are not relevant for such decisions. Their authors did not describe the use of full costs as a basis for arriving at normal or target selling prices. They either were unaware of the evidence (given in the discussion of Premise 6) that this is the usual pricing practice, or they believed that if a business priced in this way, it acted incorrectly.

Accounting authors admitted that costs were, in fact, allocated, but they ascribed this practice to the requirement of Accounting Research Bulletin No. 43. They did not recognize that if the only reason for allocation was to comply with this requirement, companies surely would use much simpler and less expensive procedures than those actually found in practice.[8]

The "arbitrary" allegation

For whatever reason, much of the academic literature continues to argue against the use of allocated costs in financial accounting. The principal argument is that allocations are arbitrary. The most widely quoted author is Arthur L. Thomas.[9]

The fallacy of this argument can be demonstrated by a simple example. Assume that several families join in buying one bag of potatoes for $20. They divide up the potatoes, and each family agrees to pay its share of the $20 cost. The rules of arithmetic say that each potato cost some portion of the $20 and that the sum of the cost of individual potatoes is $20, neither more nor less. Although there is no exact way of ascertaining the cost of individual potatoes, the families can easily agree on how to allocate the $20. If the bag of potatoes weighed 100 pounds, the potatoes that each received can fairly be said to cost 20 cents a pound, unless some of the potatoes were rotten, in which case the cost per pound would be calculated at $20 divided by the number of pounds of good potatoes. This basis of allocation is fair, and it is fairer than the alternative of calculating the cost at so much per potato, without regard to the weight of individual potatoes. Potatoes, of course, do differ in appearance and in other characteristics, and there are various grades of potatoes reflecting these differences. But reasonable people can agree on the criteria for each grade, and they buy and sell potatoes at prices related to grade.

Meaning of arbitrary.   The word *arbitrary* has two quite different meanings: (1) inexact and (2) capricious (i.e., arrived at by whim). The process of assigning costs to potatoes is arbitrary in the sense that it is inexact, but it is not arbitrary in the sense that it is capricious. There are sound rules for assigning costs to potatoes, and most people will agree that these rules are preferable to having no rules at all.[10] The Heisenberg uncertainty principle in physics states that no measurement is exact. Society nevertheless functions satisfactorily on the basis of approximations; it could not function otherwise.

An allocation that is truly capricious or whimsical cannot be defended, and no reasonable person would try to do so. The problem is to arrive at the most reasonable basis of allocation. Sound concepts for solving this problem do exist.

Notwithstanding the incorrect connotation that Thomas and his colleagues have ascribed to the word *arbitrary*, some economists have accepted the thesis and condemn all cost allocations. Recently, some courts have taken the same attitude.[11] The fact remains that although cost allocations are by one definition arbitrary, this does not imply that they are not useful. Only capricious allocations are useless.

In recent years, sophisticated allocation techniques, some derived from game theory, have been developed to apply the basic idea of fairness in rigorous ways.[12] These techniques are far from being arbitrary in the sense of being capricious.

Variable costing

Another argument against the allocation of indirect costs is made by the proponents of what is called *variable costing*. In a variable cost system, goods in inventory are assigned only the variable cost of producing them; fixed production costs are called period costs and are assigned as expenses in the period in which they are incurred.[13] Variable costing questions both object allocation and temporal allocation—object allocation because of the division of a period's cost between the inventory cost object and the period cost object, and temporal allocation because the more costs that are held in inventory, the larger will be the reported income of the current period.

Arguments for variable costing. The basic argument for counting fixed production costs as period costs is that these costs represent the cost of "being in business" during the period and are therefore not related to the specific goods produced during that period.[14] The fallacy of this argument is that being in business is not a relevant cost object for production costs. An entity does not incur these costs for the purpose of being in business; it incurs them for the purpose of producing goods. Except in unusual circumstances, such as when an entity maintains an idle plant, the goods produced in the period did use the resources represented by the fixed production costs: the production supervision, the depreciation and maintenance of plant, the insurance, and so on. Since cost is defined as the monetary amount of resources used for a cost object, and since the cost object is the production of goods, these resources are part of the cost of the goods produced.

The rationale is similar to that in the potato example, given above. If all the products collectively caused the total of these fixed costs, then it follows that each product caused some fraction of this total. Although there can be differences of opinion about how the amount allocated to each product should be measured, there can be little room for disagreement on the broad concept that the cost of producing the goods included not only the variable costs but also a share of the other production costs. To argue otherwise is to assert that these costs were unnecessary. (The issue of idle plant *is* a controversial point, but it is best addressed at the level of standards rather than of concepts.)

A second argument for variable costing is the benefit/cost argument. In calculating the total cost of a cost objective, measuring the direct costs and adding a specified percentage for indirect costs is less expensive than going through the elaborate bookkeeping that is sometimes required for cost allocations. As is the case with any accounting shortcut, this argument is valid only if approximately the same results would be obtained by the less expensive method. Such would be the case in a company that produces a single product or a family of products, each member of which uses the same quantity of similar production facilities, and the company has an insignificant amount of inventory. It is not valid if the amount of indirect costs equitably allocated to products, or other cost objects, varies substantially.

Most of the controversies and litigation surrounding the standards of the Cost Accounting Standards Board related to Standards 403 and 410, the two standards dealing with the allocation of indirect costs. And in the future there will be controversy about Standard 418, the most recent standard on this topic. However, neither the government nor contractors as a class would be willing to do away with these standards and substitute the simple rule that indirect costs should be allocated to contracts as a percentage of direct costs. Such a rule would obviously lead to undercosting contracts that used more than an average amount of indirect resources, and overcosting those that used less than an average amount. The only supporters of such a rule would be those contractors who used less than an average amount of indirect resources on government work as compared with commercial work.

A third argument in favor of variable costing is that a full cost system may permit manipulation of reported income. By "selling overhead to inventory," that is, by building up inventory beyond an optimum amount, management could hold fixed overhead costs in inventory rather than having them flow through to the operating statement.[15] This practice would increase reported income in the current period. In the structure of this framework, this is not an acceptable argument. If management does produce for inventory, accounting should report this fact. If the full costs of goods in inventory exceed their realizable value, the inventory amounts should be reduced to market. As a practical matter, the situations in which management deliberately can manipulate income in this fashion are uncommon. Deliberately producing more than the market requires is a risky proposition; if the goods cannot be sold, the unpleasant consequences will come to light in the very next accounting period.[16]

Arguments against variable costing. A strong argument against variable costing is that it increases the noncomparability of costs. Consider a company that at various times follows different production policies for a given product. It may (a) purchase the completed product from another manufacturer, (b) purchase components and assemble these into the product, or (c) manufacture both the components and the product in-house. Variable costs might be $100 for (a), $60 for (b), and $40 for (c). The cost of the purchased product in (a) includes the fixed costs of the other manufacturer, the cost of the components in (b) includes the fixed cost of the components manufacturer, but the variable cost of the product made in-house includes no fixed costs. It would be unreasonable to report that the "costs" of these products were so dissimilar. Would anyone claim that if three physically identical products were in inventory, one produced under each of these policies, one should be reported at a cost of $100, the second at $60, and the third at $40?

Types of allocation

As noted earlier, there are two allocation problems. First, there is the problem of allocating costs to the proper accounting period; this is the problem of *temporal allocation*. Second, after the costs applicable to a given accounting period have been measured, there is the problem of allocating costs to the cost objects that used resources during that period; this is the problem of *object allocation*. The second problem is the specific province of cost accounting.

Temporal allocation. Temporal allocation is required by the basic concept of entity equity maintenance (Concept 3.03) and the concept that financial statements should articulate (Concept 3.08). This fact can be seen most clearly in the case of long-lived, depreciable assets. If the cost of such an asset were not allocated to the accounting periods involved, the cost either would be written off entirely in the period in which the expenditure was made, or it would be held as an asset until it was disposed of; these are the only alternatives to allocation. If the cost were written off in the period of acquisition, the entity's income in that period would be understated; at the end of that period, the entity still has a valuable resource, and any accounting that did not recognize that fact would be misleading. If held as an asset until disposition, the income of the intervening periods would be overstated because some part of the resource represented by the asset was in fact used up in each of these periods. Thus, the only way in which entity equity maintenance can be measured is to charge some part of the cost to the periods in which the asset was used.

A second reason for temporal allocation is the premise that users need comparable information (Premise 19). If a building is rented during a period, the rent is a direct cost of the period; if a building is owned, its depreciation is an allocated cost. In either case, a resource was used during the period, and this resource had a cost. To record the cost in one case but not the other would lead to noncomparable results.

Object allocation.   Allocating costs to cost objects is similar to the process, already described, of allocating the cost of a bag of potatoes to individuals. By definition, indirect costs apply to more than one cost object. Some fraction of the total of an indirect cost item must apply to each of these cost objects. The cost of heating a factory is an indirect cost of all the products made in the factory, and some fraction of the heating cost is therefore a cost of each of these products.

The premise that users want comparable information is also relevant here. Suppose that in one period a factory produced 100 desks and that the product cost object was this lot of desks. If, in addition to material and labor costs, the factory incurred $5,000 of general operating costs, this $5,000 would be a direct cost of the desks since they were the only product cost object. Now, suppose that in the following period the factory produced 50 desks and 50 file cabinets, each lot of desks and of file cabinets being a cost object, and that the general operating costs continued to be $5,000. In the second period these general operating costs would be indirect costs with respect to the two cost objects. Unless some fraction of the $5,000 is allocated to desks, it would appear that the desks cost less in the second period than in the first, which makes no sense.

ALLOCATION CONCEPTS

Basic criterion

The basic idea governing allocation methods is that of fairness (Premise 18).[17] The objective should be to allocate the costs to accounting periods and to cost objects within accounting periods as fairly as possible.

The criterion of fairness was discussed in the 1960s and early 1970s, notably by Leonard Spacek, managing partner of Arthur Andersen & Co.[18] Spacek's thesis, however, was that the "economic rights" of the various claimants to the assets of an entity should be measured fairly.

The premises on which this framework is built do not permit such an approach. They suggest that accounting cannot measure directly the value of many assets (Premise 8) and that the economic rights of common shareholders, who have the residual claim on these assets, therefore cannot be measured. For this reason, the criterion of fairness cannot be made operational when it is applied to economic rights, that is, to the balance sheet.

For reasons given in the discussion of Concept 3.03, I maintain that financial accounting should focus on the measurement of income; that is, it should focus on the operating statement, rather than on the balance sheet. Given such a focus, the criterion of fairness can be made operational.[19] Although there is no precise way of measuring what is fair, there are satisfactory approximations. Courts of equity and arbitration panels apply the idea of fairness every day and to much more difficult problems than those encountered in accounting.[20]

Concepts

Two concepts for cost allocation follow, one for temporal allocation and the other for object allocation.[21] Both are based on the idea of fairness.

> **Concept 5.09.** *Temporal Fairness: if a resource is used for several accounting periods, the amount of its cost assigned to any one period should be in proportion to the estimated benefits provided in that period.*

> **Concept 5.10.** *Object fairness: indirect costs of an accounting period should be allocated to cost objects in proportion to the amount of these costs that each cost object caused. If a causal relationship cannot be identified, another equitable basis of allocation should be used.*

Many authorities, including the Cost Accounting Standards Board, use the phrase *causal or beneficial* to apply to both types of allocation. The concepts given above use the term *benefit* as the criterion for temporal allocation and *cause* as the preferred criterion for object allocation. Having incurred a cost in one year, it is inappropriate to regard activities of future years as having *caused* the cost; the cost was caused when the resource was acquired. It is appropriate, however, to think of the periods that benefit from this cost.

Conversely, the idea of *benefit* is not an adequate criterion for allocating costs to cost objects within a period. It does provide guidance in many situations, but in some of them it cannot logically be applied. For example, a property tax, although a necessary cost, does not "benefit" the entity as a whole or any cost object within it. Nevertheless, it is a cost to the entity and to cost objects that cause the tax. If a property tax levy is based on the value of a factory building, it is caused by the presence of that building and hence is a cost of products made in that building.[22]

Concept 5.10 suggests that although *cause* is the preferred basis of object allocation, a causal factor cannot be identified in all situations. If several products are made from a single raw material, for example, there may be no way of allocating the joint costs to individual products on the basis of cause. This situation arises frequently in process industries. Similarly, if a tree is cut into several grades of lumber, *cause* does not provide a basis of allocating costs to each grade. In such situations, the basic criterion remains that of fairness, and one of several alternatives is preferable in various circumstances.

In a concepts statement, it is inappropriate to discuss the various bases of allocation in detail. Suffice it to say that satisfactory bases do exist and that rationales for the appropriate basis to use in a given set of circumstances are thoroughly discussed in the literature and even more thoroughly in the many court cases in which the basis of cost allocation is an issue.[23] Devices such as *intermediate cost* objects (or *overhead pools*) to collect costs that eventually are allocated to *final cost objects* are also properly the subject of standards.[24]

By-product costing

Although Concept 5.10 provides general guidance for costing by-products, a more specific statement is desirable. Present practice is that the cost of a by-product should be equal to its net realizable value if the by-product can be sold. This means that no profit is recorded for by-products. Other by-products are costed at their direct (incremental) cost. These are sound practices, and there is no good reason to change them. The following concept states these practices:

> **Concept 5.11.** *A by-product is a secondary product from a process whose primary purpose is to produce one or more main products. If the by-product is intended to be sold, its cost should be set equal to its net realizable value. The cost of other by-products should be the direct costs of producing them.*

APPLICATION OF THE ALLOCATION CONCEPTS

To illustrate the application of the two principal allocation concepts, I shall begin with the measurement of a college's financial performance and its relation to charges made to the students; then I shall extend the analysis to profit-oriented entities. The college provides a good place to begin, because the situation is easy to visualize and is relevant to readers who are either students or parents. Since the college is a nonprofit organization, the complications associated with income taxes, shareholder equity, and equity interest, discussed in Chapter 4, do not arise. Since the college does not produce goods, there are no problems of inventory measurement.

Pullen College

Pullen College is a hypothetical four-year liberal arts college. It has an enrollment of 2,000 full-time students, 1,600 living in college dormitories and 400 living off campus. Pullen has an endowment of $40 million contributed by donors who intend that earnings on the principal of the endowment be used to help finance current operations. Its only other sources of financial support are tuition from the 2,000 students and room rent from the 1,600 dormitory residents. In order to focus the analysis, it is assumed that no operating funds are received from grants or annual alumni drives and that no students receive financial aid from the college. Food service, bookstore, athletics, and other auxiliary activities are assumed to operate on a break-even basis and therefore are disregarded.

The budget committee of the board of trustees is meeting to consider the proposed budget for the year ending August 31, 1984. It must decide on the tuition and the room rent for that year. The committee wants these charges to be fair.

Two meanings of fairness

In this situation, the two types of fairness referred to in concepts 5.09 and 5.10 have clear-cut meanings. Temporal fairness means that the 2,000 students, or their parents, should expect to pay tuition for 1984 that will finance the cost of operating the college in 1984. Requiring current students to pay some of the costs that are incurred for the benefit of future generations of students would not be fair; current students receive no benefits from these future costs. Moreover, current students have no right to expect that past generations of students will have contributed to financing their education.

Object fairness means that of the total costs incurred in 1984, the 2,000 students should pay for education costs, and the 1,600 dormitory residents should pay for the costs of operating the dormitories. It would not be fair to require the 400 off-campus students to pay any part of dormitory costs; they do not cause these costs.

The budget committee has been given a tentative budget for the coming fiscal year ending August 31, 1984, which is summarized in Exhibit 5–1. The question to be decided by the budget committee is whether the estimates used to develop Exhibit 5–1 properly reflect the education and dormitory costs for the year. If they do, the criterion of fairness leads to a

---

Exhibit 5–1

Pullen College—tentative operating statement for 1984

Education:

Tuition revenue—2,000 students @ $6,000	$12,000,000
Endowment earnings	2,000,000
Total revenues	14,000,000
Educational expenses	14,000,000
Net Income	0

Dormitories:

Room rent—1,600 residents @ $1,000	$ 1,600,000
Dormitory expenses	1,600,000
Net Income 0	

---

tuition of $6,000 per student and a room rent of $1,000 per resident. If they do not, these preliminary estimates will be changed, and the tuition and room rent will be changed accordingly. Several issues were raised in the course of discussing this question.

Case A: Additions to inventory

The administration plans to increase the inventory of fuel oil so that by August 31, 1984, the supply will be 50,000 gallons larger than on August 31, 1983. This increase is in anticipation of price increases two years hence. At $1.50 per gallon, this fuel oil will require an expenditure of $75,000. Adequate storage space is available. The $75,000 was excluded from 1984 costs in Exhibit 5–1.

A committee member argues that the $75,000 should be included in 1984 costs, because it is an expenditure in that year. He points out that the AICPA *Audit Guide on Colleges and Universities* requires that expenditures of this type be shown as deductions from revenues.[25] The audit guide is wrong. Students in 1984 receive no benefits from the $75,000 inventory increase. Students in 1985 will benefit when this fuel oil is consumed, and the 1985 students should pay this cost. To increase 1984 tuition by $25 per student for this item would be unfair.

This case illustrates the basic nature of the accrual concept in accounting. The approach used in this simple example underlies most principles relating to temporal fairness.

Case B: Indirect costs

Some of the costs of operating Pullen College are incurred jointly for both education and dormitories. In the tentative budget, some of these costs are allocated to education and the remainder to dormitories, which are the two relevant cost objects. A committee member points out that several authors advocate that these costs should not be allocated because, by definition, there is no exact way of determining how much of the total of these costs should be allocated to each cost object.

This argument is wrong. If part of these costs are not allocated to dormitories, the entire amount will be charged as a general expense of the college, and the 2,000 students will end up paying for all of it as part of tuition. The 1,600 dormitory residents should be expected to pay their fair share of these common costs. The 400 off-campus students should not be required to pay more than their share (400/2,000) of the full costs of education. There can be disagreement with the details of how the costs should be allocated, but the resolution of these disagreements should meet the test of fairness.

Case C: Basis of allocation

Of the $15.6 million of estimated operating costs, $2 million is for the maintenance of buildings and grounds. Some elements of this cost (such as the cost of janitors assigned to specific buildings) are charged directly either to the education or to the dormitory cost object. The remaining costs are allocated on the basis of the number of square feet of space occupied by education and dormitory activities, respectively. On this basis, $1.5 million of the maintenance cost is assigned to education and $0.5 million to dormitories.

A committee member objects to the recordkeeping required in order to obtain this cost allocation and advocates that maintenance costs be allocated in proportion to revenues, as the simplest solution. On this basis, $1.8 million (90 percent) of the total would be assigned to education and $0.2 million to dormitories.

Once again, the committee member is wrong. The result of this simple allocation formula would be to increase tuition and decrease room rent, as compared with the more careful method actually employed. The point is that not all bases of allocation are equally satisfactory. Within limits, there can be debate about the fairest method, such as whether cubic feet or square feet should be the basis of allocation and whether the same rate should apply to daytime educational facilities as is applied to dormitory facilities that have both day and night operation. Outside of these limits, however, there are allocation methods that produce clearly unfair results.

Relevance to financial statements

In order to sharpen the discussion, the preceding description has focused on fairness in arriving at charges for tuition and room rent. Exactly the same reasoning applies to the measurement of expenses on the operating statement. If the budget committee plans zero income for each of the two categories, education and dormitories, and if actual revenues are earned as planned and actual expenses are incurred as planned, then the operating statement should report zero income for each of these items. This will happen if, but only if, the reasoning used in the above analysis is also used in allocating costs first to the proper year and then to the two cost objects, education and dormitories.

Concretely, if accounting reports a material amount of net income when, in fact, there has been no net income, parents who read the operating statement can complain that tuition or room rents were too high, faculty can complain that their salaries should have been higher, and students can complain that they did not get the amount of education that they paid for. If, on the other hand, accounting erroneously reports a material amount of net loss, the governing board will be concerned about management's ability to keep expenses in line with revenues.

Relevance to other entities

The preceding cases demonstrate that for Pullen College there are operational, clear-cut principles for allocating indirect costs to accounting periods and to cost objects within accounting periods. Although there is no way of knowing whether the amounts allocated are exactly accurate, there is ample assurance that they are satisfactory approximations. Most importantly, the cases demonstrate that some approaches are fairer than others, contrary to the assertions of critics who say that there is no way of judging whether one allocation method is better than another.

Entities similar to colleges.   In the case of Pullen College, the criterion of fairness is obviously sensible; valid differences of opinion about its application arise only as to details. This clear-cut conclusion follows from the fact that there is a direct relationship between the costs assigned to cost objects and the prices that are charged for these cost objects.

A similar relationship exists in companies whose rates are regulated, and in companies whose revenues are derived from cost-type contracts (construction companies, professional firms, shipyards, airplane manufacturers, and the like). In these entities, temporal fairness is always an important consideration, and if the entity produces more than one product, object fairness is important also.[26]

Nonbusiness organizations of all types, including governmental units, must, on average, limit the cost of the services they provide in a year to the resources that are available for operations in that year. The cost of services provided is measured according to the concepts of fairness.

Other entities.   Nonbusiness entities and entities whose prices are directly based on costs comprise about half the economic activity in the United

States. There remains the question of whether the idea of fairness applies to profit-oriented entities, that is, to entities in which there is no necessary connection between costs and selling prices.

Part of the answer to this question is clear-cut. As in Case A for Pullen College, if costs are added to inventory in a year, they are not chargeable against revenues for that year. If depreciable assets are not written off in some way over their useful life, they either must be charged against income in the year of acquisition, or they must be held at cost until retired; either of these alternatives distorts income. If one grants that some sort of allocation is appropriate in these circumstances, it would seem that the fairness criterion suggests the most sensible way of making these allocations.

Events occur in business, however, that have no counterpart to those at Pullen College. The fairness concepts are equally applicable to these events. These unique events have nothing to do with the fact that business is profit-oriented and Pullen College is not. The overriding issue is the assignment of costs, and in both types of organizations, the purpose of assigning costs to accounting periods and to cost objects within periods is similar.

Uncertain benefits. A business incurs certain types of cost for the purpose of producing income in *future* periods. Examples are advertising and other promotional efforts,[27] research/development, store openings and similar start-up costs. Conceptually, if expenditures for these purposes benefit future periods, they are assets in the current period. This concept, however, must be qualified because of the premises that users want reliable information (Premise 20) and that managers are inclined to report favorable results (Premise 10). There are, therefore, sound reasons for requiring convincing evidence of future benefits as a criterion for capitalizing these costs.

General and administrative costs. Manufacturing companies carry on two principal types of activities, production and marketing. Conceptually, the category of costs labeled "general and administrative" are caused by both types, and an appropriate fraction of these costs should be charged to product cost objects and included in inventory. There is no question that those headquarters and other staff unit costs that are identified with production should be assigned to product cost objects if the amounts are material.

A question does arise about the costs that are incurred for the entity as a whole, including top management costs, public relations costs, corporate legal costs, costs of the finance function, and corporate accounting costs. Although a case can be made that the concept of object fairness requires that part of these costs be allocated to production (with the result that a fraction will be carried in inventory), the causal connection between the cost object and these costs may be so tenuous that allocation is not warranted.

This problem arises only in companies that produce for inventory. In other companies, these costs are clearly expenses of the current period. No distortion of net income occurs if the costs are allocated to cost objects because all the cost objects (which are called *programs* in such entities) also relate to the current period.

Income taxes. Income taxes are a cost, but the concepts stated above do not apply to income taxes. Income taxes cannot be allocated to the period benefitted because they are not a benefit at all. They cannot be allocated to product cost objects within a period because the relation between production activities and the amount of income tax usually cannot be determined. Income taxes can and should be allocated to cost objects for extraordinary gains and losses that are reported separately; this topic is discussed in Chapter 6.[28]

INTEREST AND DEPRECIATION

In most respects current practice is consistent with the concepts discussed in the preceding section. The conceptual framework does, however, require that interest, the cost of using funds, be recognized explicitly as an element of cost, and it follows that this cost should be assigned to cost objects. The fairness concepts govern how this assignment should be made.

Recognition of interest as a cost suggests a quite different depreciation concept than those now used by most entities. The Pullen College situation will be used to introduce the explanation of this difference.

Case D: Dormitory smoke detectors

Pullen has decided to install smoke detectors in its dormitories in 1984 at a cost of $200,000. They have an estimated useful life of 10 years beginning in 1985. The $200,000 will be borrowed in 1984 at 10 percent, and the loan will be amortized with 10 equal payments of $32,549 beginning in 1985. The total cost over the 10-year period therefore will be $325,490, of which $200,000 is for the cost of the smoke detectors themselves and $125,490 is for interest. How should this event affect room rents?

Dormitory residents in 1985 through 1994 will benefit from the additional fire protection, and residents in these years should pay this cost. The relevant cost is not only the $200,000 cost of the smoke detectors; it also includes the $125,490 interest cost. If only $200,000 were recovered from room rents, the remaining $125,490 would have to come from general college funds (tuition), and the effect would be that the 400 students who do not live in dormitories would be paying for a cost that they did not cause. This would not be fair. It follows that the cost of using an asset includes interest on the funds used to finance the asset acquisition.

Case E: Library storage building

The stack space in Pullen's library has reached capacity, and it has been decided to enlarge and modernize the library facilities. Planning and building the new facility will require five years. A temporary storage building will be built at a cost of $100,000 to alleviate the problem during the period 1985 through 1989. The $100,000 cost of this building will be financed by a five-year loan, with annual payments of $20,000 on the principal and 10 percent interest on the unpaid balance. (The loan is structured so that it corresponds to the usual way of accounting for this transaction; this avoids the issue of whether the accounting should correspond to the financing arrangements. The answer, needless to say, is that the pattern of financial payments should *not* govern the accounting for the asset.)

The usual practice is to depreciate the $100,000 cost on a straight-line basis at $20,000 per year and to record the interest cost as an expense of the year in which it is incurred. This practice is wrong. It leads to temporal unfairness among students who are enrolled in each of the five years, 1985 through 1989. The unfairness arises because the nature of interest is not properly recognized.

The calculations of each year's cost, according to usual accounting practice, are given in Exhibit 5–2. If these costs are reflected in tuition charges, Exhibit 5–2 shows that students will pay less for the building in 1986 than in 1985, and still less in each year thereafter. Why should this be? The building will be just as useful to the 1989 students as to the 1985 students. (If anything, it will be more useful as the years go by because more books

---

Exhibit 5–2

Effect on tuition of straight-line depreciation

Year	Unpaid loan (beginning of year)	Depreciation	Interest*	Total	Per student
1985	$100,000	$ 20,000	$10,000	$ 30,000	$15
1986	80,000	20,000	8,000	28,000	14
1987	60,000	20,000	6,000	26,000	13
1988	40,000	20,000	4,000	24,000	12
1989	20,000	20,000	2,000	22,000	11
Total		$100,000	$30,000	$130,000	$65†

* 10% of loan balance.
† $65 per student for five years = $13 average per student/year.

Exhibit 5–3

Effect on tuition of level amortization

Year	Unpaid loan (beginning of year)	Principal	Interest *	Total	Per Student
1985	$100,000	$ 16,380	$10,000	$ 26,380	$13.19
1986	83,620	18,018	8,362	26,380	13.19
1987	65,602	19,820	6,560	26,380	13.19
1988	45,782	21,801	4,578	26,380	13.19
1989	23,982	23,982	2,398	26,380	13.19
Total		$100,000	$31,900	$131,900	$65.95

* 10 percent of beginning balance.

presumably will be stored in it.) Fair treatment would seem to require that students pay the same amount each year because each year's students benefit equally from it.

Now, consider what would happen if the loan were paid off in five equal annual payments, as is the practice with the typical bank loan, and tuition in each year included the amount of these payments. The annual charges would then be as shown in Exhibit 5–3. (The total payment is higher than that in Exhibit 5–2 because the annual amount of principal reduction is less than $20,000 in the earlier years). Note that in Exhibit 5–3, the total cost is the same each year, $13.19 per student. Such a schedule would therefore appear to meet the test of temporal fairness more satisfactorily than that in Exhibit 5–2.

Relevance to depreciation

By simply changing the name, the "principal" column in Exhibit 5–3 could become "depreciation." Its total would be $100,000, which it must be to recover the cost of the building, but the amount of depreciation increases each year. The depreciation method that produces numbers like those in the principal column of Exhibit 5–3 is called *annuity depreciation*.[29] Few entities use it. Nevertheless, it is a method that will produce equal annual tuition payments over the life of the asset. In the absence of evidence that the benefits from the asset vary from year to year, the effect on tuition should be the same each year, and the annuity method accomplishes this.[30]

It would seem to follow that in the absence of evidence that an asset's benefits are likely to be different in various future periods, annuity depreciation is the proper method of depreciation. This generalization goes against practically all current practice, but it follows unequivocally from the concept of temporal fairness.[31]

General applicability

What is the relevance of the preceding analysis to accounting for depreciation and interest in a profit-oriented entity? It is said by some that there are two important differences between a business and a nonprofit entity such as a college: (1) a business has shareholders who expect a return on their investment, whereas a college does not, and (2) the purpose of a business is to earn profits, whereas this is not the purpose of a college. I shall show that neither of these differences affects the conclusions reached in the situations described above, and that these conclusions can therefore be generalized to all accounting entities.

Difference in sources of funds. Pullen College does not have shareholders; that is, it does not obtain funds by equity financing. It finances capital acquisitions by borrowing. (It does have endowment, but earnings on endowment are used for operating purposes.) A profit-oriented entity obtains funds both by borrowing and from equity investors. As I show in Chapter 4, these funds have a cost, and although the cost is not as easily measured as the cost of the $100,000 loan obtained by Pullen College, the cost can be approximated satisfactorily. Even though funds for capital acquisitions in a profit-oriented entity are obtained from both debt and equity sources, the relevant cost is the total interest cost that corresponds to the amount shown in Exhibit 5–3.

Difference in objectives. A college has maintained its entity equity if its revenues in a period equal or exceed its expenses in that period. A profit-oriented entity has maintained its entity equity if its revenues are sufficient to recoup the cost of using equity funds, as well as other expenses of the period. In conventional accounting, this is a major difference between the two types of entities. The framework proposed here removes that difference, however, because it includes the cost of using equity funds as an element of cost.

Effect on performance measurement. The conventional method of recording depreciation and omitting equity interest cost distorts the amount of income reported. In the first several periods after the acquisition of a depreciable asset, income is understated, and in later periods it is overstated. This phenomenom will be illustrated by a situation similar to the Pullen

College storage building loan described in Exhibits 5–2 and 5–3, transferred to a business setting. The calculations are given in Exhibit 5–4.

Assume that a company can isolate the profit impact of a single asset acquisition; for example, it has a profit center consisting only of this asset. In the interest of simplicity, income taxes are disregarded, and return on assets employed is calculated on the beginning book balance of the investment.

The company has analyzed a proposed acquisition that costs $100,000 and is estimated to produce net revenues (i.e., revenues less all costs except depreciation and interest) of $26,380 per year for five years. The company requires a return of 10 percent on its investments. As shown in Section A of Exhibit 5–4, at the required return of 10 percent the net present value of this proposition is zero, so its estimated return is exactly 10 percent. The company therefore acquires the asset.

Assume that revenues are earned exactly as estimated. The operating statement effect of this investment for each of the five years, as measured in conventional accounting, is given in Section B of Exhibit 5–4. Straight-line depreciation is $20,000 per year, revenue is $26,380 per year, so income is $6,380 per year. Note that a return of 10 percent of the outstanding investment is not reported for any of the five years. In the early years it is less than 10 percent, and in the later years it is more than 10 percent. Such a report is incorrect because the true return is 10 percent in each year.

If the proposed method were adopted, income would be calculated as in Section C of Exhibit 5–4. Depreciation is calculated by the annuity method. Interest in each year is an element of cost and is 10 percent of the beginning book value in that year. The reported income is zero in each year, indicating that the investment produced the required return. Note that the return is the same in each year. Note also that although the labels differ, the numbers in Exhibit 5–4 are the same as those in Exhibits 5–2 and 5–3.

In short, the use of straight-line depreciation distorts income if the depreciable asset produces equal benefits each year. Accelerated depreciation would make the distortion even worse, for it would make the reported return in the early years even lower. This is not a trivial matter. Shyam Sunder studied the impact of conventional depreciation practices on a sample of 273 manufacturing companies for the period 1946 through 1974 (all the manufacturing companies for which data were available in the Compustat file for this period). He found that "capital investment has a substantial short-run negative effect on earnings of firms."[32]

There are many reported instances of profit center managers who have been reluctant to make economically attractive investments because of the depressing effect such investments have on reported earnings in the early years. Indeed, recognizing this problem, many companies use the residual income method in their management accounting reports, a practice which gives somewhat similar results to those shown in Exhibit 5–4, Section C.

Exhibit 5–4

Distortion resulting from conventional depreciation

A. Analysis of proposed investment

Cash inflows, 5 years @ $26,380,	
discounted at 10 percent ($26,380 × 3.791)	$100,000
Investment	100,000
Net present value	$ 0

B. Straight-line depreciation; interest not a cost

Year	Book value beginning of year	Depreciation	Revenue	Income	Return on investment
1	$100,000	$ 20,000	$ 26,380	$ 6,380	6%
2	80,000	20,000	26,380	6,380	8
3	60,000	20,000	26,380	6,380	11
4	40,000	20,000	26,380	6,380	16
5	20,000	20,000	26,380	6,380	32
Total		$100,000	$131,900	$31,900	

C. Annuity depreciation; interest as a cost

Year	Book value beginning of year	Depreciation	Interest	Total expense	Revenue	Income
1	$100,000	$ 16,380	$10,000	$ 26,380	$ 26,380	0
2	83,620	18,018	8,362	26,380	26,380	0
3	65,602	19,820	6,560	26,380	26,380	0
4	45,782	21,801	4,578	26,380	26,380	0
5	23,982	23,982	2,398	26,380	26,380	0
Total		$100,000	$31,900	$131,900	$131,900	

Effect on comparability. Businesses that lease assets are typically charged a level annual amount for the lease payments. In calculating this amount, the lessor takes into account the cost of the asset and the interest cost of funds committed to the asset (including both debt and equity interest as used in this framework). This charge is therefore similar to interest plus annuity depreciation as illustrated above. The stream of annual depreciation charges on an owned asset is not comparable to this stream of lease payments.

States, municipalities, hospitals, colleges, and universities that finance capital expenditures with borrowed funds often make level debt service payments to retire this debt. They charge the debt service as an operating expense, and they do not charge depreciation. If the length of the bond issue corresponds approximately to the service life of the asset, the net effect on income is approximately the same as charging interest and annuity depreciation, as illustrated above.

Depreciation concepts

The preceding analysis leads to the conclusion that the cost of using a depreciable asset includes both a depreciation and an interest component. If the estimated benefits from the asset are equal each year, annuity depreciation reflects this cost correctly. Other assumptions as to the pattern of benefits lead to other depreciation methods, but in most cases not to straight-line depreciation and scarcely ever to accelerated depreciation. Without attempting to describe all the possibilities, I sum up the main ideas in the following concepts:[33]

> ***Concepts 5.12.*** *The cost of using a depreciable asset in an accounting period should include both depreciation and the cost of interest on the funds committed to the asset.*

> ***Concepts 5.13.*** *If the benefits of using a depreciable asset are presumed to be equal in each year of its life, the depreciation component of the cost should be calculated by the annuity method.*

INTEREST ON ENTITY EQUITY

Funds obtained from shareholders have a cost, and, for reasons given in Chapter 4, accounting should recognize the cost of using these funds. Do funds generated by the entity's own activities, and which are reported as entity equity, also have a cost?

The argument against recognizing a cost of entity funds is that these funds were obtained at no cost to the entity. Furthermore, to the extent that an interest cost for these funds were recognized as an expense, the reduction in income would be exactly offset by a credit to entity equity, so there would be no net effect. This credit is, in a sense, a profit that results from an entity dealing with itself, but this framework does not allow a profit to be generated in this manner.

The arguments for recognizing this cost are that to the extent that costs are capitalized, there is a net effect on entity equity and that the costs of cost objects are understated if this cost is not recognized.

The problem arises concretely in the example of the Pullen College storage building described above. Suppose that instead of borrowing the $100,000 cost, Pullen financed the building with funds that it had accumulated from a net excess of revenues over expenses in past years. The source of these funds is entity equity; it constitutes a rainy-day reserve and reflects prudent management. If the $100,000 is spent for the building, Pullen loses the opportunity to earn interest on the short-term investment of these funds, and this decreases its operating revenue. Furthermore, unless the cost of using entity funds is recognized, a building financed with these funds will be reported as costing less than a building financed with a loan, whereas the method of financing should not affect the actual cost of the building. This line of reasoning says that use of the funds for a capital purpose does involve a cost.

The counter to this argument is that the cost of using the funds for the building rather than to earn income is an opportunity cost, and the framework does not recognize opportunity costs.

My inclination is to conclude that entity equity funds do not have a cost (even though when faced with exactly this situation at Pullen College, I agreed to recognition of this cost in the accounts).

In most enities the amount of entity equity is likely to be small and the effect of either treatment is therefore unlikely to be material.

Appendix

SOME IMPLICATIONS OF COST CONCEPTS

(Other implications are given in the Appendix to Chapter 6.)

Labor-related costs.   The cost of labor services includes the present value of the fringe benefits, and the tax payments associated with those services. Although not easily measured, fringe benefits (including pension costs) and taxes on labor costs conceptually are part of the cost of each hour or similar unit of labor service. Some entities now account for these items as if they were separate cost objects or separate elements of the cost of a cost object. This practice is justified only if it has no material effect on the cost of cost objects.[34]

Transfer prices.   In current cost accounting systems, products are transferred from one cost center to another at a cost which does not include an element of profit, whereas products are transferred from one profit center to another at the market price or at cost plus a profit margin. If interest is included as an element of cost, the discrepancy between these two methods will be reduced. The transfer price, in the typical situation, becomes a transfer at cost.

Research/development.   Some research/development expenditures benefit future periods. Conceptually, they are assets, but FASB Statement No. 2 does not permit these expenditures to be recognized as assets. Presumably, the reasons for this conclusion were that the asset amount could not be reliably measured, or that the expenditures that benefit future periods could not be separately identified from those that do not. In order to qualify as assets, the expenditures must benefit future periods in at least an equal amount. The amount of profit to be earned on the new product or process

146

need not be estimated, so long as revenue is highly likely to at least equal all related costs. The requirement that research/development costs be expensed as incurred should be reexamined.

Expense and effort.   Expense does not necessarily correspond to effort. Expense is an expired cost, whether or not effort was involved in the period.[35]

Depreciation and administrative costs.   Cost of sales includes depreciation on assets used in the production of the goods that were sold, and it also includes that part of general and administrative costs that are caused by production activities. The practice of reporting the total amount of depreciation and general and administrative costs as period expense items is conceptually unsound.[36]

LIFO.   The LIFO inventory method is conceptually unsound unless LIFO reflects the actual flow of products out of inventory, which is unlikely. Costs associated with revenues under this method are not the costs of the goods that were sold. Nevertheless, use of LIFO can be tolerated as a practical matter so long as its use in financial statements is a condition for using LIFO for income tax purposes.

Periodic replacement.   Some assets consist of components with different useful lives. For example, the frame of a building may have a life of 50 years, but its roof a life of 10 years. Conceptually, each component should be depreciated over its useful life. Viewed in this way, it is clear that re-roofing a building actually adds a new asset, which should be depreciated in the future. The alternative of creating a reserve for reroofing is conceptually unsound.

Periodic overhaul.   The barnacles that accumulate on a ship must be removed periodically. This situation is basically different from a periodic replacement because no depreciation cost was applied during the periods in which the barnacles accumulated. An expense item for such overhaul should be recognized in the years during which the barnacles accumulated.

6

Net income measurement

Entity equity reports the amount of funds that the entity has generated through its own activities, as contrasted with funds that creditors and investors supplied. The amount of entity equity is changed by two classes of events: (1) it is increased by the net income of a period or decreased by the net loss of a period, and (2) it is changed by certain other events whose effect is excluded from net income. The latter class includes prior period adjustments, nonoperating contributions to entity equity, and certain exceptional gains and losses.

This chapter discusses the measurement of net income.[1] Other types of changes in entity equity are discussed in Chapter 7. A few topics that do have implications for net income also are deferred to Chapter 7 because they are primarily governed by concepts relating to assets and sources of funds, the subject of that chapter.

APPROACH TO THE ANALYSIS

Premise 15 states that users of financial statements are primarily interested in information about an entity's performance, and secondarily in information about status. Concept 3.03 states that financial performance should be measured primarily by an entity's success in maintaining its equity during

148

an accounting period, that is, by its income. The evidence given in support of the premise and the concept is strong.[2]

For the whole life of a profit-oriented entity, income as conventionally measured is the total amount of cash (or other resources) distributed to equity investors in excess of repayment of the funds they have contributed. Accrual accounting is not needed to measure this total; the process is often described as "cash to cash." The problem of measuring income arises because performance must be reported for short priods of time; users of information will not wait for the cash-to-cash measurement. There is no perfect way of deciding how much of the total income for the entity should be attributed to a single accounting period, and all important accounting issues are associated with attempts to do this. George O. May put it well: "The measurement of periodic income would be indefensible if it were not indispensable."[3]

The problem of periodic income measurement does not arise in evaluating a proposed capital investment. The relevant numbers are the cash inflows and outflows over the whole life of the project. Having made the investment, however, the entity must thereafter assign an appropriate amount of revenue and expense to each accounting period. Some authors fail to distinguish between these two quite different types of problems. They point out that annual depreciation charges are irrelevant in making the investment decision, without recognizing that depreciation is an essential element in measuring periodic income.

In authoritative pronouncements, in the literature, and in practice, there is a great deal of confusion and inconsistency about concepts applicable to income measurement, especially in the measurement of revenue. In a study that has been helpful to me, Henry Jaenicke described some three dozen types of events and showed how authoritative pronouncements require that some of these be treated differently from others, even though they are basically similar.[4]

I shall introduce the discussion by describing considerations that are relevant to the development of income concepts. Next, I shall describe what seem to me to be "red herrings" that lead to muddled thinking about appropriate concepts. With this material as background, I develop definitions and concepts for income in general and for revenues and expenses, which are its two components. Some implications for the development of accounting standards are given in the appendix.

RELEVANT CONSIDERATIONS

Five general observations about income follow from the premises in Chapter 2 and the basic concepts in Chapter 3: (1) net income measures an entity's success in meeting its financial goals; (2) income concepts apply to all entities; (3) income relates to all aspects of operating activities; (4) income derives from the entity's performance; and (5) income should be recognized only when the amount can be reliably measured.

Income related to financial goals

The accounting period is one year (Concept 3.04). If an entity reports zero income for an accounting period, its operating activities have neither increased nor decreased its equity (subject to the qualification that income measurement is constrained by the need for reliability). If one of its goals is to increase its equity, the amount of income indicates how well the entity has performed in terms of this goal.

Applicable to all entities

The idea of entity equity maintenance applies to all entities (Concept 3.03). Most of the literature, however, relates to profit-oriented entities. The conclusions in this literature can be broadened simply by changing the central question from "How does a given event affect profits?" to "How does a given event affect the entity's equity?"

The AICPA Audit Guides for the various types of nonbusiness organizations are based on somewhat different concepts than those described for businesses, and concepts in some Audit Guides are inconsistent with those in others. These inconsistencies are undesirable. In part they arise because the authors interpreted the term *revenue* as relating solely to the sale of goods and services. This inconsistency can be resolved simply by defining revenue so that it applies to all additions to entity equity that are associated with operations. In part, the inconsistencies arise simply because the Audit Guides are outdated.

Because most resource flows of all entities are fundamentally similar, business and nonbusiness entities are discussed together. Certain types of flows are unique or almost unique to nonbusiness organizations, and these will be pointed out.

Broad view of operating performance

An entity is basically an organization that acquires goods and services and uses them to provide other goods and services. Until fairly recently, this idea led to the narrow view that the costs of goods and services used in a period were the inputs, or expenses, of that period; the value of goods and services provided were outputs, or revenues; and income was the difference between revenues and expenses. This view, called the *current operating performance* view, has been superseded by the *inclusive income* view.

The latter view is preferable because the entity's activities are broader than providing goods and services, and the current operating performance view is not broad enough to encompass other operating inflows and outflows during the period. Losses and gains are examples of outflows and inflows not directly related to the production and sale of goods and services.

Resource inflows received without a corresponding provision of outputs are another example of revenue not directly related to goods and services produced. Transactions of this nature are common in nonbusiness organizations; they include tax revenues, contributions, and grants. They also occur in business organizations in the form of subsidies. The concept of income should be broad enough to include events of this type.

Focus on performance

Income is a measure of performance. It follows that if the entity must do something to earn income, there is no income until the entity has performed. Many problems in income measurement arise because of the difficulty of specifying when performance has occurred.

Many events during an accounting period have two aspects, a revenue aspect and an expense aspect. Sale of a product involves both sales revenue and also the related cost of sales. There is no income unless the revenue associated with an event exceeds the expense associated with the same event. This is the idea of "matching."

Manufactured goods.   In manufacturing companies, the events associated with a single sales transaction may occur over a span of many years. The process may be said to begin with the approval of production plans or the ordering of material, and it ends only when the last product liability suit has been litigated.

In some companies, the most important event in this process is the booking of a firm sales order; the subsequent production and delivery of the goods and collection of the account receivable may involve only routine effort. Our focus, however, is on an entity's performance; recognizing income before the production process has even begun is stretching the idea of performance. Thus, I rule out bookings as a basis for income recognition. Furthermore, in the usual situation the possibility of cancellations makes the bookings amount unacceptably unreliable.

Advance payments.   The idea of performance is the reason for not recognizing advance payments (such as prepaid magazine subscriptions) as revenue, even though the money already has been received and the amount of profit on the transaction can be accurately measured at the time of receipt. Advance payments (sometimes called *precollected* *revenue*) are not revenues. They are liabilities until the entity has done whatever it is required to do as a condition of the payment.

Services. Conceptually, the recognition of income for most services is straightforward. Performance takes place when the services are rendered, and income is recognized at that time. Revenue for the rental of a hotel room is recognized each day the room is rented. Interest revenue for the use of money is recognized each day the money is available for use.

Performance in more than one period. If performance occurs in more than one period, income may be recognized in each of these periods. If a one-year maintenance contract at a fixed price provides services for three months of 1982 and nine months of 1983, three months of the revenue is recognized in 1982, regardless of the amount of maintenance work done in 1982. The contract is for the readiness to provide maintenance, and this readiness is not necessarily related to the amount of maintenance actually done. If performance with respect to a single order for goods occurs in two or more periods, income is recognized in each of these periods. This applies both to deliveries of completed goods and also to performance under a contract for a single item, such as building a ship.

Performance not involving expenses. Although most income earning activities involve both revenue and expense elements, some do not. Many nonbusiness organizations, for example, receive grants, contributions, taxes, and similar items without a corresponding requirement to provide goods or services. These resource inflows are revenues, but the idea of performance does not apply to them.

Substance over form. In deciding when performance has occurred, the economic substance is more important than the legal form. Performance may have occurred prior to or after the legal transfer of title.

Reliable measurements

Accounting should report the financial effect of those events that can be reliably measured (Concept 3.02). All the important problems of income measurement arise because the effect of many events on an entity's equity is uncertain. Essentially, income measurement concepts suggest guidelines for dealing with these uncertainties. They arise for one or more of the following reasons:

- Users want timely information (Premise 19) and are unwilling to wait until all uncertainties are resolved.
- Management tends to be optimistic in reporting information (Premise 10).
- The fair value of monetary resources can be reliably measured, but the fair value of most nonmonetary resources cannot be reliably measured, except when they enter or leave the entity (Premise 8).

Because accountants must seek an appropriate balance between the need for relevance and the need for reliability (Concept 3.14), and particularly because of management bias, the recognition of increases in an entity's equity requires more reliable evidence than recognition of decreases (Concept 3.13). In the statements that follow, therefore, recognition of revenue is described in terms of being *highly likely,* whereas recognition of expenses is described in terms of being *reasonably possible.*

Also, considerable weight is given to events involving an outside party as evidence that income has occurred. Such events usually involve monetary amounts, and these can be reliably measured.

The central problem in income measurement is the amount of uncertainty that should be tolerated, and the central question is: "How much reliability is enough?" In economics, the concept of income does not include the idea of reliability in its measurement, and this is the principal reason why the economic concept of income differs from the accounting concept.

Almost all future events are uncertain. This is a simple fact. Nevertheless, the occurrence and magnitude of many events can be estimated within reasonably close limits. Accounting cannot be based on the idea that events are recorded only when their effects are known with certainty. Rather, accounting is roughly based on the idea of "certainty equivalents," a concept from statistics.

Reasonable accuracy in estimating a whole class of events, rather than of each individual member of the class, is all that is required. Loss on a given account receivable cannot be predicted; if it could be, the sale to that customer would not have been made. Loss on the aggregate of accounts receivable often can be predicted with reasonable accuracy.

RED HERRINGS

Several ideas often used in analyzing income concepts seem to me not to be helpful in arriving at sound or useful conclusions.

Eanings as a continuous process

APB Statement No. 4 (paragraph 149) describes revenue as "being 'earned' gradually and continuously by the whole of enterprise activities." The idea of earning as a continuous process appears frequently in the literature about income measurement, going back at least to William Paton and A. C. Littleton and to George O. May.[5]

This view is consistent with the utility theory of value in economics, which holds that the production process adds form, place, or time utility and hence increases value. This theory is the basis of Marxian economics, which holds that the increase in a product's value is primarily the result of the efforts of labor. There is little evidence that supports this theory as a theory. Even if there were some validity to the theory, no one has explained how the alleged increase in value throughout the production process can be reliably measured.

The amount of income earned from goods involves both production activities and marketing activities, but the separate amount attributable to each is rarely measurable. Unless the total amount of production "income" can be measured, there is no basis for assigning part of this income to each of the periods in which the goods are manufactured. Classical economic theory and many economics texts do not recognize marketing as a business function; under perfect competition, goods are delivered without selling effort. In classical economics, therefore, the problem of separating production income from marketing income does not arise.

The more generally accepted theory of value holds that the production process is essentially one of recombining materials, labor, and other resources; that the value of the specific goods increases by the amount of resources added to them; but that the process does not add to the total value of the entity. Hence production does not increase the entity's equity and does not generate income. The process adds value to the goods being manufactured but subtracts an equal amount of value from other resources. These additions and subtractions are measured as the cost of the resources involved. Income occurs when the goods are transferred to another party that is willing to pay more than their cost. This theory can easily be made operational because it requires only that production costs be assigned to goods; this is much easier than attempting to measure values.

Interest is not fully recognized as a production cost in the current accounting model. If it were recognized, the difference between these two theories of value would decrease, and in the pure competition model it would disappear. In the pure competition model, with an appropriate allowance for interest, income from the production process is zero.

The value of a football team probably increases with every day of practice, starting with spring training, but the team's performance is measured by the final score of the game. Similarly, the value of the process of producing and selling products cannot be measured on the basis of information obtainable in the course of the production process.

Critical event.   The opposite of the continuous process approach is the critical event approach. In this approach income is recognized at the moment of making the most critical decision in the cycle of production and marketing activities.[6] Except in transactions in which there is an exchange of goods for cash or receivables, this concept is difficult to relate to practice, and for such transactions it gives the same results as the APB Statement No. 4 concept, described in the next paragraph. For other events, the critical events approach leads to strange results. Booking of sales orders, especially when they are accompanied by prepayments, would count as revenue, for example. Alternatively, the critical event in some transactions eventually turns out to be a product liability suit which, although it may occur years after the sale, has far more critical consequences than any other event in the whole income earning process.

Earning process complete; exchange

APB Statement No. 4 (paragraph 150) states that revenue is recognized when "(1) the earning process is complete or virtually complete, and (2) an exchange has taken place." Although these criteria work for the great majority of events, they do not fit all of them. For a life insurance policy, the earnings process is not complete until the policyholder dies. For most goods, the entity is subject to claims under express or implied warranties for an indefinitely long period, and the earnings process is not complete until all claims have been settled. In these cases, trying to decide when the process is virtually complete is an impossible, and unnecessary, task.

"Exchange" is not a necessary criterion for revenue recognition. For many events, satisfactory evidence both as to performance and as to reliable measurement requires that an exchange has taken place. However, if exchange were an essential criterion, recognition of revenue from events such as the discovery of mineral deposits would be ruled out. These events do increase the entity's equity, the entity has performed, and the value of the deposits can in some cases be reliably measured. On the other hand, if exchange is not a criterion, an entity might recognize income from events that involve dealing with itself, which is inconsistent with Premise 3A. In most circumstances, these events should not be recognized as revenue. Thus, although exchange is not here taken as an absolute requirement, the intention is that in most circumstances revenue recognition does involve an exchange with an outside party, and there is a presumption that in the absence of an exchange, income cannot be reliably measured.

Realization

It is often said that revenue is recognized when it is realized. What is usually meant by this statement, however, is that certain criteria are set forth for the recognition of revenue, and when an event satisfies these criteria, the revenue is said to be realized. In this sense, the statement is a tautology. The event "becomes real" whenever the stated conditions are met.

In a narrower, but more meaningful, sense "realization" means to turn something into money or its equivalent. I shall use realization in this sense, and realization then becomes a condition for revenue recognition in certain circumstances.[7]

Revenue equated with output

It is sometimes said that revenue measures an entity's output. In profit-oriented entities, revenues from the sale of goods and services are usually a good approximation of the entity's output. In nonbusiness entities, however, there is no necessary connection between the value of services provided (e.g. education, police protection, welfare aid) and the revenue earned from delivering these services. Moreover, these entities have revenues from contributions, taxation, and other sources that are not directly related to the delivery of services. Thinking of revenue as an *inflow of resources,* is more realistic than thinking of revenue as an *outflow of product.*

With a focus on output, resource inflows not directly related to output are said to be "nonreciprocal transfers." This is not a necessary or useful distinction.[8]

Income is the difference between revenue and expense. The focus should be on this difference. Although the conceptual problem of revenue recognition is more difficult than that of expense recognition, both need to be considered together. For example, the *revenue* that will ultimately be realized from a sales contract with a financially sound customer usually can be reliably measured at the time the contract is signed, but the *income* can be measured only when the related expenses are known or can be reliably estimated.

Asset/liability approach

In general, the revenue/expense approach to income measures the flows during the period directly, while the asset/liability approach indirectly records the difference in stocks between the beginning and the end of the period. For reasons given in the discussion of Concept 3.04, the revenue/expense approach is preferable.

Since accounting is an articulated system (Concept 3.08), one might think that these approaches would produce identical results. In a world of certainty, this would be the case. In the real world, however, one must decide which approach is more useful. Note 16 in Chapter 3 describes some of the difficulties associated with the asset/liability approach and shows how the revenue/expense approach overcomes these difficulties. These points will not be repeated. This section is limited to a discussion of two criticisms that have been made of the revenue/expense approach.[9]

Smoothing. Critics assert that the revenue/expense approach permits, or even requires, income smoothing. The possibility that it permits a reserve for self insurance, whose size is arbitrarily determined by management, is often used as an example. There is indeed evidence that entities, particularly well-established companies, do want to smooth income. Reducing the peaks and valleys gives a desirable impression of stability or of steady progress. There is no reason to believe, however, that the revenue/expense approach does permit, let alone encourage, smoothing. The constraints to inhibit artificial smoothing can be just as effective under this approach as under the asset/liability approach.

Inadequate guidance.   It is argued that an asset is a real thing, and that one can visualize changes in the amounts of assets, whereas income is not a thing at all, and therefore concepts related to income are too nebulous to provide adequate guidance. There is little evidence in support of this argument. Accounting does not recognize all assets (e.g., internally generated goodwill), and many intangible assets are, in the literal sense, unreal. The important question is which approach leads to more useful concepts. The examples given in Chapter 3 show the difficulty of developing useful concepts from the asset/liability approach.

Distributable income

Historically, corporate income was the amount that the corporation could legally distribute to its owners as dividends or, more broadly, the amount the corporation could distribute without reducing the scale of its operating activities. Some authors continue to hold this view.[10]

As a legal concept, the amount that can be distributed is of relatively minor interest in the current environment. The typical corporation retains approximately half its income (as measured without counting the cost of equity interest) in order to provide additional equity capital. Some large and growing companies, such as Digital Equipment Corporation, have never distributed anything, while others have distributed more than 100 percent of their income in a given year. These distributions reflect management's judgment as to what the entity is "capable of distributing," which is the literal meaning of "distributable." The amount that the company theoretically or legally could distribute is not relevant in these circumstances. Nonprofit organizations cannot distribute income, so the idea is meaningless for such entities.

A corporation can distribute more than the accumulated amount of income if it decides to do so. Even though part of such a distribution is labelled as a return of capital, from the viewpoint of the recipient this is simply money, except as it affects the calculation of taxable income. It is not necessarily a return of the investor's capital; the investor's capital is the price he or she paid for the stock, which, except for the original investors, is not recorded in the accounts. The entire amount of a distribution is money that the recipient can use. The special rules for calculating income taxes are outside the boundary of financial accounting.

Although the amount of distributable income is defined in law, the amount that a given corporation can distribute may be governed by restrictions in bond indentures or other agreements, and therefore different from the legal maximum. Measuring income in accordance with the legal definition may not report these facts.

Since substance is more important than form (Concept 3.02), the legal definition would not be governing in any event. Viewed the other way around, when the law relies on accounting to distinguish between a return *of* capital from a return *on* capital, the concepts stated here are applicable.

Distributable income is a fuzzy concept. In order to make it operational, the accountant would have to know the amount of funds needed in the future to finance inventory, receivables, new plant, and other items because an entity is unable to operate without providing for these needs. Accounting cannot measure these amounts. They depend on management's judgment. Accounting reports on events that have already happened (Premise 4), whereas estimates of these amounts relate to events that are going to happen in the future.

Entry and exit values

It has become fashionable to refer to *entry values*, which are essentially costs, and *exit values*, which are amounts at which resources leave the entity. Using these terms, Staubus writes, "the accountant is said to 'recognize revenue' when he switches from one measurement approach to the other."[11] This statement is true but not helpful. It says nothing about how the period in which income should be recognized should be identified.

Transactions

Accounting is sometimes said to be based on transactions, that is, on documented evidence of changes in the accounts. This is only a partial truth. Entries made at the end of the accounting period adjust revenue and expense items for events that have not been properly recognized by the transactions recorded during the period. Recognition of unrecorded revenues, such as interest revenue, and of unrecorded expenses, such as the expiration of asset costs, are not based on transactions.

DEFINITION OF NET INCOME

The preceding analysis suggests that the following ideas should be incorporated in the definition of net income: (1) net income should relate to operating activities of an accounting period, with "operating" being broadly construed; (2) the definition should be applicable to both business and nonbusiness entities; (3) income should be recognized when the entity has performed and the amount can be realiably measured; and (4) the definition should suggest that the direct measurement of revenues and expenses is preferable to the indirect measurement of changes in assets and liabilities. The following definition incorporates these ideas:

> *Concept 6.01.*   *Net income is the increase in entity equity arising from the financial effects of those operating activities of an accounting period that can be reliably measured. Net income is measured as the difference between revenues of the period and expenses of the period.*

Gains and losses

Gains and losses are not explicitly mentioned in the above definition; they are regarded as components of revenues and expenses. The reason is convenience of exposition. Many statements apply to both revenues and gains, and many other statements apply to both expenses and losses, and the identification of gains and losses separately would unnecessarily complicate these statements. The terms *gains* and *losses* are used in this analysis to refer to certain types of revenues and expenses.[12]

MATCHING CONCEPT

Although most income measurement concepts are discussed under the separate headings of revenues and expenses, one topic—the matching concept—relates to both of them.[13] The general idea of matching is obviously sound. If a given event led to both an increase in revenue and an increase in expense, the amount of income in a period would not be correctly reported if the revenue component were reported in one period and the expense component in another period. As usually stated, however, the matching idea is narrower than it needs to be.

It is usually said that expenses are matched against revenues; that is, the revenue applicable to a period is determined first, and then the expense applicable to that revenue is matched to it. Although this description fits many situations, there are other situations in which matching is the reverse; that is, the expense applicable to the period is determined first, and then the associated revenue is matched to it. For example, if an entity receives a contribution and in exchange agrees to perform certain services, the contribution is not revenue until the period in which these services are performed, as evidenced by the incurrence of expense for the stated purpose. Until that period, there is a liability to perform the services. A similar condition exists in those situations in which revenue from long-term construction projects is recognized according to the percentage of completion of the contract, as measured by expenses incurred.

The following concept includes this broader connotation of matching:

> **Concept 6.02.** *When a given event affects both revenues and expenses, the effect on each should be recorded in the same accounting period.*

DEFINITION OF REVENUE

The definition of revenue follows automatically from the definition of income, and is stated only in the interest of completeness:

> **Concept 6.03.** *The revenues of an accounting period are those additions to entity equity resulting from operating activities of the period that can be reliably measured.*

As noted above, the term *operating activities* is construed broadly. It includes all activities that increase entity equity, except for nonoperating contributions and a few other events that are reported as direct changes in entity equity, rather than as components of income.[14] Events that have no effect on entity equity, such as the purchase of assets, are of course, irrelevant to income measurement.

REVENUE RECOGNITION: TIMING

Many concepts of income and revenue appear in the literature. Norton Bedford lists nine logically distinct concepts of business income, with several subcategories under each, and explains why even this list is by no means exhaustive.[15]

Central revenue ideas

Three ideas are, I believe, central to the development of a concept for the time at which revenue is recognized. One is the idea of performance. To the extent that the entity has to perform in order to generate income, revenue should not be recognized until this performance has occurred.[16] (Not all types of revenue require performance.) The second is the idea of reliable measurement. Revenue should not be recognized until the amount of income resulting from an event can be reliably measured. The third idea is of timeliness. Revenue should be recognized as soon as the first two conditions have been satisfied.

Because of inherent differences in the sources of revenue, these ideas cannot be incorporated in a single concept. They require three concepts: one for revenues from products, another for gains, and a third for other revenue sources.

Revenue from products

Products are the goods or services that the entity produces or acquires from other entities and then resells.[17] Some authors treat *goods* separately from *services*, but such a distinction is not necessary at the conceptual level. Services include such activities as: permitting the use of property, which is rental or lease revenue; lending money, for which the revenue is interest; and providing the use of a valuable name or production process, for which the revenue is royalty payments.

The following concept applies to revenue recognition of products.[18]

> ***Concept 6.04.*** *Revenues from products should be recognized in the earliest period in which (a) the entity has performed substantially what is required in order to earn income and (b) the amount of income can be reliably estimated.*

In most circumstances, a reliable measurement of the amount that will be realized can be made only when products are delivered (that is, when goods are shipped or services are performed). In the ordinary sales transaction, there is an agreement to exchange goods for money or for the promise to pay money, the agreement is consummated when the exchange takes place, and ordinarily this occurs when the goods are delivered. This point is often described as the time when title passes from the seller to the buyer, but a more accurate statement is the time when the benefits (or rewards) and risks of ownership pass. The passage of title is a legal concept, and it may not reflect the substance of the transaction. For example, in the usual installment sales contract, title does not pass until the last payment has been made, but, assuming payments are made when due, the buyer has the goods and the seller has performed at the time of delivery.

The concept does not imply that product revenue is recognized on an all-or-nothing basis. If an entity provides a service that extends over more than one accounting period, revenue is recognized in each period, provided the amount of income applicable to that period can be reliably measured. Similarly, the percentage-of-completion basis of revenue recognition is consistent with the concept, provided the amount of income can be reliably measured.[19]

If income from a service requires satisfactory completion of an act, income often cannot be reliably measured until the act has been completed. The revenue for repairing an automobile should not be recognized until the repairs have been completed. Revenue from a consulting contract to provide services should be recognized during each period that the services are provided, whereas revenue from a consulting contract that is contingent on the satisfactory completion of a report should not be recognized until a satisfactory report has been completed.

The emphasis is on the measurement of income, not the measurement of revenue itself. The amount of revenue from a fixed-price production contract can be reliably measured at the time the contract is signed, but the amount of income depends on the costs incurred in performing under the contract, and these costs are usually not known until they actually are incurred. (Income can be either positive or negative.)

Gains

Two types of gains are discussed: those resulting from the discovery of mineral resources, and those associated with increases in the value of recorded assets.

Discoveries. Accounting does not now recognize the increase in equity resulting from the discovery of mineral resources. The amount of income that eventually will be realized from the sale of these resources is uncertain, and full performance has not occurred until these resources are sold. Consequently, if a company purchases a proven oil field, the asset amount reflects the value of the field, whereas if a company discovers a field with its own resources, only the exploration costs are capitalized. Although the point is debatable, it seems to me that this treatment of discoveries is less desirable than the alternative of recognizing the gain when its existence has been well established. The discovery itself is performance, and modern techniques permit its measurement. This leads to the following concept:

> **Concept 6.05.** *Gains from the discovery of a mineral resource should be recognized in the earliest period in which a reasonable value for the resource can be reliably estimated.*

It should be emphasized that this concept applies to the initial recognition of the asset and the corresponding gain. Concept 3.13 prohibits increasing the asset amount for any subsequent increase in the estimates. If the revised estimates are lower than the net realizable value of the reserves, Concept 6.08, given below, requires that the asset amount be reduced. To permit changes in the asset amounts for each reestimate would involve the unsolvable problems that were discovered in attempts to implement Reserve Recognition Accounting.

Other nonmonetary gains. The basic revenue criterion requires that other gains be recognized only when they have been realized because only at that time can the amount of the gain be reliably measured. This criterion works well for nonmonetary gains, but for monetary gains it can lead to a lack of symmetry in income recognition because the corresponding concept for losses does not require realization. In order to avoid this lack of symmetry, the following concept applies only to nonmonetary gains, and a separate concept for monetary gains and losses is given as Concept 6.11.

> ***Concept 6.06.*** *Other nonmonetary gains should be recognized in the period in which they are realized.*

Revenues from other sources

In addition to product revenues and gains, revenues may arise from other sources, particularly in nonbusiness organizations. These include dues in membership organizations, taxes in governments, appropriations from other entities (such as an amount appropriated by a state to a municipality), grants, and contributions. If an entity has an endowment or similar trust funds, earnings on that endowment are revenues. (As emphasized earlier, nonoperating contributions are not revenues because revenues are associated with the operating activities of the accounting period.)

Amounts realized from these sources are either unrestricted, or their use is restricted to a specified purpose. If unrestricted, they may be designated for use in a specified time period (for example, 1983 property taxes), or they may be available for use at any time. Since many of these resource inflows do not involve performance by the entity, the performance criterion is not necessarily applicable, and a different conceptual approach is required. The following concept suggests the period in which revenue is recognized in each of these circumstances:

> ***Concept 6.07.*** *Other resource inflows intended for operating purposes should be recognized as revenues in the period in which income is realized.*

The concept focuses on the realization of income, rather than of revenue. With such a focus, recognition of the various types of resource inflows becomes clear. Unrestricted, undesignated inflows should be recognized as revenues in the period in which money or a valid receivable is received. Inflows designated for use in a specified time period are revenues of that period because they are associated with the expenses of that period. Inflows restricted to a specified purpose are revenue in the period in which expenses are incurred for that purpose because the matching concept (Concept 6.02) states that expenses and revenue for the same event should be recognized in the same period.

Recall that an amount is realized when money or money equivalents have been received. This concept therefore suggests that undesignated cash contributions or grants should be recognized in the year of receipt, but that undesignated pledges or similar intentions to make payments should not be recognized as revenue until the amounts have been received, unless the pledge is approximately as enforceable as an account receivable.

RECOGNITION OF REVENUE: AMOUNT

The preceding section addressed the problem of determining the accounting period in which revenue should be recognized. There remains the problem of determining the amount of revenue that should be recognized in that period.

Problems of deciding on the amount of revenue that should be recognized are caused by two facts: (1) the amount that eventually will be collected may be uncertain and (2) the amount may not be realized until much later than the revenue has been recognized. In an uncertain world, there is no perfect solution to the first problem; in view of management bias (Premise 10), the governing idea should be that the amount is the amount that is highly likely to be realized. The second problem is easily solved by including the idea of present value in the concept.

The term *highly likely* is imprecise; it should be made more precise in standards relating to various types of events. The term suggests that the probability of realizing at least the recognized amount should be greater than 0.5, just as the term *reasonably possible* used for expenses suggests that the probability need not be as great as 0.5.

The concept is as follows:

> **Concept 6.08.**   *The amount of revenue should be the present value of the amount that is highly likely to be realized.*

Several units of service

If services are performed for more than one period, revenue should be recognized in each of these periods. The amount of revenue recognized in each period usually should be in proportion to the units of service rendered. For an annual subscription to a monthly magazine, $1/12$ of the subscription revenue should be recognized in each month. By contrast, advertising revenue can be associated with each specific issue of the magazine.

Since the matching concept requires that revenue be recognized in the same period as the related expense, this practice assumes that expenses are proportional to the number of units of service. In many situations this is a valid assumption, but in some cases it is not. For example, a franchisor may incur more expenses at the beginning of an agreement than are incurred in later periods. In these circumstances, the amount of related expense in a given period is a better guide to the amount of revenue recognized than is the number of units of service.

Amount when income is uncertain

In certain types of installment sales and long-term construction contracts, the amount of income that will be realized is less certain than that suggested by the term *highly likely*. Income should not be recognized in these circumstances until the evidence indicates that revenue is highly likely to exceed expenses. Nevertheless, if the circumstances warrant, revenue can be recognized, so long as the amount of revenue does not exceed the amount of expenses incurred in the period for the same contract.

EXPENSES

Most of the concepts for expense recognition are given in Chapter 5. The concepts given below can be deduced from the definition of expenses and from concepts relating to cost. They are stated primarily for the purpose of clarifying the significance of the definition of expense. The basic concept is Concept 5.03: Expenses are costs that are applicable to the current accounting period. The following flows logically from that concept:

> **Concept 6.09.** *If there is a reasonable possibility that an asset will not be associated with revenue in a future period in an amount at least equal to its recorded cost, the difference between its recorded cost and the probable future revenue should be reported as an expense.*

This concept provides the rationale for writing inventory and monetary assets down to market.

APB Statement No. 4 includes three types of costs as expenses: (1) costs associated with products sold during the period, (2) costs of the period, and (3) costs that do not benefit future periods. The concepts given here cover the same types of cost: the first by the matching concept (Concept 6.02) and the second and third by the basic expense concept (Concept 5.03). If costs do not benefit a future period, they must be costs of the current period.

Losses

The concept for losses is not parallel with the concept for gains because less reliable evidence is required to recognize losses than is required for gains. The following applies to nonmonetary losses:

> **Concept 6.10.** *If there is a reasonable possibility that a loss (other than a loss on a monetary asset) has occurred during the current period, or if a loss occurring in a prior period is discovered during the current period, the amount of loss that is reasonably possible should be recognized as an expense of the current period.*

Since a loss is here classified as one type of expense, Concept 6.10 follows closely from the basic expense concept, Concept 5.03. If a loss occurs in the current period, it clearly is an expense. If the loss occurred in an earlier period but was discovered in the current period, (e.g., an embezzlement), the choices are either to make a direct debit to equity or to classify the item as an expense. Since in this framework, direct entries to equity are made very sparingly, the latter practice is preferable; this is consistent with current practice.

As a practical matter, measuring the amount of loss that is "reasonably possible" is often difficult, especially if litigation is involved. The concept, however, is clear.

MONETARY GAINS AND LOSSES

The concepts given above are not symmetrical with respect to the treatment of gains and losses. Losses are recognized whenever they occur or are discovered, whereas most nonmonetary gains are recognized only when they are realized. This difference in treatment is consistent with Concept 3.13, which requires better evidence for recognizing revenues than for recognizing expenses. This concept recognizes management's optimistic bias (Premise 10).

Management can do little to manipulate amounts reported for monetary items, however, because, as stated in Premise 8, the fair value of monetary items can be realiably measured. Therefore, a principal reason for the lack of symmetry in the treatment of gains and losses does not exist for monetary items. Monetary gains and monetary losses can both be reliably measured.

Moreover, a report of the performance of entities such as mutual funds would be seriously distorted if all losses in a period were recognized but only realized gains were recognized. Such a requirement would open the door to manipulation because management could influence net income by its decisions as to what securities to sell.

On the other hand, some monetary gains and losses are ephemeral. If an entity holds debt securities for investment purposes, fluctuations in the general level of interest rates cause changes in the current value of these securities, but such changes are irrelevant if the entity plans to hold the securities to maturity, or even for a long time. At maturity, they will be worth their face amount, and fluctuations in value in the interim have no significance.[20]

The problem is further complicated by the fact that securities are held for different reasons. Although some entities hold fixed-income securities to maturity, others seek to profit from changes in their market prices.

These considerations suggest that under certain circumstances, both gains and losses on monetary assets should be recognized, whether or not they are realized, and that under other circumstances, neither gains nor losses should be recognized. Neither of these principles is consistent with the concepts stated above, and they require an additional concept:

Concept 6.11. Monetary gains and losses should be recognized as revenues or expenses in the period in which they occur unless they are unlikely to be realized, in which case they should not be recognized until realized.

This is a general statement, but it is the function of standards, not of concepts, to spell out its application under various conditions. This is in fact done in FASB Statement No. 12, *Accounting for Certain Marketable Securities*, and that statement is generally consistent with the concept stated above.

Appendix

SOME IMPLICATIONS OF INCOME MEASUREMENT CONCEPTS

Listed below are certain implications that follow from the income measurement concepts.[21]

REVENUE

Timing of recognition

Ordinary sale of property.   Revenue from the sale of property or property rights should be recognized in the period in which most of the benefits and risks of ownership are transferred to another entity. This does not mean that *all* the risks of ownership have been transferred from the seller, because in most cases the seller remains liable for defects in the product, and in other cases the goods are returned and the seller assumes the risks again. Criteria for deciding how strong the evidence of transfer should be in various circumstances are appropriately the subject of standards.[22]

Installment sales.   Ordinarily, revenue should be recognized on an installment sale when the goods are delivered. However, if income that will be realized on an installment sale cannot be reliably estimated at the time of sale, revenue for a period should be the amount collected from the customer during that period. The estimate is for installment sales as a class, not for individual transactions. This is consistent with current practice.[23] As is the case with any sale on credit, there is the possibility that the cash will not be received.

Long production process.   If production under a contract occurs during substantial parts of two or more accounting periods, and if the amount of income applicable to the fraction produced in each period can be reliably estimated, revenue should be recognized in each of these periods.[24]

Discoveries. Revenue from the discovery of minerals should be recognized in the period in which the amount of the discovered minerals is proven.[25] When a company discovers oil, gas, or other minerals on property whose mineral rights it controls, it is certainly better off than it was before the discovery occurred.

Certain agricultural products. Revenue from agricultural products that can be sold at a support price should be recognized in the period in which production is completed. These products include grains and other products that can be sold at support prices fixed by the federal government, and other products, such as milk, that can be sold at prices fixed by state governments. The farmer has earned income that can be reliably measured when the production process has been completed, that is, when the products have been harvested. Farmers who decide to hold the products do so in anticipation that prices will increase. The gain or loss from holding them is treated in accordance with the concepts for gains and losses.[26]

Precious metals. The concepts do not permit revenue recognition for precious metals at the time the production process has been completed unless the amount to be realized is assured. At one time, gold could always be sold at a government guaranteed price, but this is no longer the case.[27]

Services, the ordinary case. Revenue from services should ordinarily be recognized in the period in which the services are performed.

Revenue contingent on final act. If the amount to be realized for services depends significantly on the satisfactory performance of a final act, such as the acceptance of a satisfactory report or an architect's drawings, revenue should be recognized when that act is performed. Costs incurred in such circumstances are recorded as inventory until completion of the final act.

Low down-payment. Sales revenue should not be recognized when real property is sold with such a low down payment and such inadequate security for the balance due that realization of the total amount is not highly likely. Such transactions are conceptually the same as installment sales.

Right of return. The concepts suggest that if goods are sold with a right of return, revenue should be recognized at the time of sale only if it is possible to make a reasonable estimate of the amount of returns.[28]

Marketing cooperatives. The practice of recognizing revenue when a member transfers goods to a marketing cooperative is not consistent with the concepts. Even though title passes to the cooperative at that time, the amount that is likely to be realized cannot be measured until the cooperative sells the goods.

Franchise fee revenue. The practice of recognizing franchise fee revenue when received is consistent with the concepts if, but only if, the franchisor is not obligated to perform a significant amount of services in return for the fee. A standard should define what is a significant amount of services.

Bookings; executory contracts. The concepts contain the idea of performance in the case of both goods and services. They therefore rule out the possibility of recognizing revenue when sales are booked, and they rule out revenue recognition for unperformed executory contracts.

Designated period. Resource inflows designated for operating purposes in a specified period should be recognized as revenues in that period. It follows that the 1983 property tax levy is revenue in 1983, even though invoices may be sent out in 1982 and even though payment may not be received until 1984. It also follows that amounts appropriated by a legislature for use in a specified period are revenues to the receiving entity in that period. If the period is not specified, judgment is required to determine the period that the appropriating body intended.

Restricted contributions. If the use of contributions is restricted to a specified purpose, revenue should be recognized in the period or periods in which expenses are incurred for that purpose. Until expenses are incurred for the specified purpose, there is a liability, corresponding to advance payments on an unperformed contract. If expenses are incurred over two or more periods, revenue is recognized in proportion to the amount of expense in each period. If the contribution exceeds the amount of expense incurred for the specified purpose, the excess is revenue (unless the donor requires its return).

Endowment earnings. Earnings on endowment, trust, or similar funds should be recognized as revenue in the period in which they are earned. This implication is subject to the requirement of the preceding paragraph; that is, if the endowment is for a specified purpose, its earnings are not revenue unless expenses have been incurred for that purpose. The term *earned* is not defined here; it is discussed in Chapter 7.

Amount of revenue

Accretion. Accretion does not result in revenue because the amount of income that will be realized cannot be reliably estimated until the growing process has been completed and the product has been harvested and sold. Accretion is similar to work-in-process inventory, which is reported at its cost. The inclusion of interest as part of the cost of timber, nursery stock, and livestock does increase the cost of these assets, but this increase is not recognized in current practice. Recognition of interest would make the recorded cost come closer to the value added by accretion.[29]

Sales and excise taxes.   If these taxes are collected and separately identified by the seller they are not revenue. The seller is acting as a collection agent for the government and incurs a liability equal to the amount of tax collected. Equity is not affected by these tax collections.[30]

Capitalized interest.   Capitalizing interest cost does not result in revenue. The offsetting credit for the debit amount of interest cost is to a liability account (in the case of debt interest) or to shareholder equity (in the case of equity interest). There is no effect on revenue. (Some public utilities do record equity interest as revenue, and this practice is, incorrectly, approved by FASB Statement No. 71.)

Borrowing and advance payments.   Proceeds of borrowing and advance payments for goods and services are not revenues. These proceeds are accompanied by an equal increase in liabilities.

Dividing service revenue between periods.   If a service agreement covers services for more than one accounting period, revenues should be recognized in proportion to the related expenses assigned to each period. This implication does not address the difficult question of what is meant by "related expenses," particularly as to the treatment of selling costs and other front end costs. Resolution of this question is left to standards that will take into account the circumstances of various types of transactions, all within the matching concept (Concept 6.02). Basically, these standards should seek to arrive at a constant gross margin in each period, unless circumstances indicate that the gross margin is inherently uneven.

Uncertain income.   If there is not a high likelihood that income ultimately will be earned from an event, or from a class of similar events, the amount of revenue recognized in a period should not exceed the amount of related expense recognized in the period. The phrase "a class of similar events" is added to make it clear that the concept does not necessarily apply to a single event. In installment sales, for example, the probability of earning income on a single specified sale may be relatively low, but the probability of earning income on all installment sales collectively may be relatively high.

Adjustments to sales amount. The amount reported as revenue is the sales value less adjustments for the likely amount of sales returns and allowances, bad debts, and cash discounts. These adjustments reduce the sales value to the amount highly likely to be realized. The concepts permit warranty costs to be recorded either as an adjustment in revenue or as an expense. The issue of which practice is preferable should be resolved by a standard.[31]

Interest. The amount of revenue recognized on money loaned to another entity is measured by the effective interest rate of the loan applied to the amount outstanding during the period, adjusted downward, if necessary, if some lesser amount is likely to be received or if the present value of the amount to be received is less than this amount.

Nonmonetary revenues. If revenues are not in the form of money or its equivalent, the amount recorded should be the fair value of the resources received.

Insurance contracts. Revenue on insurance contracts of short duration (casualty, liability, and nonrenewable term contracts) should be recognized in the periods covered by the contract. Revenue on contracts of long duration (whole life, endowment, annuity, and renewable term contracts) should be recognized in the period in which the premiums are due from the policyholder, and the present value of expected benefits shoud be deducted from the revenue in arriving at income for the period.[32]

Equity investments. The amount of revenue earned on an equity investment is the present value of equity interest earned on that investment during the period, if there is a high likelihood that this amount eventually will be received. If receipt is not highly likely, the amount of revenue is the amount of dividends.

EXPENSES

Selling costs. Conceptually, selling costs should be associated with the revenues resulting from the selling effort. However, since the benefit to future periods resulting from these efforts often cannot be estimated, these costs ordinarily should be recorded as expenses when incurred.

Write-down to market. Unsold goods and costs of performing services are assets (inventory) until the period in which the revenue from these products is recognized. If the cost exceeds the highly likely amount of revenue, the asset should be reduced to the appropriate amount. Some argue that the practice of writing inventory down to market is inconsistent, because writing inventory up to market is prohibited. If one recognizes that better evidence is required for revenue recognition than for expense recognition (Concept 3.13), the apparent inconsistency disappears.[33]

Research/development cost. If it is highly likely that revenue on newly developed products or processes will be at least as much as their research/development costs, these costs should be capitalized.[34]

Plant closing. When a plant is closed, costs of closing the plant are costs in the period in which the decision to close the plant was made. These include any unfunded vested pension costs.[35]

Matching. Expenses are matched with activities of the period. This is often, but not always, the same as matching expenses with revenues. Some descriptions of the matching process associate it strictly with revenues. Such an association is unrealistic when applied to general and administrative expenses because these are only remotely, if at all, associated with revenues of the current period. Expensed research/development costs are not matched with revenues. Many expenses in nonbusiness organizations are not related to revenues as such. Tying the matching idea to the period eliminates all these apparent inconsistencies.

Contingency Reserves. Creation of a reserve for possible, but unidentified, contingencies is not consistent with the concepts. However, recognition of a class of losses that are statistically measurable, though not individually identifiable, is consistent with the concepts because on a statistical basis an identifiable amount of such losses has occurred during the period. Such losses are insurable, and the credit to the reserve is not conceptually different from insurance payments for the same class of losses.

Preoperating costs. Preoperating costs are not expenses of the period in which they are incurred, provided that they are highly likely to generate income in succeeding periods at least equal to their amount.[36]

GAINS AND LOSSES

Nonmonetary. Nonmonetary gains are recognized only if they are realized. Nonmonetary losses are recognized whether realized or not.

Debt restructuring. The treatment of the loss or gain on troubled debt restructuring required in FASB Statement No. 15 is consistent with this framework.[37] Debt is monetary liability. Therefore a gain or loss from restructuring debt is recognized in the period in which it occurs.

Purchasing power gain or loss. Recognition of the purchasing power gain or loss on net monetary assets is not consistent with this framework. As stated in Concept 3.02, accounting reports in units of money, not units of purchasing power.[38]

Market value of debt. Changes in the market value of a company's own debt should be disregarded. The debt is carried at the present value of the obligation, and this is in no way affected by changes in the market value of a company's bonds.[39]

Transactions on futures. Transactions involving commodity futures, forward contracts, puts and calls on securities, and foreign exchange are essentially monetary and should be recognized in accordance with this concept.[40]

Losses on plant. An uninsured loss on plant from fire or other reasons is a loss. A decline in the market value of plant is not a loss. Accounting does not attempt to measure changes in the market value of assets that are held for use, as contrasted with assets (such as inventory) that are held for eventual sale.

Sales commitments. If there is a reasonable possibility that performing a firm sales contract will result in a loss to the seller (as is the case when the price of material included in the contract has risen substantially), the loss should be recognized in the period in which it is discovered. The buyer, however, should not recognize a gain, because no gain has been realized.

7

Assets and sources of funds

This framework describes the items on the two sides of the balance sheet somewhat differently from the definitions in FASB concepts statements and the descriptions in most texts. Except for the new concepts on shareholder equity and entity equity, however, the description here is consistent with what the amounts reported on current balance sheets actually represent. Items on the right-hand side summarize the sources of an entity's funds, and items on the left-hand side summarize the things in which these funds were invested as of the date of the balance sheet. This chapter defines the main categories of these items and describes concepts for their recognition and measurement. The appendix describes some of the implications of these concepts for accounting standards.

BALANCE SHEET

Ambiguous terms

Capital. As explained in Chapter 2, the word *capital* is used with any of four meanings in accounting. It is used (1) for all the items on the left-hand side of the balance sheet, (2) for some items on theleft-hand side (e.g., "capital assets"), (3) for all the items on the right-hand side (e.g. "capital structure"), and (4) for some items on the right-hand side (e.g., as synonymous with shareholder equity). These different uses cause confusion.[1] In this framework I use *capital* only in the first sense, which corresponds closely to its meaning in economics; that is, an entity's capital is its wealth. In order to indicate that accounting does not report all items that qualify as capital in the economists' definition (e.g., human capital, social capital), I use *assets* for those items of capital that are reported in financial statements.

Equity.   The word *equity* is used with three different meanings in accounting. It is used (1) in the sense of fairness, (2) as a name for all the items on the right-hand side of the balance sheet ("equities"), and (3) as a name for one category of these items ("equity capital").[2] To reduce the confusion, I have used *fair*, rather than *equitable* in discussing cost allocations in Chapter 5. I do not use *equity* in the sense of all right-hand balance sheet items. As used here, *equity* refers to certain items on, but not the complete, right-hand side.

Balance sheet concept

Resolving these conflicts in the definitions leaves unambiguous meanings of *capital* and of *equity* that are useful in describing balance sheet items. The left-hand side reports an entity's assets, which are those items of its capital that are recognized in accounting. Asset items show the nature of the various types of capital and the amounts invested in each type. The right-hand side shows the sources of the funds used to acquire this capital. One of these sources is the shareholders, and the amount of capital supplied by this source is called *shareholder equity*. Although this term may give the erroneous impression that equity is the shareholders' claim on or interest in the assets, the term is so commonly used that it seems unwise to discard it. Its use in terms such as *debt/equity ratio* continues to be valid.

Capital providers did not directly provide most of the assets reported on the left-hand side. Rather, they provided the funds that the entity then used to acquire the assets. Thus, the right-hand side is best described as reporting the sources of funds. Exhibit 7–1 is a schematic diagram of the balance sheet that follows from this approach. The definition is as follows:

> **Concept 7.01.**   *A balance sheet reports the amount of funds supplied to the entity from various sources and the forms in which its capital existed as of the balance sheet date.*

Trust funds excluded.   The definition refers to funds supplied to the entity. Funds for which the entity acts as trustee, custodian, agent, or in a

Exhibit 7–1

ANY CORPORATION
Schematic Balance Sheet
as of December 31, 19x1
(as proposed)

Assets	*Sources of funds*
Items on this side report the forms in which the entity's capital exists and the amount invested in each form as of December 31, 19x1.	Items on this side report the sources of the entity's funds and the amount obtained from each source as of December 31, 19x1.

Assets consist of:

1. *Monetary assets.* These are money or claims to specified amounts of money. The amounts are the present value of these claims.

2. *Unexpired costs.* These are nonmonetary assets to be used in future periods. The amounts are that part of their cost that has not yet been charged as expenses.

3. *Investments.* These are investments in other entities. The amounts are the amounts originally invested plus amounts due from the other entities.

Fund sources consist of:

1. *Liabilities.* Funds supplied by external parties other than equity investors. These parties include, among others:

   Lenders (consisting of amounts supplied directly plus unpaid debt interest).

   Vendors.

   Employees (accrued wages and unfunded benefits).

   Government (deferred income taxes).

2. *Shareholder equity.* Funds supplied by equity investors, consisting of amounts supplied directly plus unpaid equity interest.

3. *Entity equity.* Funds obtained by the entity's own efforts. The cumulative difference, through December 31, 19x1, between revenues (including gains) and expenses (including losses).

Note: For display, assets and liabilities may be classified as either current or noncurrent.

---

similar fiduciary capacity are not funds of the entity and should not be reported on its financial statements. For convenience the balance sheet may include certain such funds, such as withholding taxes collected from employees. It may not be worth the bookkeeping cost to set up separate accounting entities for these funds.

Assets

> ***Concepts 7.02.*** *Assets are the forms in which an entity's capital exists. Assets consist of monetary items, unexpired costs, and investments. The amounts reported are the amount of capital tied up in each form.*

Capital means "wealth" or "resources," and assets are those items of capital that are recognized in accounting.[3] Three types of assets are listed: monetary assets, unexpired costs, and investments. Each type represents a form in which an entity's capital exists. They are listed separately because, as will be explained in a later section, the amounts of each type are measured in different ways.

With rare exceptions (such as discoveries described in Chapter 6), assets arise as a result of events that involve an external party. Although an entity's goodwill is real, whatever its source, goodwill is an accounting asset only if it is measured by a purchase. Changes in the form of assets, such as those that occur in the production process, are recognized, but these internal changes do not affect the total amount of assets.

Measured property. In discussing Premise 2, I described two essential characteristics of any valid measurement system: (1) the system should make it possible to array objects according to the property measured and (2) the amounts of separate items should be additive. A 10-pound package weighs more than an 8-pound package, and the combined weight of the two packages is approximately 18 pounds. I say "approximately," because measurements are never exact; the closeness with which they approximate reality depends on the accuracy of the measuring device.

The property of "assets" stated in Concept 7.02—forms in which an entity's capital exists—meets both these measurement criteria. An asset reported at the amount of $10,000 had more of the entity's funds committed to it than an asset reported at the amount of $8,000; if these were the only two assets, the total assets of the entity were approximately $18,000.

I know of no other approach to asset measurement that meets these two criteria. Certainly, the "future-benefits" approach of the FASB does not. Monetary assets do represent future benefits. However, except at the moment of acquisition, accounting does not, and cannot, measure the amount of future benefits associated with nonmonetary items. Although each item listed has *some* future benefit, for most of them the amount of these benefits cannot be measured (Premise 8).

For inventory items, the amount of probable future benefits is *at least* as much as the amount stated, but accounting could measure how much the benefits are only if the ultimate amount to be realized could be approximated, and this is not ordinarily possible. For plant assets, the measurement of future benefits is out of the question. Thus, if accounting reports Machine A as having a book value of $10,000 and Machine B has having a book value of $8,000, there should be no implication that Machine A has more future benefits than Machine B, nor that the total future benefits of the two machines is $18,000.

Moreover, the future benefits from all assets collectively are not the sum of the amounts for individual assets, even if these amounts did represent future benefits. Future benefits to the entity are the results of its entire activities, which is not the sum of individual assets (except in entities such as mutual funds whose assets are primarily monetary). For the same reasons, a system of asset measurement based on "value," in any sense that I can think of, is not possible.

The FASB staff might react to the above comment by stating that defining assets as "probable future benefits" does not necessarily mean that this is the property of assets that accounting tries to measure. I do not understand this line of reasoning. Presumably, the definitions of accounting elements should suggest the properties that accounting measures. One can define a human being in any of a number of ways, but if one is describing a measurement system for humans, the description should include the property—weight, age, height, and so on—that the system is supposed to measure.

Put another way, the idea of assets as "forms in which capital existed" meets the criterion of being "representationally faithful", as described in FASB Concepts Statement No. 2 on Elements, because the amounts represent what they purport to represent. A concept of assets as future benefits or values cannot be representationally faithful because these properties cannot be measured.

Sources of funds

Two of the three types of sources of funds were defined in Chapter 4. *Shareholder equity* is the amount of funds supplied by shareholders and consists of their direct contributions plus any interest that has not yet been distributed to them. *Entity equity* is the amount of capital that the entity has obtained from sources other than liabilities and shareholders, principally as the result of its operating activities. There remains the definition of liabilities. Recall from Chapter 4 that entity equity is an internal source of funds and that liabilities and shareholder equity are external sources, that is, funds from these sources come from parties outside the entity. Liabilities, therefore, are all external sources of funds other than from the entity's shareholders. This discussion leads to the following definitions:[4]

> **Concept 7.03.** *Liabilities report the amounts of funds supplied by those external parties who do not receive equity rights in return.*

This definition corresponds more closely to reality than one that refers to "obligations" or "claims." Some liabilities represent claims, but others, such as deferred income taxes, do not. All liabilities, however, represent a source of funds. In the case of lenders, the source is direct and obvious. Others who furnish funds are vendors who are willing to wait for payment; employees who are not paid immediately the amount they have earned, including the present value of future pension benefits; and the government to the extent it is willing to defer the payment of taxes. Even the liability for warranty payments is a source of funds; it represents the amount provided by customers (probably unknowingly) until the warranty costs are incurred.

Moreover, there is not an exact correspondence, in all cases, between the amount of a liability reported on the balance sheet and the amount claimed by the party who supplied the funds. The exact nature of each party's rights and claims is spelled out in underlying documents, such as loan agreements, or in law, such as the priority of the claims of wages payable. The rights may change, depending on the circumstances. For example, in a going concern, a bondholder may have only the right to periodic interest payments, whereas if certain covenants are violated, the bondholder may have the right to the full amount of the bond. The specific rights should be summarized in notes to the financial statements.

RECOGNITION CONCEPTS

Most of the concepts relevant to the recognition and measurement of assets and sources of funds were described in earlier chapters. One source of funds is income, and as stated in Concept 3.03, the measurement of income is of primary importance in accounting. A journal entry that includes a debit or credit to an income account has an equal credit or debit to some other account, and in most cases this is an asset or liability account. Thus, concepts for the recognition and measurement of income automatically resolve most of the issues relating to the recognition and measurement of amounts of assets and liabilities.

These relationships hold because of the articulation concept (Concept 3.08).[5] In Chapter 6, revenue was defined, and concepts for measuring revenue were stated. These concepts establish the credit portion of entries involving revenue. If the debit portion of the entry is to an asset account, which ordinarily is the case, there is no need to think about the period in which the amount is recognized; it is recognized in the same period as the credit amount. Similarly, concepts for the measurement of expenses establish the debit portion of an entry, and the corresponding credit to an asset or liability account is given automatically. Concepts in Chapter 5 similarly guide the recognition and measurement of expenditures and the related asset amounts.

There remain three issues relating to assets and sources of funds: (1) unperformed contracts, (2) changes in entity equity caused by nonoperating events, and (3) other changes in assets and sources of funds.

Unperformed contracts

Contracts between the entity and an outside party involve rights and obligations. Concept 6.04 states that revenue is recognized for products only when the entity has performed; therefore, if there has been no performance, revenue is not recognized. There can be a loss, and hence an expense, under an unperformed contract, however. If, for example, the seller agreed to deliver goods at a specified price, and the cost of these goods increases substantially above the cost that was estimated before the time this increase occurred, the seller has incurred a loss in the priod in which this increase becomes known. A striking example of this situation was the Westinghouse Electric Corporation contract to deliver uranium over a period of 20 years to 27 utility companies at a price averaging $9.50 per pound. By 1976, the world market price of uranium had risen to $40 per pound.[6]

Two accounting treatments for this problem are possible: (1) the contract could be unrecognized at the time it was signed and the loss could be recognized as an expense when its occurrence became reasonably possible (Concept 6.10). Or (2) the contract could be recorded as an asset and an offsetting liability at the time it was signed and the loss recorded as a write-down of the asset when the reasonable possibility of loss was discovered (Concept 6.09). Either treatment leads to the correct measurement of income. In the former, however, the primary financial statements would not reveal the possible liability that results from entering into such a contract (although disclosure of such contracts could be required in the notes).

Finding an operational way of implementing the latter approach is difficult. Yuji Ijiri suggests the possibility of recognizing only a "firm commitment" which he defines as a commitment for which "it is unlikely that its performance can be avoided without a severe penalty."[7] Many sales contracts, purchase contracts, and employment contracts fit this definition, however, and in the great majority of cases, these contracts are completed routinely. The principal problems arise in take-or-pay contracts that cover a long future period, and in most circumstances even these contracts do not result in a loss whose possible occurrence can be identified in advance of performance. Recording the usual type of contracts in the accounts would serve no useful purpose and would require additional bookkeeping, which may be inconsistent with the benefit/cost appraisal required in Concept 3.15. The following concept therefore seems appropriate:[8]

> **Concept 7.04.** *Contracts, the two sides of which are proportionately unperformed, should not be recognized.*

Nonoperating contributions

In addition to revenues from the sale of goods and services, an entity may have resource inflows from gifts, contracts, contributions, appropriations, and similar sources. If these inflows are associated with operations of the period, they are revenues. If not, they should be reported as direct additions to entity equity, collectively called nonoperating contributions.

Contributions used to finance activities of the current period clearly add to the income of that period. If a contribution is designated for a specified operating purpose, it is income in the period in which costs are incurred for that purpose. If these costs are incurred in a subsequent period, receipt of the contribution creates a liability to incur these costs, and there is no revenue in the current period. These operating contributions were discussed in Chapter 6.

Nonoperating contributions are different. In nonbusiness organizations, the principal types are contributions to an endowment fund in which only the earnings can be used for operating purposes, and contributions for capital assets (e.g., buildings, equipment, museum collections). Nonoperating contributions also are made to profit-oriented entities; for example, a municipality may contribute land improvements as an inducement to a business to locate a plant. Although these nonoperating contributions increase an entity's equity, the report of the entity's financial performance would be misleading if they were included in the measurement of income of the period in which they are received.

If in a certain accounting period a college has revenues of $19 million and expenses of $20 million, it has not maintained its equity—it has not broken even. If during the period, it received a $2 million contribution to its endowment, and if this $2 million were counted as revenue, the income statement would indicate that the college had generated income of $1 million. The more realistic view is that the college has incurred a loss of $1 million, the difference between the $19 million of revenues and the $20 million of expenses. If the college's operating activities continue at these levels of revenues and expenses, it is heading for trouble. For this reason, nonoperating contributions should be excluded from the measurement of income in the period in which they were received.

The distinction between operating and nonoperating contributions is not always clear. For example, a donor's will may include a bequest to a charitable organization, without specifying what use is to be made of it. In this case a judgment must be made as to whether the contribution is for operating or nonoperating purposes. If the amount is sizable in relation to normal operating contributions, the problem of judging the donor's intent is difficult and is likely to provoke discussion beyond the accountant's authority to resolve. (Recall that Concept 3.02 states that substance takes precedence over legal form.) The distinction between operating and nonoperating contributions can, to some extent, be spelled out in a standard, but judgment will be required in resolving questions such as the above. The governing criterion is the donor's intent.[9]

The following is therefore the concept for the recognition of nonoperating contributions:

> **Concept 7.05.** *Contributions intended for nonoperating purposes should be credited to entity equity.*

Conversion of contributed equity to expense. If a nonoperating contribution consists of a building or other depreciable asset, or if it consists of money used to acquire such an asset, a problem arises in deciding how, if at all, depreciation of this asset should enter into the measurement of the entity's income. Some people argue that there is no expense associated with such an asset because its acquisition did not require the use of the entity's resources; that is, the entity's cost was zero. Consequently, the entity has operated so as to maintain its equity if its revenues are sufficient to meet its expenses, not counting this depreciation. To include depreciation as an expense would indicate that operations generated less income than in fact was the case, it is said.

On the other hand, if depreciation is omitted, the costs of carrying out the entity's programs are understated. This reduces the comparability of one entity's program costs with those of another entity that acquired similar assets with its own resources and thus is contrary to Premise 21, which states that users need comparable information

A way out of this dilemma is to record depreciation as an expense and to record an equal amount as revenue. If this is done, there is no net effect on income, and the cost of using these assets is reported. The initial reaction to this proposal is usually that it involves additional recordkeeping that is not worth the effort. Actually, the entry to record the revenue offset to depreciation requires little effort. Basically, I think the opposition stems from Premise 22, the natural reluctance to accept changes in accounting standards. In any event, I do not state this idea as a concept; it is best stated at the level of standards.

If depreciation is recorded as an expense with an offsetting credit to revenue, there is an equal impact on the amount of contributed equity and on the asset amount. Both the amount of contributed equity and the book value of the asset will decrease.[10] If no depreciation is charged, the contributed capital and the related asset remain at the amount of the original contribution. The concept for the recognition of contributed equity allows for this possibility.

Other changes in entity equity

Net income measures the net financial effect of operating activities during an accounting period, and, as emphasized in Chapter 6, "operating" should be construed broadly so as to incorporate almost all events that happened in, or were discovered in, the period. Nevertheless, present practice requires that the effect of a few unusual events be recorded as a direct charge or credit to entity equity, and with good reason.

Prior period adjustments. Since income reflects the events of an accounting period, events that happened in prior periods should be excluded. An example is an accounting error that occurred in the prior period. (However, accounting errors usually are immaterial and are therefore included in income in order to avoid the separate reporting that otherwise would be necessary.) No concept is necessary to deal with this situation. The change in entity equity merely reflects the fact that the amount is now known to be different from the amount previously reported.

However, the concept should not be used as justification for charging entity equity with costs that actually should be reported on some income statement. For this reason, the narrow definition of prior period adjustments in FASB Statement No. 16, *Prior Period Adjustments*, is appropriate.

Prior service costs of pension plans. When a defined benefit pension plan is amended to increase its benefits, the act of amending the plan creates an additional expenditure beyond that previously recognized. The entity is required to pay larger future benefits than those that were required before this amendment was made. The present value of the increased benefits can be calculated, and the calculation is as accurate as the calculation of the amount of expenditure before the decision to sweeten the plan occurred. The offsetting credit for this expenditure is a liability.

APB Opinion No. 8, *Accounting for the Cost of Pension Plans*, does not recognize this additional liability in the period in which it became known. Instead, it requires that the amount be disclosed in a note and that the additional amount be charged as an expense in future years, not less than 10 years nor more than 40. This treatment is conceptually unsound, and as of 1983, the FASB was reexamining what should be done to change the requirement in APB Opinion No. 8.

Mechanically, the debit offsetting the credit to the liability account could be an asset, an expense, or a charge to entity equity. The amount is not an asset because it is not an unexpired cost; the work to which the additional expenditure is related was performed in the past. The argument for recording the amount as an expense is that it reflects an event that occurred in the current period, namely the amendment to the pension plan. An argument for charging the amount to entity equity is that equity has been reduced by this event, that the reduction will be made up by increased revenues over future periods, and that the matching concept requires that expenses be recorded in the same period as the associated revenues. Since selling prices tend to be based on full cost (Premise 5), and since selling prices in the current and earlier periods did not reflect the increase, the argument has some validity.[11]

An even stronger argument for charging entity equity stems from Concepts 5.03 and 5.05 regarding expenditures. The cost of an hour of labor includes all the expenditures involved in obtaining that hour of labor. When a pension plan is amended to provide additional benefits, the cost originally estimated turns out to have been understated. If at the time the hour was worked, the fact that the plan subsequently would be changed were known, the expenditure for that hour would have incorporated the increased amount, just as it incorporates estimates of future investment earnings, salary increases, mortality, terminations, and other factors.

Discovery in a subsequent year of this understatement means that the amount of expenditure initially recorded was incorrect. Literally, correction of this error is a prior period adjustment in the year of discovery. However, if this adjustment were recorded as an expense, even an extraordinary expense, the income in the year of discovery may be seriously distorted. Therefore, a good case can be made for relaxing the requirement of Statement No. 16 and permitting the amount to be charged initially to entity equity.

If this is done, entity equity would be charged and the pension liability would be credited for the full amount of the increment in the year the plan was amended. In succeeding years a portion of the prior service benefit would be reversed and charged against income (a credit to entity equity and a debit to pension cost). The effect on income would therefore be the same as the APB Opinion No. 8 treatment; the difference is that the full amount of the liability would appear on the balance sheet. The number of years over which this charge would be made is entirely arbitrary; in order to provide comparability, it should be stated in a standard.

Other events that affect entity equity.   The conceptual basis for charging or crediting entity equity for certain other events is debatable. Examples from current practice are a gain on certain sales of marketable securities, the recognition of income tax benefits from the carry-forward of operating loss under certain circumstances, and the gain or loss on foreign exchange translation.

In part, resolution of these questions reflects a political compromise. Some people argue that including these items in the measurement of income would distort income, and others argue that failure to recognize them at all would be inappropriate. The compromise is to recognize them, but in a way that does not affect income in the current period. Realistically, the necessity for such compromises must be admitted, and the following concept takes this possibility into account:

> *Concept 7.06.   A direct entry to entity equity should be made only if it corrects an error in the amount of entity equity at the beginning of the period, or if the effect of including the amount in net income would be to distort seriously the measurement of net income.*

OTHER BALANCE SHEET EVENTS

The preceding concepts cover many of the events relating to assets and sources of funds. They do not, however, address events such as borrowing and repaying loans, receiving and paying for inventory, receiving cash from credit customers, issuing debt and equity securites, and the like. Most of these events are routine, and their treatment is noncontroversial. As a part of the framework, a concept is necessary to guide the recognition of these other events:

> *Concept 7.07. Events involving increases in assets whose recognition is not guided by other concepts should be reported in the period in which the entity acquires the right to use the resources. Events involving increases in liabilities whose recognition is not guided by other concepts should be reported in the period in which the entity becomes obligated to pay another party.*

In accordance with this concept, dividends are recorded in the period in which they are declared, whether or not they are paid in that period; and contributions are recorded when the entity has the right to use them, even if not received in cash in that period.

MEASUREMENT CONCEPTS

Most issues relating to the amount of assets or sources of funds to be recognized are settled by concepts already discussed. Concepts governing the amounts recognized for revenues and expenses are given in Chapter 6, and the offsetting part of these entries record the same amount in asset and sources-of-funds accounts. The amount recorded as the acquisition cost of productive assets is governed by concepts in Chapter 5. The measurement of entity equity is governed by the concepts for income measurement and the concepts for the recognition of other changes in entity equity (Concepts 7.05, 7.06, and 7.07). Concepts for the measurement of unexpired costs have been stated in Chapters 5 and 6. Note that no single concept applies to the measurement of the whole class of assets.

These concepts, however, do not address all the issues that arise with respect to (1) monetary assets (2) investments, (3) liabilities, and (4) shareholder equity.

Monetary assets

The measurement of monetary assets differs from the measurement of unexpired costs and from the measurement of investments. The concept is consistent with present practice and with Premise 8:

> *Concept 7.08. Monetary assets are money and claims to specified amounts of money. They should be reported at the present value of the amounts highly likely to be received.*

Investments

Since capital existing in the form of debt securities involves a promise to receive money, this capital is a monetary asset. As used here, therefore, the term *investments* is limited to equity investments because these do not involve a promise to pay money. There are two types of such investments: (1) securities held to produce income and (2) equity investments in other entities made in order to have an influence on these entities. (The distinction between these two types is not always clear, but this fact does not affect the analysis made here.) Changes in the market value of securities held to produce income are governed by the concepts on the recognition of nonmonetary gains and losses (Concepts 6.06 and 6.10). Thus, a concept is needed only for other types of investments.

Since my framework recognizes equity interest as a cost, one possibility would be to report the amount of an equity investment at the amount originally invested plus any unpaid equity interest. However, unpaid equity interest has not been realized, and its recognition would be inconsistent with the concepts that require realization as a condition of revenue recognition. The alternative is the conservative one of recording the investment at the amount originally invested plus dividends declared but not received. The same principle applies to other unpaid obligations of the investee, such as royalties.

> *Concept 7.09.* *Investments are interests in other entities. Investments that do not involve a promise to pay money should be reported at the amount originally invested plus amounts due from the other entity.*

Liabilities

Measurement of the amount of many liabilities is governed by concepts for expenditures and expenses. For the remainder, the following concept applies:

> *Concept 7.10.* *Liabilities whose amount is not governed by other concepts should be reported at the present value of the entity's obligation to those who supplied the funds.*

The discount rate. If obligations come due at some considerably distant future time, their present value is determined by application of a discount rate. The relevant rate is the rate on obligations of similar risk as of the date that the obligation was incurred. This was the rate that was at least implicit in management's decision to assume the obligation, and in many cases it was an explicit rate. Subsequent changes in interest rates do not change the amount of the obligation incurred.

If bonds were issued at par in a market transaction, the stated interest rate is the rate on obligations of similar risk; the rate was validated by the marketplace. If issued at a premium or a discount in a market transaction, the real interest rate is similarly established. A problem arises when debt is contracted in a nonmarket transaction (e.g., purchase of an asset in exchange for a note) at a stated interest rate that differs from the rate prevailing at that time. In such a transaction, the stated rate may be unrealistically low, or zero. In this case, the amount of the obligation should be found by using an implicit rate of interest, and this rate corresponds to the prevailing rates for obligations of similar risk. This is current practice. The following concept addresses these points:

> **Concept 7.11.** In measuring the amount to be reported for a liability, the future amount of the obligation should ordinarily be discounted at the interest rate implicit in the amount of funds received. If this rate is not apparent from the transaction itself, the discount rate should be the interest rate on obligations of similar risk prevailing at the time the obligation was entered to.

Shareholder equity

The amount reported as shareholder equity is a straightforward consequence of concepts already stated:

> **Concept 7.12.** The amount reported for shareholder equity should be the fair value of the funds originally supplied by equity investors, calculated at the time the funds were committed, plus equity interest, less dividends or other distributions to shareholders.

Endowment earnings

Although a contribution to an entity's endowment does not affect income in the current period, earnings on that endowment are an element of revenue in succeeding periods. Discussion of earnings measurement was deferred to this chapter because an understanding of the nature of nonoperating contributions is needed as a background. There is disagreement as to how the amount of endowment revenue should be measured. The predominant practice is to measure endowment revenue at the sum of rents, royalties, interest income on fixed income investments, and dividends on equity investments. Realized gains in the market value of equity investments are added to the corpus of the endowment; they are not revenues.

Some entities, however, use the *spending rate* approach (also called the *total return* approach). They measure endowment revenue—the amount available for spending in the current period—as a stated percentage of the average market value of the endowment portfolio. The percentage is low, usually about 5 percent. The difference between the amount calculated at the spending rate and the actual amount of dividends, interest, and other inflows remains in the corpus and tends to keep the purchasing power of the corpus intact. The spending rate approach is based on the premise that the earnings on equity investments include the growth in market value, as well as dividends.[12]

The conditions under which each of these approaches is appropriate is not a conceptual matter and should be set forth in a standard.

Appendix

SOME IMPLICATIONS OF ASSETS AND FUNDS SOURCES CONCEPTS

Assets

Value implications. The amounts for monetary assets are essentially the fair value of these items. The amounts for other types of assets do not represent the values of these items. The total of assets does not represent the values of these items. The total of assets does not represent the total amount of an entity's wealth.

Capital leases. Capital leases are assets. A noncancellable long-term lease provides capital to the lessee. The corresponding source of this capital is a liability. This is in accordance with the basic concept that accounting recognizes substance over form (Concept 3.02). Difficult problems arise in drawing the line between capital leases and operating leases and in handling related events such as sale-leaseback transactions. Resolution of these problems is a matter for standards; no conceptual issue is involved.[13]

Human resource accounting. The asset concept does not permit the recognition of human resources as assets, except to the limited extent that expenditures for recruiting or training can be said to benefit future periods. No external party has provided the capital that constitutes human resources. This is unfortunate because human resource accounting may well be the next important development in accounting. The practical application awaits some reliable way of measuring the asset amounts. Amounts spent for recruiting or for training programs do not provide the answer because these amounts are only tenuously related to the actual asset amounts for the persons involved.

190

Monetary and nonmonetary assets.   The distinction between the recognition and measurement of monetary and nonmonetary assets can be used to develop standards that are different for one category than for the other. The distinction between monetary and nonmonetary assets could also lead to different balance sheet classifications. It could for example, lead to a classification of current monetary assets (quick assets), rather than current assets. The topic is discussed in Chapter 8.

Unusual assets.   Some issues are difficult to resolve. For example, Gellein has described an unusual situation about streetcar tracks. An investor-owned transit company possessed streetcar tracks that were completely paved over when the company shifted from trolley cars to busses. At that time the tracks had a substantial book value, but they had no future value as tracks. Nevertheless, a regulatory commission promised that the transit company could recover the book value of the streetcar tracks in its rate structure, and because of this promise, the company's rates, and hence its revenues, are higher than they otherwise would be. The tracks provided a future benefit because without them future revenues would be lower. The tracks were therefore an asset; they benefit the future and are unexpired costs. By its promise, the regulatory agency has provided capital to the transit company.[14]

Sources of funds

Warranties.   The liability for warranty repairs or replacement arises when the sale is made and is so recorded in present practice. However, in present practice the amount is the estimated dollar cost of the future repairs or replacements. The amount should be the present value of these future disbursements.

Income and shareholders' contributions.   The concepts clarify the distinction between income and shareholders' contributions. Transactions with shareholders do not affect entity equity; they affect shareholder equity. Dividends, including preferred dividends and stock dividends, do not affect income. Stock options that are compensation do affect income. The conversion of convertible bonds to stock does not affect income at the moment of conversion, although it may affect the measurement of income thereafter because the event may give rise to a change in the amount of liabilities and shareholder equity on which interest is charged.

Nonbusiness organizations.   In present practice, a description of accounting for nonbusiness organizations is awkward because these organizations have no owners' equity. All organizations have entity equity, as defined here. Nonbusiness organizations simply disregard the concepts relating to shareholder equity because they are irrelevant in these organizations.

Convertible debt. The classification of convertible debt is debatable. Some people argue that convertible debt is a liability because the investor does not have equity rights until conversion takes place, but others reason that the conversion feature is in itself a right to equity at any time that the holder chooses to exercise it. Still others view convertible debt as having characteristics of both a liability and a shareholder equity. Standards are required to resolve this issue, and they should state the characteristics of convertible debt issues that determine how a given issue should be classified. The important point is, however, that whichever way they are classified, there is no effect on income.

Treasury stock. The idea that shareholder equity reports the amount of capital supplied by equity investors clarifies the treatment of treasury stock. When an entity obtains stock by paying its owner, the amount of shareholder equity has decreased. If the stock is reissued, the amount of shareholder equity increases by the amount received or by the fair value of services rendered, if the stock is reissued for services. Under no circumstances is treasury stock an asset. Although the amount should be disclosed separately in the shareholder equity section of the balance sheet, disclosure does not affect the net amount of the entity's sources of funds.

Redeemable preferred stock. If cash is received in exchange for redeemable preferred stock, the amount of additional capital is clearly the amount of cash. If, however, redeemable preferred stock is issued in exchange for an asset whose fair value is difficult to measure, a problem arises. Is the amount of additional capital the par value of the stock, its redemption value, or somewhere in between? The SEC (in Accounting Series Release 268) requires that redeemable preferred stock be carried at its redemption value.[15] Preferred stock is often issued as part of the price of an acquisition, and the seller may value it at the redemption value, although the par value may be set lower for estate for income tax reasons. In these circumstances, the SEC position is correct. In other circumstances, the redemption value may have little real significance.

Common stock. If stock is issued in exchange for cash, the amount of additional capital provided is the net amount of cash received (after issuance costs). If a corporation's stock has a reliable market price and if it issues stock in exchange for noncash assets, the amount of additional capital represented by these assets is measured by the market price of the stock (with an allowance for dilution in some circumstances). The seller of the noncash assets could sell the stock at this price; alternatively, the corporation could buy the stock at the market price and transfer it to the seller.

A problem arises when there is no reliable way of determining either the fair value of the stock or the fair value of the assets acquired. This happens when a company whose stock is thinly traded acquires another company in exchange for stock. The measurement concept is still applicable: the amount of new capital should be measured at its fair value. A standard is required for measuring this amount in various circumstances. This standard would state that in the absence of any better criterion, the stock should be measured at its book value.

Stock subscriptions.   To the extent that amounts of stock subscriptions are enforceable, they are receivables, equal in amount to the additional shareholder equity.

Income taxes.   This framework gives some guidance in resolving accounting issues relating to the investment tax credit and deferred taxes, but it by no means suggests all the answers.[16] As used in this framework, "matching" (Concept 6.02) is not a relevant consideration. The matching concept states that expenses for a transaction should be reported in the same period as the revenues for the same transaction, and no revenues are involved in income taxes. Thus, matching should not be used as an argument in accounting for income taxes. The framework also states that liabilities should be recorded at the present value of the obligation (Concept 7.10). For deferred taxes, this would mean the present value of the additional future amount to be paid to the government; for many depreciable assets, the expected future payment is small and its present value even smaller.

The framework does not, however, suggest whether the flow-through method for the investment tax credit is preferable to the deferral method. Neither does it suggest whether the liability approach is preferable to the net-of-tax approach for timing differences.

Financial statements

This chapter deals primarily with how the information in financial statements should be displayed. It suggests no basic change in the number or general content of financial statements.

The discussion provides an opportunity to summarize the import of the concepts this book describes, particularly concerning the information that users should and should not expect to obtain from the statements.

A set of financial statements for an accounting period consists of (1) an operating statement, (2) a balance sheet (actually, one balance sheet at the beginning of the period and another at the end), (3) a funds flow statement, and (4) if necessary, one or more statements of changes in equity.

Terminology

As a relatively minor matter, and not a necessary part of a conceptual framework, there are real advantages in requiring the use of standard terms in financial statements. Currently, entities use several dozen titles for the financial statements that report the results of operations.[1] Users of the information might justifiably infer that these differences reflect subtle differences in meaning, but this usually is not the case. A project to standardize terms was undertaken by the AICPA Committee on Terminology in the 1950s, but its bulletins were never made authoritative.

The terms should be both descriptive and short. The following is an example of an unnecessarily cumbersome title: "All Governmental Funds: Statements of Sources and Uses of Financial Resources and Changes in Fund Equity."[2]

OPERATING STATEMENT

The statement described in this section has the title, "Operating Statement." I think this is slightly more descriptive than "Income Statement." Although income is the central theme for profit-oriented organizations, income is not central to nonbusiness organizations. "Operating" applies to all organizations equally well and suggests the important distinction between operating and nonoperating events, described in Chapter 7.

Nature of the operating statement

Some people criticize the concept of an operating statement, maintaining either that it does not report what it is supposed to report or that what it reports is misleading or meaningless.[3] I do not think these criticisms are warranted.

The framework described here leads to an operating statement that reports the entity's success in maintaining or increasing its equity through operations. As is the case with most measurements, the statement does not do this perfectly, but it does provide a useful approximation. As stated in Premise 4, maintaining or increasing equity is a primary financial goal of profit-oriented entities, and the operating statement reports how well the entity performed with respect to this goal.

The primary goal of a nonbusiness organization is to provide services. If the monetary value of the services it provides cannot be measured, which is the case with many nonbusiness organizations, the operating statement cannot report how well the organization performed, and no informed user should expect it to do this. Nevertheless, the operating statement of a nonbusiness organization reports useful information, namely the entity's success in operating so as to maintain its equity. An organization that did not break even in an average year is in financial difficulty. The operating statement can also report how much the entity spent for various programs and thereby indicate the magnitude of its efforts on these programs; this is "service effort." The operating statement cannot report "service accomplishments," however, and the user must not expect it to do so.[4]

No one should expect a performance report for a complex activity to be completely accurate. The higher up an entity is on the hierarchy of systems described in Chapter 2, the less accurate any quantitative measure of performance becomes. In an individual sports competition, both the relative and absolute performance of participants can be measured accurately: who ran the fastest; who jumped the highest. In team competition, the score tells which team won, but experts can argue for a long time thereafter about which team actually played better.

Team competition is restricted in space (about an acre for football) and in time (each game ends at a discrete time, and each season ends after a specified number of games). The team's competitors are clearly identified. In contrast, a business entity may operate in global space, it competes continuously rather than within discrete time intervals, and its competitors are often not known. Reports of its performance are correspondingly less accurate than those for a team, and users of accounting statements should not expect them to be otherwise.

Significance of the bottom line

With the recognition of equity interest, the bottom line on an operating statement, labeled net income, indicates approximately whether financial performance has been satisfactory for both nonbusiness and business entities. In both cases, a bottom line of zero indicates satisfactory performance. For a nonbusiness entity, zero net income means that if the factors that resulted in this relationship hold in the future, the entity can continue to operate indefinitely. For a business entity, zero net income means that the entity has operated so as to recover all its expenses, including the cost of using funds supplied by equity investors, and if this relationship holds in the future, it also can continue to operate.

For a nonbusiness entity, no generalization about the significance of a positive amount of net income can be made. Positive net income may indicate that the entity generated an addition to its equity that will benefit future operations, which is good. Alternatively, it may mean that the entity did not provide as much service as it should have provided with available resources, which is bad.

For a business, a positive amount of net income is good since it indicates success toward its financial goal. This impression is qualified by limitations inherent in financial accounting. The operating statement tends to focus on the short run and to omit the effect of some important events that affect future performance. For example, it does not attempt to report the value of an important new product development.[5]

For both business and nonbusiness entities, a negative amount of net income indicates poor performance, subject to the qualification that in a given year the negative income may be deliberate—a start-up situation in a business or the use of equity built up in prior years in a nonbusiness organization. No entity can survive indefinitely if, on average, its revenues do not at least equal its expenses.

In any event, users want an operating statement, and they want a bottom line. As Robert Sprouse, vice chairman of the FASB, stated: "For the foreseeable future the Financial Accounting Standards Board's deliberations and pronouncements are likely to be primarily concerned with measuring earnings."[6] The function of the accountant is not to judge whether the users' focus on the bottom line is right or wrong. Rather, the accountant's task is to satisfy the users' needs.

Cash basis.   Some people go so far as to say that net income is a meaningless number because it is subject to manipulation. They argue that the amount of cash cannot be manipulated and that the difference between cash receipts and cash disbursements is therefore a more reliable measure of performance. The assertion that a cash-based report is reliable is just plain wrong. Some state and local governments do report on a cash basis. If they want to report a surplus for a period, they can simply postpone payment of outstanding invoices until the next period. If they think the surplus is going to be too high, they can reduce it by putting incoming checks for taxes or grants in a desk drawer until the beginning of the next period.[7] In any event, the evidence for Premise 16 shows that users want a report of net income measured on the accrual basis.

Operating statement concept

The basic concept for the operating statement is straightforward:[8]

> *Concept 8.01.*   *An operating statement should summarize the revenues and the expenses of an accounting period and the difference between them.*

Operating statement categories

Operating versus nonoperating.   Some people suggest that the operating statement should distinguish between events that are related to the entity's "ongoing major or central operations" and those that are related to "peripheral or incidental" transactions. In this context, "operating" is defined narrowly, and nonoperating activities would include, essentially, the effect of external events that are unrelated to the activities of the entity in seeking to accomplish its goals. Examples are the sale of buildings and equipment at more or less than book value; uninsured losses from fire, flood, or other natural occurrences; and a decline in the value of inventory.

Operating income, measured as the difference between revenues and expenses in this narrow sense, would be useful information. It would indicate the entity's performance in terms of its own efforts, separated from the influence of external, presumably uncontrollable events. Unfortunately, however, there does not seem to be any way of drawing a reasonably clear line between these two types of events. If an entity insured against fire, the cost would be an operating expense; if the entity were uninsured, a fire loss would be a nonoperating loss. If inventory were sold at less than its cost, there would be a decrease in operating income; if written down to market prior to sale, there would be a nonoperating loss. To regard these events as fundamentally different would lead to a wrong impression of operating income.

Holding gains.   A similar, but by no means identical, distinction is that between operating income and holding gains. Holding gains are those arising from holding nonmonetary assets and net monetary liabilities in periods of inflation. The conceptual framework of Edgar Edwards and Philip Bell and that of Robert Sprouse and Maurice Moonitz incorporate such a distinction.[9]

Although this distinction is widely discussed in the literature, it is not consistent with one of the basic premises underlying this framework. Implementation of this concept would require that reliable estimates of the fair value of nonmonetary assets be available, and Premise 9 states that such estimates are rarely available. Nevertheless, reporting holding gains as supplementary information, outside the basic financial statements, may be useful.

Extraordinary gains and losses.   Although there is no operational way either of separating operating gains and losses from nonoperating gains and losses or of separately identifying holding gains and losses, an operational distinction can be made if gains and losses are limited to extraordinary items. This is a useful distinction because the extraordinary items, although components of income, can give a misleading impression of financial performance during a period if they are not reported separately from other revenues and expenses.

Extraordinary items are those that are unusual, infrequent, and of substantial size. They are therefore exceptional items. It is often easier to specify the criteria for an exception to a general rule than it is to describe all the characteristics of the general case. For this reason, operational criteria for extraordinary items are easier to state than the alternative of defining "operating" in the sense of relating to the central operations of the entity. This is done satisfactorily in APB Opinion No. 30.[10]

Reporting net amounts.   APB Opinion No. 30 requires that the net effect of an extraordinary event, including its income tax consequences, be reported, and this is sensible. If a manufacturer of desks sells one of the desks in its product line for $500 and the inventory cost of that desk is $300, the $500 is reported as revenue, and the $300 is reported as expense. If the same manufacturer sells one of the desks in its office for $500 and the book value of that desk is $300, only the gain of $200 is reported. The former practice is useful in disclosing the entity's gross margin, whereas gross margin is meaningless with respect to sales of an entity's productive assets.

The following concept does no more than state current practice:

> **Concept 8.02.** *The net effect on entity equity of each principal type of extraordinary gains and losses should be reported separately and below other items on an operating statement.*

Information about programs

Although the operating statement of a nonbusiness organization cannot report what the entity accomplished, it can provide useful information about the magnitude of its various activities by summarizing the amounts spent on each major program. Also, if revenues are specifically identified with programs, reporting these revenues with the related expenses provides useful information. This leads to the following concept:

> **Concept 8.03.** *If the principal activities of an entity are to carry out identifiable programs, the operating statement should summarize the expenses and, if applicable, the revenues for each major program.*

Other categories

In its Exposure Draft, "Reporting Income, Cash Flows, and Financial Position of Business Enterprises" (November 16, 1981), the FASB proposed three additional bases for classifying components of income: (1) distinguishing "amounts affected in various ways by changes in economic conditions," (2) distinguishing among items the "measurement of which is subject to different levels of reliability," and (3) distinguishing among expenses that vary with volume, expenses that are discretionary, and expenses that are stable over time or that depend on other factors.[11] Examples of the first two categories are not given, and I do not understand how these distinctions are intended to be made or how they are to be incorporated in the operating statement.

It seems unlikely that an operational distinction can be drawn between variable, discretionary, and fixed costs. For one thing, discretionary costs can be either fixed or variable. For exampe, an entity may decide to permit research/development costs to be x percent of sales volume, which makes them "vary with volume," or it may limit research/development costs to a specified amount per year, which makes them fixed. The word *discretionary* is extremely difficult to define in an operational way. Except for non-cancellable contractual commitments, most cost elements are discretionary in some sense. Even the material and labor components of a product can be changed by changing the specifications of the product. Sunk costs can be changed by disposing of the assets that they represent.

A useful distinction between variable and fixed costs can be made within an entity by detailed rules adopted by that entity, but it seems unlikely that operational definitions can be formulated for entities generally. Even if definitions could be written, their application would greatly complicate the operating statement. This is because some components of a period's fixed costs are in inventory and are not reported on the current operating statement at all. The fixed component of cost of sales depends considerably on whether products were produced internally or purchased externally. In the latter case, the vendor's fixed costs become part of the buyer's variable costs.

Fixed costs are, at most, "more or less" fixed. The longer the time period involved, the fewer elements of cost are fixed. Taking one year as the relevant period, many elements of production and administrative costs are normally regarded as being fixed, but these costs are subject to change if conditions warrant. The number of administrative personnel may be increased or decreased. Plant and equipment may be disposed of or increased. Fixed costs may be incurred by making contracts for services for fixed quantities at fixed prices; conversely, fixed costs can be turned into variable costs by converting such contracts to reimbursement on a per-unit basis.

Curiously, the Exposure Draft did not mention gross margin as a useful component of an operating statement. For entities that produce and/or sell products, the difference between revenues and cost of sales is generally regarded as being an important piece of information. Some entities do not now report cost of sales.

The FASB sent this Exposure Draft back to the drawing board, and as of 1983 it remains there. It should be buried.

Value-added statement. In West Germany, companies are required to report the results of operations in a value-added format. From the sales revenue, there is subtracted the amount of purchased materials and services to give the amount of value added by the entity. Other costs and expenses are then deducted to arrive at net income. With such a format the gross margin is not disclosed, and this seems to be more useful information than the value added.[12]

BALANCE SHEET

The balance sheet (or statement of changes in financial position) was defined in Concept 7.01.[13] In the discussion of that concept, I described the left-hand and right-hand sides differently than the FASB description, but I believe my description reflects what the balance sheet represents, as currently prepared, and also what it should represent. The balance sheet is used for two principal purposes: (1) as part of the measurement of performance and (2) to provide information on the entity's liquidity or solvency.

Relation to performance measurement

Currently, a key measure of financial performance in profit-oriented entities is a ratio in which net income (or some component of income) is the numerator and fund sources (or some component thereof) is the denominator. The denominator may be either total fund sources (which is the same as total assets), total "permanent" fund sources (i.e., amount of funds obtained from debt and equity investors), or shareholder equity. In the framework suggested here, the nature of these ratios will change because of the inclusion of equtiy interest as a cost and of entity equity as a source of funds, but users presumably will continue to want some way of relating the income of a period to the funds used in generating that income.

Concepts discussed in chapter 4 lead to a separation of liabilities from shareholder equity. They do not, however, provide for a separation of permanent capital from circulating capital. The latter requires separate reporting of current and noncurrent liabilities.

Liquidity and solvency

Premise 17 states that users want information that helps them make judgments about an entity's liquidity or solvency. In making these judgments users study various components o the balance sheet.[14] In most cases, they are more interested in monetary assets than in unexpired costs (e.g., plant and various intangibles) or equity investments. For many purposes, they want a separation of current assets and current liabilities. Rarely are they interested in the total assets or the total sources of funds, except for financial institutions. Amounts of unexpired costs do not provide information about the entity's ability to meet its obligations, especially its current obligations (except that for some purposes inventory, which is an unexpired cost, is useful in judging liquidity).

Balance sheets for financial institutions—banks, insurance companies, mutual funds, trust funds—are meaningful when taken as a whole because most of the amounts are monetary. The assets are essentially values, and the liabilities are essentially the amounts of these values that are claimed by creditors. Information provided by these balance sheets may be as important as the information provided by the operating statements of these institutions.[15]

Balance sheet format

Rather than considering the balance sheet as a whole, users usually select various balance sheet items according to whatever analysis they are making. This selectivity is in contrast with the operating statement, in which users primarily focus on a single number, the bottom line, and only secondarily on the components.

Some of the desirable components of the balance sheet are identified in the concepts discussed in Chapters 4 and 7. Chapter 7 classifies asset categories as monetary, unexpired costs, and investments, and it listed three categories of sources of funds: liabilities, shareholder equity, and entity equity. These categories meet the informational needs suggested above, except that they do not provide for a separation between current and noncurrent items. Current items are important, especially for the analysis of liquidity. This requires an additional concept.

> **Concept 8.04.** *A balance sheet should identify* current assets and current liabilities *separately from* noncurrent assets and noncurrent liabilities.

Combined with the categories already identified, this concept leads to the following permutations of assets: current monetary assets, current nonmonetary assets (e.g., inventory), noncurrent nonmonetary assets (e.g., plant), monetary investments (e.g., debt instruments held for investment purposes), and nonmonetary investments (equity securities held in order to obtain an interest in another entity). These categories are conceptual, and the actual terms used could often be more descriptive. For example, *inventory* would usually be used rather than *nonmonetary current assets*.

The concept does not define the word *current*. The definition is properly stated as a standard, and the present standard seems satisfactory.[16]

Other categories

The FASB Exposure Draft states that the balance sheet should report information that is "useful in assessing liquidity and financial flexibility," and information "about the nature and amounts of assets and liabilities, the measurements of which differ in terms of relative reliability."[17] These criteria seem to lead to the classifications currently used, rather than suggesting new classifications. For example, an entity with relatively large cash equivalents is more flexible than one with relatively large inventories; plant is less reliably measured than monetary assets. Assuming that no new classifications are intended, I do not discuss these criteria.

Shareholder equity

In current practice the funds directly contributed by shareholders is divided into two items, the amount of stock outstanding, measured at its par or stated value, and "other paid-in capital," which is the additional amount contributed above the par or stated value. Since shareholders may be liable for making up the discount on stocks issued at par, this separation would seem to be significant. In recent years, however, the par value of stock has been invariably set far below the issue price, and therefore the distinction no longer has any practical meaning.[18]

Information about the amount of funds obtained from various classes of common and preferred stock is useful, and a standard should describe how much detail should be reported on the balance sheet and how much should be disclosed in the notes. Similar requirements should be stated for bond issues.

The item "undistributed equity interest" is a part of the shareholder equity section, as described in Chapter 4.

Nonoperating assets and equity

Many entities, principally nonbusiness orgnizations, have assets that were obtained from contributions, grants, or appropriations intended for nonoperating purposes and therefore not available to finance operating activities in the period in which they were contributed. These include contributions of plant and equipment or of money to acquire plant and equipment, contributions to endowment funds, and contributions of art or other museum objects. These are here called nonoperating assets.[19]

Nonoperating assets should be distinguished from contributions made for a specified operating purpose. Although a restricted operating contribution requires that money be spent for the specified purpose, the money received can be mingled with other operating funds. The restriction of these contributions is on the use of operating assets in general, and there is a liability to use some funds (but not necessarily the money actually contributed) to carry out the specified purpose.[20]

On the balance sheet, nonoperating assets should be segregated from operating assets, and the sources of nonoperating funds should be distinguished from the sources of funds available for operations. If an entity has $100,000 of cash equivalents available for operations and $200,000 of cash equivalents in an endowment fund, it would be misleading to combine these two amounts; only the $100,000 is available for the payment of operating liabilities.

In order to provide this segregation, an entity should report, in effect, two balance sheets—one associated with its operating activities and the other with its nonoperating activities.[21] This segregation can be accomplished either by actually reporting separate balance sheets or by reporting two clearly defined and self-balancing sections in a single balance sheet. It may be desirable to divide the nonoperating assets into categories—one for plant and another for endowment.

As explained in Chapter 7, the use of depreciable nonoperating assets in operations can be reported by charging depreciation as an operating expense with a corresponding credit to revenue.

With the exception of the depreciation charge, the practices of many nonbusiness organizations are consistent with the above description.[22] This discussion leads to the following concept:

> **Concept 8.05.**   *Nonoperating assets are assets acquired with non-operating contributions. Nonoperating assets should be reported separately from operating assets and the related sources of funds should be reported separately from the entity equity generated by operating activities.*

FUNDS FLOW STATEMENT

For many years some companies reported a statement entitled "Funds Flow Statement." In 1971 APB Opinion No. 19 was published; it specified in some detail the nature of such a statement and gave it a new title, "Statement of Changes in Financial Position." "Funds Flow Statement" seems. equally descriptive, and it is shorter. "Funds Statement" is not an accurate title. The balance sheet is a funds statement; it shows the *status* of funds. The title should indicate that the statement describes the *flow* of funds. The following concept is intended to be consistent with current practice:

> **Concept 8.06.**   *An entity should report a funds flow statement that summarizes investing and financing activities associated with its operations during an accounting period if these activities have been significant.*

The phrase "associated with its operations" suggests that the regular funds flow statement should exclude nonoperating flows. These are discussed in the next section.

The final qualifying clause is given because there seems to be an impression that a funds flow statement should be prepared by all entities. In many small entities, the significant items of funds flow are apparent from the operating statement and the comparative balance sheets for the beginning and the end of the period. In these circumstances, preparations of an additional statement serves no useful purpose.

In a conceptual framework, it is unnecessary to describe the circumstances in which the funds flow statement should report working capital flows as contrasted with cash flows. This distinction is properly the subject of a standard. APB Opinion No. 19 is not entirely clear on this point, but it easily can be revised so as to clarify the distinction.

Recently, the Financial Accounting Standards Board, a committee of the Financial Executives Institute, a commissioner of the SEC, and several others have proposed that the preparation of a funds flow statement on the working capital basis no longer be permitted. They have not made a convincing case. Indeed their comments indicate an unfamiliarity with the nature of a statement prepared on the working capital basis. Since a large majority of companies use the working capital basis, and since few users of financial statements have expressed dissatisfaction with that basis, it seems unlikely that the working capital basis will be outlawed.[23]

STATEMENT OF CHANGES IN EQUITY

Although mentioned in authoritative pronouncements, there is no specific requirement currently that a "statement of retained earnings" be reported. "Retained earnings," as such, does not appear in this framework; its substance is now divided between shareholder equity and entity equity. Nevertheless, if significant changes in shareholder equity or entity equity have occurred, and if they are not obvious from information reported on the other three required financial statements, these changes should be reported separately.

Changes of this nature happen frequently in nonbusiness organizations, particularly in organizations that have endowment or contributed plant. Transactions affecting these categories do not appear on an operating statement. They should be reported on one or more separate statements. They are, in effect, funds flow statements for nonoperating assets and the related equity items, but it seems desirable to limit the title "Funds Flow Statement" to the operating flows with which this term traditionally has been associated.

In business organizations, certain changes in shareholder equity do not involve a flow of funds. A stock dividend is one example; conversion of preferred stock to common stock is another. Such changes should be reported on a statement of changes in equity. Declaration of dividends is not, by itself, a reason for reporting such a statement because dividends are reported on the funds flow statement. Thus, the statement described here need be prepared only when it discloses significant information not reported on other statements.

The concept that describes this statement and limits its required use to situations in which the same information is not readily apparent in other statements is:

> *Concept 8.07.* *If the causes of significant changes in shareholder equity or entity equity are not readily discernible from other statements, these should be reported on one or more statements of changes in equity.*

CONCLUSION

The four financial statements described above constitute the required financial statements in this framework. For reasons given in Chapter 1, this framework is limited to information in the financial statements. Financial reports also include notes and other supplementary information.

The description of the financial statements in this chapter summarizes the thrust of the proposal. The framework differs from current practice principally in: the recognition of shareholder equity as a source of funds, rather than as the difference between assets and liabilities; the separate recognition of entity equity, and the recognition of equity interest as the cost of using shareholder equity funds. To readers whose experience is with business enterprises, the material about program costs and nonoperating assets may also seem novel, but this is because these items are found primarily in nonbusiness organizations. Concepts for these items are consistent with those currently used by nonbusiness organizations, except governments.

My intention has been to develop financial accounting concepts that follow from the premises stated in Chapter 2. If the concepts are inconsistent with these premises, or if the premises themselves are wrong, the analysis is open to criticism. If neither of these errors have been committed, I hope the framework will be accepted.

Notes to chapter 1

1. "Conceptual Framework: Needs and Uses," address given at the FASB Symposium, June 24, 1980. Excerpts were published in *FASB Viewpoints*, August 19, 1980.

2. In many disciplines, scientists develop concepts and engineers apply them. In accounting there are very few "scientists," that is, theorists. The closest approximation is the microeconomist, but few economists are interested in accounting. There is practically no academic research in theory except by doctoral candidates. But few doctoral candidates study theory as such because manipulation of data is ordinarily not helpful in theory construction, and most doctoral supervisors do not consider research respectable unless it involves the manipulation of data.

3. In his *Fund Theory of Accounting* (1947), William J. Vatter vividly states the need for a conceptual framework:

> Every science, methodology, or other body of knowledge is oriented to some conceptual structure—a pattern of ideas brought together to form a consistent whole or a frame of reference to which is related the operational content of that field. Without some integrating structure, procedures are but senseless rituals without reason or substance; progress is but a fortunate combination of circumstances; research is but fumbling in the dark; and the dissemination of knowledge is a cumbersome process, if indeed there is any 'knowledge' to convey (p. 1).

See also Donald J. Kirk, "Concepts, Consensus, and Compromise: Their Roles in Standard Setting," *Journal of Accountancy,* April 1981. For a particularly thoughtful analysis, see Charles T. Horngren, "Uses and Limitations of a Conceptual Framework," *Journal of Accountancy,* April 1981.

4. Current discussions about accounting for pensions illustrate this point. Some argue that the pension cost in a given year is the amount paid in that year. Others argue that the current pension cost is the present value of the future pension payments caused by the work done in the year. Until there is agreement on the concept for cost, these arguments get nowhere. These arguments therefore prevent a discussion of what should be the relevant *standard* for pension cost, given an agreed upon cost concept. The FASB Discussion Memorandum on pensions is described later in this chapter. For a summary of this memorandum that shows the difficulty of discussing pension issues in the absence of agreement on concepts, see Timothy S.

Lucas and Betsy Ann Hollowell, "Pension Accounting: the Liability Question," *Journal of Accountancy,* October 1981.

5. A few people disagree with this statement. See, for example, George J. Benston, "The Value of the SEC's Accounting Disclosure Requirement," *The Accounting Review,* July 1969, pp. 515–32. Benston claims that the forces of the marketplace will require entities to disclose appropriate information; otherwise, investors will be unwilling to provide capital. His analysis of the relationship of stock market prices to published information leads him to conclude that additional reporting requirements have had no identifiable effect. I believe that this analysis, like most analyses based on the "efficient markets" model, fails to identify effects because of inadequacies in its statistical tools, and that the data therefore neither substantiate nor repudiate his proposition. In any event, standards are necessary to increase the comparability of data for various reporting entities.

6. In most respects, management accounting practices are consistent with financial reporting standards. Presumably, the standards that are most useful in reporting to external parties are also useful in conveying information to management. Furthermore, the objectives of individual managers within an entity should be consistent with those of the entity as a whole, and reports on the performance of individual managers should therefore be consistent with reports on the performance of the entire entity. Unless there is good reason to do so, an entity will therefore avoid the extra effort involved in maintaining a management accounting system that is inconsistent with its financial accounting system.

Management accounting information is more detailed than that in general purpose financial statements, but the detail is generally an elaboration of what is contained in the financial statements. If management is willing to pay the extra cost of operating a management accounting system that is inconsistent with its financial accounting, this is an indication that the financial accounting standards need to be reexamined. For example, many companies treat the cost of using capital as a cost in their management accounting systems even though this practice is, except in limited circumstances, uncommon in financial accounting. This fact should encourage a reconsideration of the financial accounting practice.

In earlier books I have argued that management accounting was inherently different from financial accounting because top management had stronger enforcement capability than external bodies and could therefore tolerate more subjective practices than was appropriate for financial accounting. This argument now seems weak to me, and I am coming to believe that there is almost as much risk of biased internal reporting within a large organization as there is in biased reporting to external parties.

7. Requiring disclosure in notes is a useful device for dealing with a problem for which there is not yet agreement on the appropriate treatment. The FASB did this in 1980 for "Disclosure of Indirect Guarantees of Indebtedness of Others," "Disclosure of Unconditional Obligations," and "Disclosure of Interest Rate Futures Contracts and Forward and Standby Contracts." This was a temporary solution, however. At some time the board has to resolve the questions of whether or not these items are to be included in the primary financial statements, and if so, how.

8. Eldon S. Hendriksen, *Accounting Theory,* 4th ed. (1982).

9. Most securities for nonbusiness organizations are issued by state and local governments. In 1979, issues for new capital by these entities totalled $41.5 billion. New corporate debt issues in 1979 totalled $40.1 billion. Corporations also issued some equity securities in 1979, but few nonbusiness organizations issue equity securities. See *Federal Reserve Bulletin*, January 1981, p. A34.

10. Committees of the American Accounting Association have written reports containing conceptual material about nonprofit organizations. The most recent is the "Report of the Committee on Nonprofit Organizations," *The Accounting Review* (Supplement 1975), pp. 3–49. The leading texts have some conceptual material: Leon E. Hay, *Accounting for Governmental and Nonprofit Entities*, 6th ed. (1980); Edward S. Lynn and Robert J. Freeman, *Fund Accounting Theory and Practice*, 2d ed. (1983); Malvern Gross and William Warshauer, *Financial and Accounting Guide for Nonprofit Organizations*, 3d ed. (1979). These materials emphasize the differences between nonbusiness and business accounting rather than the similarities.

11. The American Institute of Certified Public Accountants (AICPA) Trueblood report, *Objectives of Financial Statements*, by Robert M. Trueblood, chairman, (1973), did have a brief chapter on "Objectives of Financial Statements for Governmental and Not-for-Profit Organizations," but this was treated as a separate topic. The other parts of the document related primarily to business. Chapters 1 and 2 were not explicitly limited to business, but they had a strong business orientation.

Much of William J. Vatter's writing relates to both business and nonbusiness organizations, and his *Fund Theory of Accounting* has much to say about business and nonbusiness accounting. However, it does not purport to be a complete conceptual statement.

This separation of business and nonbusiness accounting is rapidly fading. For example, FASB Concepts Statement No. 1, published in 1978, was explicitly limited to businesses; whereas FASB Concepts Statement No. 3, published in 1980, says "Although this Statement is entitled *Elements of Financial Statements of Business Enterprises*, the Board has tried to word several of the definitions so that they could also apply to organizations other than business enterprises" (paragraph 2). In FASB Concepts Statements No. 4, also published in 1980 but developed later than Concepts Statement No. 3, the Board correctly concluded (paragraph 1) that "it is not necessary to develop an independent conceptual framework for any particular category of entities (e.g., nonbusiness organizations or business enterprises)."

12. This authority was legislated in the Accounting and Auditing Act of 1950 (31 U.S.C. 66). A sovereign state can prescribe accounting standards for the state itself and for the municipalities and other entities over which it exercises control. However, since there are 50 states, there is a need for general purpose reports for governmental entities that are prepared according to a single set of standards. In the absence of such a set of standards, the reports of municipalities in various states are not comparable.

13. For a discussion of this question, see FASB Discussion Memorandum, *Effect of Rate Regulation on Accounting for Regulated Enterprises* (1979), and the resulting FASB Statement 71 (December 1982).

14. Professor Robert R. Sterling argues that accounting is not, but should become, a science. See his *Toward a Science of Accounting* (1979). He regards art as the antithesis of science (p. 3). Most of his analogies with science relate to concepts of elementary physics. The fallacy of his argument is that accounting, like all of the social sciences, is fundamentally different from physics and the other natural sciences. In the social sciences, there are few laws that can be empirically tested. Moreover, accounting "laws," unlike physical laws, are made by man and can be changed by man. For a thorough analysis of Sterling's book, see Edward Stamp, "Why Can Accounting Not Become a Science Like Physics?" *Abacus*, June 1981.

15. Accountants tend to think that their problems are unique. In fact, standards are developed in many areas, and a study of the standards setting process and the nature of the resulting standards in other disciplines is useful in thinking about accounting. Any example from engineering can illustrate. In 1904 the entire business district of Baltimore was destroyed by fire because the screw threads on the city's fire hydrants would not fit couplings on the hoses of fire engines rushed from other cities and towns. This dramatized the need for uniform standards, and the American Society of Mechanical Engineers undertook to develop them. The first major uniform standard that resulted was for steam boilers, effective in 1914. It replaced separate codes of 10 states and 19 municipalities. See Bruce Sinclair, *A Centennial History of the American Society of Mechanical Engineers* (1980). The principal nongovernmental standards setting agency now is the American National Standards Institute which establishes new standards at a rate of over 1,000 a year. The magnitude of its activity is indicated by the fact that it generates over $10 million in revenues from the sale of its publications.

16. The three-step process is considerably simpler than that used by the FASB. The FASB approach is illustrated in Exhibit 1–1.

Exhibit 1–1

FASB conceptual framework

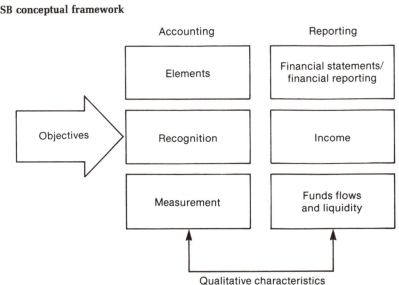

Qualitative characteristics

17. For an extensive discussion of the nature of concepts, see Charles Christenson, "Proposals for a Program of Empirical Research into the Properties of Triangles," *Decision Sciences*, October 1976. As Christenson points out, the use I give to the word *concepts* is not quite accurate because concepts relate to things themselves, where I use the word to refer to sentences about things. A conceptual framework necessarily consists of sentences about things, however.

18. This point is developed in depth in Thomas S. Kuhn, *The Structure of Scientific Revolutions*, 2d ed., International Encyclopedia of Unified Science (1970).

19. Three such sources of concepts are: the previously cited Eldon S. Hendriksen, *Accounting Theory*; Philip E. Meyer, *Applied Accounting Theory* (1981); and Kenneth S. Most *Accounting Theory*, 2d ed. (1982).

20. Maurice Moonitz, *The Basic Postulates of Accounting*, Accounting Research Study No. 1 (1961); and Robert T. Sprouse and Maurice Moonitz, *A Tentative Set of Broad Accounting Principles for Business Enterprises*, Accounting Research Study No. 3 (1962).

21. *Inventory of Generally Accepted Accounting Principles for Business Enterprises*, Accounting Research Study No. 7 (1965).

22. For a strong criticism of APB Statement No. 4, see Yuji Ijiri, "Critique of the APB Fundamentals Statement," *Journal of Accountancy*, November 1971. In a dissent published with Statement No. 4, George R. Catlett said, "the concepts and principles set forth in this Statement are . . . vague generalizations which are noncontroversial but serve no useful purpose . . . circular reasoning with undefined terms being defined by other undefined terms . . . and reverse logic by summarizing a wide variety of customs and practices . . . and then rationalizing back to principles that presumably support what now exists."

23. AICPA, Study Group on the Objectives of Financial Statements.

24. Commenting on the report of the Trueblood committee, Ross M. Skinner wrote, "we have the good grey dignified prose of the committee, the fuzzy abstractions triumphing over the concrete examples, the careful balancing of the one hand and the other." "The Trueblood Report: Brave New Beginning or Dead End?" *CA Magazine*, December 1973.

25. The most complete set of multinational accounting standards is the Fourth Directive of the European Economic Community, adopted in 1978. Another group is the International Accounting Standards Committee, whose members are representatives of accounting professional bodies in many countries. It has issued several standards, but most of them are on noncontroversial topics. The United Nations Commission on Transnational Corporations has plans to develop accounting standards, but as of 1982 it has not done so. See also Adolf Enthoven, *Accounting Systems, Developments and Requirements in Third World Economies* (1976).

26. FASB Discussion Memorandum, *Employers' Accounting for Pensions and Other Postemployment Benefits* (1981).

27. For other criticisms of the work of the FASB, see Nicholas Dopuch and Shyam Sunder, "FASB's Statements on Objectives and Elements of Financial Accounting: A Review," *The Accounting Review*, January 1980; and American Accounting Association, *Report of the Subcommittee to Respond to FASB Exposure Draft: Objectives of Financial Reporting by Nonbusiness Organizations* (1980).

28. Robert R. Sterling and Arthur L. Thomas, eds., *Accounting for a Simplified Firm Owning Depreciable Assets* (1979).

29. For a discussion of this view see papers in David Solomons, ed., *The Conceptual Framework of Accounting* (1977). See especially the comments by Nicholas Dopuch and the exchange between Dopuch and Paul Rosenfield, pp. 19–27, and the comment by Dopuch on p. 77. See also David Solomons, "The Politicization of Accounting," *Journal of Accountancy,* November 1978.

30. For the argument that it is impossible to develop accounting standards that satisfy the informational needs of different groups, see Joel S. Demski, "The General Impossibility of Normative Accounting Standards," *The Accounting Review,* October 1973; and "Choice among Financial Reporting Alternatives," *The Accounting Review,* April 1974. In the first paper, Demski considers attempts to establish accounting principles by using "standards, such as relevance, usefulness, objectivity, fairness, and verifiability to delineate the desired alternatives" (p. 718). He develops an "impossibility theorem" to show that "generally speaking, we cannot rely on standards to provide a normative theory of accounting. No set of standards exist that always will rank alternatives in accordance with preferences and beliefs—no matter what these preferences and beliefs are" (p. 721). In the 1974 paper, Demski concludes that the selection of financial reporting alternatives "ultimately must entail trading off one person's gains for another's" (p. 232).

William H. Beaver and Joel S. Demski in "The Nature of Financial Accounting Objectives: A Summary and Synthesis," *Journal of Accounting Research* Supplement (1974), also use Arrow's social choice framework. They examine the Trueblood report and conclude that the role of objectives is to delineate the relationship between individual preferences and social preferences "that wil form the basis for resolution of financial reporting controversies" (p. 175). However, since optimal accounting principles do not exist, the role of an accounting policymaker is said to be strictly a political role of trading off conflicting objectives of financial statement user groups.

Barry E. Cushing, "On the Possibility of Optimal Accounting Principles," *The Accounting Review,* April 1977, rejects the above argument. Cushing concludes that "rational choice theory does not preclude the possibility of optimal accounting principles" (p. 321). He challenges the basic assumption which is fundamental to the conclusions reviewed above, namely, that financial statement users have heterogeneous tastes and beliefs. "Considered in the extreme, this assumption requires that an information system is not socially optimal even though it is preferred by all users save one who is possessed of bizarre tastes and preferences" (p. 311). He questions such an unduly restrictive definition of optimality and also the empirical validity of the assumption. Another point made in his analysis is that Arrow's assumptions underlying the general impossibility theorem (and accounting extensions of it) "have not been accepted universally and, in fact, have generated substantial controversy in the literature of welfare economics" (p. 313). Cushing proceeds to show that rational choice theory does allow the resolution of five specific accounting issues in an optimal manner.

Raymond J. Chambers, "The Possibility of a Normative Accounting Standard," *The Accounting Review*, July 1976, argues against Demski's notion that individual preferences, beliefs, and opportunities have to be admitted into the analysis in order to rationalize choices between accounting (or information) alternatives. Reliance on qualities such as relevance, usefulness and fairness of accounting information allows one to single out the most preferred alternative; this "rests firmly on the proposition that individual users *prefer* relevant to irrelevant information, useful to useless information, and fair to unfair information" (p. 647). He shows that "the general and uninterpreted use of the phrase 'beliefs and preferences' lies at the root of Demski's conclusion" (p. 647). Chambers separates the total problem, or choice situation, into two questions: (1) What information shall be drawn upon? (2) Given the information, what course of action is feasible and preferred? He then argues against treating all information en bloc and rebuts Demski's "impossibility" conclusion by showing that within the general setting of financial problems, there is a class of information (called accounting information) "which is invariant with respect to potential decisions and relevant to them all" (p. 649). He concludes, therefore, that the impossibility theorem, stemming from the view that information (en bloc) is variant, or dependent, on the decision maker's individuality and choice problems, must be rejected.

31. The argument is made in two articles by Ross L. Watts and Jerold L. Zimmerman: "Toward a Positive Theory of the Determination of Accounting Standards," *The Accounting Review*, January 1978; and "The Demand for and Supply of Accounting Theories: The Market for Excuses," *The Accounting Review*, April 1979.

As Charles Christenson has pointed out, the arguments in these papers confuse theories about accounting with theories about the behavior of people who develop and use accounting information—quite a different topic. Professor Christenson also shows that the assertion that normative theories are "unscientific" is wrong. All sciences have theories about appropriate methodology, and these correspond to normative theories in accounting; "The Methodology of Positive Accounting," *The Accounting Review*, January 1983.

32. This position is developed in *Corporate Reporting: Its Future Evolution*, a Research Study of the Canadian Institute of Chartered Accountants (1980). Professor Edward Stamp, the author of the final draft, has also written on the same theme in "Accounting Standards and the Conceptual Framework: A Plan for Their Evolution," *The Accountant's Magazine*, July 1981; "Accounting Standard Setting: A New Beginning," *CA Magazine*, September 1980; "First Steps towards a British Conceptual Framework," *Accountancy*, March 1982; and the previously cited "Why Can Accounting Not Become a Science Like Physics?" Professor Stamp regards the FASB as a "costly white elephant." A similar view is developed in Professor Richard Macve's report to the British Accounting Standards Committee: "A Conceptual Framework for Financial Accounting and Reporting: The Possibilities for an Agreed Structure," October 1981.

33. *The Emmanual Saxe Distinguished Lectures in Accounting 1977–1978* (1978).

34. The following also advocate expanding the boundaries of accounting to the so-called data-base concept in management information systems: Claude S. Colantoni, Rene P. Manes, and Andrew Whinston, "A Unified Approach to the Theory of Accounting and Information Systems," *The Accounting Review,* January 1971; and John E. Butterworth, "The Accounting System as an Information Function," *Journal of Accounting Research,* Spring 1972.

35. For a description of these studies, see William H. Beaver, *Financial Reporting: An Accounting Revolution* (1981), Chapter 5. See also, Edward B. Deakin, "Accounting Reports, Policy Interventions and the Behavior of Securities Returns," *The Accounting Review,* July 1965. Unlike most studies, Deakin's shows that there is some evidence supporting the view that accounting disclosures actually affect stock market prices, in particular the disclosures required by the SEC in 1935. He also shows that a widely quoted study by Benston that concludes that there is no such evidence is deficient because Benston selected an inappropiate date at which to measure the phenomenon.

36. Generalizations cannot be made about practice in nonbusiness organizations as a class. The AICPA has five audit guides: *Colleges and Universities* (1973); *Voluntary Health and Welfare Organizations* (1974); *Hospitals* (1972); *State and Local Governmental Units* (1980); and *Other Nonprofit Organizations* (1981). These guides are inconsistent with one another in important respects. In particular, the audit guide for state and local governmental units (which accepts Statements 1 and 2 of the National Council of Governmental Accounting as authoritative) is fundamentally different from the others.

37. Although depreciation was introduced in the British income tax code in 1878, it was not common in the United States until early in the 20th century. This proposal is much less drastic than some others. Reed K. Storey, the principal architect of the FASB's conceptual framework, has said: "I think the handwriting is already on the wall for the present model (which is often mislabeled 'historical cost accounting') because, among other things, it can't cope with everyday complications, such as changing prices and fluctuating foreign exchange rates." (*Conditions Necessary for Developing a Conceptual Framework, FASB Viewpoints,* March 3, 1981). Scrapping the historical cost model would be a much more drastic change than anything I suggest. My framework basically accepts the historical cost model, and I don't think this model is mislabeled.

Notes to chapter 2

1. "On the Uncertainty of Science," *Harvard Magazine,* September–October 1980.

Not only does human knowledge not stay put, but also many people do not believe the evidence that leads to changes in it. As late as 1979, a public opinion poll revealed that half the adults in America continued to believe that "God created Adam and Eve to start the human race": Ronald L. Numbers, "Creationism in 20th-Century America," *Science,* 5 November 1982.

2. For a description of the impact of these developments on business organizations, see Alfred D. Chandler, *Strategy and Structure* (1962).

3. See, for example, Robert S. Kaplan, *The Information Content of Financial Accounting Numbers: A Survey of Empirical Evidence* (1978). Kaplan summarizes dozens of studies. He concludes that financial statements do provide some information, which is scarcely a world-shaking observation; and he explains that the reason some studies do not show affirmatively that financial statement information is useful may be that other factors than those recognized in the study influenced the results. He concludes with the comment that we should not expect that empirical research "will resolve many of the fundamental disclosure and reporting issues addressed by the FASB and the SEC."

In an unpublished paper, "Empirical vs. Non-Empirical Contributions to Accounting Theory Development," Nicholas Dopuch reviewed 104 empirical studies related to financial accounting that appeared from 1965 through 1979 in *Journal of Accounting Research* (of which he was editor). He writes, "normative income theories are difficult to verify or refute empirically." He concludes by stating that although he does not want to imply that normative theories are dead, "we are fairly certain that flogging a dead horse will not produce any benefits in the future so why not discontinue these tired old approaches to accounting theory development?" Coming from the editor of a leading journal of "scientific" studies of accounting theory, this pessimistic appraisal is noteworthy.

4. Thomas S. Kuhn, *The Structure of Scientific Revolutions* (1970).

5. In his *Essays in Positive Economics* (1953), Friedman writes:

> Under a wide range of circumstances, individual firms behave as if they were seeking to maximize their expected returns (generally if misleadingly called profits) and had full knowledge of the data needed in this attempt; as if, that is, they knew the relevant cost and demand functions, calculated marginal cost and marginal revenue from all actions open to them, and pushed each line of action to the point at which the relevant marginal cost and marginal revenue were equal. Confidence in the maximization-of-returns hypothesis is justified by evidence. Unless the behavior of businessmen in some way approximated behavior consistent with the maximization of returns, it seems unlikely that they would remain in business for long (pp. 21–22).

6. "Rational Decision Making in Business Organizations," *The American Economic Review* (1979).

7. Kenneth E. Boulding, "Economics and Accounting: The Uncongenial Twins," in *Studies in Accounting Theory* ed. W. T. Baxter and Sidney Davidson (1962).

8. Wassily Leontief, another Nobel laureate in economics, has written:

> Page after page of professional economic journals are filled with mathematical formulas leading the reader from sets of more or less plausible but entirely arbitrary assumptions to precisely stated but irrelevant theoretical conclusions. Year after year economic theorists continue to produce scores of mathematical models . . . without being able to advance, in any percep-

tible way, a systematic understanding of the structure and the operations of a real economic system (letter to *Science*, 9 July 1982, pp. 104, 107).

9. For a recent summary of research on information theory, see James A. Ohlson and A. Gregory Buckman, "Toward a Theory of Financial Accounting," *The Journal of Finance*, May 1980. See also Theodore Mock, *Measurement and Accounting Information Criteria*, AAA Accounting Research Study No. 13 (1976); and Joel S. Demski, *Information Analysis* (1980). Although the Demski book has many examples, not one relates to a real world situation. I do not mean to imply that authors claim that information theory has practical applications; the most they claim is that it may lead to practical applications at some time in the future.

10. For a realistic description of how business organizations function, see Chester L. Barnard, *The Functions of the Executive* (1936).

11. For summaries of this research see: American Accounting Association, "Report of the 1976–77 Committee on Human Information Processing"; Robert Libby and Barry L. Lewis, "Human Information Processing Research in Accounting: The State of the Art," *Accounting, Organizations, and Society* (1977), pp. 245–68; and Anthony Hopwood, *Accounting and Human Behaviour*, (1976), Chapter 8. For an example of the difficulty of obtaining worthwhile evidence from a laboratory experiment involving human information processing, see A. Rashad Abdel-khalik and Thomas F. Keller, *Earnings or Cash Flows: An Experiment on Functional Fixation and the Valuation of the Firm*, AAA Studies in Accounting Research No. 16 (1979). See also the references in Note 9.

12. Most of this research is based on the capital asset pricing model (CAPM) and its cousin, the efficient market hypothesis. Most tests of accounting alternatives using the CAPM give inconclusive results. At most, these tests can be applied to alternatives that have a major effect on income, such as LIFO versus FIFO. For less drastic alternatives, the effect of factors that have not been taken into account swamp the influence of the factor being tested. A study by Alan P. Mayer-Sommer, "Understanding and Acceptance of the Efficient Market Hypothesis and Its Accounting Implications," *The Accounting Review*, January 1979, found low levels of understanding and acceptance of the efficient market hypothesis (which underlies the capital asset pricing model) by controllers, CPAs, and financial analysts. Relevant studies will be referred to in later chapters.

Although the AICPA Trueblood report (1973) referred to this research, there is no discernible connection between the research findings and the concepts developed by the Trueblood committee.

For a lengthy discussion, see A. Rashad Abdel-khalik and Thomas F. Keller, eds., *The Impact of Accounting Research on Practice and Disclosure* (1978). The paper by Robert S. Kaplan, "The Information Content of Financial Accounting Numbers: A Survey of Empirical Evidence," is on pp. 134–73. The quotation by Robert K. Mautz is on page 177. Mautz shows that the conclusions in these studies are obvious. An example is Kaplan's statement: "The studies demonstrate that accounting numbers do have information content." In the same book (pp. 26–31), Norton M. Bedford analyzes 183 articles and papers appearing in the decade 1965 to 1975 and judges the impact they had on accounting practice. He found only 12 that preceded a new accounting practice, and even for these, the connection between the research and the practice was tenuous.

Shyam Sunder, "Proof That in an Efficient Market, Event Studies Can Provide No Systematic Guidance to Revision of Accounting Standards and Disclosure Policy" (1982), has an elegant mathematical proof of the proposition given in the title.

The stock market's reaction to a 1974 article by Abraham J. Briloff is sometimes cited as evidence for market efficiency. In that article, Professor Briloff alleged that the financial statements of McDonald's (the fast-food chain) were misleading, and the price of McDonald's stock fell immediately from 47½ to 38½. I regard this as evidence of the market's stupidity rather than of its efficiency. Informed persons know that Professor Briloff's analyses are unreliable; the price of McDonald's stock recovered within a week.

A basic flaw with the efficient market hypothesis is that it makes no allowances for differences in the ability of human beings who use information in making investment decisions. Although it seems reasonable (without fancy mathematics) that the average investor will not outperform the market, it also seems reasonable that particularly able investors will do better than average. The performance of individual investors does not show up in the calculations based on the efficient market hypothesis or even in the calculations of the return earned by individual mutual funds, because decisions in these funds are made by different individuals over time.

One may ask why unproductive research of the type described above is undertaken. The reason is that such research is useful in training doctoral candidates. It requires a rigorous analysis, an ability to use complicated tools for manipulating data, an ability to interpret the results properly, and an ability to understand and comment critically on the results of prior research. Unfortunately, the research has produced a voluminous literature which those interested in developments in accounting theory feel some obligation to read. Unfortunately also, it leads many doctoral candidates to the erroneous conclusion that this body of research has some relevance to the real world, and this handicaps them when they try to deal with real world problems.

There may be no feasible alternative to this method of educating doctoral candidates. Research into the functioning of the human body is expensive. Research into the functioning of an organization is much more expensive because organizations are vastly more complicated than individuals.

13. Paul A. Griffin, *Usefulness to Investors and Creditors of Information Provided by Financial Reporting: A Review of Empirical Accounting Research* (1982), p. 163. This quotation from the last page of the book is almost the opposite of the first two sentences on page 1: "A quiet revolution has taken place in accounting during the past two decades. Accounting researchers, by adopting scientific methods of inquiry, have generated a substantial body of empirically based knowledge."

14. See the Appendix to Chapter 1 for frameworks by Chambers, Ijiri, Mattessich, and Paton in which premises are explicit.

15. Material in this section is based primarily on James G. Miller, "Living Systems: Basic Concepts," *Behavior* (vol. 10), pp. 1932–36.

16. William Vatter's *The Fund Theory of Accounting and Its Implications for Financial Reports* (1947) is built on the premise that the entity theory is unsatisfactory because it "adopts a personality as its focus of attention." He suggests the idea of "funds" as a way of getting around this defect. Actually, the premise stated above, which is consistent with the entity theory, has nothing to do with a personality. Vatter's excellent framework can be restated as an entity framework and thereby avoid the weaknesses inherent in the literal meaning of funds, namely that they are artificially defined groups of accounts. Vatter does not state what should constitute a fund; he accepts whatever composition an organization chooses to make. Under such a concept the financial report for the State of New York could contain 5,000 balance sheets because it has 5,000 separate funds.

17. In a letter of May 14, 1980, to the FASB, the chairman of the AICPA Accounting Standards Division put it this way (p. 4): "Financial statements and financial reporting of a business enterprise should deal with financial aspects of that enterprise, for example, *its* interests, *its* rights, and *its* duties, and not with financial aspects of other entities, such as its owners" (AICPA, Accounting Standards Division, Letter to the FASB, File Reference 1004–01g). In a thorough analysis of case law, Homer Kripke demonstrates that the law does not support the idea that corporations exist for the benefit of their shareholders: "The SEC, Corporate Governance, and the Real Issues," *The Business Lawyer*, January 1981. See also Eugene F. Fama, "Agency Problems and the Theory of the Firm," *Journal of Political Economy*, April 1980. Fama makes the point that both equity investors and lenders provide funds to the firm and that the principal difference between these investors is in the different weight they give to risk and reward.

18. *Value and Capital*, 2d ed. (1939), p. 176. Hicks does not rely on this analogy in building up his argument, and a few pages after the passage quoted, he shifts to a discussion of organizations. Nevertheless, many people quote this sentence as an acceptable definition of organization income.

19. For a discussion of this point, see Paul Rosenfield and Steven Rubin, "Personal and Business Financial Statements: How Their Objectives Differ," *Journal of Accountancy*, July 1981; and the 1982 Statement of Position of the American Institute of CPAs on this subject.

20. This discussion is based principally on the writings of C. C. Stevens and Norman R. Campbell. See especially Stevens' paper in Churchman and Ratoosh, eds., *Measurement: Definitions and Theories* (1959), pp. 18–61; and the chapter from Campbell's *What is Science* reprinted in James R. Newman, ed., *The World of Mathematics* (1956), pp. 1797ff. The statement quoted is from Stevens, p. 24.

One characteristic of a measurable property is that elements are additive. If one pail contains two gallons of water and another pail contains three gallons, the two pails together contain five gallons. This idea must be used very carefully when applied to accounting. For example, if each asset is measured at its net realizable value, the sum of the assets is the sum of their individual net realizable values. This sum is not the net realizable value of the *entity*, however, because the value of the entity is quite different from the sum of the values of individual assets. In *Toward A Science of Accounting* (1979), Sterling seems to accept this limitation (p. 173); he nevertheless argues for the use of replacement values, implying that they do measure the value of the firm in some meaningful way.

21. Campbell, *What Is Science*, p. 1809.

22. This idea is thoroughly developed by Irving Fisher in *The Nature of Capital and Income* (1906). He wrote: "A stock of wealth existing at a given instant of time is called *capital*; a flow of benefits from wealth through a period of time is called *income."* This idea is clear enough as to the meaning of capital, but it can lead to confusion unless one recognizes that income is one source of capital and that the two ideas are therefore related. As an example of imprecision, Paul Samuelson, in *Economics,* 11th ed. (1980), writes that capital is "the elaborate machinery, large-scale factories and plants, stores and stocks of finished and unfinished materials" (p. 44) thus implying that monetary assets are not capital. And on the same page: "Capitalism got its name because this capital, or productive wealth, is primarily the private property of somebody, the capitalist," thus relating the left-hand side of the balance sheet to one item on the right-hand side.

Kenneth S. Most, *Accounting Theory,* 2d ed. (1982) discusses the confusion about the word *capital,* pp. 207–10.

23. For a discussion of the physical capital maintenance concept, see paragraphs 288–316 of FASB Discussion Memorandum on *A Conceptual Framework for Financial Accounting and Reporting,* (1976). This discussion illustrates the error of equating capital with equity capital. See also the appendix to Chapter 3.

24. The Trueblood report, *Objectives of Financial Statements,* is inconsistent with this premise. It states: "An objective of financial statements is to report on those activities of the enterprise affecting society which can be determined and described or measured and which are important to the role of the enterprise in its social environment" (p. 55). Having made this statement, however, the report provides no guidance on how this objective can be accomplished. However laudable such an objective may be, there is no way of attaining it within the framework of financial accounting, and to hold out an expectation that this can be done is unrealistic.

A report of the AICPA Committee on Social Measurement, *The Measurement of Corporate Social Performance* (1977), takes a similarly unrealistic view of what can be accomplished by financial accounting. Accountants have a difficult enough job in their own territory; they have no competence, as accountants, in the area of social measurement.

25. The pioneer modern work in microeconomics is that by Joel Dean, *Managerial Economics* (1951). A somewhat similar book is Eugene L. Grant, *Principles of Engineering Economy* (1950). Not all economists, even classical economists, accept the propositions described in the following paragraphs. Alfred Marshall, in *Principles of Economics* (1891), p. 443, recognized and accepted the practice of using full costs, including cost allocations, as a basis for arriving at selling prices; cost allocations are unnecessary in classical economics. John M. Clark wrote in *Studies in the Economics of Overhead Costs* (1923), p. 222, that the allocation of costs was "obvious and quite indispensable."

26. An interesting example of an unsupported assertion is the case of the lighthouse. Many economics texts describe the lighthouse as a public good. Since there is no way of prohibiting passing ships from obtaining the benefit of the lighthouse, there is no way of charging a price for the use of lighthouse services, and therefore the government must finance lighthouses, the texts state. In a fascinating article, R. H. Coase shows that this theory does not jibe with the facts. He describes the history of lighthouses in the United Kingdom since the 17th century. During that whole period, lighthouses were, in fact, owned and operated profitably by private companies. They negotiated prices with shipowner companies and with their trade associations: R. H. Coase, "The Lighthouse in Economics," *Journal of Law and Economics*, October, 1974, pp. 357–76.

27. One of the few economists who has taken the trouble to analyze the accountant's position is Churchman. See Charles W. Churchman, *Prediction and Optimal Decisions* (1961). Mattessich has an excellent discussion and critique of the weakness of Churchman's analysis in his *Accounting and Analytical Methods* (1964), Chapters 5 and 6.

28. "Rational Decision Making," p. 510. In "A Comparison of Organization Theories," *Models of Man* (1957), Chapter 10, Simon points out that classical economic theory assumes that a firm is controlled by a single entrepreneur whose aim is to maximize the firm's profits, and he notes that this assumption is inconsistent with the assumptions of organization theory. Organization theory holds that the behavior of employees is also essential to an understanding of how the firm functions; when these behaviors are taken into account, the single-minded idea of profit maximization breaks down.

Although the majority of economists embrace the profit-maximization view, a significant minority disagrees with it. In addition to Simon, see John Kenneth Galbraith, *The Affluent Society* (1958), and *American Capitalism* (1952). Even Samuelson admits in one place that satisficing is a more realistic description of how companies actually behave (*Economics*, 11th ed., pp. 479–81), but this does not affect the central ideas of his book, which are rooted in profit maximization.

29. For a discussion of this point, see Robert N. Anthony, "The Trouble with Profit Maximization," *Harvard Business Review*, November–December 1960.

30. *The Visible Hand: The Managerial Revolution in American Business* (1977). Chandler sums up the propositions that his analysis supports as follows:

1. Individual business units grew into multiunit enterprises when administrative coordination permitted more effective operation than the coordinations provided by market mechanisms.
2. A managerial hierarchy had to be created before the advantages of internalizing many activities within a single firm could be realized.
3. Modern business enterprises first appeared when the volume of economic activities reached a level at which administrative coordination was more efficient and profitable than market coordination.
4. Once successfully formed and functioning, a managerial hierarchy in and of itself becomes a source of power, growth, and permanence.
5. The salaried managers in these managerial hierarchies shifted increasingly toward technical and professional careers.
6. As the multiunit firm grew in size and diversity and its managers became more professional and career oriented, management of the firm became separated from ownership.
7. In these larger firms, career managers tended to make decisions that led to long-term stability and growth rather than short-term profits.
8. As these large enterprises grew into positions of dominance in sectors of our economy, they altered the basic structure of these sections as well as that of the economy as a whole.

31. For example, see James R. Nelson, ed., *Marginal Cost Pricing in Practice* (1964). Although the authors in this book of readings generally defend the classical position, their examples are all of highly unusual situations.

In articles advocating replacement costs, authors often assume, without evidence, that prices are based on replacement costs. Examples: Robert R. Sterling, "Relevant Financial Reporting in an Age of Price Changes," *Journal of Accountancy*, February 1975; Richard F. Vancil, "Performance Measurement During Inflation," *Harvard Business Review*, March–April 1976.

In an excellent survey, Silberston summarizes 153 British and American studies of pricing covering the period through 1968: Aubrey Silberston, "Surveys of Applied Economics: Price Behavior of Firms," *The Economic Journal*, September 1970. These studies provided practically no support for the premise that businesses use marginal-cost pricing. Other references are: Otto Eckstein, ed., *The Econometrics of Price Determination Conference* (1972); William D. Nordhaus, *The Falling Share of Profits* (1974); U.S. Council on Wage and Price Stability, *A Study of Steel Prices* (1975).

Robert Dorfman, *Prices and Markets*, 2d ed. (1972), is based entirely on the classical economic model: full costs are irrelevant. The book contains no studies of price behavior that are relevant to the issue of whether full costs are more useful than marginal costs, and it has little empirical evidence of any kind.

See also R. L. Hall and C. J. Hitch, "Price Theory and Business Behavior," *Oxford Economic Papers* (1939); A. D. H. Kaplan, Joel B. Dirham, and Robert F. Lanzillotti, *Pricing in Big Business* (1958); Robert F. Lanzillotti, "Pricing Objectives in Large Companies," *American Economic Review*, December 1958; W. W. Haynes, *Pricing Decisions in Small Business*, (1962); and James S. Earley, "Marginal Policies of Excellently Managed Companies," *American Economic Review*, March 1956.

Although they presented some evidence that companies do use full-cost pricing, these authors nevertheless argue that the actual pricing practices do not contradict microeconomic theory of the firm. They argue that the structure of markups among different products for firms using full-cost pricing provides clear evidence that demand analysis does, in fact, play an important role in price determination. James S. Earley, for example, reports that most of the firms he examined differentiated their markups for different product lines on the basis of competitive pressure and demand elasticities. Kaplan, Dirham, and Lanzillotti report a similar finding in their study of pricing practices.

For an argument in support of full-cost pricing, see my "A Case for Historical Costs," *Harvard Business Review*, November–December 1976.

Full-cost pricing does not imply that competitive conditions (including demand and other factors) are irrelevant for price determination. However, the above noted authors do not provide evidence to show that markups used in full-cost pricing result in the same prices that would be established through marginal analysis, that is, by setting marginal revenue equal to marginal cost. Unless this relationship is established (which is definitely not the case in multiproduct firms), the case for marginal-cost pricing is not made.

In view of the lack of empirical evidence, Vijayaraghavan Govindarajan and I undertook a study of how Fortune 1000 companies used cost information in arriving at selling prices: "Use of Costs in Price Decisions," *Management Accounting*, July 1983. Of the 509 respondents, 83 percent reported that they typically used full costs rather than variable costs. We view this result as a devastating rejection of the classical view.

Managers place great store by the following (source unknown):

> Count that day lost
> Whose low descending sun
> Sees quotations made at cost,
> And business done for fun.

32. Another reason, not strictly necessary for the argument being made here, is that prices are only one aspect of the "marketing mix" that the manager takes into account in making marketing decisions. For examples of other factors, see Robert D. Buzzell and Frederik D. Wiersema, "Modelling Changes in Market Share: A Cross-Sectional Analysis," *Strategic Management Journal* (1981).

33. For a recent analysis, see Robert J. Gordon, "A Consistent Characterization of a Near-Century of Price Behavior," *American Economic Review*, May 1980.

34. I have stated this argument in terms of direct and indirect costs because this provides a closer tie to the cost allocation issue to which it relates. It could be stated equally well in terms of variable and fixed costs.

35. For references, see Note 31. A carefully done attempt to use the marginal-cost approach is the report by C. James Koch and Robert A. Leone, "The Clean Water Act: Unexpected Impacts on Industry," *The Harvard Environmental Law Review* (1979). The study was limited to the tissue industry (facial and bathroom tissues, disposable diapers, paper napkins). It reached some tentative conclusions about this industry but said that the study of this small segment would cost $500,000 to duplicate, that many millions of dollars would be required to make similar studies of the impact of the clean water act on all industry, and that even with the best available techniques, the results would not be sufficiently reliable to serve as a basis for policy decisions.

36. Some people think that the amounts reported for monetary items on financial statements are the face amount of the receivable or the obligation. This is not so. The amount of a $1,000 bank loan due two years hence with 12 percent interest due at the end of each year is $1,000, but it is $1,000 because this is the present value of the stream of payments, not because the face amount is $1,000. This is shown in the following calculation:

Payment	Present value
$120 interest, Years 1 and 2	$ 202.80
$1,000 principal, end of Year 2	797.20
Total present value	$1,000.00

37. Internal Revenue Service, *Revenue Ruling 59–60*, C.B. 1959–1237. The joint definition of the American Institute of Real Estate Appraisers and the Society of Real Estate Appraisers is more detailed but essentially similar: "Market value is the highest price estimated in terms of money which a property will bring in a competitive and open market under conditions requisite to a fair sale, the buyer and seller each acting prudently, knowledgeably, and assuming the price is not affected by undue stimulus."

When a company is sold to another company as a going concern, the parties must agree on the amount to be paid. This amount may be arrived at as a multiple of current earnings, or of the average of past earnings, or of an estimate of future earnings for a specified number of years; it may be arrived at as book value, book value with certain assets eliminated, adjusted, or added, or book value plus an increment for earning power; it may be arrived at as the market value of certain assets; or it may be arrived at in any number of other ways. (Revenue Ruling 59–60 suggests these approaches.) The final amount may change by as much as 50 percent over a period of a few weeks if there is a bidding war (as in the case of Conoco's acquisition by Du Pont) even though there has been no change in the real value of the firm during the period. *The Wall Street Journal,* February 12, 1981, p. 1, reports with respect to a company that planned to go private: "Depending upon who is talking, the value of American Financial Corp's common stock is somewhere between $5 and $75 a share."

Neil W. Chamberlain, in *Enterprise and the Environment: The Firm in Time and Place* (1968), p. 166 ff, argues that a firm simultaneously has two values. To the investor, its value is a discounted stream of anticipated future earnings. To management, its value is the amount of current earnings capitalized at an appropriate rate. Although I do not accept the validity of the latter point, it illustrates the difficulty at arriving at an operational concept of value. Thus, although a value is necessarily established when a business is sold, the variations in the way it is arrived at demonstrates that there is no single, objective way of measuring the value of a going concern.

See also Robert T. Sprouse, "The Importance of Earnings in the Conceptual Framework," *Journal of Accountancy,* January 1978, pp. 64–71. Although the FASB gave wide latitude to companies in experimenting with current costs in Statement No. 33, it did not include insurance values as a permissible alternative.

38. The classic is Edgar O. Edwards and Philip W. Bell, *The Theory and Measurement of Business Income* (1961). For a thoughtful analysis of this book, accompanied by an extensive bibliography, see Lawrence Revsine, "The Theory and Measurement of Business Income: A Review Article," *The Accounting Review,* April 1981.

39. Leonard Spacek, in "The Need for an Accounting Court," *The Accounting Review,* July 1958, p. 372, observes that in 99 out of 100 cases in arguing over alternative accounting methods, "you [the auditor] are arguing for a procedure that will show a lower profit than the practice the client wants to follow" (p. 372). In an analysis of management attitudes, Ross L. Watts and Jerold L. Zimmerman state that except in very large firms, managers tend not to support proposed accounting standards that would result in a decrease in reported income: "Toward a Positive Theory of the Determination of Accounting Standards," *The Accounting Review,* January 1978.

40. FASB Concepts Statement No. 1, paragraph 28.

41. The FASB analysis is in paragraphs 24–27 of Concepts Statement No. 1. The nonbusiness analysis is in Robert N. Anthony, *Financial Accounting in Nonbusiness Organizations* (1978), pp. 39–47.

42. For amplification of this point, see paragraphs 46–90 and 145–51 of FASB Concepts Statement No. 2.

43. This idea is well put by Howard J. Snavely, Jerome J. Kesselman, and Wayne A. Label: "The purpose of accounting is providing information which the business participants . . . can use to increase their chances of making correct decisions": *Financial Accounting: Concepts, Uses, and Problems* (1977), p. 1. This statement is correct. The premise states *why* accounting data help users to make decisions.

44. Recently, several articles have referred to an "agency" theory of accounting as if it were a new idea. The agents in this theory are managers. Except for the jargon, there is nothing new about this theory. It merely describes how managers behave in organizations, which, insofar as it relates to accounting, has been a topic in management accounting texts for 30 years. So far as financial accounting is concerned, the old idea of "stewardship" suffices.

45. Few people want the primary financial statements to be forecasts or to have forecast information included as a part of these statements. At most, forecasts are advocated as supplementary information, which is outside the boundaries of this framework.

Moreover, managers tend not to favor the publication of forecasts, even as supplementary information. Evidence of managers' attitudes is found in two studies conducted just after the Securities and Exchange Commission lifted its ban on the publication of earnings forecasts in 1973. The two separate surveys polled members of the Financial Executives Institute and controllers of Fortune 500 corporations. Overwhelming opposition to being required, or even encouraged, to forecast income was cited by the respondents. They claimed that the average investor would misunderstand or misinterpret such projections. See Richard J. Asebrook and D. A. Carmichael, "Reporting on Forecasts: A Survey of Attitudes," *Journal of Accountancy*, August 1973; and Charles G. Carpenter and Austin R. Daily, "Controllers and CPAs: Two Views of Published Forecasts," *Business Horizons*, August 1974.

In a more recent survey, over 90 percent of 375 chief financial officers stated that they would cease issuing projections to all outsiders if they were required to file the disclosures with the SEC. See George Foster, *Financial Statement Analysis* (1978), pp. 538–39.

46. An historical note on the shift from the balance-sheet approach to the income-statement approach is given in Chapter 3, Note 7. A few writers disagree with this premise. For example: "Accountants, economists, and financial analysts all agree that the book value of a firm's equity is a number that roughly measures market value or perhaps what the market value of the equity should be": Fischer Black, "The Magic in Earnings: Economic Earnings versus Accounting Earnings," *Financial Analysts Journal*, November–December 1980, p. 7. The evidence in the literature is overwhelmingly against this conclusion.

47. Some people argue that a conflict cannot exist. In *Toward a Science of Accounting*, Sterling argues against the "ancient, persuasive myth . . . that one can have an accurate measure of flows while having an inaccurate measure of stocks." A moment's reflection will show that it is possible to have an accurate measure of the flow of water out of a reservoir without an accurate measure of the volume of water in the reservoir. The latter requires measures of the contours of reservoir, which is not necessary in order to measure the former. Similarly, one can measure the income of an entity during a period directly, that is, without knowing the beginning and ending amounts of all its assets and equities.

48. *Reporting Changes in Financial Position* (1971), paragraph 15.

49. SEC Accounting Series Release No. 142, "Reporting Cash Flow and Other Related Data," March 15, 1973.

50. References to cash flows dominate the report. For example, on the first page of Chapter 1: "Users of financial statements seek to predict, compare, and evaluate the cash consequences of their economic decisions." The de-emphasis of earnings is indicated by this sentence from the concluding section on the topic: "The determination of periodic earnings may develop in stages toward a methodology based on changes in discounted cash flows."

51. Harold M. Williams, "Adequate Information: Prerequisite to an Effective Board," address given in Philadelphia, September 16, 1980. Note that Chairman Williams's emphasis is exactly the opposite of that in APB Opinion No. 19.

52. Joel Stern writes about "free cash flow," which he defines as aftertax income plus depreciation less capital expenditures. (See, for example, his piece in *The Wall Street Journal*, January 29, 1979, "Annual Reports and Stock Prices," p. 16.) Chairman Williams means aftertax income plus depreciation. In a conference on August 10, 1980, held in proximity to the American Accounting Association annual conference (but with no resulting publication), on the subject of cash-flow accounting, the papers dealt with at least six different meanings of cash flows. William L. Ferrara proposes that cash flows be arrived at by adjustments to inventory, receivables, payables, and corporate costs. "A Cash Flow Model for the Future," *Management Accounting*, June 1981.

53. "The Objectives of Financial Statements: An Empirical Study of the Use of Cash Flow and Earnings by Security Analysts," *Accounting, Organizations, and Society* (1980).

54. Louis Harris and Associates, Inc., *A Study of the Attitudes toward and an Assessment of the Financial Accounting Standards Board* (1980).

55. Question 3a of the Harris study asked, "How do you feel about the relative importance of earnings per share, cash flows, changes in a company's financial position, and return on investment?" The assertion as to the relative importance of cash flows is based on the fact that 67 percent of the respondents ranked cash flows as "highly important," compared with only 49 percent who so ranked earnings per share.

There are several things wrong with this conclusion. First, the term *cash flow* was nowhere defined. Those who took it to mean earnings adjusted for depreciation or some other amount need an earnings number to arrive at the cash flow amount. More importantly, cash flows are dollar amounts, whereas both earnings per share and return on investment are ratios. Respondents may have meant only to indicate that they preferred dollar amounts to ratios. Finally, both earnings per share and return on investment are derived from earnings. Since 66 percent responded that return on investment was "highly important," it is clear that at least this many do not want to abandon the measurement of earnings. I regard the wording of this question as most unfortunate and its responses as not in any way supporting the thesis that earnings should no longer be calculated.

56. John G. Cragg and Burton G. Malkiel, *Expectations and the Valuation of Shares* (1980). See also Vijayaraghavan Govindarajan, "Objectives of Financial Reporting by Business Enterprises: Some Evidence of User Preference," *Journal of Accounting, Auditing and Finance*, Summer 1979.

See also Joe D. Icerman, *The Prediction of Corporate Cash Flows: An Analysis of Relevant Models and Presently Available Financial Statement Information* (1977). William H. Beaver, in Section 5–5 of *Financial Reporting: An Accounting Revolution* (1981), summarizes several earlier studies.

A study by David F. Hawkins and Walter J. Campbell did show that some investment analysts used cash flow information, but they did not use it exclusively, nor was it emphasized by the majority of analysts. *Equity Valuation: Models, Analysis, and Implications* (1978).

Robert L. Warren and Jackson A. White obtained responses from the vice president of 175 of the nation's 300 largest banks, 165 chartered financial analysts, and controllers of 225 of the Fortune 500 companies. Less than 5 percent of any group believed that "cash earnings per share" is more useful than "net income per share." "Cash Information: Toward a More Useful Statement of Changes in Financial Position," *The National Public Accountant*, February 1975, pp. 30–34.

If cash flow were more important than earnings, a company's stock price should increase when it shifts to LIFO because the savings in income taxes increases its cash flow. Similarly, its stock price should increase when it discontinues an unprofitable division. There is no evidence that these relationships exist. (Studies of LIFO shifts indicate that the stock price does not decrease substantially, but this is quite different from showing that it increases.) Investors want information about cash flows to *themselves*, but it does not follow that they regard cash flows to the *company* as more important than earnings.

The best case for cash-flow accounting that I know of is Yuji Ijiri, "Recovery Rate and Cash Flow Accounting," *Financial Executive*, March 1980. Ijiri's argument is based on two premises: (1) projects are evaluated in terms of their cash flow, but performance is measured by earnings, which is inconsistent; and (2) the primary objective of a business enterprise is cash flow, and performance measurement therefore should be changed to cash flow. The first premise is correct. The second premise is not supported by the evidence I cited above, however. There is another way to reconcile the measurement of performance with the technique for evaluating projects. It involves the use of annuity depreciation, which I describe in Chapter 5.

57. See A. Rashad Abdel-khalik and K. El-Sheshai, "Information Choice and Utilization in an Experiment on Default Prediction," *Journal of Accounting Research*, Autumn 1980; and E. B. Deakin, "A Discriminant Analysis of Predictors of Failure," *Journal of Accounting Research*, Spring 1972.

58. For an excellent summary of the nature of these inadequacies, see J. S. Hunter, "The National System of Scientific Measurement," *Science*, 21 November 1980.

59. When an accounting rule is changed, some users continue to attach the former meaning to the new numbers. This is the psychological phenomenon called "functional fixation." For a review of the extensive literature on this phenomenon as it applies to accounting information, see Davis Chang and Jacob B. Birnberg, "Functional Fixity in Accounting Research: Perspective and New Data," *Journal of Accounting Research*, Autumn 1977.

60. Louis Harris and Associates, *Attitudes and Assesment of the FASB* (1980), p. 69.

A 1981 study by the National Association of Corporate Directors reported that of 1,110 shareholders responding to a questionnaire, 79 percent were satisfied with the information in annual reports. However, 63 percent said they spent less than 30 minutes reading an annual report, and only 38 percent said they were influenced most by corporate documents in making investment decisions. It seems reasonably clear that dissatisfaction, if it exists, originates with groups other than shareholders—probably investment analysts.

Lauren Kelly-Newton in *Accounting Policy Formulation: The Role of Corporate Management* (1980) described four categories of forces that influence management attitude towards a proposed change in accounting standards: (1) resistance to change inherent within the individual and social system, (2) aspects specific to the innovation, (3) communication channels used to diffuse the proposed change, and (4) social system effects. She found that the primary influence on management's attitude towards adoption of a proposed change was the relative advantage of the change or the benefits that management believes will accrue from adopting the innovation.

See also Eugene E. Comiskey and Roger E. Groves, "The Adoption and Diffusion of an Accounting Innovation," *Accounting and Business Research,* Winter 1972; Maruice Moonitz, *Obtaining Agreement on Standards in the Accounting Profession,* AAA Studies in Accounting Research No. 8 (1974); James O. Hicks, "An Examination of Accounting Interest Groups' Differential Perceptions," *The Accounting Review,* April 1978; Ross L. Watts and Jerold L. Zimmerman, "Toward a Positive Theory of the Determination of Accounting Standards," *The Accounting Review,* January 1978; and Stephen A. Zeff, *Forging Accounting Principles in Five Countries: A History and Analysis of Trends* (1972).

Mie Nakayama and others analyzed the 307 respondents who submitted position papers on accounting for leases to the FASB in 1974. They found that 47 percent of the respondents opposed *any* change in the five existing pronouncements relating to leasing, even though some aspects of these pronouncements were clearly unsatisfactory. They concluded that "the due process procedures of the FASB do not seem to be working." "Due Process and FAS No. 13," *Management Accounting,* April 1981. My own impression is that these results are approximately what is to be expected for any proposal that involves change.

Reluctance to accept the metric system in the United States is a striking example of resistance to change. Even though the metric system is clearly better than our present measurement system, and even though most of the world uses this system, there is great opposition to it. Rational opponents (as contrasted with those who believe that the metric system is somehow un-American) must believe that the metric system is not *enough* better to warrant the costs and inconveniences associated with changing to it.

61. Harvey Kapnick, former chairman of Arthur Andersen & Co., in a speech in February 1976, entitled "Value-Based Accounting—Evolution or Revolution," described APB Statement No. 4 as a "meaningless attempt to rationalize from existing practices back to concepts and principles."

62. In refusing to accept Accounting Research Studies Nos. 1 and 3, the Accounting Principles Board stated in APB Statement No. 1 that the recommendations therein were "of a speculative and tentative nature." This characterization, if true, is a valid reason for rejecting a proposed change. The board also stated that the recommendations were "too radically different from present generally accepted accounting principles for acceptance at this time." This is not a valid reason for re-jecting a sound proposal. It is, at most, a reason for delaying implementation for a reasonable period.

63. This point is developed briefly in FASB Concepts Statement No. 2, para-graph 90. It warrants more than one paragraph out of the 144 paragraphs that dis-cuss qualitative characteristics. These conflicts are at the heart of the problem of developing a good conceptual framework.

For an excellent description of how conflicting premises were resolved in the development of FASB Statement No. 2 on research and development costs, see Rob-ert T. Sprouse, "Prospects for Progress in Financial Reporting" (Address given at the College of Business Administration, Texas Tech University, April 19, 1979).

64. For a strong statement of Sterling's position, see the interview, "Companies are Reporting Useless Numbers," *Fortune*, January 14, 1980, pp. 105–7. When asked how practical his proposal is, Sterling replied, "I have found that there are a lot more prices out there than people realize." He suggested that accountants could learn to "develop synthetic prices through regression analysis" for those that were missing. This view is extraordinarily naive.

65. Maurice Moonitz, *The Basic Postulates of Accounting*, Accounting Research Study No. 1, (1961).

66. Richard V. Mattessich, *Accounting and Analytical Methods*, Chapter 2.

67. William A. Paton, *Accounting Theory* (1922).

68. Robert N. Anthony, "Two Ways to Control Estimated Figures in the Income Statement," *Journal of Accountancy*, April 1949.

69. David Hawkins presented a strong statement of the opposite point of view in his 1973–74 Emmanuel Saxe Distinguished Lecture in Accounting, Baruch Col-lege, City University of New York: "Corporate reporting standards should result in data that are useful for economic decisions provided that the standard is consistent with the national macroeconomic objectives and the economic programs designed to reach these goals." I strongly disagree with this proviso.

For other views on this question, see David Solomons, "The Impact of Politics on Accounting Standards," *Journal of Accountancy*, November 1978; and Alfred Rappaport, "Economic Impact of Accounting Standards—Implications for the FASB," in *Proceedings of the Second Annual Accounting Research Convocation* (1976).

70. Following is a description of the FASB Concepts Statements, with a list of the premises therein that I have omitted:

Concepts Statement No. 1

The format of Statement No. 1 is such that the premises are not explicitly sepa-rated from the discussion of them. The premises are given in paragraphs 9 through 39. They can be distinguished from the concepts in the later paragraphs because the premises are descriptive statments (what the world *is*), whereas the concepts are normative statements (what accounting *should be*)—this is the same distinction I have made. In general, each FASB premise corresponds to a topic sentence of a numbered paragraph. I list these topic sentences (or portions of them) for those topics I have not specificaly discussed:

9. Financial reporting is not an end in itself.
10. The United States had a highly developed exchange economy.
11. Production and marketing of goods and services often involve long, continuous, or intricate processes.
12. Most productive activity in the United States is carried on through investor-owned business enterprises. (Although agreement with this premise depends on how much is "most," there is no need to debate the point.)
13. Business enterprises raise capital for production and marketing activities.
14. In the United States, productive resources are generally privately owned rather than government owned.
15. Moreover, government is a major supplier of economic statistics.
17. The objectives of financial reporting are affected not only by the environment in which financial reporting takes place but also by the characteristics and limitations of the kind of information that financial reporting, and particularly financial statements, can provide.
18. The information provided by financial reporting is primarily financial in nature.
20. The information provided by financial reporting often results from approximate, rather than exact, measures.
22. Financial reporting is but one source of information.
24. Many people base economic decisions on their relationships to and knowledge about business enterprises.

Concepts Statement No. 2.

This Statement describes the qualitative characteristics of accounting information. Although agreeing with these qualitative characteristics (except for the material on conservatism), I believe that they are actually premises about the characteristics of the information that users need; so I have included them as premises. I do not discuss "relevance" as a separate premise, because several of the premises in this chapter describe what information is relevant.

Concepts Statement No. 4

This statement of objectives for nonbusiness organizations is supposed to parallel Concepts Statement No. 1 on objectives for business enterprises. In general, No. 4 does parallel No. 1, and to this extent, my comments on No. 1 apply. To the extent that Statement No. 4 goes beyond Statement No. 1, reaction to it is difficult. The construction is such that there is no clear separation between those sentences that are premises, and hence are supposed to govern accounting concepts, and those that are not relevant for this purpose.

Also, there are some internal inconsistencies. For example, paragraph 22 says, "budgets are particularly significant in the nonbusiness environment," but paragraph 26 says, "financial reporting largely reflects the effects of transactions and events that have already happened," which is a clear indication that paragraph 22 is irrelevant because the information contained in budgets has not already happened. As another example, paragraph 40 says that users want to know "how managers of a nonbusiness organization have discharged their stewardship responsibilities and about other aspects of their performance"; whereas paragraph 42 says "it is usually not possible to determine the degree to which managers . . . have affected the result," which means, I think, that financial reporting cannot be expected to provide information on management performance separate from that on organization performance.

In general, allowing for these inconsistencies, I find nothing in Concepts Statement No. 4 that is different from the premises stated in this chapter.

Notes to chapter 3

1. Those who develop frameworks define broad terms such as *assets*, *liabilities*, *revenue*, and *expense*, but there continues to be a lack of agreed-upon definitions for several more specific terms. This unnecessarily complicates an understanding of financial reports, and in this study I shall be fairly specific about some of these terms.

2. This list draws on, but is not exactly the same as, the list in the thoughtful paper by Norton M. Bedford, "The Impact of A Priori Theory and Research on Accounting Practice," in *The Impact of Accounting Research on Practice and Disclosure*, ed. A. Rashad Abdel-khalik and Thomas Keller (1978).

3. For example, according to the 1980 proxy statement of Russell Stover Candies, Inc., its chief executive officer (CEO) owned 49 percent of its common stock. The CEO also owned all the common stock of Ward Paper Box Company, from whom Russell Stover Candies bought substantially all its candy boxes. Ward manufactured some of these boxes in Russell Stover Candies plants, using space it leased from Russell Stover Candies. It is a reasonable inference that these two corporations were controlled by a single person and therefore were a single economic entity. The financial statements of Russell Stover Candies did not consolidate Ward because the corporation did not own any stock in Ward. Perhaps there is no feasible way of framing a consolidation rule that applies to individual control, as distinguished from stock ownership.

4. This definition of the accounting entity is similar to Ijiri's: "an identifiable unit empowered to control resources," *Theory of Accounting Measurement*, AAA Studies in Accounting Research No. 10 (1975), p. 52. It is similar to the "commander" viewpoint of Louis Goldberg, *An Inquiry Into the Nature of Accounting*, AAA Monograph No. 7 (1965), pp. 162–74. It is consistent with the concept of the public accountability enterprise discussed in the Canadian Institute of Chartered Accountants Report, *Financial Reporting for Non-Profit Organizations* (1980), pp. 1–2. It is similar to the definition in the proposed Seventh Directive of the European Economic Community (1978). It is similar to AICPA, Statement of Position 81–82, *Reporting Practices Concerning Hospital-Related Organizations*. A more specific set of criteria is given in Harold I. Steinberg, "A New Look at Governmental Accounting," *The Journal of Accountancy*, March 1979. It is similar to National Council on Governmental Accounting (NCGA), Statement No. 3, *Defining the Governmental Reporting Entity* (1981). But for a criticism of NCGA Statement No. 3, see Robert J.

Freeman and Craig Douglas Shoulders, "Defining the Governmental Reporting Entity," *Journal of Accountancy*, October 1982.

5. With regard to the shift to the entity theory, Vatter states: "The second viewpoint called the entity school is of comparatively recent origin," William J. Vatter, *The Fund Theory of Accounting and Its Implications for Financial Reports*, (1947), p. 2. In a footnote, he adds:

> Littleton (in *Accounting Evolution to 1900*, 1933, p. 133) would seem to disagree with this statement, for he writes: "Continental writers of the last decade of the nineteenth century labored under the impression that the origin of the entity theory reached back only into the eighties. But later researchers tend to show that the basis at least extends much further back than that period."

However, the earlier references that Vatter discusses seem to be minor. Later Vatter quotes Littleton:

> It can hardly be said that the entity theory had achieved its full structure as an organized exposition of the nature of double-entry bookkeeping prior to 1900. Much that was necessary to round out the early notions was added after the turn of the century (p. 200).

Vatter's explanation of the shift from the proprietary view to the entity view is indicated by the following:

> The advent of the corporate form of business enterprise marks a change in the basic pattern, because corporate proprietorship is quite a different kind of thing from the simpler of business units . . . the proprietary interest is not that of one or a few men, but it refers to a constantly changing group of people (p. 3).

In their monograph, *An Introduction to Corporate Accounting Standards* (1940), which is one of the earliest expositions of the entity view, W. A. Paton and A. C. Littleton give this explanation:

> The simple notion of profit expressed as the personal gain of the proprietor cannot be applied to the corporate situation in which owner-stockholders are constantly moving in and out of the area of proprietary interest. This state of affairs lays the scene for the entity theory of accounting. . . . The basic position of the entity theorist is perhaps best expressed in the following terms: The business undertaking is generally conceived as an entity or institution in its own right, separate and distinct from the parties who furnish the funds, and it has become almost axiomatic that the business accounts and statements are those of the entity rather than those of the proprietor, partner, investors, or other parties or groups concerned (p. 8).

For additional references supporting the entity view, see Premise 1 in Chapter 2, and the related notes.

6. A leading proponent of this view is W. A. Paton. The 1957 report of the Committee on Concepts and Standards of the American Accounting Association also took this narrow view of the entity, stating, "interest charges, income taxes,

and true profit-sharing distributions are not determinants of enterprise net income,''
(p. 5). The 1966 American Accounting Association report did not mention the entity question.

7. Kenneth S. Most points out that a German writer, Eugen Schmalenbach, argued for the primacy of the income statement as early as 1916: *Accounting Theory*, 2d ed. (1982), p. 41. However, statistics on New York Stock Exchange companies indicate that previous to 1926 only 54 percent of them published net income amounts, whereas 100 percent published a balance sheet: George J. Benston, ''The Value of the SEC's Accounting Disclosure Requirement,'' *The Accounting Review*, July 1969, pp. 515–32. See also Note 46 in Chapter 2.

Prior to 1930 the general concern was with ''adequate'' and ''understandable'' balance sheets, on the grounds that for credit purposes, the balance sheet was of primary importance. Neither the Investment Bankers Association nor the accounting profession seem to have had investors' needs for financial information as their primary concern. On at least six occasions between 1920 and 1928, the Investment Bankers Association issued reports on minimum standards for financial disclosure in prospectuses, and in each the emphasis was on a detailed balance sheet, with only a one-line number for income.

During the 1917 to 1926 period, the American Institute of Accountants (AIA)—later AICPA—directed its main efforts towards encouraging business executives to use balance sheet audits for credit purposes. An example is the document, *Uniform Accounting*, prepared under George O. May's direction for the AIA in 1917, revised several times, and republished by the Federal Reserve Board (approved also by the Federal Trade Commission) in 1929 and renamed *Verification of Financial Statements*. Most of this document related to balance sheet audits; only the last three pages gave ''some suggested forms'' of comparative income statements and balance sheets.

During the period 1926 to 1932, the AIA undertook two cooperative efforts to bring about improved corporate disclosure, but they were not fruitful. In 1930, with the urging of J. M. B. Hoxsey and influenced by the effects of the stock market crash, the Institute appointed a committee, with George O. May as chairman, to cooperate with the New York Stock Exchange ''in consideration of all problems which are of common interest to investors, exchanges, and accountants.'' This undertaking represented a significant change in outlook by the accounting profession. *Uniform Accounting* had been prepared by persons connected with institutions concerned with the quality of credit, and its recommendations were made with the credit grantor in mind. But this new undertaking was with the New York Stock Exchange, and the accounting problems were therefore considered from the standpoint of investors in equity securities.

The report of this special committee was published in 1933 under the title *Audits of Corporate Accounts*. It listed four principal objectives the committee thought the exchange should ''keep constantly in mind and do its best to gradually achieve.'' These goals were (1) to bring about a better recognition by the public that balance sheets did not show present values of the assets and liabilities of corporations, (2) to encourage the adoption of balance sheets which more clearly showed on what basis assets were valued, (3) to emphasize the cardinal importance of the income account, and (4) to make universal the usage by listed corporations of certain broad principles of accounting that had won fairly general acceptance. (These historical observations are taken from David F. Hawkins, *Corporate Financial Reporting* (1977).)

In 1936, The American Accounting Association published *A Tentative Statement of Accounting Principles Affecting Corporate Reports*. The statement centered "chiefly on the following aspects of corporate accounting: Costs and values, measurement of income, and capital and surplus": *The Accounting Review*, June 1936.

In 1940, William A. Paton and A. C. Littleton in *An Introduction to Corporate Accounting Standards*, p. 67, emphasized the relative importance of the income statement as compared with the balance sheet:

> The fundamental problem of accounting, therefore, is the division of costs incurred between the present and the future in the process of measuring periodic income. The technical instruments used in reporting this division are the income statement and the balance sheet. Both are necessary. The income statement reports the assignment to the current period; the balance sheet exhibits the costs incurred which are reasonably applicable to the years to come. The balance sheet thus serves as a means of carrying forward unamortized acquisition prices, the not-yet-deducted costs; it stands as a connecting link joining successive income statements into a composite picture of the income stream.

The appendix to Paton and Littleton's book contains a selected bibliography through June 1939.

Subsequent official pronouncements of the AICPA stress the importance of the income statement. See also Paul Frishkoff, *Reporting of Summary Indicators: An Investigation of Research and Practice* (1981). This report concludes that earnings per share, an income statement concept, is the most widely used summary indicator.

8. An earlier authoritative statement of this view was in Accounting Research Bulletin No. 43: "The fairest possible presentation of periodic net income with neither material overstatement nor understatement, is important." Unfortunately, APB Statement No. 4 (1970), which, although not an authoritative document, is widely quoted, took an equivocal position. Paragraph 12 states: "The information presented in an income statement is usually considered the most important information provided by financial accounting." Yet in paragraph 75, the results of operation are defined in terms of changes in economic resources and obligations, which harks back to the balance sheet view. The flavor of paragraph 75 permeates the document and is also evident in many of the documents issued by the FASB.

A few authors question the importance of the income statement. See David Solomons, *The Accounting Review*, July 1961; and Maurice Moonitz, "Should we Discard the Income Concept?" *The Accounting Review*, April 1962, pp. 175–80.

9. See Thomas F. Keller and Stephen A. Zeff, eds., *Financial Accounting Theory: Issues and Controversies* (1969); Eldon S. Hendriksen and Bruce P. Budge, eds., *Contemporary Accounting Theory* (1974); Robert H. Parker and G. C. Harcourt, eds., *Readings in the Concept and Measurement of Income* (1969).

10. Irving Fisher, *Elementary Principles of Economics*, 3d ed. (1919), p. 38; James R. Hicks, *Value and Capital*, 2d ed. (1946), p. 176. For a critical analysis of this approach, see Keith Shwayder, "A Critique of Economic Income as an Accounting Concept," *Abacus*, August 1967, pp. 23–35; reprinted in Hendriksen and Budge, *Contemporary Accounting Theory*, pp. 83–96.

11. Alfred Marshall, *Principles of Economics,* 8th ed. (1920). Murray C. Wells traces the idea back to 1886 in *Accounting for Common Costs* (1978), pp. 103–5.

12. For an expanded discussion of this point, see Robert N. Anthony, *Financial Accounting in Nonbusiness Organizations* (1978), especially Chapters 1 and 3. An analysis made for the FASB by Paul K. Brace et al. of Peat, Marwick, Mitchell & Co. concluded that it was not feasible to measure the amount of services performed, even as supplementary information: *Reporting of Service Efforts and Accomplishments* (1980).

13. Renato Mazzolini describes the importance of the break-even point in government organizations in some depth in "Government Controlled Enterprises: What's the Difference?" *Columbia Journal of World Business,* Summer 1980. Some authors state the earnings concept in words that are applicable to both profit-oriented and nonprofit entities. For example, Paton states: "The essential problem in accounting is, and for a long time has been, to decide what events affect the current period and what affect future periods": *Accounting Theory* (1922).

14. Those favoring the revenue/expense approach included six of the largest public accounting firms and 52 of 58 corporate respondents. (These data were obtained from an analysis of the responses made by Michael Mikolayczyk.) For an excellent discussion of the two approaches, see David Solomons, ed., *Proceedings of the Conference on the Conceptual Framework of Accounting* (1977).

Although in its conceptual writing the FASB takes the asset/liability approach, in its standards it often takes the revenue/expense approach. See, for example, Statement No. 48, *Revenue Recognition When Right of Return Exists* (1981), and Statement No. 49, *Accounting for Product Financing Arrangements* (1981).

15. See L. Todd Johnson and Reed K. Storey, *Recognition in Financial Statements: Underlying Concepts and Practical Conventions* (1982), Chapter 12. The authors, who are members of the FASB staff, argue that a firm sales order is an asset, as defined. Although the authors do not say so, at the moment the order is booked, the entity has an obligation to deliver the goods, which is a liability. The amount of the liability is only the *cost* of these goods, however. Thus, net assets increase by the difference between the increase in the asset and the increase in the liability, and this difference, which is the gross margin on the order, is, by definition, income.

16. Examples of difficulties with the asset/liability approach are as follows:

a. Convertible bonds. Before conversion, convertible bonds are liabilities. When they are converted to stock, the corporation's liabilities are correspondingly reduced, and this increases net assets. Thus, if the definition were followed literally, the conversion of convertible bonds would increase income. Most people would agree that no income results from this transaction; all it does is to convert one type of funds source into another type. The only way that this absurd effect on income could be avoided is to view the conversion as involving two separate transactions: (1) the exchange of the bonds for cash and (2) the subsequent investment of this cash in stock. This is not what happened.

b. Preferred stock. Preferred stockholders are owners. However, some preferred stock issues also meet the definition of liabilities. Redeemable preferred stock, for example, (1) entails a legal responsibility to transfer assets at a specified date, (2) affords the enterprise no discretion, and (3) results in an obligation that has already happened. These are the three characteristics of liabilities given in the FASB Concepts Statement No. 3, paragraph 29. Indeed, the obligation is much clearer and more immediate than the obligation to pay deferred income taxes, which is specifically classified as a liability, and it may be discharged sooner than mortgage bonds with a distant maturity. If preferred stockholders are owners, their dividends are a distribution of capital, and income is unaffected. If preferred stock is a liability, dividends are a charge against income, just as is interest on bonds.

By straining the definitions, it might be possible to classify each variant within the preferred stock and convertible bond categories as either liabilities or owners' equity, but the fact that such straining is required demonstrates the conceptual weakness of the definitions.

In a symposium sponsored by the FASB on June 24, 1980, three distinguished panelists were asked whether redeemable preferred stock was a *liability,* as the FASB defined this term in its conceptual framework. The panelists agreed that redeemable preferred stock was a liability and that the obligation to pay it was more immediate than a bond with a more distant maturity. They balked, however, at accepting the inevitable consequence of this classification, namely, that in the context of the FASB conceptual framework, preferred dividends are an expense.

c. Compensation stock options. Some companies issue stock options to employees as a part of their compensation for services rendered. If an employee can purchase stock at less than its market value, there is a cost to the entity; the option certainly is not a gift to the employee. Conceptually, this is an expense of the period in which the services were performed. In the framework of FASB Concepts Statement No. 3, this cost would not be recognized. When the option is granted, neither assets nor liabilities are affected, there is no change in net assets, and hence no effect on income. When the option is exercised, the cash received is a contribution by owners, and this does not affect income.

d. The asset/liability approach suggests that depreciation is a decrease in the value of assets. Depreciation cannot measure a change in an asset's value in any meaningful sense; rather, depreciation is an allocation of an asset's cost to accounting periods.

e. In order to fit into the asset/liability approach, deferred income taxes (if a credit balance) must come within the definition of a liability. Yet the obligation to pay deferred income taxes at some indefinite time in the future is nowhere near as strong as obligations that are not recognized as liabilities, such as the obligation to make pollution control expenditures in response to legislation.

f. A loss on purchase commitments does not affect either assets or liabilities, since the FASB framework does not imply that the commitment itself should be recorded. Nevertheless, it is definitely a loss.

g. Repairing a machine increases its value over what it was before the repair was made. In the asset/liability approach, repairs would therefore be capitalized.

h. Land improvements donated by a municipality to a company in order to encourage building a plant is an asset. In the asset/liability approach, such a donation increases assets and therefore results in revenue.

i. A sale/leaseback transaction often results in an increase in net assets since the cash received is often greater than the book value of the assets sold. In the asset/liability approach, this transaction therefore would result in revenue.

j. Internally generated goodwill increases assets as much as does purchased goodwill. If a company received a tender offer at greater than book value, this is valid evidence of the amount of internally generated goodwill. This amount therefore results in revenue in the asset/liability approach.

k. Bond issue costs decrease net assets. They therefore would be an expense in the asset/liability approach. ~not ~of accted for as reduction in proceeds

17. Paton and Littleton, in *Corporate Accounting Standards*, describe nonmonetary assets as "charges awaiting future revenues" (p. 26). However, at a 1970 symposium, Paton said, "I am firmly convinced that the most significant measure of any resource is what it is currently worth": Williard E. Stone, ed., *Foundations of Accounting Theory* (1971), p. xi. Paul Grady in *Inventory of Generally Accepted Accounting Principles for Business Enterprises*, Accounting Research Study No. 7 (1965), describes the balance sheet as simply "a summary of balances in the books of account."

18. Stone, *Foundations of Accounting Theory*, pp. 102–3.

19. Perhaps the controversy could be resolved if there were agreement on the meaning of "value." In the analysis, I have implicitly taken it to mean what something is worth, in some sense. Richard Mattessich, however, states in *Accounting and Analytical Methods* (1964): "In a broad sense, all proposals for accounting relate to value because in a broad sense numerals are assigned to objects or events in order to express preferences, and these are values" (p. 144). The classical economics concept of "value in exchange" then becomes only one type of value. Mattessich also states, referring to Boulding, that economists no longer say that a person maximizes value; rather, a person maximizes utility (p. 156). Boulding points out, however, that this elegant sounding statement "means no more than a person does what he thinks best."

20. Study Group on the Objectives of Financial Statements, *Objectives of Financial Statements* (1973), pp. 27–40.

21. FASB Discussion Memorandum, December 2, 1976, paragraphs 71–86. The memorandum includes several quotations by authors who oppose the articulation concept. See also George J. Staubus, "Revenue and Revenue Accounts," *Accounting Research*, January 1956.

22. For a summary of these views, see Chapter 1, Note 30.

23. The concepts on comparability, consistency, materiality, and conservatism given here are discussed in much greater depth in FASB Concepts Statement No. 2.

24. For a thorough discussion of the materiality concept, see James W. Pattillo, *The Concept of Materiality in Financial Reporting* (1976).

25. For attempts to measure the value of information, see Joel S. Demski, *Information Analysis* (1972), and Gerald A. Feltham, *Information Evaluation* (1972). Several American Accounting Association committee reports have addressed this problem (see Supplements to the *Accounting Review* for 1972, 1973, 1974). After reviewing all this material, Charles T. Horngren concludes: "The cost-benefit approach does not take us very far when we try to apply it in the multiperson setting of large organizations": "Management Accounting: Where are We?" in *Management Accounting and Control* ed. W. S. Albrecht (1975), pp. 9–26. See also Note 9 in Chapter 2.

26. Yuji Ijiri, *Historical Cost Accounting and its Rationality* (1981), pp. 27–30.

27. Shortly after the Russian Revolution, the Soviet Union attempted to develop an accounting system in which a unit of human effort was the basic unit of measurement. The purpose was to avoid units of money because money was regarded as a capitalistic device. The effort failed. The Soviet accounting system, like most accounting systems, now has a monetary basis.

Charnes, Colantoni, and Cooper have proposed a multidimensional accounting system that would include both monetary and nonmonetary amounts. It would report such nonmonetary benefits as the number of minority persons hired, training given, and housing provided at less than market rates, and it would report such costs as the cost of removing sulfur particulates from the environment. I doubt that reliable estimates of these amounts can be obtained or that they can be aggregated in some way in an overall accounting system. See Abraham Charnes, Claude S. Colantoni, and William W. Cooper, "A Futurological Justification for Historical Cost and Multi-Dimensional Accounting," *Accounting, Organizations and Society* (1976).

28. For a recent discussion of corporate responsibility reporting, see the report of the AICPA Committee on Social Measurement, *The Measurement of Corporate Social Performance,* (1977) and Marc J. Epstein, Eric G. Flamholtz, and John J. McDonough, *Corporate Social Performance: The Measurement of Product and Service Contributions* (1977). Neither report describes feasible ways of making social measurements.

The AICPA Trueblood committee report, *Objectives of Financial Statements,* had a chapter, "The Relationship of Enterprise Goals to Social Goals," which concluded with the recommendation that social activities be included in financial statements to the extent that "they can be determined and described or measured" (p. 55). Since reliable measurement is usually not feasible, this recommendation has little practical import.

In its March 14, 1980, Exposure Draft, *Objectives of Financial Reporting by Nonbusiness Organizations,* March 14, 1980, the FASB stated (paragraph 45): "Financial reporting should provide information about the service efforts and *accomplishments* of a nonbusiness organization" (italics added). However, the final Statement eliminated the requirement about accomplishments because "the ability to measure service accomplishments, particularly program results, is generally undeveloped": FASB Concepts Statement No. 4, paragraph 53.

29. The literature on this subject is vast. For an excellent short history, see Paul Rosenfield's section, in Seidler and D. R. Carmichael, eds., *Accountants' Handbook,* 6th ed. (1981), Chapter 24. Excerpts from his piece are in *Journal of Accountancy,* September 1981, pp. 95–126. The classic book is Edgar O. Edwards and Phillip W. Bell, *The Theory and Measurement of Business Income* (1961). The discussion in Statement No. 33 covers the principal points. The readings book by Eldon S. Hendriksen and Bruce P. Budge, *Contemporary Accounting Theory,* has some excellent articles.

30. Lawrence Revsine, "Let's Stop Eating Our Seed Corn," *Harvard Business Review,* January–February 1981. For a contrary conclusion see William C. Norby, "Inflation Accounting Revisited" *Financial Analysts Journal,* November –December 1981. Norby analyzed the financial statements of 111 industrial companies for the period from 1973 to 1980. He concluded that these companies collectively were able to maintain their physical capital and also expand their physical volume by a combination of retained earnings and new debt and equity financing.

31. Definitions and classifications in this section correspond to those in FASB Statement 33, *Financial Reporting and Changing Prices* (1979), unless otherwise noted.

32. For a summary of the situation in European and British Commonwealth Countries, see I. Kleerekoper, "Information Reflecting the Effects of Changing Prices," *Technical Papers of the International Congress of Accountants* (1982) pp. 39–56.

33. For a list of these studies, see Seidler and Carmichael, eds., *Accountants' Handbook,* Chapter 24, Note 40. For more recent studies see my Note 42.

34. See Richard F. Vancil and Roman L. Weil, *Replacement Cost Accounting* (1976); Lawrence Revsine, *Replacement Cost Accounting* (1973). The Rosenfield section in the Seidler and Carmichael *Accountants' Handbook* has 67 footnotes.

35. In an American Accounting Association address, "Accounting and Financial Reporting—The Challenges of the 1980s," (FASB, November 3, 1980), Reed K. Storey said: "I think the handwriting is already on the wall for the present accounting model (which is often mislabeled 'historical cost accounting') . . . it can't cope with everyday complications, such as changing prices and fluctuating foreign exchange rates . . . these changes are inevitable."

David Solomons has gone so far as to write, "it is impossible to think of a decision for which historical cost information is relevant unless it is specifically stipulated by statute, regulation, or contract": in a book review, *Journal of Accountancy,* April 1982, p. 100.

For a contrary view, see William J. Schrader, Robert E. Malcolm, and John J. Willingham, "Accounting for What Might Have Been," *Financial Executive,* September 1982.

36. For an expansion of these points, see Yuji Ijiri, *Historical Cost Accounting and its Rationality.* See also Alfred Rappaport, "Inflation Accounting and Corporate Dividends," *Financial Executive,* February 1981; Yuji Ijiri, *Theory of Accounting Measurement,* especially Chapter 6; Howard J. Snavely, "Current Cost for Long Lived Assets: A Critical View," *The Accounting Review,* April 1969; A. C. Littleton, "Factors Limiting Accounting," *The Accounting Review,* July 1970. Littleton makes this cogent comment: "Accounting has no facility for reporting 'what might have been'. . . . Present prices cannot change the amounts of recorded transactions already completed."

37. For a demonstration of the validity of this point, see Robert N. Anthony, "A Case for Historical Costs," *Harvard Business Review,* November–December 1976, pp. 69–79.

38. *Federal Power Commission v. Hope Natural Gas Co.* 320 U.S. 591.

39. For a discussion of the limitations of assessed or appraised values, see Robert T. Sprouse, ed., *The Meaurement of Property, Plant and Equipment* (1964).

40. Although the idea is probably old, I learned it from Walter F. Frese, who uses it frequently as the basic rationale for historical cost inventory accounting.

41. Lawrence Revsine, "Inflation Accounting for Debt," *Financial Analysts Journal*, May–June 1981.

42. According to an article in *Fortune*, General Electric Company does use current costs in its management accounting system: Carol J. Loomis, "How GE Manages Inflation," *Fortune* May 4, 1981, pp. 121–24. In reporting current cost information in its 1980 annual report, General Electric also endorsed the concept strongly but emphasized the considerable subjectivity involved in the calculations: "These types of adjusted data are likely to be more useful in reviewing trends over a period of time, rather than in making comparisons of restatements for any one period or in specific analyses of one period compared with another". To me, this statement suggests that General Electric supports reporting current costs as supplementary information but not for the primary financial statements. In a speech before the 1981 annual meeting of the American Accounting Association, Terence E. McClary, vice president of GE, said: "Current cost recognizes the specific cost to replace an asset and requires that we recover enough to replace the asset consumed. This view of profit, the one we favor, gets to the heart of managing a business." This suggests that GE would like to recover current costs, but it does not say that GE is, in fact, able to do so.

A study of the relationship of disclosure of replacement cost information to stock market volume showed that no significant relationship existed and that the replacement cost accounting data made public under ASR 190 "did not contain new information pertinent to holding decisions by investors": Byung T. Ro, "The Disclosure of Replacement Cost Accounting Data and Its Effect on Transaction Volumes," *The Accounting Review*, January 1981. See also a criticism of this study in the same issue.

A questionnaire survey with responses from 201 *Fortune* 500 companies reported that less than 40 percent believed that the inflation accounting data prepared in accordance with Statement 33 in 1980 annual reports were worth the cost of preparing it, and that 96 percent thought that these data, if prepared at all, should be supplementary information: Arthur Young & Company, "Financial Reporting and Changing Prices," August 1981.

Other surveys of Fortune 500 or Fortune 1000 companies report a similar lack of interest: Charles H. Gibson, "How Industry Perceives Financial Ratios," *Management Accounting*, April 1982, Dale L. Flesher, "Controllers Say FAS 33 is not Very Useful," *Management Accounting*, January 1983, pp. 50–53. Although acknowledging this lack of interest, Allen H. Seed believes it reflects a lack of understanding: "Managing More Effectively with Inflation Adjusted Data," *Financial Executive*, November 1982, pp. 15–20.

A survey of 90 senior financial executives reported that in only 25 of the companies were the data used internally and in none did Statement 33 disclosures have an effect on the company's ability to raise capital: The Conference Board, *Experience with Inflation Accounting in Annual Reports* (1982).

Kenneth Most, *Accounting Theory*, 2d. ed. (1982) Chapters 10 and 11 has additional material, including the results of other user surveys.

43. Hospital Financial Management Association (1980).

Notes to chapter 4

1. As explained in Chapter 3, there are two versions of the entity theory. The analysis here is consistent with the version that regards debt financing and equity financing as two sources of funds and that regards income as being earned only after the cost of using these funds has been recouped. It is not consistent with the view that income is an amount earned before any distributions to bondholders, shareholders, or the government as income taxes. No authoritative body supports the latter view, nor is it implied in any accounting standard.

2. For a thorough discussion of these views, see Eldon S. Hendriksen, *Accounting Theory*, 4th ed. (1982), Chapters 1 through 5, and 17.

3. Not all liabilities are claims. Some are legally enforceable claims, but others, such as deferred income tax liability, are not owed currently to anyone, and they may never become claims. This inconsistency is a further defect of the "resources equals claims" interpretation of the balance sheet equation, but it is not a necessary part of the argument for the changes suggested here.

4. Yuji Ijiri has a similar view of the balance sheet. He describes the left-hand side of the balance sheet as "unrecovered investments," that is, the forms in which cash has been invested; and he describes the right-hand side as "unpaid financing," that is, the sources from which cash has been obtained. If "funds," were substituted for "cash," Ijiri's description would be the same as that given here. Yuji Ijiri, "Cash Flow Accounting and its Structure," *Journal of Accounting, Auditing and Finance*, Summer 1978.

In a letter to FASB (File reference 1004–Olg, May 14, 1980) the AICPA also developed the entity view. However, this letter recommended that the "duties of the enterprise to its owners should be set out in the notes to the financial statements." This conclusion is not consistent with its analysis because the analysis demonstrates that owners' equity is a separate category of equity and should be reported as such *within* the financial statements.

The statement of financial position of the Broken Hill Proprietary Company Limited, the largest company in Australia, reflects the view that one section shows the source of funds and the other section shows the form in which they are now invested. The heading of one section is "Funds have been provided from," and the heading of the other section is "These funds are represented by." (The first section is placed above the second section, rather than to the right of it, as is customary in the United States.)

In socialist countries, no great distinction is made between debt and equity. Entities obtain funds from the government. Some of these funds are furnished with a specified obligation to pay principal and interest; they correspond to debt. Other funds are furnished without such specified obligations; they correspond to equity. In the accounting system, entities are charged for the use of both types of funds.

5. Although unlikely, it is conceivable that dividends could exceed the cumulative amount of equity interest. If this should happen, the question arises as to whether the excess should be debited to shareholder equity or to entity equity. I think the preferable practice is to charge entity equity, so as to keep intact the amount of the shareholders' original contribution of funds. This point is debatable, however.

6. The terminology is relatively unimportant. I use the word *equity* so as to relate the new terms as closely as feasible to terms with which readers are familiar and thus to retain such ideas as the debt/equity ratio, equity financing, and the like. More precise labels would be "funds supplied by shareholders" and "funds generated by the entity." In an unincorporated business, the item corresponding to shareholder equity would be labeled "partner equity" or "proprietor equity." For further discussion of this terminology, see Chapter 7.

Also, for brevity, I use *liabilities* as a general term for all funds furnished by outside parties other than shareholders. Some liabilities, such as deferred income tax, are not obligations. I use *creditors* as a general term for all the parties who supply these funds, although I recognize that some, such as unpaid employees, are not normally classified as creditors.

Since nonprofit organizations do not have shareholders, the problem of separating shareholder equity from entity equity does not arise in such organizations. The amount they report as operating equity already corresponds to entity equity. Nonprofit organizations may also add to their equity by contributions for plant and endowment. These contributions are not associated with operations. They are discussed in Chapter 7.

7. The idea that equity interest should be explicitly recognized as an element of cost was extensively discussed in the early decades of the 20th century. In an April 1913 article, "Interest on Investment in Equipment," *Journal of Accountancy*, William Morse Cole wrote: "To exclude interest charges from cost of . . . jobs is to ignore one of the most important matters that we should know, namely, how far this use of capital is economically justified" (p. 240). See also American Institute of Accountants, "Report of the Special Committee on Interest on Relation to Cost," *Yearbook* (1918), pp. 110–12; W. P. Hilton, "Interest on Capital," *Journal of Accountancy*, October 1916; C. H. Scovell, "Interest on Investment," *American Economic Association Papers and Proceedings*, March 1919, pp. 22–40; and C. H. Scovell, *Interest as a Cost* (1924).

For a more thorough review of this history, see Robert N. Anthony, *Accounting for the Cost of Interest* (1975), pp. 21–25; and S. Paul Garner, *Evolution of Cost Accounting to 1925* (1954), pp. 142–61.

For recent discussions, see Philip L. Defliese, *Should Accountants Capitalize Leases?* (1973); "Defliese Calls for 'Cost of Capital Disclosures'," *The Journal of Accountancy*, May 1975, p. 25; and David Harold Silvern, "Enterprise Income: Measuring Financial Management," *Financial Executive*, April 1975, pp. 56–61. In

"Interest and Profit Theory—Amended from an Accounting Stance," *Michigan CPA*, January–February 1976, William A. Paton develops the idea that equity interest should be accounted for as a cost. However, his method of reporting this cost differs from the method to be described here. Paton's article is reprinted in *Journal of Accountancy*, June 1976.

8. Dividends would be debited to shareholder equity. The distinction between dividends declared and dividends paid becomes less important in this framework than in current practice. Probably it would be desirable to continue the present practice of debiting shareholder equity when dividends are declared, and crediting a liability account. The liability account would be debited when the dividends were disbursed. Stock dividends and treasury stock transactions would be treated the same as in current practice. Shareholder equity would be divided into paid-in capital and accrued equity interest. I see no reason to retain the distinction between par value and other paid-in capital, even in current practice.

9. The amount of dividends on common stock usually is far less than the return that shareholders expect to earn on their investment. In 1980 the annual dividend yield on the Standard & Poor's 500 common stocks was about 5 percent, and the composite yield on AAA bonds was about 11.5 percent. Because the risk to the investor is lower, the cost of debt funds is clearly lower than the cost of equity funds. Therefore, the cost of equity funds must be much higher than the 5 percent dividend yield.

10. Sara A. Lutz, "Pension Plan Disclosures: What They Mean," *Management Accounting*, April 1982; and Katherine Schipper and Roman Weil, "Alternative Accounting Treatments for Pensions," *The Accounting Review*, October 1982. Differences reported in the latter study for the pension obligation computed under two different methods averaged three times the annual pension cost.

The FASB analyzed the financial statements of 1,100 companies and reported that the interest rates assumed in computing the actuarial amount of pension expense in 1980 ranged from 4 percent to 12 percent: FASB, *Highlights of Financial Reporting Issues* October 14, 1981, p. 4. This range results in a difference of 300 percent in reported pension expense, other things being equal.

11. There is much discussion in the theoretical literature about measuring the cost of capital. (In this literature "capital" means shareholder equity, rather than assets as used in this framework.) For a readable book, see James H. Lorie and Mary T. Hamilton, *The Stock Market: Theories and Evidence* (1973). The collection edited by Eugene F. Brigham, *Readings in Managerial Finance* (1971), has five articles on this subject, and there are references to many others. None of them suggests a solution that could be implemented by most companies.

One of the four terms in the capital asset pricing model is *beta*, which is a measure of risk. In a careful analysis, Burton G. Malkiel demonstrates that this measure is significantly inferior to the simple alternative of measuring the dispersion of analysts' forecasts of earnings: *Risk and Return, A New Look*, NBER Working Paper No. 700 (1981).

Another approach to arriving at the cost of equity funds is the dividend-growth model. It assumes that the value of stock is the present value of the future stream of dividends. A crucial term in this model is *g*, the assumed rate of dividend growth through time. Since there is no reliable way of estimating g, this model is not of practical use.

For an empirical analysis based on this model, see Franco Modligliani and Richard A. Cohn, "Inflation, Rational Valuation, and the Market," *Financial Analysts Journal*, March–April 1979, pp. 24–44. This article has interesting implications. The authors make a careful analysis of the relation of stock prices to inflation-adjusted earnings. They conclude that stock prices in the late 1970s were only about 50 percent of what they should have been if investors acted rationally. This leaves them in a quandary.

If their conclusion is correct, then the capital asset pricing model does not describe an efficient market. Indeed, the model is useless as a basis for decision making because it does not include an allowance for the investor's irrational behavior, and there is no way of making such an adjustment except on the unrealistic assumption that investors will behave as irrationally in the future as they have behaved in the past. Rather than attempt to make such an adjustment, investors would be better off to scrap the model and use a model that does explain market behavior. On the other hand, if the conclusion is wrong, then the model must also be wrong— it does not represent what it is supposed to. Since Professor Modigliani is one of the leading proponents of the capital asset pricing model, this study provides special food for thought.

There have been other recent studies on the effect of inflation adjusted earnings. Some reach conclusions similar to that given above; others end up with the conclusion that stocks are not underpriced.

See Notes 35 and 36 for empirical applications of the capital asset pricing model.

For an approach to estimating the equity interest rate for hospitals (which is a component of reimbursable costs), see Richard W. Furst and Rodney L. Rosenfeldt, "Estimating the Return on Equity Capital," *Hospital Financial Management*, June 1981.

12. Statement No. 34, *Capitalization of Interest Cost*, contains some qualifications, the most important one being that the total amount of capitalized interest cost in a year cannot exceed the amount of debt interest cost in that year. In the present accounting model, such a restriction is necessary; otherwise, the difference between capitalized cost and debt interest would show up as income. As I stated in Corollary 3A to Premise 3, an entity cannot earn income by dealing with itself. A company cannot earn income by the act of *acquiring* an asset.

Some people doubt that Statement No. 34 actually does require the capitalization of interest on both debt and equity. Indeed, Paragraph 53 of that standard indicates that Board members disagreed among themselves on this point. I think the Statement is clear. Paragraph 13 states: "The amount capitalized in an accounting period shall be determined by applying an interest rate(s) ('the capitalization rate') to the average amount of *accumulated expenditures for the asset* during the period" (emphasis added). "Accumulated expenditures" are *all* the expenditures; there is no way in most circumstances of separating expenditures made with debt financing from expenditures made with equity financing, nor does the standard suggest such a separation. The capitalization rate is the pretax debt rate, but it is applied to all expenditures.

Statement No. 34 (paragraph 15) prohibits the capitalization of interest in excess of the total amount of debt interest. This prohibition would be unnecessary if only debt interest were capitalized.

Despite the argument in the first paragraph above, some people believe that interest in excess of debt interest should be recorded as a revenue item on the operating statements of public utilities. They state that when a rate regulatory body permits the capitalization of interest on construction work in process (CWIP), it implicitly guarantees that the utility can recover this cost through its prices. In Chapter 7, I shall argue that revenue recognition requires performance. In this case, the utility has not performed until it has delivered the services to customers; it had not done this at the time the asset was under construction.

Statement No. 34 uses a rate derived from "borrowings outstanding during the period" (paragraph 13). I think this overstates the cost of all funds because some funds—accounts payable, accrued wages, deferred income taxes—were obtained at zero interest cost. These funds should be incorporated in calculating the average interest cost. See the appendix for the technique of doing this. Some people argue that accounts payable and other funds sources that have no explicit interest cost actually have an implicit interest cost. Although this point is debatable, even if it were valid, there is no feasible way of identifying this cost. For certain liabilities, such as notes payable with zero stated interest, the implicit amount of interest can be, and should be, calculated.

13. Income tax regulations also specify rates that apply to related party loans, to certain types of installment payments, and for other transactions in which the rate is not directly observable. Although stated as numerical rates, these are changed from time to time as the general level of interest rates changes.

14. See Note 16 in Chapter 3. In Concepts Statement No. 3, the FASB admitted that drawing a line between liabilities and equities "may involve practical problems" (paragraph 49), although it claims that the line is "clear in concept." A few of the problems described in Note 16 are mentioned. It has pushed the discussion of these problems forward to its project on recognition, but as of this writing (early 1983), it has not published recognition concepts.

15. In Concepts Statement No. 3 (Note 34), the Board notes that equity interest (which it calls "imputed interest") is a problem, states that it does not intend to foreclose recognition of equity interest, but defers the issue to a future concepts statement.

16. See, for example, Paul A. Samuelson, *Economics*, 11th ed. (1980), Chapter 30.

17. Intermediate accounting texts give a description of these instruments. See, for example, Glenn A. Welsch, Charles T. Zlatkovich, and Walter T. Harrison, *Intermediate Accounting*, 5th ed. (1979), Chapters 15, 17, and 19. Finance texts also describe various types of instruments. See for example, James C. Van Horne, *Financial Management and Policy*, 5th ed. (1980).

For recently developed instruments, see Holly A. Clemente, "Innovative Financing," *Financial Executive*, April 1982. One reason for the development of these instruments is the issuer's desire to make its obligation as unrestrictive as the investor will tolerate, but to make the instrument sufficiently like debt so that its interest cost will qualify as a tax-deductible expense. Another reason is that the issuer would like to have the instrument classified as equity so as to improve its debt/equity ratio, while the investor wants a stronger assurance of payment than the usual equity security provides. This is why redeemable preferred stock is sometimes issued as part of the payment for an acquisition.

18. This topic is discussed in depth in finance texts. The essential point is that debt securities put a more onerous burden on the company, but because of the lower risk to the lender and because debt interest is tax deductible, they have a lower cost to the company than does equity. Equity securities, for opposite reasons, have a lower risk to the company and a correspondingly higher cost.

A few authors deny that the debt/equity ratio has any significance. The best known article is Franco Modigliani and M. H. Miller, "The Cost of Capital, Corporate Finance, and the Theory of Investment," *American Economic Review*, June 1958. However, their finely spun arguments do not fit the facts in the real world. For an article demolishing the Modigliani and Miller thesis, see Robert H. Litzenberger and James C. Van Horne, "Elimination of the Double Taxation of Dividends and Corporate Financial Policy," *The Journal of Finance*, June 1978.

19. Techniques for this analysis are described in most texts on management accounting. See, for example, Robert N. Anthony and James S. Reece, *Accounting Principles*, 5th ed. (1983), Chapter 22. The only situation in which the specific types of funds are relevant in analyzing capital investment proposals is one in which the proposal itself involves a specified mixture of debt and equity. This happens, for example, in the purchase of income producing property that is to be financed in part by a mortgage loan. After the decision to accept an investment proposal has been made, alternative ways of financing it may be considered (e.g., lease versus purchase), but this financing decision is made separately from the decision to acquire the asset.

20. A 1977 survey of the 1,000 largest American companies found that 74 percent had investment centers: James S. Reece and William R. Cool, "Measuring Investment Center Performance," *Harvard Business Review*, May–June 1978. By definition, an investment center is a responsibility center in which the amount of capital employed is explicitly measured, either by measuring the return on assets employed or by including a charge for the use of funds as an element of cost.

21. See Edward N. Rausch, *Financial Management for Small Business* (1979); and Ernest W. Walker and J. William Petty II, *Financial Management of the Small Firm* (1978).

22. The classic text on rate regulation is James C. Bonbright, *Principles of Public Utility Rates* (1961). A more recent text is Alfred E. Kahn, *The Economics of Regulation: Principles and Institutions* (1970–71).

23. The history of Statement No. 34 illustrates both the resistance to change (Premise 22) and also how this resistance can be overcome. I proposed the recognition of equity interest in "Accounting for the Cost of Equity," *Harvard Business Review*, November–December 1973. In a chance conversation with John C. Burton, chief accountant of the Securities and Exchange Commission, I learned that he had read the article and was strongly against the proposal. In June 1974, the SEC proposed a moratorium on interest capitalization, and this proposal became binding with the issuance of Accounting Series Release 163 on November 14, 1974. The moratorium was to be reconsidered "at such time as the Financial Accounting Standards Board develops standards for accounting for interest cost."

The FASB did not have this topic on its agenda, and until the SEC action, had no plans to add it. The FASB added the topic to its agenda on November 25, 1974. Statement No. 34 was issued in 1979, not an unusually long interval as such projects go. It has seemed to me that ASR 163 turned out to be counterproductive to the SEC's goals; if the release had not been issued, the topic might still be absent from the FASB agenda.

As an indication of FASB inaction in the absence of pressure, one of the issues in the discussion memorandum regarding interest (issued December 1977) was the recognition of equity interest as a cost under all the circumstances described in this chapter. As of 1983, six years later this issue has not been added to the FASB agenda, let alone worked on.

Cost Accounting Standard 414 (discussed in Note 24) provides another example of how standards result from pressure. The Cost Accounting Standards Board (CASB) was created in 1970. Its original agenda listed the principal items that it decided should be considered, and interest was not one of them. In March 1975, CASB issued CAS 409, Depreciation of Tangible Capital Assets, which required straight-line depreciation over the service life of the asset. This principle was strongly opposed by defense contractors, who succeeded in getting the Congress to hold hearings on it in April and May 1975. (The Congress could veto any CASB pronouncement within 60 days of its publication.)

At these hearings, some witnesses advocated adjusting depreciation by an allowance for inflation. At the request of Elmer Staats, the CASB chairman, I testified and advocated the recognition of interest as an allowable cost of using capital. Dr. Staats promised that both possibilities would be considered, and the congressional committees therefore did not veto the implementation of CAS 409.

The CASB staff developed a standard for an inflation adjustment (proposed CAS 413) and another for the recognition of interest cost. The Board soon agreed that the inflation adjustment was both conceptually unsound and impracticable, and CAS 413 was dropped. The other approach became CAS 414, *Cost of Money as an Element of the Cost of Facilities Capital*, issued July 1976.

The original proposal included recognition of the cost of using working capital, as well as plant. Developing a workable way of incorporating working capital turned out to be complicated (although, in my opinion, not overly complicated), and this aspect of the project was deferred. It was still on the CASB agenda when the Board went out of existence in 1981. The principles of CAS 414 were extended to all federal procurement by Federal Procurement Regulation 61, May 1981; the five-year delay is another indication of how slowly change occurs in the absence of pressure.

24. Cost Accounting Standard 414 applies to facilities capital (that is, plant and equipment). The rate is the rate specified by the U.S. Treasury as the rate on medium-term fixed income securities (CAS 414.40 (b)). The Cost Accounting Standards Board was developing a similar approach to calculating the interest cost of current assets (or working capital) but did not publish a standard on this topic prior to its dissolution in 1981. A similar approach is used in pricing cost-type government contracts in the United Kingdom and the Federal Republic of Germany.

25. T. D. 7747, *Federal Register* 45 (December 31, 1980), p. 86738.

26. For a discussion of this point, see Robert N. Anthony, *Financial Accounting in Nonbusiness Organizations* (1978), Chapter 3; and Robert N. Anthony and Regina E. Herzlinger, *Management Control in Nonprofit Organizations,* 2d ed. (1980), Chapters 4 and 5.

27. For an elaboration of this point, including references that discuss it as early as 1788, see D. A. R. Forrester, "Holding Costs or Holding Gains," *Management Accounting* (United Kingdom) March 1977.

28. The SEC attempted to deal with this problem in the petroleum industry by a practice called reserve recognition accounting. The idea of this approach was to recognize the present value of petroleum reserves and of changes in this value resulting from reestimates of the size of the reserves and of the present value of the ultimate sales proceeds. It found that there was no reliable way of measuring these amounts and abandoned the system. The approach suggested here will not incorporate the value of reserves, but it will make the asset amount higher the longer the reserves are held.

29. For a discussion of this point, see Philip L. Defliese, "What Makes Profits Look 'Obscene'," *Business Week*, August 4, 1975.

30. David W. Young, "Accounting for the Cost of Interest: Implications for the Timber Industry," *The Accounting Review*, October 1976.

31. James A. Hayes and Robert N. Anthony, *Accounting for the Cost of Interest,* Working Paper HBS 75–47 (1975).

32. Cornelius J. Casey, *Capitalization of Interest Costs: Empirical Evidence of the Effect on Financial Statements,* Working Paper HBS 78–59. (1975).

33. George J. Benston, "The Value of the SEC's Accounting Disclosure Requirement," *The Accounting Review,* July 1969.

34. In addition to these two studies, another study tested the usefulness of the information. Baruch Lev and Kenneth W. Taylor studied the association between stock returns and conventional performance measures, particularly earnings per share, and the association between stock returns and earnings net of the cost of equity funds, calling the latter amount "residual earnings:" Baruch Lev and Kenneth W. Taylor, "Accounting Recognition of Imputed Interest on Equity," *Journal of Accounting, Auditing and Finance,* Spring 1979. The test did not show an association. However, the model used was such that an association was unlikely to be revealed by it.

The tests were performed for two five-year periods: 1962–1966 and 1969–1973. The residual earnings amount was computed by deducting from reported income an estimate of the cost of equity funds. This cost was estimated as the product of the expected rate of return on common stock derived from the capital asset pricing model, applied to the book value of common equity. Lev and Taylor concluded that the empirical evidence "does not lend support" to the proposition that entity residual earnings is a more efficient source of information as a basis for arriving at market price of stocks than conventional performance measures.

Unfortunately, the question addressed in this study was not the relevant question. Stock market prices should reflect *both* the residual earnings *and also* the addition of interest to shareholder equity. This study omitted the latter component. The amount of residual earnings reflects the performance of the entity as an entity. It does not fully reflect the shareholders' stake in that performance. The residual earnings amount affects stock prices only in the sense that it incorporates some assessment of risk; that is, it allows for the effects of leverage and business risk.

This study, and the other two studies that are summarized next, do not incorporate the idea of separating shareholder equity from entity equity. They assume that the amount of equity interest (which they tend to call "imputed interest") for a year is credited to retained earnings. This creates a little difficulty in relating the results to the framework that I describe. This difference does not affect the relevance of the results to my argument, however.

35. Jon W. Bartley, "Accounting for the Cost of Capital: An Empirical Examination," *Journal of Business Finance and Accounting* 9, no. 2 (1982). Bartley applied the same interest rate to the book value of all companies. Several rates were examined, including a risk-free rate, a risk-free rate plus an estimated risk premium, the prime rate, and Aaa and Baa corporate bond rates. For comparison, estimates of each company's cost of equity capital were calculated, based on the dividend valuation model of Gordon and Shapiro, and the ex post statement of the capital asset pricing models of Sharpe and Lintner. Bartley's conclusions were:

> The results of this study appear to support the position that entity residual income measures contain information which is not present in either proprietary income or entity operating income. Specifically, entity residual income may be more useful for the assessment of market risk. However, the evidence is not conclusive, and the important issue of predictive ability is not directly addressed.
>
> A secondary finding which could have implications for policy makers is that entity residual income measures based upon a simple uniform imputed interest rate have characteristics similar to those based upon more sophisticated unique rate estimates. The levels of correlation between accounting and market risk measures were fairly uniform over a range of imputed interest rates. This indicates that the choice of a specific uniform rate may not be critical in the context of risk assessment. These findings suggest that the old issue of choosing between a reliable measure of entity residual income and a subjective but theoretically superior measure may pragmatically be a nonissue.

This study is particularly important because it is one of very few efficient market studies which has indicated that one accounting practice may be superior to another in the sense that the reported number more accurately reflects a variable (e.g., security returns or systematic risk) that the investor considers important.

This article contains an excellent bibliography.

36. Jon W. Bartley and Lewis F. Davidson, "The Entity Concept and Accounting for Interest Costs," *Accounting and Business Research*, Summer 1982.

In this study, interest was treated as a period cost; that is, none of the interest cost was capitalized. In each iteration, a single uniform interest rate was applied to the book or market value of common equity of all companies, letting the rate vary over time. As a basis for comparison for the uniform rate measures (the same as in Bartley's study), forward extensions of the Gordon/Shapiro dividend model, and of the ex post statement of the capital asset pricing model were used to generate unique estimates of each company's cost of equity capital. The conclusions of the study were that:

> entity residual income measures based upon uniform imputed interest rates are likely to be good surrogates for more sophisticated measures based upon unique cost of capital estimates for each company. The cross-section distributions and rankings of companies based upon uniform and unique rate estimates were surprisingly similar for comparable aggregate levels of imputed interest costs. This seems to resolve the most difficult issue relating to the implementation of an entity residual income measure. . . . Although further research is needed, the results of this study clearly suggest that the objective, uniform imputed interest approach to estimating the cost of equity capital may result in an entity residual income measure very similar to that based on a theoretically more sound estimate.
>
> The selection of an appropriate imputed interest rate to be applied to the equity base of all companies has always been a major problem for advocates of this simple approach to imputing the cost of equity capital. The results of this study suggest that the choice of a specific imputed interest rate is less crucial than previously thought. The differences between the cross-sectional distributions of entity residual income were small within a range of imputed interest rates of roughly six percent. Of course, the average level of entity residual income of all companies is affected by the choice of an imputed interest rate.

37. Conceptually, the value of a profit-oriented entity is the present value of its future earnings. Although a few writers advocate a conceptual framework that measures this amount, almost everyone would agree that no reliable estimate of it can be made. Articles advocating such an approach or suggesting that it is worth consideration include: J. W. Coughlan, "Funds and Income," *NAA Bulletin*, September 1964; George J. Staubus, "The Relevance of Evidence of Cash Flows," in *Asset Valuation and Income Determination*, ed. Robert R. Sterling (1971); and Joshua Ronen, "A Test of the Feasibility of Preparing Discounted Cash Flow Accounting Statements," in *Objectives of Financial Statements: Selected Papers* ed. J. J. Cramer and G. H. Sorter (1974).

38. In his Chapter 30, titled "Interest and Capital," Paul Samuelson neither states nor implies that interest is related to debt funds only. He refers at various points to common stock, savings bank deposits, and bonds as all involving interest cost. In his Chapter 31, "Profits and Incentives," Samuelson writes that reported profits include interest: Samuelson, *Economics*, 11th ed. (1980).

39. See Note 20.

40. For a description of the proposed accounting concepts in Common Market countries, see the *Fourth Directive* of the European Economic Community, August 1978.

41. Professor Benjamin M. Friedman, in a working paper report (1979) of a project for the National Bureau of Economic Research, "The Changing Role of Debt and

Equity in Financing U.S. Capital Formation," estimated that only 4 percent of external corporate financing is equity and 96 percent is debt.

Another source estimated that in 1979 additional funds for nonfinancial corporations came from the following sources: retained earnings, $68.3 billion; equity sold, $3.2 billion; and debt, $109.8 billion. Malcolm A. Salter and Wolf A. Weinhold, *Merger Trends and Prospects for the 1980s*, Working Paper HBS 80–49 (1980).

42. For a discussion of this point, including the advantages of an equity interest deduction over other proposals for encouraging capital formation, see my articles, "Equity Interest: A Cure for the Double Taxation of Dividends," *Financial Executive*, July 1977; and "Recognizing the Cost of Interest on Equity," *Harvard Business Review*, January–February 1982, pp. 91–95. For an excellent discussion of income taxes in general, see Dan Throop Smith, "Issues in Tax Policy," in *The United States in the 1980s*, ed. Peter Duignan and Alvin Rabushka (1980).

43. In hearings held by the House Ways and Means Committee on November 19, 1979, Dan Throop Smith agreed with most aspects of Chairman Al Ullman's bill (H.R. 5665) to reform the income tax but expressed disappointment that the bill did not provide relief from double taxation of dividend income. Chairman Ullman responded: "Elimination of double taxation would be in the package were it not for the fact that the corporate world is divided on the subject."

44. In addition to recognition in financial accounting, authoritative bodies are increasingly recognizing interest for special purposes. In each case, the parties have found some reasonable way of arriving at the rate. Recognition of interest in setting regulated rates, in reimbursement for cost-type defense contracts, and in certain income tax calculations has already been mentioned. The FASB requires estimates of interest rates in capitalizing leases, in exchange transactions between related parties, and in notes given for noncash considerations when the stated rate is unreasonable.

Government contracts with hospitals, colleges and universities, and state and municipal governments increasingly provide for the recognition of interest as a cost. See Note 47.

Some of those who are unwilling to accept an approximation of equity interest cost are the very people who advocate versions of current cost or replacement cost accounting, for which the approximations are much less exact.

45. Ross M. Skinner, *Accounting Principles: A Canadian Viewpoint* (1972), p. 91.

46. Three members of the Financial Accounting Standards Board voted against Statement No. 34. In their dissenting opinion they said they "consider interest to be a cost of a different order from the cost of materials, labor and other services."

47. For an excellent description of the historical development and current status of interest recognition in contracts of all types, see the 130-page opinion of the Armed Services Board of Contract Appeals in the Pennsylvania Blue Shield case (ASBCA No. 21113), July 20, 1982. The traditional government attitude is stated in 28 U.S.C. Section 2516(a):

> Interest on a claim against the United States shall be allowed in a judgment of the Court of Claims only under a contract or Act of Congress expressly providing for payment thereof.

The regulations referred to are Office of Management and Budget (OMB) Circular A–21, relating to educational institutions, 1982 revision; OMB Circular A–87, relating to contracts with state and local governments, 1980 revision; and Medicare and Medicaid regulations. However, OMB Circular A–122, applying to nonprofit organizations generally, does not permit interest as an allowable cost.

Notes to chapter 5

1. The AICPA's Accounting Research Bulletin 43 (Chapter 4) states: "As applied to inventories, cost means in principle the sum of the applicable expenditures and charges directly or indirectly incurred in bringing an article to its existing condition and location." This definition has the same thrust as that given here. APB Statement No. 4 (Paragraph 164) states that cost can be defined in several ways, but it ends up defining only acquisition cost. FASB Concepts Statement No. 3 relegates the definition of cost to a brief, vague footnote in paragraph 20. The FASB did not, as of early 1983, have a project whose purpose is to develop cost concepts. The definition used here is substantially the same as that used by the Cost Accounting Standards Board.

The framework developed by Yuji Ijiri is an axiomatic approach to the subject matter of this chapter. Although stated somewhat differently, its thrust is entirely consistent with the approach I describe. See Yuji Ijiri, *Historical Cost Accounting and Its Rationality* (1981), Chapter 5.

2. Loose use of these terms can cause confusion. For example, Sidney Davidson et al. in *Accounting: the Language of Business*, 4th ed. (1979), defines *expenditure* as follows: "Payment of cash for goods or services received. Payment may be made either at the time the goods or services are received or at a later time. Virtually synonymous with 'disbursement.' . . ." This definition is incorrect; "expenditure" is fundamentally different from "disbursement." When an employee works, the entity makes an *expenditure* for the cost of labor services. When the entity pays the employee, either in the near future for salary or a long time in the future for pension benefits, there is a *disbursement*. It is an unfortunate fact that some entities, particularly nonprofit organizations, publish an operating statement that lists items labeled "expenditures" that actually are disbursements. Such a statement is misleading if unpaid expenditures are material.

Ralph Estes, in *Dictionary of Accounting* (1981), defines "expenditure" as follows: "Something of value spent, paid, or consumed, most commonly a payment of cash." This definition manages to mix the ideas of "expense," "expenditure," and "disbursement" in a single sentence!

In the federal government, "expenditure" was at one time defined as being synonymous with "disbursement." This was because the government did not use accrual accounting and recorded acquisitions as of the time of disbursement and in the amount disbursed. Currently, the federal government uses "outlays" as the term for disbursements, a practice which is approximately correct. The federal government also uses the term "obligation." An obligation is recorded at the time the government contracts to acquire goods or services. This term has no counterpart in business accounting; obligations are not recorded in the accounts. Many state and municipal governments use "commitment" for this same idea.

3. FASB Concepts Statement No. 3 is not entirely clear on this point. In paragraph 65 it defines expenses as "outflows or other using up of assets or incurrences of liabilities (or a combination of both) during a period from delivering or *producing goods*" (italics added). Statement No. 3 justifies equating production costs with expenses in a footnote that states that in the percentage-of-completion method, production costs are expenses in the period. As I shall show in Chapter 6, although costs are charged as expenses in the percentage-of-completion method, this is not because they are production costs of the period. It is because they are applicable to revenue that is earned in accordance with a contractual agreement.

The implication that all production costs of a period are expenses of that period is misleading. As an example of the confusion it causes, see page 39 of the FASB Discussion Memorandum, *Employers' Accounting for Pensions and Other Post-Employment Benefits* (1981). The pension cost of a year is there equated with pension expense, which is clearly incorrect. Part of the pension cost remains in inventory, and only the remainder is an expense.

4. See, for example, APB Opinion No. 29, *Accounting for Nonmonetary Transactions* (1973).

5. Unfortunately, the Cost Accounting Standards Board in CAS 402, (Sec. 402.30) used the term *allocate* for the broader idea that is here called *assign*. Once it adopted this definition, the CASB was unwilling to change it. This use has resulted in some awkwardness in later pronouncements because having used *allocate* in the broader sense, the CASB had no meaningful word to use for the assignment of indirect costs. Following the example set by CASB, others use *allocate* in the broader sense, but this practice leads to unnecessary confusion.

6. For development of a conceptual framework for cost accounting that is based on general systems theory, see George J. Staubus, *Activity Costing and Input-Output Accounting* (1971).

7. One school of economists argues for the "utility theory" of value, which states that the production process does add value to the entity. This may perhaps be the case, but there is no way of making this idea operational in accounting. The value of a manufactured product cannot usually be reliably measured until the product is sold, and even then the division of the profit margin between the amount attributable to production and the amount attributable to marketing is usually not feasible.

Despite the impracticality of measuring increases in value during the production process, some staff members of the Financial Accounting Standards Board believe that this approach is "a more promising area for obtaining real improvement in recognition practice than does more tinkering with the sales basis . . .": L. Todd Johnson and Reed K. Storey, *Recognition in Financial Statements* (1982), p. 201. Perhaps the recognition of equity interest as a cost would accomplish a result similar to what they have in mind. In any event, situations in which the *value* added by production (in contrast to the *cost* added by production) can be reliably measured are so rare that they could not conceivably form the basis for a generalization. These exceptional situations will be discussed in Chapter 6.

8. Murray C. Wells, in *Accounting for Common Costs* (1978), concludes that "the allocation of overhead costs is wrong." In his analysis, Wells refers to 150 sources, including 11 cost accounting texts published since 1969. The analysis has fatal flaws.

Although 10 of the 11 cost accounting texts say that the allocation of overhead costs is not wrong in appropriate circumstances, Wells asserts, "the arguments used in support of allocation procedures are confused and inconclusive." He bases this assertion primarily on his analysis of three editions of Charles T. Horngren, *Cost Accounting: A Managerial Emphasis,* and two editions of Robert N. Anthony and James Reece, *Management Accounting Principles.*

As a professor who has used Horngren's text in class and as co-author of the other book, I can say that both books emphasize the fact that different cost constructions are appropriate for different purposes. Disregarding this basic point, Wells quotes from the Anthony/Reece text's discussion of circumstances in which allocations are *not* appropriate (for example, in alternative choice decisions) and gives the impression that we mean them to apply to *all* circumstances, including those in which allocations are appropriate (for instance, normal pricing decisions).

In his summary, Wells does not even mention pricing as a possible use of cost information. He specifically excludes temporal allocations from the whole study (p. 3), yet the problem of inventory costing is primarily a matter of temporal allocation.

Some economists have a cute way of getting around the undeniable fact that in the real world costs are allocated. They argue that the only relevant costs are incremental costs; that in problems involving pricing, rate setting, and contract costing, the relevant incremental costs are long-run costs, and the closest approximation to long-run incremental costs are allocated historical costs. This approach permits them to castigate allocated costs, beat the drum for incremental costs, and end up with numbers that although labeled incremental are in fact allocated.

The fallacy of this argument is that if one really tried to find long-run incremental costs, allocated costs would usually be a poor approximation. Incremental costs are supposed to indicate what costs will be in the future, whereas allocated costs are what costs have been in the past. In an environment in which there is inflation, productivity improvements, and technological change, historical costs are unlikely to correspond to future costs.

The arguments for cost allocation are made in literature that dates from the 19th century. Murray C. Wells, *Accounting for Common Costs* (1981), has an excellent summary of early developments, in contrast with my above criticism of his analysis of recent developments. See also Paul Garner, *Evolution of Cost Accounting to 1925* (1954).

9. For a lengthy discussion, see Arthur L. Thomas, *The Allocation Problem in Financial Accounting Theory,* and *The Allocation Problem: Part Two,* which are respectively AAA Studies in Accounting Research Nos. 3 and 9 (1969 and 1974). Shorter and more understandable versions of his basic argument appear in several publications: "The FASB and the Allocation Fallacy," *Journal of Accountancy,* November 1975, pp. 65–68; and "Matching: Up from Our Black Holes," in *Accounting for a Simplified Firm Owning Depreciable Assets,* ed. Robert R. Sterling and Arthur L. Thomas (1979), pp. 11–33.

In addition to the basic fallacy of equating "arbitrary" with "capricious," the principal example that Thomas uses does not relate to the usual cost allocation situation but rather to the reverse of that situation; the example is backwards. He describes the process of baking sourdough bread, which requires ingredients, labor, equipment, and a source of heat; and he states that it is impossible to allocate the price of the bread to these components. This is not the usual allocation problem; rather, the problem is to assign ingredients, labor, equipment, and other costs to the bread. To the extent that the cost elements are used only to make bread, the costs are direct, and there is no allocation problem. It seems likely that many of those who cite Thomas with approval have not studied his writings in sufficient detail to recognize the fallacies in them. His use of terms such as "corrigible" and of elaborate but irrelevant equations do not facilitate such a study.

In "Reporting of Faculty Time: An Accounting Perspective," *Science* 1 January 1982, pp. 27–32, Thomas demonstrates the weakness of his thesis. After the usual diatribe against allocation, Thomas comes up against the undeniable fact that in deciding on the reimbursable costs for a university research contract, indirect costs *must* be allocated. His solutions to this problem are incredibly naive: (1) the government and the university should "negotiate" the allocation; (2) divide the costs in proportion to the number of contracts (for example a 50/50 split if there are two contracts); or (3) establish an indirect cost rate. He does not give the slightest clue as to *how* the negotiation should be conducted or *how* the indirect cost rate should be arrived at.

For another argument against allocation, see Joel Demski and Gerald Feltham, *Cost Determination: A Conceptual Approach* (1976). This monograph was intended as a guide to concepts for the then newly established Cost Accounting Standards Board. Because the monograph rejects the idea of cost allocations as a basis for contract costing, and because most informed persons recognize that such allocations are essential in arriving at contract costs equitable to contracting parties (for example, the federal government and a contractor), the Cost Accounting Standards Board did not seriously consider the monograph.

10. This is approximately the idea of the 1971 American Accounting Association Committee on Foundations of Accounting Measurement. Its report in *The Accounting Review* (Supplement 1971), pp. 1–48, presented this definition: "A measurement process is arbitrary if (1) another numeral could have been assigned instead, (2) the economic decision to be made is sensitive to the difference between the two numerals, and (3) no conclusive argument is invoked to defend the numeral that actually was chosen."

The committee report goes on to say, however, "that any assignment of joint costs to two or more resulting products is arbitrary" according to these criteria. It gives no support for this assertion and thus slips into the notion that any inexact cost is arbitrary. The committee does conclude that cost allocations are necessary for the purposes of financial accounting, even though they are arbitrary.

11. Until recently, full cost (that is, the sum of direct and indirect costs) was regarded as the governing principle in price discrimination cases under the Robinson-Patman Amendment to the Clayton Act and in antitrust cases under the Sherman and Clayton Acts. However, a 1975 article focused attention on variable costs, which in this context are approximately the same as direct costs: Philip Areeda and Donald F. Turner, "Predatory Pricing and Related Practices Under Section 2 of the Sherman Act," *Harvard Law Review*, February 1975. This article has been widely quoted, both in the literature and in court decisions.

Critics of it have pointed out, quite correctly, that although prices below variable costs are discriminatory ("predatory" in the current jargon), the article does not demonstrate that prices above variable costs are nondiscriminatory; therefore, the article is not a demonstration that allocated costs are irrelevant. Furthermore, the logic of the article itself has been attacked. For a summary of the criticisms, see F. M. Scherer, "Some Last Words on Predatory Pricing," *Harvard Law Review*, March 1976.

The courts continue to rely on allocated costs in rate regulation cases. Lawyers, however, have uncritically picked up the Areeda/Turner theme in other contexts. For example, Robert C. Clark in a generally excellent article, "Does the Nonprofit Form Fit the Hospital Industry?" *Harvard Law Review*, May 1980, writes:

> Hospital activities benefit from large shared costs (indirect costs); yet no practical, economically sound means exist for allocating these costs to the several activities. Accountants' methods of allocating 'overhead' are arbitrary . . . (p. 1481).

This argument is wrong. As hospital managers and those who pay for hospital care will attest, there are indeed practical, economically sound allocation methods; they are used routinely for pricing millions of invoices for patient care.

12. A development with considerable promise is the "Shapley value." It has been advocated, for example, as a way of allocating state income taxes to divisions of a corporation doing business in California and in other states as well. California calculates the California taxable income of such a corporation by applying a percentage to the total income of the corporation. This percentage is the corporation's "business activity" in California as a percentage of its total business activity. Business activity is a simple average of its sales, its payroll, and the book value of its property.

Thus, each division in California caused the California taxable income in two ways: (1) it caused part of the total corporation income and (2) it caused part of the California business activity. There is no exact way of weighting the importance of these two causes, because their effect is joint. The usual practice, therefore, was either to attribute all of the tax to one of these causes or to assume that each cause should be weighted equally. The Shapley value produces a result that is certainly better than ignoring one of the joint causes, and that is probably more equitable than assigning equal weights, although its results are usually quite close to the simple solution of assigning equal weights.

The Shapley value is based on propositions from game theory, in particular that part of game theory that relates to negotiations. For its use in negotiations, see Howard Raiffa, *The Art and Science of Negotiations* (1982), pp. 269–73. Raiffa's comments on the uses and limitations of the Shapley value also apply to cost allocations.

The Shapley value method is needed only in situations in which there are joint causes. If the costs are attributable to a single cause (such as activity), then it gives the same result as straightforward allocation methods, but with much more work.

The original article was L. Shapley, "A Value for N-Person Games," in *Contributions to the Theory of Games,* ed. H. W. Kuhn and A. W. Tucker (1953). The first association of the idea to cost allocation was M. Shubik, "Incentives, Decentralized Control, the Assignment of Joint Costs, and Internal Pricing," *Management Science,* April 1962. The California income tax problem is described in R. E. Verrecchia, "An Analysis of Two Cost Allocation Cases," *The Accounting Review,* July 1982.

The most lucid explanation of the application of the Shapley value to the allocation problem that I know of is *Sharing Costs Fairly,* Executive Report No. 5, of the International Institute for Applied Systems Analysis (1981). This report describes an equitable way of allocating the cost of a proposed water supply system to the several cities that will use it. As an indication of the practical difficulty, however, even in this relatively straightforward problem, the decision makers decided that the results were unreliable and allocated the costs on the basis of the relative population of the cities rather than on the basis of the Shapley value.

Shane Moriarity, ed., *Joint Cost Allocations* (1981), has some excellent papers on cost allocation as well as papers repeating the tired arguments against allocation.

13. Most elementary accounting and cost accounting texts and handbooks have material on variable costing often, but erroneously, referred to as "direct costing." For a good analysis and summary of the literature, see James M. Fremgen, "The Direct Costing Controversy: An Identification of Issues," *The Accounting Review,* January 1964. Although Fremgen's paper is not recent, I know of no new arguments on the question. Since the topic is a favorite theme of the research arm of the National Association of Accountants, current material is likely to be found in their Research Reports and in their journal, *Management Accounting.*

Variable costing was first described by Jonathan Harris in "What Did We Earn Last Month?" *NACA Bulletin,* January 15, 1936. Since then it has been widely discussed in the literature. Although it is not acceptable either for general purpose financial statements or for calculating taxable income, many authors recommend its use for management accounting purposes, particularly in arriving at selling prices. Notwithstanding much endorsement in the literature, there is no evidence that variable costing is widely used in practice.

Some researchers are not convinced even by their own evidence. A study made for the National Association of Accountants found a strong tendency to use full costs in arriving at selling prices, but the authors found this surprising. See Lawrence A. Gordon et al., *The Pricing Decision* (1981). Another study for the same organization found that "indirect cost allocations are far more widely used than the accounting literature suggests they should be" but recommended that "allocations should nevertheless be limited to variable costs" for purposes such as cost-based pricing: James M. Fremgen and Shu S. Liao, *The Allocation of Corporate Indirect Costs* (1981), p. 80. In this study 84 percent of 123 respondents reported that they used allocated costs.

Article 35 (2) of the *Fourth Directive* of the European Economic Community takes an equivocal view on this matter. It states that the inclusion of indirect costs in product costs is optional. A sound conceptual framework should not have options on major topics, unless the conditions under which each option should be applied are spelled out.

I emphasize that this conceptual framework is limited to financial accounting. Variable costs are useful in management accounting.

14. For development of this point, see David Green, Jr., "A Moral to the Direct-Costing Controversy?" *The Journal of Business*, July 1960; and George H. Sorter and Charles T. Horngren, "Asset Recognition and Economic Attributes: The Relevant Costing Approach," *The Accounting Review*, July 1962. The arguments of these authors rely heavily on the erroneous idea that cost is a sacrifice.

15. Although recognizing the conceptual superiority of absorption costing, Skinner does not endorse it for the reason given in this paragraph: R. M. Skinner, *Accounting Principles* (1972), p. 344.

16. The Sterling Homex case (SEC Release 34–11514) is often cited as a case in point. Actually, this case did not involve selling overhead to inventory. Rather, the management recorded as revenues amounts for products that had not been sold. No accounting principle permits such a practice.

17. The word *equity* is also used for this idea, but in accounting, equity is also used as the name of a certain type of funds source and as a collective name for all sources of funds.

Some authors include the ability to bear the cost as a criterion of cost allocation. I see no rationale for such a criterion and do not discuss it. Another criterion is the independence of the cost object, meaning that actions taken with respect to one cost object should not affect the amount of cost allocated to other cost objects. There is some merit to this idea, particularly in cost assignments made for the purpose of measuring the performance of responsibility centers. This purpose, however, is a management accounting purpose, not related to financial accounting. The problem implied by this criterion can be avoided by proper application of the concepts given in this framework.

Several researchers have made studies of "fairness," using the approach suggested in the social choice literature. Basically, these are mathematical analyses of the preference of division managers for various allocation schemes. In all of them, it is assumed that a division manager will prefer an allocation scheme that is likely to give the division the lowest amount of allocated cost. This is a cynical assumption. It seems more reasonable to assume that managers will prefer a scheme that allocates costs in proportion to causal relationships. Because of this basic assumption, none of these studies seem to me to produce useful results. Some studies, which are worth reading only if one takes into account the above assumption, are: Shane Moriarity, "Another Approach to Allocating Joint Costs," *The Accounting Review*, October 1975; D. V. Balachandran and R. T. S. Ramakrishnan, "Joint Cost Allocation: A Unified Approach," *The Accounting Review*, January 1981; and D. L. Jensen, "A Class of Mutually Satisfactory Allocations," *The Accounting Review*, October 1977.

Raiffa, *The Art and Science of Negotiation*, Chapter 19, has an excellent discussion of the concept of fairness.

A good way of making the idea of fairness operational is to listen to discussions between a defense contractor and the contracting officer of the Department of

Defense. The contractor, assuming it also has commercial work, wants to allocate as much as possible of the common costs to a cost-reimbursement defense contract. The contracting officer wants the opposite; a disinterested third party can learn much from the arguments that each party puts forth.

18. Fifty-two of Spacek's speeches are collected in *A Search for Fairness in Financial Reporting to the Public* (1969). The idea of fairness as being the "basic postulate of accounting" was the theme of several of these speeches. In 1960 Arthur Andersen & Co. filed a brief with the Accounting Principles Board with the title, *The Postulate of Accounting;* the postulate was fairness.

19. Ijiri classifies accounting into *equity accounting* and *operational accounting.* In equity accounting, data are used to solve conflicting interests, and the system must be operated in the most objective, consistent, and unambiguous manner because the data it provides "directly affect the way in which conflicting interests are solved, e.g., in income tax accounting or in divisional accounting involving transfer of goods and services among divisions." In operational accounting, the accountants' objective is primarily to provide useful data for decision makers. Ijiri's concept of equity accounting is similar to that discussed in this section. See Yuji Ijiri, *The Foundations of Accounting Measurement: A Mathematical, Economic, and Behavioral Inquiry* (1977), p. 67.

The American Accounting Association Committee on Foundations of Accounting Measurement used the same classification in its 1971 report. It should be emphasized that both Ijiri and the AAA committee were discussing accounting in general, rather than that part of accounting called financial accounting, which is the subject of this framework. Although not precisely labeled in this way, these authors probably intended "equity accounting" as being equivalent to financial accounting and "operational accounting" as being equivalent to management accounting. It is unquestionably true that allocated costs are not relevant to many types of problems that arise in management accounting, particularly short-run, alternative choice decisions.

20. For a development of this idea, see James W. Pattillo, *The Foundations of Financial Accounting* (1965).

21. In nonprofit accounting, the term *generational equity* is used for the concept here labeled *temporal fairness.* It is a descriptive term because it indicates that a practice is equitable when costs are charged to the generation that benefits from them. See Emerson O. Henke, *Accounting in Nonprofit Organizations,* 3d ed. (1983).

22. In a case involving a tax on inventories, The Boeing Company based its argument on the benefits approach (U.S. Armed Services Board of Contract Appeals, The Boeing Company, ASBCA No. 19224). Two cost objects were involved: products made for the Department of Defense and products made for commercial customers. The city of Seattle levied a tax on the inventory associated with the commercial products but not on the inventory associated with the defense products (federal property was not taxed by the municipality). Boeing argued that the proceeds of the tax were used for education, fire protection, and other municipal services, and that the tax therefore benefitted all those who received these services. These included employees in plants making defense products as well as employees in plants making commercial products. Boeing therefore proposed to allocate the tax in proportion to the number of employees of these two cost objects. The Court quite properly rejected this argument. It found that the inventory associated with the commercial products *caused* all of the tax, and that the tax should therefore be assigned entirely to the commerical cost object.

For Boeing's position on this problem, and also for a thorough discussion of other aspects of cost allocation, see The Boeing Company, *Towards Common Concepts of Cost Allocations in Cost Accounting* (1978).

23. These bases are discussed in cost accounting texts. For recent developments, not incorporated in some texts, see Note 12.

One way of thinking about the appropriate basis of allocation is to consider what would cause the indirect costs of a cost object to vary if they were direct costs. Most items of indirect cost could be converted to a direct cost if the entity chose to do so. For the production of a single product, plant facilities could be built or leased for that product only; personnel, accounting, and other overhead services could be set up for that product alone; and so on. If these elements were direct costs, what would cause them to change in the moderately long run? Perhaps the quantity of products produced, perhaps the number of direct employees, and so on.

24. "Cost objects" must be distinguished from "cost elements." Cost elements are items of material, labor, and various types of services that together constitute the cost of cost objects. For example, in the sometimes asked question, "Is interest a cost of constructing a new plant, or is interest a financing cost?" the "either-or" implication is incorrect. Interest is a cost element in the construction of a new plant. The cost object is the plant. Financing is not a cost object. Treating fringe benefits as if they were cost objects is another example of failure to make this distinction.

25. AICPA, *Audits of Colleges and Universities* (1975), Chapter 6.

26. For example, telephone companies provide a variety of services, some of which are monopolistic and others are competitive. Rate regulators want each service to bear its fair share of costs. If the assignment is unfair, prices for the monopoly services may be too high, and the resulting extra profit may be used to subsidize the competitive services. This is the phenomenon known as cross-subsidization.

27. For a discussion of advertising see A. Rashad Abdel-khalik, "Advertising Effectiveness and Accounting Policy," *The Accounting Review*, October 1975.

28. Recall that this framework is limited to general purpose financial statements. It excludes problems of segment reporting, which is supplementary information, and it excludes principles of contract costing; these are not necessarily consistent with the standards of general purpose financial statements. The comments made here do not necessarily apply to these problems.

29. The idea of annuity depreciation is not new. Ladelle recommended it in the 19th century. See Richard P. Brief, "A Late Nineteenth Century Contribution to the Theory of Depreciation," *Journal of Accounting Research*, Spring 1967.

Hector R. Anton discussed annuity depreciation in 1956 in "Depreciation, Cost Allocation, and Investment Decisions," *Accounting Research*, April 1956. In addition to demonstrating the superiority of annuity depreciation when annual benefits are equal, Anton described several other patterns of benefits and developed the appropriate depreciation schedule for each.

The annuity method was favored in Maurice Moonitz and Louis H. Jordan, *Accounting—An Analysis of its Problems* (1963); and also by Philip L. Defliese, "Should Accountants Capitalize Leases?" (1973).

T. R. Dyckman has developed a technique that incorporates both annuity depreciation and the income tax effect of depreciation. See his "A Return-Reporting Framework," in *Accounting for a Simplified Firm*, ed. Sterling and Thomas.

William H. Beaver and Roland G. Dukes report the results of an empirical study which suggests that adjusting reported income for annuity depreciation improves the association between income and stock market prices (although this was not the purpose of the study): "Interperiod Tax Allocation and Delta-Depreciation Methods: Some Empirical Results," *The Accounting Review*, July 1973.

A search of the 1979–80 annual reports of 4,170 companies revealed only 11 that mentioned the use of annuity depreciation (or sinking-fund depreciation, which is similar); 10 were public utilities and 1 was a life insurance company: Accounting Standards Division, American Institute of CPAs, *Depreciation of Income Producing Real Estate* (1981).

For a bibliography, see Keller and Zeff, *Accounting Theory*, vol. 2, pp. 305–6.

30. Oscar Gellein, in correspondence, asks whether a quite different result might be obtained by applying the concept in another way. He suggests that investors advance funds for plant with the expectation of recovering these funds (plus interest) over the life of the plant. The longer this recovery period, the greater the amount of interest they expect. Thus, it can be argued that the cost of the plant increases each year by an amount of additional interest. This approach does not fit into my framework because it is inconsistent with Concept 5.05, which states that the cost of the plant is the total of the expenditures that make the plant ready for its intended use. The accumulation of cost stops when plant construction has been completed.

31. Currently, the only authoritative requirement is that the cost of a facility "be spread over the expected useful life of the facility in such a way as to allocate it as equitably as possible to the periods during which services are obtained from the use of the facility": Accounting Research Bulletin No. 43, Chapter 9, paragraph 5. However, the Securities and Exchange Commission has stated informally that it will not accept the annuity method (reported by Defliese; see Note 29).

Most authors advocate either the straight-line method or an accelerated method, the latter on the grounds that the presumed higher maintenance costs in later years should be offset by a lower depreciation charge in those years. The annuity method discussed in this section leads to an opposite depreciation pattern from an accelerated method; in the annuity method, the annual depreciation charge increases in the later years. The reason for this discrepancy is that my analysis considers the depreciation charge and the interest cost as together constituting the cost of using the asset. The cost of maintaining the asset is a separate matter. Furthermore, available evidence suggests that maintenance costs for many items do not increase as a function of time in the pattern implied by accelerated depreciation; they tend to increase for some years and then become level.

Mathematical arguments are advanced in support of both straight-line and accelerated methods. See Baruch Lev and Henri Theil, "A Maximum Entropy Approach to the Choice of Asset Depreciation," *Journal of Accounting Research*, Autumn 1978.

For an extended discussion of depreciation methods, including several variations of the annuity depreciation concept and their application to various patterns of income streams, see Eldon S. Hendriksen, *Accounting Theory*, 4th ed. (1982), Chapter 14. This reference also contains an extensive bibliography.

For the applicability of annuity depreciation to the measurement of divisional performance (as distinguished from financial reporting), see Charles T. Horngren, *Cost Accounting*, 4th ed. (1977), pp. 724–27.

For the relevance of annuity depreciation to rate making, see Ezra Solomon, "Alternative Rate of Return Concepts and Their Implications for Utility Regulation," *The Bell Journal of Economics and Management Science*, Spring 1970, pp. 65–81.

This framework does not deal with all aspects of depreciation and the related problems of amortization. Although the argument given here leads to annuity depreciation in the absence of evidence for a better method, there are circumstances in which other methods (such as units of production) are appropriate. One or more standards, consistent with the concept of temporal fairness, should address these issues.

32. Shyam Sunder, "Corporate Capital Investment, Accounting Methods and Earnings: A Test of the Control Hypothesis," *The Journal of Finance*, May 1980, p. 560.

For a more thorough discussion of this phenomenom, see Robert N. Anthony and John Dearden, *Management Control Systems*, 4th ed. (1980), Chapter 8.

33. These concepts are silent as to the treatment of income taxes. Taken literally, they do allow for the effect of income taxes because tax provisions related to depreciable assets almost always make the aftertax benefits unequal from year to year and the concepts apply only when the benefits are equal. As a practical matter, I think it highly unlikely that a standard would require the inclusion of income tax effects in the calculation of depreciation. This would be extremely complicated, and I doubt that the benefits would be worth the cost.

34. An essential part of the definition of liability in the FASB concepts statement on elements of financial statements is that the event "has already happened." This fact leads to confusion about such matters as pension payments, sick pay, holiday pay, and similar personnel benefits. These payments have not already happened, so it can be argued that they are not liabilities. With the framework given here, there should be less ambiguity about these topics. The cost of one hour of work includes these costs, so they are expenditures. The expenditures have already happened. Even if there is no contractual obligation to pay the sick pay or the vacation pay, and even if they are not paid to employees who leave, the amount of these payments that is caused by current hours of work can be estimated actuarily. Since they are expenditures not yet paid for, the corresponding amounts are also liabilities. Conversely, payments for vacations or sick leave in a subsequent period have nothing to do with the operations of that period. They therefore are not expenses of that period.

35. Paton and Littleton, *Introduction to Corporate Accounting Standards* (1940), describe revenues as "accomplishments" and expenses as "effort." Although these descriptions are approximately correct, they can cause problems in reporting certain types of transactions. For example, depreciation expense in a period involves no "effort" in that period; the effort was expended when the asset was acquired.

36. The AICPA Accounting Standards Division draft standard on *Accounting for Certain Service Transactions* includes this statement: "General and administration costs ordinarily should be charged to expense as incurred but may be charged to contract costs under the percentage-of-completion method if the costs are clearly identifiable with contract revenue." This requirement is inconsistent with the cost and expense concepts. If cost elements are part of the cost of producing goods or services, they should be so reported, whether or not the revenue arises under a contract.

Notes to chapter 6

1. I shall use *net income* for the bottom line on the operating statement. Net income has the same connotation as *earnings*, as used in FASB Concepts Statement No. 1 on *Objectives*, but *earnings* is inappropriate for nonbusiness organizations. Entity equity is changed both by income and also by certain other events described in Chapter 7, and in FASB Concepts Statement No. 3 on *Elements*, the aggregate of both types of changes is called *comprehensive income*. I have not found it necessary to use this term.

For a thorough discussion of the nature of income, see Edgar O. Edwards and Philip W. Bell, *The Theory and Measurement of Business Income* (1961); and Robert T. Sprouse and Maurice Moonitz, *A Tentative Set of Broad Accounting Principles for Business Enterprises*, Accounting Research Study No. 3 (1962).

Some theorists question whether an income concept has any meaning. William H. Beaver and Joel S. Demski, for example, express "deep concern over the role of the income concept" and over the idea that "more income is better than less." See their "The Nature of Income Measurement," *The Accounting Review*, January 1979. I do not understand their argument. In any event, it seems clear that in the real world, users of accounting information want to know how well the entity performed, even though the accounting measure of performance is less than perfect.

2. In addition to the evidence given in Chapters 2 and 3, a recent FASB Research Report confirms the importance of income measurement: Paul Frishkoff, *Reporting Summary Indicators: An Investigation of Research and Practice* (1981).

3. Philip Defliese gave me this quotation. He is sure it comes from George O. May, but neither he nor I can track its source. The idea is expressed, but not so succinctly, on pp. 30–31 of George O. May, *Financial Accounting: A Distillation of Experience* (1943).

Kenneth E. Boulding says that the measurement of income is the most important function of financial accounting: "otherwise accountancy would be mere arithmetic": *Economic Analysis*, 3d ed. (1955), p. 852.

William A. Paton and A. C. Littleton make a similar statement: "The fundamental problem of accounting is the division of the stream of costs incurred between the present and the future in the process of measuring income": *An Introduction to Corporate Accounting Standards* (1940), p. 67.

4. Henry R. Jaenicke, *Survey of Present Practices in Recognizing Revenues, Expenses, Gains, and Losses* (1981).

5. Paton and Littleton wrote "that revenue is 'earned' during the entire process of operation": *Corporate Accounting Standards*, p. 48. May wrote: "Manifestly, when a laborious process of manufacture and sale culminates in the delivery of the product at a profit, that profit is not attributable, except conventionally, to the moment when the sale or delivery occurred: *Financial Accounting*": *A Distillation of Experience* (1943), p. 30.

This idea is perpetuated in FASB Concepts Statement No. 3, footnote 23 which refers to:

> the concept that value added by productive activities increases assets as production takes place, which is the basis for the common observation that revenues are *earned* by the entire process of acquiring goods and services, using them to produce other goods and services, selling the output, and collecting the sales price or fee (italics in original).

Reed K. Storey's paper delivered at the 1980 American Accounting Association annual meeting (1980) states that "almost everybody knows that revenues result from the whole process of buying, converting, and selling assets or services and collecting the selling price." (I don't want to be counted as one of the "almost everybody".) A FASB Research Report develops this theory at great length but gives no indication as to how it can be made operational: L. Todd Johnson and Reed K. Storey, *Recognition in Financial Statements* (1982), especially Chapters 9 and 10.

6. John H. Myers, "The Critical Event and Recognition of Net Profit," *The Accounting Review*, October 1959, pp. 528–32. A similar idea was contained in the 1964 American Accounting Association on Concepts and Standards Committee report, "The Realization Concept," in *The Accounting Review*, April 1965. This idea is not to be confused with the "events" concept advocated by George Sorter. As explained in Chapter 1, the Sorter approach does not attempt to arrive at a single amount for revenue; in his approach the disaggregated components of income are reported.

7. For an excellent discussion of this point, see Charles T. Horngren, "How Should We Interpret the Realization Concept?" *The Accounting Review*, April 1965.

For a summary of statements about realization, see Yuji Ijiri *Historical Cost Accounting and its Rationality*, Research Monograph No. 1 (1981), p. 50.

8. An early reference to "nonreciprocal transfers", as distinguished from "exchanges" was in APB Statement No. 4, paragraph 62. Exchanges are transactions between one entity and another entity in which each entity gets something and gives up something else, and nonreciprocal transfers are transactions in which an entity gives or gets something, without getting or giving something else in return.

I do not find this distinction helpful. The distinction suggests that there is something fundamentally different between resource inflows from the sale of goods or services and resource inflows of other types, such as taxes in a municipality, contributions, donations, and grants. In fact, many nonbusiness organizations make such a distinction in their operating statement, labeling the first type as "revenue" and the second as "other support." Actually, both types of inflows add to an entity's equity; they make it better off.

Kenneth S. Most, *Accounting Theory*, 2d ed. (1982), pp. 430–33, equates revenue with output. With the broader view of revenue, his criticisms of existing revenue principles would, I believe, disappear.

9. For an argument in favor of the asset/liability approach, see Robert T. Sprouse, "The Importance of Earnings in the Conceptual Framework," *Journal of Accountancy*, January 1978. The main points are that the revenue/expense approach requires definitions of *matching* and *nondistortion*, and that these terms are difficult to define in an operational way. I believe that my definitions in this chapter are operational.

Many examples of erroneous reasoning about income arising from the asset/liability approach could be cited. For example, the firm of Ernst & Whinney argue that an allowance for compensated absences during the period in which the employee works is not properly counted as an expense for the reason that the "event" is the employee's illness, that this is not an expense until it happens, and that there is no liability until that time (letter to FASB, February 15, 1980). A focus on revenue/expense makes it clear that it is the work done in the current period that gives rise to the right to a compensated absence and that the expense should therefore be recognized in the period in which the work is done. Kenneth Most points out that the FASB concept of revenue was not helpful in arriving at its Statement No. 48: *Accounting Theory*, 2d ed., p. 429.

10. Yuji Ijiri goes so far as to state that "income should be distributable, hence, should be recognized only when money (cash or receivables) is acquired": *Historical Cost Accounting*, p. 81.

11. George J. Staubus, *Making Accounting Decisions* (1977), p. 172.

12. This idea is not new. Similar definitions were used by the AICPA Committee on Terminology, in Accounting Terminology Bulletin No. 2 (1955). However, in APB Statement No. 4 (paragraph 198) and in FASB Concepts Statement No. 3, gains and losses are separated from revenues and expenses.

13. According to Kenneth Most, the concept of matching was not specifically mentioned in the literature until the 1940s: *Accounting Theory*, 2d ed., p. 431.

Failure to appreciate the importance of the matching concept has led to some untenable conclusions. In 1981 and 1982 the FASB staff working on the nonbusiness project agonized at great length over the revenue recognition of contributions. The problem can be stated as follows: A university receives a $30,000 contribution in 1983 for the purpose of financing a conference to be held in 1984. Should the revenue be recognized in 1983 or in 1984?

Reasoning from the asset/liability approach, the staff concluded that if there was no legal obligation to spend $30,000 on the conference, there was no liability at the end of 1983, and the $30,000 was therefore revenue in 1983. The matching concept leads to the opposite conclusion. The expenses for the conference are incurred in 1984, and the corresponding revenue should therefore be recognized in 1984. To do otherwise would overstate income in 1983 by $30,000 and understate income in 1984 by the same amount.

14. "Operations" is used here in the broad sense in which it was used in APB Opinion No. 30. *Reporting the Results of Operations* (1973), not in the narrower sense of "continuing operations" or "ongoing major or central operations:" FASB Concepts Statement No. 3, Paragraph 64.

15. Norton M. Bedford, *Income Determination Theory* (1965), Chapter 3.

16. Standards apply the general idea of "performance" to specific situations. When considered in conjunction with the criterion of "reliable measurement" the two ideas suggest the proper resolution of many issues. Although producing goods is performance, the amount of income realized from these goods usually cannot be measured until the goods have been sold. Although installment sales represent performance, income from some installment sales is not sufficiently measurable until the installment payments have been received. Conversely, receipt of an advance payment is not revenue, even though the amount of income can be reliably measured because the entity has not yet performed by delivering the goods or services for which the advance payment was made.

17. Exposure Draft 20 of the International Accounting Standards Executive Committee (April 1, 1981) has three categories for the idea here labeled as "products": sales of goods, rendering of services, and holding of assets. The third category includes interest, dividend, and royalty revenue. Its proposed standard for each category is, I believe, entirely consistent with the concept to be stated here.

18. This statement is similar to that in the 1974 American Accounting Association Committee on Concepts and Standards report: "income should be reported as soon as the level of uncertainty has been reduced to a tolerable level": *The Accounting Review* (Supplement 1974), p. 209.

The same general idea is contained in earlier American Accounting Association Committee Statements: AAA Executive Committee, *Accounting Principles Underlying Corporate Financial Statements* (1941); AAA Executive Committee, *Accounting Concepts and Standards Underlying Corporate Financial Statements* (1957); and AAA Committee on Concepts and Standards, "A Discussion of Various Approaches to Inventory Meaurement," *The Accounting Review*, July 1964. As an indication of the relatively short time that accounting has focused on income measurement, the 1936 statement of the AAA, "A Tentative Statement of Accounting Principles Underlying Corporate Financial Statements," *Accounting Review*, June 1936, did not give criteria for revenue recognition.

19. Acceptance of the percentage-of-completion method is sometimes used as evidence that revenue may be recognized as a function of the "earning process." This is not so. The percentage-of-completion method is used only when there is a contract and when the income resulting from the performance of part of the contract can be reliably measured. Such contracts usually specify the points at which partial performance has been achieved and often provide for payment at these points. Production of goods under such contracts is inherently different from producing goods for inventory. In the latter case, the entity has not performed until it has sold the goods.

A standard for the percentage-of-completion method might well specify that income should be recognized only when the entity has a right to receive payment under the contract. This variation of the percentage-of-completion method is known as the "progress payment method." Such a standard might be interpreting the "highly likely" criterion too narrowly, however.

20. In 1980, interest revenue on the typical fixed-income portfolio was just about equal to the decline in market value of the portfolio, so if losses were taken into account, the net performance (called the "total return") would be approximately zero; nevertheless, entities that planned to hold fixed-income securities rather than sell them did, in fact, earn the interest revenue on such instruments. Article 35 of the *Fourth Directive* of the European Economic Community, August 1978, permits recognition of unrealized monetary losses if they are permanent.

21. The implications given here are consistent with the 21 implications listed in the Appendix to Exposure Draft 20 of the International Accounting Standards Committee, April 1, 1981.

22. For real estate sales, see the AICPA Accounting Guide, *Accounting for Profit Recognition on Sales of Real Estate* (1973); and the AICPA Audit Guide, *Accounting for Sales of Real Estate* (1979). For the record and music industry, see FASB Statement No. 50. For cable television systems, see FASB Statement No. 51. For sales with a right of return, see AICPA Statement of Position 75–1, *Revenue Recognition When Right of Return Exists* (1975). For leases, see FASB Statement No. 13 and its subsequent amendments and interpretations. For films, see the AICPA Accounting Guide, *Accounting for Motion Picture Films* (1979). These pronouncements are generally consistent with the concept.

The Sterling Homex case is sometimes cited as an example of the looseness of accounting standards with respect to revenue recognition. This is not a valid example. Sterling Homex recognized revenue on 10,000 finished modular houses in the period in which these modules were produced, even though only 900 of these modules were, in fact, sold in that period. This was a deceptive practice, not in accordance with any revenue recognition concept, and resulted in convictions for fraud.

23. Some people argue that the installment basis is unsound. See Richard A. Scott and Rita K. Scott, "Installment Accounting: Is it Inconsistent?" *Journal of Accountancy*, November 1979. The basic argument is that if income can be reliably measured, there is a sale, but that if it cannot be reliably measured, there is no income until the installment agreement has been carried out. I think a middle ground is desirable: the amount cannot be estimated with sufficient reliability to warrant income recognition on the sales basis, but income is sufficiently likely so that revenue need not be deferred until the completion of the transaction.

24. The percentage-of-completion method is permitted in AICPA, *Accounting for Performance of Construction-Type and Certain Production-Type Contracts* (1981).

25. FASB Statement No. 19 rejected the discovery basis on the grounds of the difficulty in measuring it (paragraph 133). This Statement has been withdrawn, however.

26. APB Statement No. 4 (paragraph 152) permits but does not require revenue recognition for agricultural products "with assured sales prices" when production is completed. That statement also permits the production basis for precious metals, but this is not consistent with Concept 6.04. (At the time Statement No. 4 was written, gold had an assured sales price.)

27. Although APB Statement No. 4 (paragraph 152) permits the production basis for precious metals, a 1976 study by Peat, Marwick, Mitchell & Co. found only 2 of 39 mining companies using this basis, and a 1978 study of Coopers & Lybrand found none of 21 companies using it. These studies are summarized in Jaenicke, *Survey of Present Practices*, p. 92.

28. The type of transaction described in AICPA Statement of Position (SOP) 75–1, *Revenue Recognition When Right of Return Exists*, is excluded from revenue but not because of the existence of a right of return. SOP 75–1 discusses the transaction in which a seller transfers inventory but agrees to buy it back at a later date. The seller's purpose is to create revenue in the period in which the transfer takes place. The importance of substance over form is the reason why this transaction does not generate revenue.

29. For a discussion of accretion, see Eldon S. Hendriksen, *Accounting Theory*, 3d ed. (1977), pp. 185–86.

30. It can be argued that sales and excise taxes are often part of accounts receivable and that if they are excluded from revenue, the sales/receivables ratio will be distorted. If such a distortion does occur, it can be corrected by excluding sales and excise taxes from the amount of receivables.

Article 28 of the EEC *Fourth Directive* states: "The net turnover [revenue] shall comprise the amounts derived from the sale of products and the provision of services falling within the company's ordinary activities, after deduction of sales rebates and of value added tax and other taxes directly linked to the turnover."

31. Most countries require deductions of sales rebates, but New Zealand, Switzerland, and the United States have no standard on this topic. Japan defines rebates as selling expenses: Organization for Economic Co-operation and Development (OECD), *Accounting Practices OECD Member Countries* (1980), pp. 17–19. Such differences confuse users of financial statements.

32. These principles are consistent with current practice. An alternative would be to recognize income from long-duration contracts over the life of the contract. However, this is regarded by many people as being inconsistent with the concept that income should be recognized as soon as it can be reliably measured. Present practice suggests that the key aspects of insurance are the sale of the policy, earning of premiums, and investment earnings. Subsequent payments of benefits can be reliably measured from mortality tables. Although investment earnings may be different from amounts assumed in arriving at the premium amounts, these differences can be recorded as revenues (or losses) in the period in which they occur. This treatment is debatable, however.

33. Article 39 of the EEC *Fourth Directive* requires a reduction of inventory amounts to market, but the reduction can subsequently be written up if the value increases. This write-up is not consistent with the framework described here. Article 40 permits FIFO, LIFO, or other inventory methods.

34. This principle is inconsistent with FASB Statement No. 2, which requires that research/development costs be expensed. Statement No. 2 should be re-examined. See Gary W. Burns and D. Scott Peterson, "Accounting for Computer Software," *Journal of Accountancy*, April 1982.

35. For an excellent discussion of this topic, see Lawrence C. Best and Paul A. Gewirtz, "Plant Closings: The Pension Cost Controversy," *Financial Executive*, November 1980.

36. Article 34 of the EEC *Fourth Directive* permits capitalization of "formation expense" and write-off over not more than five years. Article 37 applies Article 34 to research/development costs and requires that they be written off over not more than five years. Article 37 also applies Article 34 to goodwill, but the write-off period may be longer than five years.

37. FASB Statement No. 15, *Accounting by Debtors and Creditors for Troubled Debt Restructuring.*

38. For a discussion of this point, see Richard Mattessich, *Accounting and Analytical Methods* (1964), pp. 168–80. See also Prem Prakash and Shyam Sunder, "A Case Against Separation of Current Operating Profit and Holding Gains" (Unpublished working paper, March 1977).

39. For an argument against this conclusion, see Robert S. Kaplan, "Purchasing Power Gains on Debt," *The Accounting Review*, April 1977.

40. Although the FASB has issued statements on interest rate futures contracts, forward contracts and standby contracts, these statements relate to disclosure only and do not take a position on when, if ever, these contracts affect income.

Notes to chapter 7

1. An example is the FASB Exposure Draft, *Reporting Income, Cash Flows, and Financial Position of Business Enterprises*, November 16, 1981. Paragraph 7 explicitly defines capital as "the amount of owners' interest in the enterprise (owners' equity)." However, Paragraph 11 refers to "cost of capital" in the usual sense of a weighted average of the cost of using both debt and equity funds. There are several references to the "return on capital," in the sense of a return on the equity investment only. Paragraph 26 refers to an entity's "ability to raise new capital, perhaps by issuing debt securities. . . ." There are several references to an entity's "capital structure," which presumably refers to all items on the right-hand side of the balance sheet. Paragraph 99 refers to physical capital maintenance, and Paragraph 100 states that one definition of this term "focuses on the actual physical assets of the enterprise." Paragraph 101 refers to "working capital." Thus, the document uses "capital" to mean all items on the left-hand side, some items on the left-hand side, all items on the right-hand side, the sum of debt and equity, and (the explicit definition) shareholder equity.

2. *Equity* comes from the Latin word meaning "equal" or "fair." In general usage, this is understood to be its meaning, and it is one of its meanings in accounting. In accounting, however, *equity* has taken on the additional connotation of "claim." Equities are thought of as claims against the assets, and owners' equity as the owners' claim against the assets. Both these meanings derive from the common law related to equity, rather than to the concept of equity itself. Equity law and courts of equity are intended to provide fair treatment in situations not covered by statute. These courts aim to resolve the claims of litigants in an equitable manner. Thus, the idea of "claim" relates to the work of these courts, not to the root meaning of the word *equity*.

It might be argued that the owners have a claim for the amount of capital they have furnished. This, however, is a tenuous argument. In liquidation, as I pointed out in Chapter 4, the amount paid to the owners is only coincidentally related to the amount stated as owners' equity. In a going concern, the owners have no claim on anything until the directors vote a dividend or a return of capital.

Furthermore, in the literal sense, many of the amounts reported as liabilities do not correspond to the amount of a claim as of the date of the balance sheet. The vendors whose invoices are represented by accounts payable and the bondholders who are represented by bonds payable have no claim on anything except interest until the agreed-upon payment date. In the case of the bondholders, this may be 20 to 30 years in the future. Although people are accustomed to thinking of these amounts as claims, they actually are claims only if they are past due or if covenants have been violated.

A weaker term than claim is *have an interest in*, but the meaning of equity in this sense is vague. Surely, it does not mean that if owners' equity is one third of total equities, the owners have an interest in one third of the assets. They have no interest at all in the assets until the liabilities have been settled, and the amount has only a coincidental relationship to the amount of assets.

3. The approach suggested here is much easier to apply than the FASB approach. The FASB lists three essential characteristics of an asset: (a) a probable future benefit exists, (b) the enterprise can obtain the benefit and control others' access to it, and (c) the event giving rise to the benefit has already occurred: FASB Concepts Statement No. 3, paragraph 20, amplified in paragraphs 21–24 and 103–23. In the FASB approach, each candidate for an asset must be tested against all three criteria, and there are many circumstances in which this test gives ambiguous results. In my framework, the tests relate to income, and in this context the tests are much less ambiguous. Note also that the FASB tests relate only to the recognition of assets; the tests say nothing about the measurement of asset amounts.

The principal author of Concepts Statement No. 3 was Reed K. Storey. In a talk at the American Accounting Association annual meeting, August 13, 1980, "Conditions Necessary for Developing a Conceptual Framework," he gave a thorough analysis of the reasoning behind the FASB definition and a criticism of the approach suggested here. He correctly traces my approach back to Paton and Littleton. Storey says that it leads to a nebulous concept of assets; they are "What-you-may-call-its." Debits that are recorded "without much consideration of whether they refer to anything in the real world."

As my discussion implies, I do not especially care whether assets do or do not represent real world things. The important task of the accountant is to measure income, and certain assets are merely a fallout consequence of doing that job properly.

4. The FASB defines liabilities as "probable future sacrifices of economic benefits arising from present obligations of a particular entity to transfer assets or provide services to other entities in the future as a result of past transactions or events": Concepts Statement No. 3, paragraph 28. This is fundamentally different from the definition given here.

Richard Scott proposes that the right-hand side of the balance sheet be labeled "Sources of Capital" and that it consist of two categories: (1) *transitory sources of capital*, representing the entity's commitment to satisfy future demand on resources that are certain or highly likely and (2) *standing sources of capital*, representing sources presently uncommitted to the settlement of obligations. The first category is similar to liabilities and the second is similar to owners' equity, both as used in current practice, except that items such as convertible bonds expected to be converted would be in the "standing sources" category. See Richard A. Scott, "Owners' Equity, the Anachronistic Element," *The Accounting Review*, October 1979.

5. Although FASB concepts statements specifically refer to articulation, their structure is such that standards setters are encouraged to consider the debit element of a transaction separately from the credit element, which creates confusion.

The FASB Discussion Memorandum on pensions, February 19, 1981, provides an example of this confusion. Chapter 2 raises issues about the liability aspect of the pension transaction, and Chapter 3 raises issues about the expense aspect. In paragraphs 189–95, the possibility is recognized that resolution of these issues may lead to an amount for the debit to expense that differs from the amount for the credit to the liability account, and the respondent is asked to reconcile these two views. The only possiblity suggested is that if the liability is larger than the pension expense, the difference be treated as an intangible asset. Such an asset would be most peculiar.

In the approach suggested in this framework, the focus is on the measurement of expense (more precisely, in this case, of expenditure). Once the proper amount of expense has been determined, the liability part of the entry follows automatically. The 53 paragraphs in the Discussion Memorandum that discuss the nature of liabilities would not even be considered. (One special case about pension liability is given in a later section of this chapter; it does not affect the general approach given above.)

Some of the problems of measuring income in accordance with the FASB concepts were described in Chapter 3. A further weakness of the FASB concepts is that they provide little guidance in measuring balance sheet items. In Concepts Statement No. 3 (paragraph 19), assets are defined as "probable future economic benefits obtained or controlled by a particular entity as a result of past transactions or events." Under this definition, almost any conceivable item that anyone wanted to call an asset would qualify.

Furthermore, paragraph 16 states: "All matters of recognition, measurement, and display have purposely been separated from the definitions of the elements of financial statements in the Board's conceptual framework project." Thus, the Statement provides no guidance as to which of the qualifying items are to be recognized in accounting, and no guidance as to how the amounts of these items are to be measured. For example, if stockholders receive a tender offer for twice the book value of their stock, this is a valid indication that past events have generated goodwill that is worth at least an amount equal to the book value of the recorded assets, and this internally generated goodwill surely would qualify as an asset under the FASB definition. Although other parts of the FASB conceptual framework project are supposed to address these issues, they have not yet done so.

The definition of liabilities in Concepts Statement No. 3 (see Note 4) also provides no guidance as to which items are to be recognized or how amounts are to be measured. For example, the receipt of a sales order creates a liability to ship the goods under this definition (accompanied by an offsetting asset, presumably.) Or (the other side of the same coin) when an entity places a purchase order, it incurs an obligation to accept delivery and pay for the goods, and thus incurs a liability under this definition.

In Concepts Statement No. 3 (paragraph 43) equity is defined as "the residual interest in the assets of an entity that remains after deducting its liabilities." This is a purely arithmetical definition that says nothing directly about what equities actually are.

Although Concepts Statement No. 3 has many paragraphs amplifying the above definitions, none of them even hints at how future work can solve the recognition or measurement problems.

6. In 1975, Westinghouse Electric Corporation was sued for a total of $2.5 billion for suspending its contracts to supply uranium to 27 utility companies. Westinghouse had contractual commitments to deliver 80 million pounds of uranium, over a 20–year period, at an average price of $9.50 a pound. At the time Westinghouse made the commitment, it had only 15 million pounds of uranium in inventory. Uranium prices rose sharply in 1973 and 1974 and by 1976 reached $40 a pound. In its defense of this suit Westinghouse cited a section of the Uniform Commercial Code which releases a party from its contractual obligation if it can prove the commercial impracticability of fulfilling its end of the bargain. Westinghouse blamed its failure to cover supply commitments on Arab oil producers, on OPEC pricing policies, on the oil embargo, on government regulators, on alleged price rigging by an international uranium cartel, and on other unexpected events that forced up the price of uranium and reduced its availability. At the same time, Westinghouse sued 17 American uranium producing companies, accusing them of forming a cartel with 12 foreign (Australian, French, South African, and Canadian) companies to rig uranium prices and control world supplies. By 1981 Westinghouse had settled these suits. According to *The Wall Street Journal,* March 18, 1981, p. 6, its loss was $950 million.

7. For a thorough discussion of the topic analyzed in this section, see Yuji Ijiri, *Recognition of Contractual Rights and Obligations* (1980). The quotation is on p. 63.

8. The wording is taken from John B. Canning, *The Economics of Accountancy* (1929), p. 22.

9. The AICPA Audit Guides for hospitals, for colleges and universities, and for voluntary health and welfare organizations, and its Statement of Position 78–10 for certain nonprofit organizations all require that contributions be recorded as revenue (or other support, which amounts to the same thing) unless they are legally restricted to nonoperating purposes. This is inconsistent with Concept 3.02 which states that substance, rather than legal form, is governing. Statement No. 1 of the National Council on Governmental Accounting (1980), however, makes the same distinction between operating and nonoperating contributions that is suggested in Concept 7.05.

10. For example, assume that a depreciable asset with a fair value of $100,000 is contributed to the entity. The contribution is recorded by the following journal entry:

```
Contributed asset ................................................. 100,000
      Contributed entity equity .......................................         100,000
```

If the asset has a life of 10 years, the following entries are made each year:

```
Expense ......................................................... 10,000
      Contributed asset .............................................          10,000
Contributed entity equity ......................................... 10,000
      Revenue ....................................................          10,000
```

At the end of the first year, the book value of the contributed asset is $90,000, and the amount of contributed entity equity (which is a component of entity equity) is $90,000. The decrease in the total amount of entity equity equals the depreciation of the contributed asset and recognizes that $10,000 of the contribution provides revenue of the current period.

11. The requirements for recognition and amortization are given in paragraphs 16 and 17 of APB Opinion No. 8, and the disclosure requirements are given in paragraph 46. See also FASB Interpretation No. 3 (1974) and FASB Statement No. 36. As this is written, the whole topic of accounting for pensions is under review. It seems likely that the basic concept will be preserved but that less latitude will be allowed in applying the concept than is permitted in APB Opinion No. 8.

12. For further discussion of this point, see Robert N. Anthony, *Financial Accounting in Nonbusiness Organizations* (1978), pp. 126–34.

Some people propose that endowment interest and dividends be recognized as revenues and that the difference between this amount and the amount calculated at the spending rate be subtracted, either as an expense or as a "transfer" back to the endowment. Although the net effect on income would be the same as the direct recognition of the spending rate amount, this alternative is unnecessarily cumbersome. Furthermore, my framework does not use the concept of "transfers" for transactions of this type; if an item is an expense, it belongs on the operating statement, and if it is a transfer, it does not belong on the operating statement.

13. The basic standard is FASB Statement No. 13, *Accounting for Leases*. This statement has been modified and expanded by Statements Nos. 17, 22, and 23, and by several FASB Interpretations.

14. Oscar Gellein, remarks at FASB symposium, June 1980. Gellein concluded that these streetcar tracks were a receivable because customers would eventually pay for them. In this framework, however, a receivable is a monetary asset representing amounts already owed, not amounts that will be owed from sales that will take place in the future.

15. The Accounting Series Release relating to redeemable preferred stock is one of the few requirements of the SEC that specifies how amounts reported in financial statements are to be measured, as contrasted with matters relating to disclosure.

16. Accounting for income taxes is the subject of APB Opinion No. 11. Accounting for the investment tax credit is the subject of APB Opinion No. 4. For an excellent analysis of the current situation, see R. D. Nair and Jerry J. Weygandt, "Let's Fix Deferred Taxes," *Journal of Accountancy*, November 1981. See also Eldon S. Hendriksen, *Accounting Theory*, 4th ed. (1982) pp. 430–44; and Kenneth S. Most, *Accounting Theory*, 2d ed. (1982) pp. 391–96.

Notes to chapter 8

1. *Accounting Trends and Techniques* (AICPA, 1981), which summarizes the accounting practices of 600 large business enterprises, lists these titles: "Statement of Income," "Consolidated Statement of Income," "Statement of Consolidated Income," "Statement of Consolidated Income and Retained Earnings," "Consolidated Statements of Earnings and Retained Earnings," "Consolidated Statement of Earnings," "Consolidated Statements of Earnings," "Statements of Consolidated Earnings and Earnings Reinvested," "Statements of Operations," "Statement of Operations and Accumulated Deficit," "Consolidated Statements of Operations," and "Consolidated Statement of Operations."

A study of income-type statements of 67 nonprofit associations reports that 23 different titles were used: E. Lewis Bryan, *A Financial Reporting Model for Not-for-Profit Associations* (1981).

A study of the financial statements of 102 foundations identified 28 different titles for the statement that most closely resembles an operating statement: Jack Traub, *Accounting and Reporting Practices of Private Foundations* (1977), p. 71.

"Revenue" is defined differently by different companies, even in the same industry, as illustrated by the treatment of federal excise taxes in the petroleum refining industry. Following are the 1978 practices of 32 large petroleum companies:

Nine companies definitely *did not* include excise taxes in revenues.

Ten companies *did* include excise taxes in revenues but did not identify the amount.

Four companies reported "gross revenues," "excise taxes," and "net revenues."

Nine companies made *no mention* of excise taxes in the income statement or in the footnotes (for some of them, taxes may not have been applicable or material).

Although such inconsistencies do not affect the bottom line, they result in non-comparability of information about companies' size and gross margin percentage.

The *Fourth Directive* of the European Economic Community (1978) specifies the terms that are to be used on the balance sheet and operating statement. This may be going farther than is desirable, but standardization of broad categories would be helpful, and there is no sound reason for perpetuating the variety of titles used for the statements themselves.

2. National Council on Government Accounting, Statement 1, *Governmental Accounting and Financial Reporting Principles* (1979).

3. For example: "it [the financial capital maintenance concept] is not subject to real-world interpretation because of the reliance on depreciation allocations and a concept of realization. The resulting income computation is based on structural rules rather than reality." Eldon S. Hendriksen, *Accounting Theory*, 3d ed. (1977), p. 154.

T. A. Lee, "Enterprise Income: Survival or Decline and Fall," *Accounting and Business Research*, Summer 1974, pp. 178–92, discusses in detail "the elusive concept of reported enterprise income." He concludes (p. 180) that the current "income measure . . . presents an incomplete and misleading mixture of income elements." He adds (pp. 189–90) that the concept of enterprise income "is subject to a great deal of variation in both its conception and practice; its measurement is open to criticism; its meaning is imprecise and it does not appear to be entirely appropriate to the economic factors it is intended to symbolize; nor does it appear to be entirely relevant to the majority of persons who may be assumed to be using it."

For similar statements, see Gerald H. Lawson, "Cash Flow Accounting," *The Accountant*, October 28, 1971, pp. 586–622.

Proponents of the events approach to accounting theory advocate replacing the operating statement with a disaggregated set of numbers. William J. Vatter states: "The point to be made is that there is no reason why the [operating] statement has to be arranged in such a way as to . . . calculate an annual net income figure. . . . The aim of [operating] statements is broader than the mere production of a single amount to represent the income for the year. . . . There is a good reason to argue that the accountant should confine himself to the reporting of business events, without attempting to report in a single figure, or a set of calculations directed at that single figure, the final result of operations." Vatter does not, however, argue for the abolition of the operating statement: *The Fund Theory of Accounting and Its Implications for Financial Reports* (1947), pp. 35–36.

4. In its Exposure Draft, *Objectives of Financial Reporting by Nonbusiness Organizations* (1980), the FASB stated (paragraph 45): "Financial reporting should provide information about the service efforts and accomplishments of a nonbusiness organization" (paragraph 45). Subsequently, the FASB commissioned Peat, Marwick, Mitchell and Co. to study the feasibility of measuring service accomplishments. Peat Marwick's Research Report, *Reporting of Service Efforts and Accomplishments* (1981), concluded that although such measurements were highly desirable, the state of the art was not developed to the point where they were feasible in most nonbusiness organizations. FASB Concepts Statement No. 4, the pronouncement on objectives for nonbusiness organizations, stated: "Ideally, financial reporting also should provide information about the service accomplishments of a nonbusiness organization. . . . However, the ability to measure service accomplishments, particularly program results, is generally undeveloped" (paragraph 53). The FASB encouraged further research, but it is unlikely that any methods of measuring in monetary terms the value of such services as a college education, the performance of a symphony orchestra, or the police and fire protection in a municipality will be developed.

5. This is one important reason why growth company stocks trade at high price/earnings ratios. Investors are, quite properly, judging the future effect of these new products, even though this is not reflected in the operating statement. Currently, companies that are believed to be successful in manipulating genes are in this category.

6. Robert T. Sprouse, "The importance of Earnings in the Conceptual Framework," *Journal of Accountancy*, January 1978, pp. 64–71. Sprouse gives sound reasons for providing a bottom line: managers, auditors, and users want an earnings number; it is widely published, and it is not practical to provide disaggregated data that users can use to construct their own idea of a bottom line.

7. For several years, the State of New York has concealed its financial status by deferring until after the beginning of the fiscal year payments of cash that it owed to local school districts. On a cash basis its budget was balanced. The magnitude of this manipulation is indicated by the size of the bond issue that was made shortly after the beginning of the year in order to raise cash for these disbursements. In 1983, this bond issue was more than $3.9 billion.

8. Premise 22 states that users do not want a change in current practice unless there is a good reason to do so. For this reason, I do not discuss concepts that I believe are consistent with current practice, are sound, and are relatively noncontroversial. The AICPA Audit Guide for colleges and universities does not meet these criteria. It describes a report that is somewhat similar to the operating statement described here but states that this report "does not purport to present the results of operations." An operating statement that does not present the results of operations is not useful. Other AICPA Audit Guides for nonbusiness organizations contain financial statements that either implicitly or explicitly purport to report the results of operations, but, with the exception of hospitals, they focus on expenditures rather than on expenses. The state and local government Audit Guide (incorporating Statement 1 of the National Council on Governmental Accounting) does not have a statement that comes close to reporting the operating performance of a governmental entity.

9. Edgar O. Edwards and Philip W. Bell, *The Theory and Measurement of Business Income* (1961); Robert T. Sprouse and Maurice Moonitz, *A Tentative Set of Broad Accounting Principles for Business Enterprises*, Accounting Research Study No. 3 (1962).

10. APB Opinion No. 30 states the criteria for extraordinary items as follows:

1. The event must be unusual; that is, it should be highly abnormal and unrelated to, or only incidentally related to, the ordinary activities of the entity.
2. The event must occur infrequently; that is, it should be of a type that would not reasonably be expected to recur in the foreseeable future.

11. These points are taken from paragraph 48 of the Exposure Draft. Additional distinctions are suggested in Appendix B, Paragraphs 137–51. For an analysis of the FASB position, see Norman N. Strauss and Alex T. Arcady, "A New Focus on the 'Bottom Line' and its Components," *Journal of Accountancy*, May 1981, pp. 66–77.

12. For a discussion of value-added statements, with examples, see Kenneth S. Most, *Accounting Theory*, 2d ed. (1982), pp.416–18.

13. The officially recommended term is *statement of financial position*. This term is often found as the title in formal financial statements and in accounting texts. However, in reports by financial analysts, in the financial press, and in ordinary conversation, use of the longer term is rare. Moreover, the longer term can give the impression that the statement reports financial position in some broader sense than is actually the case. As George Sorter has written (unpublished paper), "the balance sheet reports the effect of accounting events that have occurred and are awaiting events that have not occurred."

14. See Lloyd C. Heath and Paul Rosenfield, "Solvency: The Forgotten Half of Financial Reporting," *Journal of Accountancy*, January 1979, pp. 48–54. See also Lloyd C. Heath, *Financial Reporting and the Evaluation of Solvency*, Accounting Research Monograph No. 3 (1979); Lloyd C. Heath, "Is Working Capital Really Working?" *Journal of Accountancy*, August 1980, and comments on that article in *Journal of Accountancy*, December 1981, p. 82 ff; and Lloyd C. Heath, "Solvency Reporting in a Changing World," *International Congress of Accountants Technical Papers* (1982), pp. 3–22. Perhaps the rearrangements proposed in these articles are more significant than meet the eye; to me, they seem trivial.

15. Many texts describe the analysis of the financial statements of financial institutions. An interesting way of viewing these statements is in Donald S. Howard and Gail M. Hoffman, *Evolving Concepts of Bank Capital Management* (1980).

16. The present definitions are in Chapter 3A of Accounting Research Bulletin 43. Current assets are defined as:

> . . . cash and other assets or resources commonly identified as those which are reasonably expected to be realized in cash or sold or consumed during the normal operating cycle of the business.

Usually, the normal operating cycle is presumed to be one year, unless the nature of the production process clearly indicates that a longer period is appropriate. Current liabilities are defined as:

> . . . obligations whose liquidation is reasonably expected to require the use of existing resources properly classifiable as current assets, or the creation of other current liabilities.

Rather than continuing the current/noncurrent dichotomy, the possibility of making monetary/nonmonetary the basic distinction should be considered. Yuji Ijiri stresses the importance of the monetary/nonmonetary distinction in *Theory of Accounting Measurement*, Studies in Accounting Research No. 10 (1975), Chapters 4 and 5. Ijiri criticizes APB Statement No. 4 for not making this distinction in "Critique of the APB Fundamentals Statement," *Journal of Accountancy*, November 1971. See also Anson Herrick, "Current Assets and Liabilities," *Journal of Accountancy*, January 1944.

For an excellent analysis of the rationale for separating current from noncurrent assets and liabilities, see Vatter, *Fund Theory of Accounting*, pp. 60–65. See also Canning, *The Economics of Accountancy*, p. 207.

The practice of identifying current assets and current liabilities originated with the centuries-old legal requirement in England for a double account form of balance sheet, in which fixed assets were distinguished from "floating assets." In this concept, profits were related only to flows of floating assets. Depreciation, being a write-off of fixed assets, was not recognized as a charge against revenue. The leading British case is *Lee v. Neuchatel Asphalte Company*, in which the court held that "the current balance of current revenue might be distributed as a dividend without reference to depletion." Although the double account form has not been used in the United Kingdom for many years, the idea governs the system currently recommended by the National Council on Governmental Accounting. As recently as 1940, Paton stated that he thought "it might help our understanding if the practice were revived of dividing the balance sheet horizontally into two sections, the current account balance sheet and the capital account statement": William A. Paton, *Recent and Prospective Developments in Accounting Theory* (1940), p. 7.

As used here "current monetary assets" corresponds to "quick assets," that is, current assets minus inventory and deferred charges.

17. FASB Exposure Draft, *Reporting Income, Cash Flows and Financial Position of Business Enterprises*, November 16, 1981, paragraph 37.

18. The proposed Uniform Companies Act provides for only two components of shareholder equity: contributed capital and retained earnings.

19. Although not available to finance operating activities, these assets are related to operating activities. Nonoperating plant is used in operations, and the earnings from restricted endowment are revenues for operations. At the time the contributions were received, however, they were not available for operating purposes. Subsequently, they may or may not be available for operating purposes.

20. FASB Concepts Statement No. 4 has a reference to a "restricted resources" (paragraph 46). It says that information about them should be provided, but that how this should be done is "outside the scope of this Statement and may be the subject of future Board projects."

21. The idea of two balance sheets for one entity is not new. It is the basic idea behind fund accounting as practiced in many nonbusiness organizations. In the United Kingdom, the double account balance sheet was used, as described in Note 16. This balance sheet separated the accounts on a different basis than that described here, however. See Lawrence R. Dicksee, *Advanced Accounting*, 7th ed. (1932), p. 149.

22. The National Council on Governmental Accounting Statement No. 1, for state and municipal governments, takes an entirely different approach. Restricted assets are recorded in a "group of accounts," which is not a fund and is self balancing only in the sense that whenever the asset side is debited, a meaningless credit is made to a fund balance account. The practices in Statement No. 1 are cumbersome and lead to confusing financial statements. Federal government accounting has no mechanism for accounting for restricted capital assets in a meaningful way. Strange as it may seem, capital expenditures are debited to a capital account, and there they remain indefinitely. Thus, the capital account for the U.S. Navy shows the cumulative total amount expended for the Navy's capital items since 1789.

23. Paragraph 45 of the Exposure Draft (see Note 17) states: "The objectives of financial reporting indicate that users need information about cash inflows and out-flows. . . ." The basis for this conclusion is summarized in paragraphs 38 and 39 of FASB Concepts Statement No. 1 on objectives. Paragraph 38 states that investors need information about prospective cash flows to *themselves*, and paragraph 39 states that *therefore* they need information about cash flows of the enterprise. This is a non sequitur. Cash flows to investors are dividends and proceeds from their sale of securities. Cash flows of the enterprise may or may not be useful in predict-ing the investor's cash flows. In fact, paragraph 43 states that the primary focus of financial reporting should be on earnings, not on cash flows. Nevertheless, cash flows are mentioned on almost every page of the Exposure Draft.

The FASB does not cite evidence to support its premise that users want cash flow information. I present evidence that users want information about income more than they want information about cash flow in the discussion of Premise 16. Only a minority of respondents to the Exposure Draft commented on this item, and of these a small majority (56 out of 92) supported the cash basis. Of 3,582 Statements of Changes in Financial Position for 1981 contained in the NAARS data base, at least 2,872, or 80 percent, used the working capital basis. (Not all of the other 20 percent used the cash basis.) Presumably, the overwhelming majority of public cor-porations believe that the working capital basis is more useful than the cash basis. In many entities, the circulation of cash among the various items of current assets and current liabilities is relatively unimportant; the important information is how the net current asset position changed and how this change was financed. This information is highlighted in a funds flow statement that focuses on working capi-tal.

Advocates of the cash flow basis tend to use adjectives as a substitute for evi-dence. Barbara S. Thomas, commissioner of SEC, states that the working capital basis is "outmoded" and "more confusing than informative" but gives no evidence: *Journal of Accountancy*, November 1982, p. 99. Commissioner Thomas has a simi-lar diatribe in *Financial Executive*, January 1983. The Financial Executives Institute Committee on Corporate Reporting states that the cash basis is "more understand-able and useful" but gives no evidence (response to the FASB Discussion Memo-randum). That committee has urged Financial Executives Institute members to shift to a cash basis, but as of 1983, relatively few have done so.

For an excellent discussion of the controversy, see Kenneth S. Most, *Accounting Theory*, 2d ed., pp. 449–71.

The whole controversy is about a trivial point. A user who prefers a report on cash flows can easily convert a working capital basis report to a cash basis report. The information is the same on both; only the arrangement is different.

Yuji Ijiri's conceptual framework, as set forth in *Historical Cost Accounting and its Rationality* (1981) and elsewhere, is interpreted by some as focusing on cash flow accounting. As I read it, the cash flow focus is on the total life of a project, cash-to-cash, rather than on the cash flow in an accounting period. Ijiri describes the cash recovery rate, which is the amount of cash recovered in a given period per dollar of cash invested, as a useful basis for measuring performance. In order to find and use the cash recovery rate, however, one must estimate the total life of each project undertaken during the period (or at least the average future life of all projects). This problem is equivalent to that of arriving at a depreciation rate, which is said to be a principal cause of the inadequacy of income measurement in the conventional system. The measurement of income proposed in my framework will give substantially the same result as that obtained by Ijiri's proposal because the sum of interest plus annuity depreciation (Concepts 5.12 and 5.13) is the true amount of capital recovery that must be earned in the period.

Bibliography

"Accounting and Auditing Act of 1950" (31 U.S.C. 66).

Abdel-khalik, A. Rashad. "Advertising Effectiveness and Accounting Policy." *The Accounting Review*, October 1975, pp. 657–70.

—————. "Advertising Effectiveness and Accounting Policy: A Reply," to Dale L. Flesher, "Advertising Effectiveness: A Comment." *The Accounting Review*, January 1977, pp. 261–65.

—————. "The Entropy Law, Accounting Data and Relevance to Decision Making." *The Accounting Review*, April 1974, pp. 271–83.

Abdel-khalik, A. Rashad; and K. El Sheshai. "Information Choice and Utilization in an Experiment on Default Prediction." *Journal of Accounting Research*, Autumn 1980, pp. 325–42.

Abdel-khalik, A. Rashad; and Thomas F. Keller. *Earnings or Cash Flows: An Experiment on Functional Fixation and the Valuation of the Firm.* Studies in Accounting Research No. 16. Sarasota, Fla.: American Accounting Association, 1979.

Abdel-khalik, A. Rashad; and Thomas F. Keller, eds. *The Impact of Accounting Research on Practice and Disclosure.* Durham, N.C.: Duke University Press, 1978.

Alexander, Sidney S. "Income Measurement in a Dynamic Economy." Revised by David Solomons in *Studies in Accounting Theory*, ed. W. T. Baxter and Sidney Davidson. Homewood, Ill.: Richard D. Irwin, 1962, pp. 126–17.

American Accounting Association. "A Tentative Statement of Accounting Principles Affecting Corporate Reports." *The Accounting Review*, June 1936, pp. 187–91.

—————. Executive Committee. *Accounting Principles Underlying Corporate Financial Statements.* Sarasota, Fla.: AAA, 1941.

————. Committee on Concepts and Standards. "A Discussion of Various Approaches to Inventory Measurement." *The Accounting Review,* July 1964, pp. 700–14.

————. Committee to Prepare a Statement of Basic Accounting Theory. *A Statement of Basic Accounting Theory.* Evanston, Ill.: AAA, 1966.

————. Committee on Concepts and Standards. *Accounting and Reporting Standards for Corporate Financial Statements.* Sarasota, Fla.: AAA, 1957.

————. Committee on Foundations of Accounting Measurement. "Report." *The Accounting Review,* Supplement 1971, pp. 1–48.

————. Committee on Human Resource Accounting. "Report." *The Accounting Review,* Supplement 1973, pp. 169–85.

————. Committee on Human Information Processing. "Report of the 1976–77 Committee." *Committee Reports,* August 1977.

————. Committee on Concepts and Standards. "The Realization Concept." *The Accounting Review,* April 1965, pp. 312–22.

————. Committee on Research Methodology in Accounting. "Report." *The Accounting Review,* Supplement 1972, pp. 399–520. Also published with comments in Robert R. Sterling, ed., *Research Methodology in Accounting.* Houston, Tex.: Scholars Book Co., 1972.

————. "Statement of Accounting Theory and Theory Acceptance." Committee Report. Sarasota, Fla.: AAA, 1977.

————. Committee on Concepts and Standards—Internal Planning and Control. "Report." *The Accounting Review,* Supplement 1974, pp. 79–96.

————. Committee on Nonprofit Organizations. "Report." *The Accounting Review,* Supplement 1975, pp. 3–49.

————. *Report of the Subcommittee to Respond to FASB Exposure Draft on Objectives of Financial Reporting by Nonbusiness Organizations.* Sarasota, Fla.: AAA, 1980.

American Institute of Certified Public Accountants (AICPA). Special Committee on Interest in Relation to Cost. "Report." *Yearbook,* 1918, pp. 110–12.

————. *Accounting for Sales of Real Estate.* Audit Guide. New York: AICPA, 1979.

————. *Accounting for Performance of Construction-Type and Certain Production-Type Contracts.* New York: AICPA, 1981.

————. Accounting Standards Division. *Depreciation of Income Producing Real Estate.* New York: AICPA, 1981.

————. Committee on Terminology. *Accounting Terminology Bulletins.* Reprinted in Financial Accounting Standards Board. *Accounting Standards.* Stamford, Conn.: Annual.

————. *Uniform Accounting.* New York: American Institute of Accountants, 1917.

―――. *Audits of Hospitals.* Audit Guide. New York: AICPA, 1972.

―――. Special Committee Report. *Audits of Corporate Accounts.* New York: AICPA, 1933.

―――. *Accounting Research Bulletins.* Reprinted in Financial Accounting Standards Board. *Accounting Standards.* Stamford, Conn.: Annual.

―――. *Accounting Principles Board Opinions* and *Statements.* Reprinted in Financial Accounting Standards Board. *Accounting Standards.* Stamford, Conn.: Annual.

―――. Statement of Position 81–2. *Reporting Practices Concerning Hospital-Related Organizations.* New York: AICPA, 1981.

―――. Study Group on the Objectives of Financial Statements. Robert M. Trueblood, Chairman. *Objectives of Financial Statements.* New York: AICPA, 1973.

―――. Statement of Auditing Standards No. 6. *Related Party Transactions.* New York: AICPA, 1975.

―――. Statement of Position 75–1. *Revenue Recognition When Right of Return Exists.* New York: AICPA, 1975.

―――. Statement of Position 76–8. *Accounting Practices in the Record and Music Industry.* New York: AICPA, 1976.

―――. Statements of Position 79–2. *Cable Television Companies.* New York: AICPA, 1979.

―――. *Accounting for Profit Recognition on Sales of Real Estate.* Audit Guide. New York: AICPA, 1973.

―――. *Accounting for Retail Land Sales.* Audit Guide. New York: AICPA, 1973.

―――. *Audits of Colleges and Universities.* Audit Guide. New York: AICPA, 1973.

―――. *Audits of Voluntary Health and Welfare Organizations.* Audit Guide. New York: AICPA, 1974.

―――. *Accounting for Motion Picture Films.* Accounting Guide. New York: AICPA, 1979.

―――. *Audits of State and Local Governmental Units.* Audit Guide. New York: AICPA, 1980.

―――. *Audits of Other Nonprofit Organizations.* Audit Guide. New York: AICPA, 1981.

―――. Committee on Social Measurement. *The Measurement of Corporate Social Performance.* New York: AICPA, 1977.

―――. *Accounting Trends and Techniques.* New York: AICPA, Annual.

Anderson, Arthur & Co. *The Postulate of Accounting—What It Is, How It Is Determined, How It Should Be Used.* Chicago: 1960.

Anthony, Robert N. *Accounting for the Cost of Interest.* Lexington, Mass.: Lexington Books, 1975.

―――――. "A Case for Historical Costs." *Harvard Business Review,* November–December 1976, pp. 69–79.

―――――. "Equity Interest: A Cure for the Double Taxation of Dividends," *Financial Executive,* July 1977, pp. 20–23.

―――――. *Financial Accounting in Nonbusiness Organizations.* Stamford, Conn.: FASB, 1978.

―――――. "The Trouble with Profit Maximization." *Harvard Business Review,* November–December 1960, pp. 126–34.

―――――. "Two Ways to Control Estimated Figures in the Income Statement." *Journal of Accountancy,* April 1949, pp. 298–306.

―――――. "Accounting for the Cost of Equity." *Harvard Business Review,* November–December 1973, pp. 88–102.

Anthony, Robert N., and John Dearden. *Management Control Systems,* 4th ed. Homewood, Ill.: Richard D. Irwin, 1980.

Anthony, Robert N., and Regina E. Herzlinger. *Management Control in Nonprofit Organizations.* Rev. ed. Homewood, Ill.: Richard D. Irwin, 1980.

Anthony, Robert N., and James S. Reece. *Accounting Principles.* 5th ed. Homewood, Ill.: Richard D. Irwin, 1983.

Anton, Hector R. "Depreciation, Cost Allocation and Investment Decisions." *Accounting Research,* April 1956, pp. 117–34.

―――――. "Objectives of Financial Accounting: Review and Analysis." *Journal of Accountancy,* January 1976, pp. 40–51.

Areeda, Philip, and Donald F. Turner. "Predatory Pricing and Related Practices under Section 2 of the Sherman Act." *Harvard Law Review,* February 1975, pp. 697–733.

Arnett, Harold E., *Proposed Funds Statement for Managers and Investors.* New York: National Association of Accountants, 1979.

Asebrook, Richard J., and D. A. Carmichael. "Reporting on Forecasts: A Survey of Attitudes." *Journal of Accountancy,* August 1973, pp. 38–48.

Balechandran, D. V., and R. T. S. Ramakrishnan, "Joint Cost Allocation: A Unified Approach." *The Accounting Review,* January 1981, pp. 85–96.

Barden, Horace G., *Accounting Research Study No. 13,* "The Accounting Basis for Inventories." New York: AICPA, 1973.

Barnard, Chester L. *The Functions of the Executive.* Cambridge Mass.: Harvard University Press, 1936.

Bartley, Jon W. "Accounting for the Cost of Capital: An Empirical Examination." *Journal of Business Finance & Accounting* 9, no. 2 (1982), pp. 239–54.

Bartley, Jon W., and Lewis S. Davidson. "The Entity Concept and Accounting for Interest Costs." *Accounting and Business Research,* Summer 1982, pp. 175–87.

Baxter, W. T., *Depreciation.* London: Sweet & Maxwell, 1971.

Beaver, William H. *Financial Reporting: An Accounting Revolution.* Englewood Cliffs, N.J.: Prentice-Hall, 1981.

————. "The Nature of Income Measurement." *The Accounting Review,* January 1979, pp. 38–43.

Beaver, William H., and Joel S. Demski. "The Nature of Financial Accounting Objectives: A Summary and Synthesis." *Journal of Accounting Research,* Supplement 1974, pp. 170–87.

Beaver, William H., and Roland E. Dukes. "Interperiod Tax Allocation and Delta-Depreciation Methods: Some Empirical Results." *The Accounting Review,* July 1973, pp. 549–59.

Bedford, Norton M. *Income Determination Theory.* Reading Mass.: Addison-Wesley Publishing, 1965.

————. "The Impact of A Priori Theory and Research on Accounting Practice." In *The Impact of Accounting Research on Practice and Disclosure,* ed. A. Rashad Abdel-khalik and Thomas F. Keller. Durham, N.C.: Duke University Press, 1978, pp. 26–31.

Benston, George J. "The Value of the SEC's Accounting Disclosure Requirement." *The Accounting Review,* July 1969, pp. 515–32.

Best, Lawrence C., and Paul A. Gewirtz. "Plant Closings: The Pension Cost Controversy." *Financial Executive,* November 1980, pp. 12–19.

Bevis, Herman W. *Corporate Financial Reporting in a Competitive Economy.* New York: Macmillan, 1965.

Black, Fischer. "The Magic in Earnings: Economic Earnings versus Accounting Earnings." *Financial Analysts Journal,* November–December 1980, pp. 19–24.

The Boeing Company. *Towards Common Concepts of Cost Allocations in Cost Accounting.* Seattle: The Boeing Company, 1978.

Bonbright, James C. *Principles of Public Utility Rates.* New York: Columbia University Press, 1961.

Boulding, Kenneth E. *Economic Analysis.* 3d ed. New York: Harper & Bros., 1955.

————. "Economics and Accounting: The Uncongenial Twins." In *Studies in Accounting Theory,* ed. W. T. Baxter and Sidney Davidson. Homewood, Ill.: Richard D. Irwin, 1962, pp. 44–55.

Brace, Paul K., et al. *Reporting of Service Efforts and Accomplishments.* Stamford, Conn.: Financial Accounting Standards Board, 1980.

Brief, Richard P. "A Late-Nineteenth-Century Contribution to the Theory of Depreciation." *Journal of Accounting Research,* Spring 1967, pp. 27–38.

Brigham, Eugene F., ed. *Readings in Managerial Finance*. New York: Holt, Rinehart & Winston, 1971.

Briloff, Abraham J. "Let Many Flowers Bloom." Emmanual Saxe Distinguished Lectures in Accounting, 1977–78. New York: Bernard M. Baruch College, City University of New York, 1978.

Bryan, E. Lewis. *A Financial Reporting Model for Not-for-Profit Associations*. Ann Arbor, Mich.: UMI Research Press, 1981.

Burns, Gary W., and D. Scott Peterson. "Accounting for Computer Software." *Journal of Accountancy*, April 1982, pp. 50–58.

Burton, John C.; Russell E. Palmer; and Robert S. Kay, eds., *Handbook of Accounting and Auditing*. Boston: Warren, Gorham & Lamont, 1981.

Butterworth, John E. "The Accounting System as an Information Function." *Journal of Accounting Research*, Spring 1972, pp. 1–27.

Buzzell, Robert D., and Frederik D. Wiersema. "Modelling Changes in Market Share: A Cross Sectional Analysis." *Stategic Management Journal* 2 (1981), pp. 27–42.

Byrne, Gilbert R. "To What Extent Can the Practice of Accounting Be Reduced to Rules and Standards." *Journal of Accountancy*, November 1937, pp. 364–79.

Byung, T. Ro. "The Disclosure of Replacement Cost Accounting Data and Its Effect on Transaction Volume." *The Accounting Review*, January 1981, pp. 70–84.

Campbell, Norman R. "Measurement." In *The World of Mathematics*, ed. James R. Newman. New York: Simon & Schuster, 1956, pp. 1797–1813.

Canadian Institute of Chartered Accountants (CICA). *Financial Reporting for Non-Profit Organizations*. Toronto: CICA, 1980.

————. *Corporate Reporting: Its Future Evolution*. Research Study. Toronto: CICA, 1980.

Canning, John B. *The Economics of Accountancy*. New York: Ronald Press, 1929.

Carpenter, Charles G., and Austin R. Daily. "Controllers and CPAs: Two Views of Published Forecasts." *Business Horizons*, August 1974, pp. 73–78.

Casey, Cornelius. *Capitalization of Interest Costs: Empirical Evidence of the Effect on Financial Statements*. Working Paper HBS 78–59. Boston: Division of Research, Graduate School of Business Administration, Harvard University, 1978.

Catlett, George R. Dissent to Accounting Principles Board Statement No. 4, October 1970. Reprinted in FASB, *Accounting Standards*.

Chamberlain, Neil W. *Enterprise and the Environment: The Firm in Time and Place*. New York: McGraw-Hill, 1968.

Chambers, Raymond J. *Accounting, Evaluation and Economic Behavior*. Englewood Cliffs, N.J.: Prentice-Hall, 1966.

————. "Towards a General Theory of Accounting." *The Australian Society of Accountants Annual Lecture, 1961*. Adelaide, Australia: The University of Adelaide, 1961.

————. "Accounting Principles and Practices—Negotiated or Dictated?" In *Proceedings of the Second Annual Accounting Research Convocation*. Tuscaloosa: The University of Alabama, 1977, pp. 1–21.

————. "The Possibility of a Normative Accounting Standard." *The Accounting Review*, July 1976, pp. 646–52.

Chandler, Alfred D. *Strategy and Structure: Chapters in the History of the Industrial Enterprise*. Cambridge, Mass.: MIT Press, 1962.

————. *The Visible Hand: The Managerial Revolution in American Business*. Cambridge, Mass.: Belknap Press, Harvard University Press, 1977.

Chang, Davis, and Jacob B. Birnberg. "Functional Fixity in Accounting Research: Perspective and New Data." *Journal of Accounting Research*, Autumn 1977, pp. 300–12.

Charnes, Abraham; Claude S. Colantoni; and William W. Cooper. "A Futurological Justification for Historical Cost and Multi-Dimensional Accounting." *Accounting, Organizations and Society* 1, no. 4 (1976), pp. 315–37.

Christenson, Charles. "Proposals for a Program of Empirical Research into the Properties of Triangles." *Decision Sciences*, October 1976, pp. 631–48.

————. "The Methodology of Positive Accounting." *The Accounting Review*, January 1983, pp. 1–22.

Churchman, Charles W. *Prediction and Optimal Decisions: Philosophical Issues of a Science of Values*. Englewood Cliffs, N.J.: Prentice-Hall, 1961.

Churchman, Charles W., and P. Ratoosh, eds. *Measurement: Definitions and Theories*. New York: John Wiley & Sons, 1959.

Clark, John M. *Studies in the Economics of Overhead Costs*. Chicago: University of Chicago Press, 1923.

Clark, Robert C. "Does the Nonprofit Form Fit the Hospital Industry?" *Harvard Law Review*, May 1980, pp. 1416–89.

Clemente, Holly A. "Innovative Financing." *Financial Executive*, April 1982, pp. 14–19.

Coase, R. H., "The Lighthouse in Economics," *Journal of Law and Economics*, October 1974, pp. 357–76.

Colantoni, Claude S.; Rene P. Manes; and Andrew Whinston. "A Unified Approach to the Theory of Accounting and Information Systems." *The Accounting Review*, January 1971, pp. 90–102.

Cole, William Morse. "Interest on Investment in Equipment." *Journal of Accountancy*, April 1913, pp. 232–36.

Comiskey, Eugene E., and Roger E. Groves. "The Adoption and Diffusion of an Accounting Innovation." *Accounting and Business Research*, Winter 1972, pp. 67–77.

The Conference Board. *Experience with Inflation Accounting in Annual Reports.* New York, 1982.

Cost Accounting Standards Board (CASB). *Cost Accounting Standards.* Code of Federal Regulations, Title 4, U.S. Government Printing Office, Annual.

Coughlan, J. W. "Funds and Income." *NAA Bulletin,* September 1964, pp. 23–34.

Coughlan, Joseph D. and William K. Strand. *Depreciation: Accounting, Taxes, and Business Decisions.* New York: Ronald Press, 1969.

Cragg, John G., and Burton G. Malkiel. *Expectations and the Valuation of Shares.* Cambridge, Mass.: National Bureau of Economic Research Working Paper No. 471, 1980.

Cramer, J. J., and G. H. Sorter, eds. *Objectives of Financial Statements: Selected Papers.* New York: ALCPA, 1974.

Cushing, Barry E. "On the Possibility of Optimal Accounting Principles." *The Accounting Review,* April 1977, pp. 308–21.

Davidson, Sidney, et al. *Accounting: The Language of Business.* 4th ed. Glen Ridge, N.J.: Thomas Horton and Daughters, 1979.

Deakin, E. B. "A Discriminant Analysis of Predictors of Failure." *Journal of Accounting Research,* Spring 1972, pp. 162–69.

———. "Accounting Reports, Policy Interventions and the Behavior of Securities Returns." *The Accounting Review,* July 1965.

Dean, Joel. *Managerial Economics.* Englewood Cliffs, N.J.: Prentice-Hall, 1951.

Defliese, Philip L. "Defliese Calls for 'Cost of Capital Disclosures.' " *Journal of Accountancy,* May 1975, p. 25.

———. "Ideas and Trends: What Makes Profits Look 'Obscene.' " *Business Week,* August 4, 1975, pp. 10–11.

———. *Should Accountants Capitalize Leases?* New York: Coopers and Lybrand, 1973.

Demski, Joel S. "Choice Among Financial Reporting Alternatives." *The Accounting Review,* April 1974, pp. 221–32.

———. "The General Impossibility of Normative Accounting Standards." *The Accounting Review,* October 1973, pp. 718–23.

———. *Information Analysis.* Reading Mass: Addison-Wesley, 1980.

Demski, Joel S. and Gerald A. Feltham. *Cost Determination: A Conceptual Approach.* Ames: Iowa State University Press, 1976.

Dicksee, Lawrence R. *Advanced Accounting.* 7th ed. London: Geeble, 1932.

Dorfman, Robert. *Prices and Markets.* 2d ed. Englewood Cliffs, N.J.: Prentice-Hall, 1972.

Dopuch, Nicholas. "Empirical vs. Non-Empirical Contributions to Accounting Theory Development." Unpublished paper.

Dopuch, Nicholas, and Shyam Sunder. "FASB's Statements on Objectives and Elements of Financial Accounting: A Review." *The Accounting Review,* January 1980, pp. 1–21.

Dyckman, T. R. "A Return-Reporting Framework." In *Accounting for a Simplified Firm Owning Depreciable Assets,* ed. Robert R. Sterling and Arthur L. Thomas. Houston, Tex.: Scholars Book Co., 1979, pp. 73–92.

Earley, James S. "Marginal Policies of Excellently Managed Companies." *American Economic Review,* March 1956, pp. 44–70.

Eckstein, Otto, ed. *The Econometrics of Price Determination: Conference, October 30–31, 1972.* Washington, D.C.: Board of Governors of the Federal Reserve System, 1972.

Edwards, Edgar O., and Philip W. Bell. *The Theory and Measurement of Business Income.* Berkeley and Los Angeles: University of California Press, 1961.

Edwards, Edgar O.; Philip W. Bell; and L. Todd Johnson. *Accounting for Economic Events.* Houston, Tex.: Scholars Book Co., 1979.

Enthoven, Adolf J. H. *Accounting Systems, Developments and Requirements in Third-World Economies.* Richardson, Tex.: University of Texas at Dallas, 1976.

———. *Accountancy and Economic Development Policy,* New York: American Elsevier Publishing, 1973.

Epstein, Marc J.; Eric G. Flamholtz; and John J. McDonough. *Corporate Social Performance: The Measurement of Product and Service Contributions.* New York: National Association of Accountants, 1977.

Estes, Ralph. *Dictionary of Accounting.* Cambridge, Mass.: MIT Press, 1981.

European Economic Community (EEC). *Fourth Directive.* Brussels: Council of Ministries of the European Community, August 1978.

———. [Proposed] *Seventh Directive.* Brussels: EEC, 1978.

Fama, Eugene F. "Agency Problems and the Theory of the Firm." *Journal of Political Economy,* April 1980, pp. 288–307.

Financial Accounting Standards Board (FASB). *Concepts Statements.* Reprinted in *Accounting Standards.* Stamford, Conn.: FASB, Annual.

———. *Statements of Financial Accounting Standards.* Reprinted in *Accounting Standards.* Stamford, Conn.: FASB, Annual.

———. *An Analysis of Issues Related to Reporting Earnings.* Discussion Memorandum. Stamford, Conn.: FASB, 1979.

———. *Reporting Funds Flows, Liquidity and Financial Flexibility.* Discussion Memorandum. Stamford, Conn.: FASB, 1980.

———. *Employers' Accounting for Pensions and Other Post-Employment Benefits.* Discussion Memorandum. Stamford, Conn.: FASB, 1981.

————. *Criteria for Determining Materiality*. Discussion Memorandum. Stamford, Conn.: FASB, 1975.

————. *A Conceptual Framework for Financial Accounting and Reporting: Elements of Financial Statements and Their Measurement*. Discussion Memorandum. Stamford Conn.: FASB, 1976.

————. *Reporting Income, Cash Flows and Financial Position of Business Enterprises*. Exposure Draft. Stamford, Conn.: FASB, 1981.

————. *Reporting of Service Efforts and Accomplishments: Colleges and Universities, Hospitals, Human Service Organizations, State and Local Governmental Units, Trade and Professional Associations, Philanthropic Foundations*. Research Report. Prepared by Peat, Marwick, Mitchell & Co. for the FASB. Stamford, Conn.: FASB, 1980.

Feltham, Gerald A. *Information Evaluation*. Sarasota, Fla.: AAA, 1972.

Ferrara, William L. "A Cash Flow Model for the Future." *Management Accounting*, June 1981, pp. 12–17.

Fisher, Irving. *Elementary Principles of Economics*. 3d ed. New York: Macmillan, 1919.

————. *The Nature of Capital and Income*. New York: Macmillan, 1906.

Flesher, Dale L. "Controllers Say FAS Is Not Very Useful." *Management Accounting*, January 1983, pp. 50–53.

Forrester, D. A. R. "Holding Costs or Holding Gains." *Management Accounting* (United Kingdom), March 1977, pp. 114–17.

Foster, George. *Financial Statement Analysis*. Englewood Cliffs, N.J.: Prentice-Hall, 1978.

Freeman, Robert J., and Craig Douglas Shoulders. "Defining the Governmental Reporting Entity." *Journal of Accountancy*, October 1982, pp. 50–63.

Fremgen, James M. "The Direct Costing Controversy—An Identification of Issues." *The Accounting Review*, January 1964, pp. 43–51.

Fremgen, James M., and Shu S. Liao. *The Allocation of Corporate Indirect Costs*. New York: National Association of Accountants, 1981.

Friedman, Benjamin M. "The Changing Role of Debt and Equity in Financing U.S. Capital Formation." Unpublished report for National Bureau of Economics Research. Cambridge, Mass., 1979.

Friedman, Milton. *Essays in Positive Economics*. Chicago: University of Chicago Press, 1953.

Frishkoff, Paul. *Reporting of Summary Indicators: An Investigation of Research and Practice*. Stamford, Conn.: Financial Accounting Standards Board, 1981.

Furst, Richard W., and Rodney L. Rosenfeldt. "Estimating the Return on Equity Capital." *Hospital Financial Management*, June 1981, pp. 34–44.

Galbraith, John Kenneth. *The Affluent Society.* Boston: Houghton Mifflin, 1958.

————. *American Capitalism.* Boston: Houghton Mifflin, 1952.

Garner, S. Paul, *Evolution of Cost Accounting to 1925.* (University, Ala.: University of Alabama Press, 1954), pp. 142–161.

Gellein, Oscar S. "Conceptual Framework: Needs and Uses." Address at FASB Symposium. June 24, 1980.

Gibson, Charles H. "How Industry Perceives Financial Ratios." *Management Accounting,* April 1982.

Gilman, Stephen. *Accounting Concepts of Profit.* New York: Ronald Press, 1939.

Goldberg, Louis. *An Inquiry into the Nature of Accounting.* American Accounting Association Monograph No. 7. Iowa City, Iowa: AAA, 1965.

Gordon, Lawrence A., et al. *The Pricing Decision.* New York: National Association of Accountants, 1981.

Gordon, Robert J. "A Consistent Characterization of a Near-Century of Price Behavior." *American Economic Review,* May 1980, pp. 243–49.

Govindarajan, Vijayaraghavan. "The Objectives of Financial Statements: An Empirical Study of the Use of Cash Flow and Earnings by Security Analysts." *Accounting Organization and Society* 5, no. 4 (1980), pp. 383–92.

————. "Objectives of Financial Reporting by Business Enterprises: Some Evidence of User Preference." *Journal of Accounting, Auditing and Finance,* Summer 1979, pp. 339–43.

Grady, Paul. *Inventory of Generally Accepted Accounting Principles for Business Enterprises.* Accounting Research Study No. 7. New York: AICPA, 1965.

Grant, Eugene L. *Principles of Engineering Economy.* New York: Ronald Press, 1950.

Green, David, Jr. "A Moral to the Direct-Costing Controversy?" *The Journal of Business,* July 1960, pp. 218–26.

Griffin, Paul A. *Usefulness to Investors and Creditors of Information Provided by Financial Reporting: A Review of Empirical Accounting Research.* Stamford, Conn.: Financial Accounting Standards Board, 1982.

Gross, Malvern, and William Warshauer. *Financial and Accounting Guide for Nonprofit Organizations.* 3d ed. New York: John Wiley & Sons, 1979.

Hall, R. L., and C. J. Hitch. "Price Theory and Business Behavior." *Oxford Economic Papers.* Oxford U.K.: The Calendar Press, 1939.

Harris, Jonathan. "What Did We Earn Last Month?" *NACA Bulletin,* January 15, 1936.

Harris, Louis, and Associates, Inc. *A Study of the Attitudes toward and an Assessment of the Financial Accounting Standards Board.* Stamford, Conn.: Financial Accounting Foundation, 1980.

Hawkins, David. "Financial Accounting, The Standards Board and Economic Development." Emmanual Saxe Distinguished Lecture in Accounting, 1973–1974. New York: Bernard M. Baruch College, City University of New York, 1975.

————. *Corporate Financial Reporting.* Homewood, Ill.: Richard D. Irwin, 1977.

Hawkins, David F., and Walter J. Campbell. *Equity Valuation: Models, Analysis and Implications: A Research Study and Report.* New York: Financial Executives Research Foundation, 1978.

Hay, Leon E. *Accounting for Governmental and Nonprofit Entities.* 6th ed. Homewood, Ill.: Richard D. Irwin, 1980.

Hayes, James A., and Robert N. Anthony. *Accounting for the Cost of Interest.* Working Paper HBS 75–47. Boston: Division of Research, Graduate School of Business Administration, Harvard University, 1975.

Haynes, W. W. *Pricing Decisions in Small Business.* Lexington: University of Kentucky Press, 1962.

Heath, Lloyd C. *Financial Reporting and the Evaluation of Solvency.* Accounting Research Monograph No. 3. New York: AICPA, 1979.

————. "Is Working Capital Really Working?" *Journal of Accountancy,* August 1980, pp. 55–62.

————. "Solvency Reporting in a Changing World." In *Technical Papers.* Mexico City: Twelfth International Congress of Accountants, 1982.

Heath, Lloyd C., and Paul Rosenfield. "Solvency: The Forgotten Half of Financial Reporting." *Journal of Accountancy,* January 1979, pp. 48–54.

Hendriksen, Eldon S. *Accounting Theory.* 4th ed. Homewood, Ill.: Richard D. Irwin, 1982.

Hendriksen, Eldon S., and Bruce P. Budge, eds., *Contemporary Accounting Theory.* Encino, Calif.: Dickenson Publishing, 1974.

Henke, Emerson O. *Accounting in Nonprofit Organizations.* 3d ed. Belmont, Calif.: Wadsworth Publishing, 1983.

Herrick, Anson. "Current Assets and Liabilities." *Journal of Accountancy,* January 1944, pp. 48–55.

Hicks, James O., "An Examination of Accounting Interest Groups' Differential Perceptions," *The Accounting Review,* April 1978, pp. 371–88.

Hicks, James R. *Value and Capital: An Inquiry into Some Fundamental Principles of Economic Theory.* 2d ed. Oxford U.K.: Clarendon Press, 1946.

Hilton, W. P. "Interest on Capital." *Journal of Accountancy.* October 1916, pp. 259–64.

Hopwood, Anthony. *Accounting and Human Behaviour.* Englewood Cliffs, N.J.: Prentice-Hall, 1976.

Horngren, Charles T. *Cost Accounting: A Managerial Emphasis.* 5th ed. Englewood Cliffs, N.J.: Prentice-Hall, 1982.

————. "How Should We Interpret the Realization Concept?" *The Accounting Review*, April 1965, pp. 323–33.

————. "Management Accounting: Where are We?" In *Management Accounting and Control*, ed. W. S. Albrecht. Madison: Graduate School of Business, University of Wisconsin, 1975, pp. 9–26.

————. "Uses and Limitations of a Conceptual Framework." *Journal of Accountancy*, April 1981, pp. 86–95.

Howard, Donald S., and Gail M. Hoffman. *Evolving Concepts of Bank Capital Management*. New York: Citicorp, 1980.

Hunter, J. S. "The National System of Scientific Measurement." *Science*, 21 November, 1980, pp. 869–74.

Icerman, Joe D. "The Prediction of Corporate Cash Flows: An Analysis of Relevant Models and Presently Available Financial Statement Information." Ph.D. dissertation, University of North Carolina at Chapel Hill, 1977.

Institute of Chartered Accountants in Australia and Australian Society of Accountants. *Statement of Provisional Accounting Standards, Current Cost Accounting*, October 1976 (amended August 1978).

International Institute for Applied Systems Analysis (IIASA). *Sharing Costs Fairly*. Executive Report No. 5. Laxenburg Austria: IIASA, 1981.

Ijiri, Yuji. "Cash Flow Accounting and Its Structure." *Journal of Accounting, Auditing and Finance*, Summer 1978, pp. 3–48.

————. "Critique of the APB Fundamentals Statement." *Journal of Accountancy*, November 1971, pp. 43–50.

————. *The Foundations of Accounting Measurement: A Mathematical, Economic, and Behavioral Inquiry*. Englewood Cliffs, N.J.: Prentice-Hall, 1967.

————. *Historical Cost Accounting and its Rationality*. Research Monograph No. 1. Vancouver: The Canadian Certified General Accountants' Research Foundation, 1981.

————. *Recognition of Contractual Rights and Obligations*. Stamford, Conn.: FASB, 1980.

————. "An Introduction to Corporate Accounting Standards: A Review." *The Accounting Review*, October 1980, pp. 620–30. (Includes a comment by William A. Paton.)

————. "Recovery Rate and Cash Flow Accounting." *Financial Executive*, March 1980, pp. 54–60.

————. *Theory of Accounting Measurement*. Studies in Accounting Research No. 10. Sarasota, Fla.: American Accounting Association, 1975.

Jaenicke, Henry R. *Survey of Present Practices in Recognizing Revenues, Expenses, Gains, and Losses*. Stamford, Conn.: Financial Accounting Standards Board, 1981.

Jensen, D. L. "A Class of Mutually Satisfactory Allocations." *The Accounting Review*, October 1977, pp. 842–56.

Johnson, L. Todd, and Reed K. Storey. *Recognition in Financial Statements: Underlying Concepts and Practical Conventions.* Stamford, Conn.: Financial Accounting Standards Board, 1982.

Kahn, Alfred E. *The Economics of Regulation: Principles and Institutions.* New York: John Wiley & Sons, 1970–71.

Kaplan, A. D. H.; Joel B. Dirham; and Robert Lanzillotti. *Pricing in Big Business.* Washington, D.C.: Brookings Institution, 1958.

Kaplan, Robert S. "Purchasing Power Gains on Debt." *The Accounting Review*, April 1977, pp. 308–21.

————. *The Information Content of Financial Accounting Numbers: A Survey of Empirical Evidence.* Reprint No. 833. Pittsburgh: Carnegie-Mellon University, 1978.

Kapnick, Harvey. "Value-Based Accounting—Evolution or Revolution." *Arthur Andersen & Co., Executive News Briefs.* February 1976, pp. 1–6.

Keller, Thomas F., and Stephen A. Zeff, eds. *Financial Accounting Theory: Issues and Controversies.* 2 vols. New York: McGraw-Hill, 1969.

Kelly-Norton, Lauren. *Accounting Policy Formulation: The Role of Corporate Management.* Reading, Mass.: Addison-Wesley, 1980.

Kirk, Donald J. "Concepts, Consensus, and Compromise: Their Roles in Standard Setting." *Journal of Accountancy*, April 1981, pp. 83–86.

Kleerekoper, I. "Information Reflecting the Effects of Changing Prices." *Technical Papers.* Mexico City: Twelfth International Congress of Accountants, 1982.

Koch, C. James, and Robert A. Leone. "The Clean Water Act: Unexpected Impacts on Industry." *The Harvard Environmental Law Review*, 1979, pp. 84–111.

Kohler, Eric L. *A Dictionary for Accountants.* 4th ed. Englewood Cliffs, N.J.: Prentice-Hall, 1970.

Kripke, Homer. "The SEC, Corporate Governance, and the Real Issues." *The Business Lawyer*, January 1981, pp. 173–206.

Kuhn, T. S. "The Structure of Scientific Revolutions." International Encyclopedia of Unified Science. 2d ed. Chicago: University of Chicago Press, 1970.

Lamden, Charles W.; Dale L. Gerboth; and Thomas W. McRae. *Accounting for Depreciable Assets.* New York: AICPA, 1975.

Lanzillotti, Robert F. "Pricing Objectives in Large Companies." *American Economic Review*, December 1958, pp. 921–40.

Lawson, Gerald H. "Cash Flow Accounting." *The Accountant*, October 28, 1971, pp. 586–622.

Lee, T. A. "Enterprise Income: Survival or Decline and Fall." *Accounting and Business Research*, Summer 1974, pp. 178–92.

Leontiff, Wassily. Letter to *Science*. 9 July, 1982, pp. 104–7.

Lev, Baruch, and Henri Theil. "A Maximum Entropy Approach to the Choice of Asset Depreciation." *Journal of Accounting Research*, Autumn 1978, pp. 286–93.

Lev, Baruch, and Kenneth W. Taylor. "Accounting Recognition of Imputed Interest on Equity: An Empirical Investigation." *Journal of Accounting, Auditing and Finance*, Spring 1979, pp. 232–43.

Libby, Robert, and Barry L. Lewis. "Human Information Processing Research in Accounting: The State of the Art." *Accounting, Organizations, and Society*, 2, no. 3 (1977), pp. 245–68.

Littleton, A. C. *Accounting Evolution to 1900*. New York: American Institute Publishing, 1933.

————. "Factors Limiting Accounting." *The Accounting Review*, July 1970, pp. 476–80.

Littleton, A. C., and V. K. Zimmerman. *Accounting Theory: Continuity and Change*. Englewood Cliffs, N.J.: Prentice-Hall, 1962.

Litzenberger, Robert H., and James C. Van Horne. "Elimination of the Double Taxation of Dividends and Corporate Financial Policy." *The Journal of Finance*, June 1978, pp. 737–50.

Loomis, Carol J. "How GE Manages Inflation." *Fortune*, May 4, 1981, pp. 121–24.

Lorie, James H., and Mary T. Hamilton. *The Stock Market: Theories and Evidence*. Homewood, Ill.: Richard D. Irwin, 1973.

Lucas, Timothy S., and Betsy Ann Hollowell. "Pension Accounting: The Liability Question." *Journal of Accountancy*, October 1981, pp. 57–66.

Lutz, Sara A. "Pension Plan Disclosures: What They Mean." *Management Accounting*, April 1982, pp. 48–54.

Lynn, Edward S., and Robert J. Freeman. *Fund Accounting Theory and Practice*. Englewood Cliffs, N.J.: Prentice-Hall, 2d. ed. 1983.

Macve, Richard. "A Conceptual Framework for Financial Accounting and Reporting: The Possibilities for an Agreed Structure." Report to the British Accounting Standards Committee, October 1981.

Malkiel, Burton G. *Risk and Return: A New Look*. NBER Working Paper No. 700. Cambridge, Mass.: National Bureau of Economic Research, 1981.

Marshall, Alfred. *Principles of Economics: An Introductory Volume*. 8th ed. New York and London: Macmillan 1920.

Mattessich, Richard. *Accounting and Analytical Methods: Measurement and Projection of Income and Wealth in the Micro- and Macro-Economy*. Homewood, Ill.: Richard D. Irwin, 1964.

May, George O. *Financial Accounting: A Distillation of Experience*. New York: Macmillan, 1943. (Reprinted by Scholars Book Co., 1972.)

Mayer-Sommer, Alan P. "Understanding and Acceptance of the Efficient Market Hypothesis and Its Accounting Implications." *The Accounting Review,* January 1979, pp. 88–106.

Mazzolini, Renato. "Government Controlled Enterprises: What's the Difference?" *Columbia Journal of World Business,* Summer 1980, pp. 28–37.

Meyer, Philip E. *Applied Accounting Theory.* Homewood, Ill.: Richard D. Irwin, 1981.

Miller, James G. "Living Systems: Basic Concepts." *Behavior.* Vol. 10, pp. 1932–36.

Mock, Theodore J. *Measurement and Accounting Information Criteria.* Accounting Research Series No. 13. Sarasota, Fla.: AAA, 1976.

Modigliani, Franco, and Richard A. Cohn. "Inflation, Rational Valuation and the Market." *Financial Analysts Journal,* March–April 1979, pp. 24–44.

Modigliani, Franco, and M. H. Miller. "The Cost of Capital, Corporate Finance and the Theory of Investment." *American Economic Review,* June 1958, pp. 261–77.

Moonitz, Maurice. *The Basic Postulates of Accounting.* Accounting Research Study No. 1. New York: AICPA, 1961.

————. *Obtaining Agreement on Standards in the Accounting Profession.* Studies in Accounting Research No. 8. Sarasota, Fla.: AAA, 1974.

————. "Should We Discard the Income Concept?" *The Accounting Review,* April 1962, pp. 175–80.

Moonitz, Maurice, and Louis H. Jordan. *Accounting—An Analysis of Its Problems,* 2 vols. New York: Holt, Rinehart & Winston, 1963.

Moriarity, Shane. "Another Approach to Allocating Joint Costs." *The Accounting Review,* October 1975, pp. 791–95.

————. ed. *Joint Cost Allocations.* Norman: University of Oklahoma Press, 1981.

Most, Kenneth S. *Accounting Theory.* 2d ed. Columbus, Ohio: Grid Publishing, 1982.

Myers, John H. "The Critical Event and Recognition of Net Profit." *The Accounting Review,* October 1959, pp. 528–32.

Nair, R. D., and Jerry J. Weygandt. "Let's Fix Deferred Taxes." *Journal of Accountancy,* November 1981, pp. 87–102.

Nakayama, Mie; Steven Liben; and Martin Benis. "Due Process and FAS No. 13." *Management Accounting,* April 1981, pp. 49–53.

National Council on Governmental Accounting (NCGA). Statement No. 1. *Governmental Accounting, Auditing and Financial Reporting.* Chicago: Municipal Finance Officers Association of the United States and Canada, 1980.

————. Statement No. 2. *Defining the Governmental Reporting Entity.* Chicago: NCGA, 1981.

Nelson, James R., ed. *Marginal Cost Pricing in Practice.* Englewood Cliffs, N.J.:
    Prentice-Hall, 1964.

Norby, William C. "Inflation Accounting Revisited." *Financial Analysts Journal,*
    November–December 1981, pp. 19–29.

Nordhaus, William D. *The Falling Share of Profits.* Brookings Papers on Economic
    Activity. Washington, D.C.: Brookings Institution, 1974.

Numbers, Ronald L. "Creationism in 20th Century America." *Science,* 5 November,
    1982, pp. 538–44.

Ohlson, James A., and A. Gregory Buckman. "Toward A Theory of Financial
    Accounting." *The Journal of Finance,* May 1980, pp. 537–44.

Organization for Economic Cooperation and Development (OECD). *Accounting
    Practices in OECD Member Countries.* Paris: OECD, 1980.

Parker, Robert H., and G. C. Harcourt, eds. *Readings in the Concept and
    Measurement of Income.* Cambridge U.K.: Cambridge University Press,
    1969.

Pattillo, James W. *The Concept of Materiality in Financial Reporting.* New York:
    Financial Executives Research Foundation, 1976.

————. *The Foundations of Financial Accounting.* Baton Rouge: Louisiana State
    University Press, 1965.

Paton, William A. "Interest and Profit Theory—Amended from an Accounting
    Stance." *Michigan CPA,* January–February 1976, pp. 30–35. (Reprinted in
    Journal of Accountancy, June 1976, pp. 76–82.)

————. *Recent and Prospective Developments in Accounting Theory.* Boston:
    Harvard University, Bureau of Business Research Studies No. 25, April
    1940.

————. *Accounting Theory.* New York: Ronald Press, 1922.

Paton, William A., and A. C. Littleton. *An Introduction to Corporate Accounting
    Standards.* Chicago: American Accounting Association, 1940.

Popper, Karl R. *The Logic of Scientific Discovery.* London: Hutchinson & Co.,
    1959.

Prakash, Prem, and Shyam Sunder. "A Case against Separation of Current
    Operating Profit and Holding Gains." Unpublished working paper, March
    1977.

Raiffa, Howard. *The Art and Science of Negotiations.* Cambridge, Mass.: Harvard
    University Press, 1982.

Rappaport, Alfred. "Economic Impact of Accounting Standards—Implications for
    the FASB." *Proccedings of the Second Annual Accounting Research
    Convocation, University of Alabama, November 18–20, 1976.* Tuscaloosa:
    University of Alabama, 1976, pp. 113–28.

————. "Inflation Accounting and Corporate Dividends." *Financial Executive,*
    February 1981, pp. 20–22.

Rausch, Edward N. *Financial Management for Small Business.* New York: AMACOM, 1979.

Reece, James S., and William R. Cool. "Measuring Investment Center Performance." *Harvard Business Review,* May–June 1978, pp. 28–30 ff.

Revsine, Lawrence. "Inflation Accounting for Debt." *Financial Analysts Journal,* May–June 1981, pp. 2–11.

————. *Theory of the Measurement of Enterprise Income.* Lawrence: The University Press of Kansas, 1970.

————. ed. *Asset Valuation and Income Determination.* Lawrence, Kans.: Scholars Book Co., 1971.

————. "Let's Stop Eating Our Seed Corn." *Harvard Business Review,* January–February 1981, pp. 128–34.

————. *Replacement Cost Accounting.* Englewood Cliffs, N.J.: Prentice-Hall, 1973.

————. "The Theory and Measurement of Business Income: A Review Article." *The Accounting Review,* April 1981, pp. 342–54.

Ro, Byung T. "The Disclosure of Replacement Cost Accounting Data and Its Effect on Transaction Volumes." *The Accounting Review,* January 1981.

Ronen, Joshua. "A Test of the Feasibility of Preparing Discounted Cash Flow Accounting Statements." In *Objectives of Financial Statements.* Vol. 2: *Selected Papers.* ed. J. J. Cramer, Jr., and G. H. Sorter. New York: AICPA, 1974, pp. 202–12.

Rosenfield, Paul. "History of Inflation Accounting." *Journal of Accountancy,* September 1981, pp. 95–126.

Rosenfield, Paul, and Steven Rubin. "Personal and Business Financial Statements: How Their Objectives Differ." *Journal of Accountancy,* July 1981, pp. 94–98.

Salter, Malcolm A., and Wolf A. Weinhold. *Merger Trends and Prospects for the 1980s.* Working Paper HBS 80–49. Boston: Division of Research, Graduate School of Business Administration, Harvard University, 1980.

Samuelson, Paul A. *Economics.* 11th ed. New York: McGraw-Hill, 1980.

Sanders, Thomas H.; Henry R. Hatfield; and Underhill Moore. *A Statement of Accounting Principles.* New York: American Institute of Accountants, 1938.

Sandilands, F. E. P. *Inflation Accounting—Report of the Inflation Accounting Committee.* London: Her Majesty's Stationery Office, Cmnd. 6225, 1975.

Scherer, F. M. "Some Last Words on Predatory Pricing." *Harvard Law Review,* March 1976, pp. 901–3.

Schipper, Katherine, and Roman Weil. "Alternative Accounting Treatments for Pensions." *The Accounting Review,* October 1982, pp. 806–24.

Schrader, William J.; Robert E. Malcolm; and John J. Willingham. "Accounting for What Might Have Been." *Financial Executive,* September 1982, pp. 22–29.

Scott, Richard A. "Owners' Equity, the Anachronistic Element." *The Accounting Review*, October 1979.

Scott, Richard A., and Rita K. Scott. "Installment Accounting: Is It Inconsistent?" *Journal of Accountancy*, November 1979, pp. 52–58.

Scovell, C. H. *Interest as a Cost.* New York: Ronald Press, 1924.

———. "Interest on Investment." *American Economic Association Papers and Proceedings*, March 1919, pp. 22–40.

Seidler, Lee J., and D. R. Carmichael, eds. *Accountants' Handbook.* 6th ed. 3 vols. New York: Ronald Press, 1981.

Seidler, Lee J., and L. Lynn. *Social Accounting: Theory Issues and Cases,* Los Angeles: Melville Publishing, 1975.

Shapley, L. "A Value for N-Person Games." In *Contributions to the Theory of Games,* ed. H. W. Kuhn and A. W. Tucker. Vol. 2. Princeton, N.J.: Princeton University Press, 1953.

Shubik, M. "Incentives, Decentralized Control, the Assignment of Joint Costs and Internal Pricing." *Management Science*, April 1962, pp. 325–43.

Shwayder, Keith. "A Critique of Economic Income as an Accounting Concept." *Abacus*, August 1967, pp. 23–35.

Silberston, Aubrey. "Surveys of Applied Economics: Price Behavior of Firms." *The Economic Journal*, September 1970, pp. 511–82.

Silvern, David Harold. "Enterprise Income: Measuring Financial Management." *Financial Executive*, April 1975, pp. 56–61.

Sinclair, Bruce. *A Centennial History of the American Society of Mechanical Engineers.* Toronto: University of Toronto Press, 1980.

Simon, Herbert A. "Rational Decision Making in Business Organizations." *The American Economic Review*, September 1979, pp. 493–513.

———. "A Comparison of Organization Theories." In *Models of Man: Social and Rational,* ed. Herbert A. Simon. New York: John Wiley & Sons, 1957, chapter 10.

Skinner, Ross M. *Accounting Principles: A Canadian Viewpoint.* Toronto: The Canadian Institute of Chartered Accountants, 1972.

———. "The Trueblood Report: Brave New Beginning or Dead End?" *CA Magazine*, December 1973, pp. 12–16.

Smith, Dan Throop. "Issues in Tax Policy." In *The United States in the 1980s,* ed. Peter Duignan and Alvin Rabushka. Stanford, Calif.: Stanford University Press, 1980, pp. 109–37.

Snavely, Howard J. "Current Cost for Long Lived Assets: A Critical View." *The Accounting Review*, April 1969, pp. 344–53.

Snavely, Howard J.; Jerome J. Kesselman; and Wayne A. Label. *Financial Accounting: Concepts, Uses, and Problems.* Los Alamitos, Calif.: Hwong Publishing, 1977.

————. "Economic and Accounting Concepts of Income." *The Accounting Review,* July 1961, pp. 374–83.

Solomon, Ezra. "Alternative Rate of Return Concepts and Their Implications for Utility Regulation." *The Bell Journal of Economics and Management Science,* Spring 1970, pp. 65–81.

Solomons, David, ed. *Proceedings of the Conference on the Conceptual Framework of Accounting, May 4, 1977.* Philadelphia: The Wharton School, University of Pennsylvania, 1977.

————. "The Impact of Politics on Accounting Standards." *Journal of Accountancy,* November 1970, pp. 65–72.

————. "The Politicization of Accounting." *The Journal of Accountancy,* November 1978, pp. 65–72.

————. "Economic and Accounting Concepts of Income." *The Accounting Review,* July 1961, pp. 374–83.

————. "Toward a Science of Accounting: Book Review." *Journal of Accountancy,* April 1982, pp. 99–102.

Sorter, George H. "An 'Events' Approach to Basic Accounting Theory." *The Accounting Review,* January 1969, pp. 12–19.

Sorter, George H., and Charles T. Horngren. "Asset Recognition and Economic Attitudes: The Relevant Costing Approach." *The Accounting Review,* July 1962, pp. 391–99.

Spacek, Leonard. *A Search for Fairness in Financial Reporting to the Public.* Chicago: Arthur Andersen & Co., 1969.

————. "The Need for an Accounting Court." *The Accounting Review,* July 1958.

Sprague, Charles E. *The Philosophy of Accounts.* 5th ed. New York: Ronald Press, 1923.

Sprouse, Robert T. "The Balance Sheet: Embodiment of the Most Fundamental Element of Accounting Theory." In Williard E. Stone, ed. *Foundations of Accounting Theory.* Gainesville: University of Florida Press, 1971, pp. 102–3.

————. "The Importance of Earnings in the Conceptual Framework." *Journal of Accountancy,* January 1978, pp. 64–71.

————. "Prospects for Progress in Financial Reporting." Address given at the College of Business Administration, Texas Tech University, April 19, 1979.

Sprouse, Robert T., ed. *The Measurement of Property, Plant, and Equipment in Financial Statements.* Boston: Graduate School of Business Administration, Harvard University, 1964.

Sprouse, Robert T., and Maurice Moonitz. *A Tentative Set of Broad Accounting Principles for Business Enterprises.* Accounting Research Study No. 3. New York: AICPA, 1962.

Stamp, Edward. "Why Can Accounting Not Become a Science Like Physics?" *Abacus,* June 1981, pp. 13–27.

———. "Accounting Standard Setting: A New Beginning." *CA Magazine,* September 1980, pp. 38–47.

———. "Accounting Standards and the Conceptual Framework: A Plan for Their Evolution." *The Accountant's Magazine,* July 1981, pp. 216–22.

———. "First Steps towards a British Conceptual Framework." *Accountancy,* March 1982, pp. 123–30.

Staubus, George J. *Activity Costing and Input-Output Accounting.* Homewood, Ill.: Richard D. Irwin, 1971.

———. *Making Accounting Decisions.* Houston, Tex.: Scholars Book Co., 1977.

———. "The Relevance of Evidence of Cash Flows." In *Asset Valuation and Income Determination,* ed. Robert R. Sterling. Houston, Tex.: Scholars Book Co., 1971, pp. 42–69.

———. "Revenue and Revenue Accounts." *Accounting Research,* January 1956.

———. *A Theory of Accounting to Investors.* Berkeley: University of California Press, 1961.

Steinberg, Harold I. "A New Look at Governmental Accounting." *Journal of Accountancy,* March 1979, pp. 48–50.

Sterling, Robert R. *Asset Valuation and Income Determination.* Houston, Tex.: Scholars Book Co., 1971.

———. "Companies are Reporting Useless Numbers." Interview. *Fortune,* January 14, 1980, pp. 105–7.

———. *Toward a Science of Accounting.* Houston, Tex.: Scholars Book Co., 1979.

———. "Relevant Financial Reporting in an Age of Price Change." *Journal of Accountancy,* February 1975. pp. 42–51.

———. *The Theory of the Measurement of Enterprise Income.* Houston, Tex.: Scholars Book Co., 1970.

Sterling, Robert R., and Arthur L. Thomas, eds. *Accounting for a Simplified Firm Owning Depreciable Assets.* Houston, Tex.: Scholars Book Co., 1979.

Stern, Joel. "Annual Reports and Stock Prices." *The Wall Street Journal,* January 29, 1979, sec. 4, p. 16.

Stone, Williard E., ed. *Foundations of Accounting Theory.* Gainesville: University of Florida Press, 1971.

Storey, Reed K. "Conditions Necessary for Developing a Conceptual Framework." *FASB Viewpoints,* March 3, 1981.

———. "Accounting and Financial Reporting—The Challenges of the 1980s." Address to the American Accounting Association, November 3, 1980.

———. *The Search for Accounting Principles—Today's Problems in Perspective.* New York: AICPA, 1964.

Strauss, Norman N., and Alex T. Arcady. "A New Focus on the 'Bottom Line' and Its Components." *Journal of Accountancy,* May 1981, pp. 55–62.

Sunder, Shyam. "Proof that in an Efficient Market, Event Studies Can Provide No Systematic Guidance to Revision of Accounting Standards and Disclosure Policy." Unpublished paper, University of Chicago, May 1981.

―――――. "Corporate Capital Investment, Accounting Methods and Earnings: A Test of the Control Hypothesis." *The Journal of Finance,* May 1980, p. 553–65.

Thomas, Arthur L. "Reporting of Faculty Time: An Accounting Prespective." *Science,* 1 January, 1982, pp. 27–32.

―――――. *The Allocation Problem in Financial Accounting Theory.* Studies in Accounting Research No. 3. Sarasota, Fla.: AAA, 1969.

―――――. *The Allocation Problem: Part Two.* Studies in Accounting Research No. 9. Sarasota, Fla.: AAA, 1974.

―――――. "The FASB and the Allocation Fallacy." *Journal of Accountancy,* November 1975, pp. 65–68.

―――――. "Matching: Up From Our Black Holes." In *Accounting for a Simplified Firm Owning Depreciable Assets,* ed. Robert R. Sterling and Arthur L. Thomas. Houston, Tex.: Scholars Book Co., 1979, pp. 11–33.

Thomas, Lewis. "On the Uncertainty of Science." *Harvard Magazine,* September–October 1980, pp. 19–22.

Traub, Jack. *Accounting and Reporting Practices of Private Foundations.* New York: Praeger Publishers, 1977.

U.S. Armed Services Board of Contract Appeals, The Boeing Company, ASBCA No. 19224.

U.S. Council on Wage and Price Stability. *A Study of Steel Prices.* Washington, D.C.: Brookings Institution, 1975.

U.S. Supreme Court. *Federal Power Commission* v. *Hope Natural Gas Co.* 320 U.S. 591.

U.S. Internal Revenue Service. *Revenue Ruling 59–60.* C.B. 1959–1237.

U.S. Securities and Exchange Commission (SEC) *Accounting Series Releases* (In 1982, title changed to *Financial Reporting Releases*). Washington, D.C.: SEC.

―――――. Accounting Series Release No. 142. "Reporting Cash Flow and Other Related Data." March 15, 1973.

Vancil, Richard F. "Inflation Accounting—The Great Controversy." *Harvard Business Review,* March–April 1976, pp. 58–67.

Vancil, Richard F., and Roman L. Weil. *Replacement Cost Accounting.* Glen Ridge, N.J.: Thomas Horton and Daughters, 1976.

Van Horne, James C. *Financial Management and Policy.* 5th ed. Englewood Cliffs, N.J.: Prentice Hall, 1980.

Vatter, William J. *The Fund Theory of Accounting and Its Implications for Financial Reports.* Chicago: University of Chicago Press, 1947.

Verrecchia, R. E. "A Question of Equity: Use of the Shapley Value to Allocate State and Local Income and Franchise Taxes." In *Joint Cost Allocations,* ed. Shane Moriarity. Norman, Okla.: Center for Economic and Management Research, 1981, pp. 14–40.

————. "An Analysis of Two Cost Allocation Cases." *The Accounting Review,* July 1982, pp. 579–93.

Walker, Ernest W., and J. William Petty II. *Financial Management of the Small Firm.* Englewood Cliffs, N.J.: Prentice-Hall, 1978.

Warren, Robert L., and Jackson A. White. "Cash Information: Toward A More Useful Statement of Changes in Financial Position." *The National Public Accountant,* February 1975, pp. 30–34.

Watts, Ross L., and Zimmerman, Jerold L. "The Demand for and Supply of Accounting Theories: The Market for Excuses." *The Accounting Review,* April 1979, pp. 273–305.

————. "Toward a Positive Theory of the Determination of Accounting Standards." *The Accounting Review,* January 1978, pp. 112–34.

Wells, Murray C. *Accounting for Common Costs.* Urbana, Ill.: Center for International Education and Research in Accounting, University of Illinois, 1978.

Welsch, Glenn A.; Charles T. Zlatkovich; and Walter T. Harrison. *Intermediate Accounting.* 6th ed. Homewood, Ill.: Richard D. Irwin, 1982.

Williams, Harold M. "Accounting and Financial Reporting: The Challenges of the 1980s." Address, Securities and Exchange Commission, November 3, 1980 release.

————. "Adequate Information: Prerequisite to an Effective Board." Address, Securities and Exchange Commission, September 16, 1980 release.

Young, Arthur and Company. *Financial Reporting and Changing Prices.* New York: August, 1981.

Young, David W. "Accounting for the Cost of Interest: Implications for the Timber Industry." *The Accounting Review,* October 1976, pp. 788–99.

Zeff, Stephen A. *Forging Accounting Principles in Five Countries: A History and Analysis of Trends.* Champaign, Ill.: Stipes Publishing, 1972.

————. *Asset Appreciation, Business Income and Price-Level Accounting: 1918–1935.* New York: Arno Press, 1976.

Author index

Subject index

This book has been set VIP in 10 and 9 point Melior. Chapter numbers are 60 point Melior Bold and chapter titles are 18 point Melior Bold. The size of the type page is 29 by 46 picas.